Flavius Josephus, William Shepard Walsh

Our Young Folks' Josephus. The Antiquities of the Jews

And the Jewish Wars of Flavius Josephus

Flavius Josephus, William Shepard Walsh

Our Young Folks' Josephus. The Antiquities of the Jews
And the Jewish Wars of Flavius Josephus

ISBN/EAN: 9783744769174

Printed in Europe, USA, Canada, Australia, Japan

Cover: Foto ©ninafisch / pixelio.de

More available books at **www.hansebooks.com**

OUR

YOUNG FOLKS' JOSEPHUS,

THE ANTIQUITIES OF THE JEWS

AND

THE JEWISH WARS

OF

FLAVIUS JOSEPHUS.

SIMPLIFIED BY
WILLIAM SHEPARD.

ILLUSTRATED.

PHILADELPHIA AND LONDON
J. B. LIPPINCOTT COMPANY
1905

PREFACE.

THE following pages are merely what they claim to be, a simplification of the story of the Jews as related by Josephus. In matters pertaining to the Old Testament, I have not deemed it my duty to supplement his narrative from the Bible even where he is most obviously deficient, although I have indicated the fact of such deficiency in notes. With regard to the New Testament, it must be borne in mind that Josephus makes no mention of Christ or of the Christian religion, except in one short paragraph in the Jewish Antiquities, which is held by some authorities to be an interpolation. Josephus wrote his histories for the Romans, and we need not therefore wonder at his passing over in silence the unpalatable doctrine of the Messiah, or at his modifying and toning down the historical statements of the Mosaic records to recommend them to the prejudices of his readers.

In conclusion, it only remains to express my thanks for assistance rendered by Mr. Henry C. Walsh in the preparation of the manuscript.

WILLIAM SHEPARD.

CONTENTS.

CONTENTS.

LIFE OF FLAVIUS JOSEPHUS.

FLAVIUS JOSEPHUS was born at Jerusalem A.D. 37. He was of illustrious birth, his father being a priest, which was considered a great distinction among the Jews, and his mother a member of the royal family of the Asmonæans. He received an excellent education, and profited so well by what he had learned that at the age of sixteen he was frequently consulted by the chief priests when they could not agree on difficult questions. About this time he joined the sect of the Essenes, and went to live in the desert with a celebrated hermit named Banun. After three years he returned to Jerusalem, where he abandoned the doctrines of the Essenes and became a Pharisee. In the year 63 he visited Rome to procure the liberation of some Jewish prisoners that had been sent there by the governor, Felix; was favorably received, and was successful in his mission through the influence of Poppæa, the wife of Nero. When the Jews revolted against Rome he was appointed governor of Galilee, and the story of his brave defence of Jotapata, of its final capture, and of his escape from death, alone among the Jewish warriors, through the intercession of Titus, has been told by himself in " The Jewish War," one of the works of which the following pages are an abstract. At the destruction of Jerusalem, his influence with the emperor, Vespasian, procured the liberation of his brothers and fifty of his friends. It was out of gratitude for these and other favors that Josephus about this time assumed the emperor's family name of Flavius. His history of " The Jewish War," which was finished

A.D. 75, was undertaken at the command of Vespasian, and is a noble and pathetic narrative of events that had been witnessed by himself.   His other important work, "The Antiquities of the Jews," was finished about A.D. 93, and was an attempt to familiarize the Roman people with the early history of the Jews as it is recorded in the Scripture.   He also wrote ɔ memoir of himself and two books against Apion, a great aaversary of the Jews.   The date of his death is not known with certainty, but is placed by some writers at about A.D. 95.

CHRONOLOGICAL TABLE.

A BRIEF SUMMARY OF THE LEADING EVENTS IN JEWISH HISTORY DURING THE PERIODS COVERED BY THIS WORK, WITH THEIR DATES.*

	B.C.
Abraham goes into Canaan	2078
Birth of Isaac	2053
Birth of Jacob and Esau	1993
Joseph is made ruler of Egypt	1872
Removal of Jacob to Egypt	1863
Birth of Moses	1728
Exodus of the Israelites	1648
Destruction of Jericho	1608
The Judges rule Israel	1582–1110
Saul made king	1110
David	1070
Solomon	1030
The ten tribes revolt and set up an independent government under their own kings	990–719
The kingdom of Judah lasts from	990–586
Captivity of Judah	607–538
Return of Zerubbabel to Jerusalem	535
Completion of temple at Jerusalem	515
The Jews remain under Persian rule until	333
The Jews are ruled by Alexander the Great	333–325
The Jews are ruled by the Ptolemys until	325–204
The Jews are ruled by the kings of Syria	204–165
The Jews are ruled by the Maccabees	165–63
The Romans become masters of Judea	63
Destruction of Jerusalem	A.D. 70

* In Old Testament dates the chronology known as the longer chronology, or that of the Greek Septuagint, has been followed in the above table.

13

OUR YOUNG FOLKS' JOSEPHUS.

CHAPTER I.

ABRAHAM, THE FOUNDER OF THE JEWISH RACE.

ONE of the most famous of all the nations that have ever lived on the earth is the nation of the Jews. The history of this people, how they rose from small beginnings and became great and mighty, and how, after many changes of fortune, they were finally conquered by the Romans, and scattered all over the earth, is very interesting and very remarkable. It is this history as it was written down by Josephus, one of their greatest historians, that our young readers will find in the following pages. Josephus wrote his history in the Greek language. It has been translated into English, but the translation is so full of big words and long sentences, and the history itself contains so much that is dry and dull, so much that young people would naturally skip, that you would probably find it difficult and unpleasant to read. Therefore in these pages the history has been put into simpler language, and those parts of it which are not interesting have been, as far as possible, left out.

You know, of course, that the founder of the great nation of the Jews was a man named Abraham. He was the son of Terah, a shepherd, who lived in a country called Chaldea, in Asia, where the ground was flat and open and well suited for pasturing flocks. Abraham had two brothers, named

Nahor and Haran. Nahor, who seems to have been the eldest, died early, leaving a son, named Lot, and two daughters, named Sarah and Milcah. In those days the laws in regard to marriage were not the same as they are now. God allowed men to marry their near relations, and also to have more wives than one. Therefore there was nothing strange in the marriage of the two brothers of Nahor to his daughters, who were their nieces. Haran took Milcah as his wife, and had many sons and daughters. Abraham took Sarah, and, as he had no children, he adopted Lot, his wife's brother and his own nephew, as his son.

When Abraham was seventy-five years of age, he left the land of Chaldea, by the command of God, and went into another country, called Canaan. He lived here for many years in peace and plenty. Then a famine broke out, and Abraham, learning that in the country of Egypt there was no famine, determined to move there. He did not intend to remain there, but only to stay so long as there was famine in Canaan, and after that to return to his own country. When Abraham was in Egypt he talked with the priests and learned men and showed them how wrong it was to worship false gods. He also taught them many things he had learned in Chaldea, among others arithmetic and astronomy, and the Egyptians afterwards taught these sciences to the Greeks.

As soon as the famine in Canaan was over, Abraham returned there. By this time his adopted son, Lot, had grown to be a young man. And he left Abraham's tent and went to live in a tent of his own. For in those days people did not live in houses like ours, but in tents. They did this because they moved about so much. As soon as the flocks and herds which they owned had eaten up all the grass in one place they would move to another. And, as the winters were never very cold, they did not find any inconvenience in this way of living.

Now Abraham had many servants under him, who looked after his flocks. Lot also had many servants. As the ser-

vants of Abraham frequently quarrelled with the servants of
Lot about the lands on which they wished to pasture their
flocks, Abraham decided that it would be best to make a fair
division. So he told Lot that he might go to any part of the
land he preferred and he would take the rest for himself. Lot
chose the country which lay around the river Jordan, near a
city called Sodom. And Abraham removed his tent to a place
called Hebron, and took all the land that lay around it as his
own.

Now Lot had not lived very long in his new place when the
people of Sodom were attacked by a nation called the Assyrians, who defeated them and carried many of them away to
their own land as captives. Among those carried away in this
manner was Lot himself.

When Abraham heard of what had happened, he was sorry
for his adopted son and for his neighbors, the Sodomites, who
had been made prisoners, and he determined to go to their
assistance. So he gathered his servants together and armed
them and started out in pursuit of the Assyrians. And after
journeying for five days he came upon them in the night at a
place called Dan. They had been feasting and making merry,
and were now drunk with wine, and many of them were asleep.
Abraham fell upon them in this condition and killed a great
many, and the rest ran away. He released the prisoners
from their bonds, and all returned home rejoicing. On their
way Melchizedek, the king of a city called Salem, who was
also a priest of God, came out to meet them. He supplied
Abraham and his army with food and wine, and while they
were all eating and drinking he praised Abraham and blessed
him. Abraham gave him a tenth part of the spoils,—that is,
of the sheep and cattle and money he had taken away from
the enemy.

When the king of Sodom saw Abraham returning with the
captives and the spoils that had been taken by the enemy he
was very glad. And he told Abraham to give him up the

prisoners that he might send them to their own homes, but to keep all the spoils. But Abraham would not do so, saying he would not keep anything for himself.

God spoke to Abraham and praised him for what he had done, and said,—

"Thou shalt not, however, lose the rewards which thy goodness deserves, but I will bless thee and make thee rich and prosperous."

Then Abraham answered, "And what advantage will these rewards be to me, if I have no one after me to enjoy them?" For Abraham was childless.

But God promised he would give him a son, who should have many children, and the descendants from these children should become as numerous as the stars in the heaven. Abraham was glad when he heard this, and he offered a sacrifice, as God had commanded him to do. And the way he offered the sacrifice was as follows: he took a heifer, or young ox, three years of age, and a she-goat three years of age, and a ram three years of age, and a turtle-dove, and a pigeon. He cut the animals into sections, but the birds he did not cut. And when he built his altar and burnt these sacrifices, he heard a voice telling him that his descendants should live for four hundred years in the land of Egypt and be treated cruelly there, but that afterwards they should overcome and return to Canaan to possess the land.

Several years passed away, however, and still Abraham and Sarah had no children. Now the people of Sodom had been growing very wicked during these years, and the Lord was angry with them for their wickedness.

One day Abraham sat at the door of his tent and saw three strangers coming towards him. He rose and saluted them, and asked them to stop and eat with him. And when they agreed to do so, he killed a calf and roasted it, and served it up before them. While they were eating they asked Abraham about his wife Sarah, where she was. When he said

she was in the tent, they told him they would return that way
hereafter and find her a mother. Sarah heard what they said,
and she laughed aloud, not believing them, for she was ninety
years old and her husband was a hundred. Then the strangers told Abraham they were not men, but were angels of the
Lord, and that one of them was sent to inform him about the
child, and two to announce that Sodom would be destroyed
because of its wickedness.

When Abraham heard this, he went out and prayed to God
to spare the city of Sodom for the sake of the few good men
that might be living there. But God told him that there were
not any good men among the Sodomites, for if there were ten
such men He would spare the town for their sake. So Abraham held his peace.

And the angels went to the city of the Sodomites and were
welcomed by Lot, who invited them to come and eat with
him. They told Lot of the destruction that was to visit the
city, and advised him to flee from it. So he gathered up his
possessions, and with his wife and his two daughters he fled
next morning from the city. No sooner was he safe outside
of the walls than God cast a thunderbolt upon the city and
set it on fire. The angels had warned Lot and his family not
to look back when they fled. But Lot's wife disobeyed this
warning, and was turned into a pillar of salt. Josephus tells
us that he saw this pillar, for it was still standing in his day.

CHAPTER II.

THE SACRIFICE OF ISAAC.

Now in a little time Abraham and Sarah had a son, as God
had foretold, and he was named Isaac, which in the Chaldaic
language meant laughter. For Sarah had laughed when she

heard the angels say that she was to have this child. As
Isaac grew up he endeared himself more and more to Abraham because of his many good qualities. He was zealous in
the worship of God, he was kind to all his neighbors, and he
loved and honored his parents. It was a great happiness to
Abraham to think that when he died he should leave this son
behind him to take charge of all his possessions, to continue
the good work that he was doing in the world, and to be the
founder of a race of men who would worship the true God.
God knew Abraham's thoughts and hopes, and because He
wished to try his obedience He appeared to him one day,
and after reminding him of all the blessings He had bestowed
on him, and that this son Isaac was only one of His many
gifts, He said,—

"Take this son Isaac, whom thou lovest so much, and get
thee to the mountain called Moriah, and there build an altar
and sacrifice Isaac upon it as a burnt-offering to me."

Abraham was deeply grieved when he heard this command
to kill his own son and offer him up on an altar, in the way
that lambs were offered up. But in all his great sorrow he
never thought of disobedience. He knew that God's will
must be done. He knew also that life was a gift from God,
which might be withdrawn in any way and at any time that
God saw fit. But he did not tell Sarah or any of his people
what he had been commanded to do, for he was afraid that
they might try to dissuade him from doing the will of God.

Early next morning he arose and bade Isaac and two other
young men who were members of his household to get ready
to accompany him on a journey. The wood, ready cut for
the sacrifice, was laid upon the back of an ass, and so the
little party started out on their journey towards Mount
Moriah. They travelled for two days, and on the morning
of the third day they came in sight of the place. Then
Abraham told the servants they need go no farther. He
left the ass with them and made Isaac shoulder the wood.

And when they had come up to the top of the mountain, Abraham, with the help of Isaac, built the altar for the sacrifice. While they were building, Isaac said to his father,—

" My father, you have wood and fire, but what are you going to offer, since we have no animal for a burnt-offering ?"

" My son," answered Abraham, " God will provide a lamb for the burnt-offering."

When at last the altar was finished, and Abraham had laid the wood on, and all things were ready, he told his son what God had commanded of him. And though Isaac loved life very dearly, being then a vigorous young man, twenty-five years of age, he told his father that if it pleased God that he should die he was willing to be sacrificed.

So Abraham took up the knife and lifted up his hand to kill Isaac. But at that moment God called out to him in a loud voice and ordered him to lay down the knife. He said that He did not desire the death of Isaac, but had only wished to try Abraham's obedience. Since, therefore, He was now satisfied of his readiness to do all His commands, He was glad that He had bestowed so many blessings upon him, and He would continue to watch over him and his family. He promised also that Isaac should live to a good old age, and that he should have numerous descendants, who would inherit the land of Canaan and be envied of all men, and that through these descendants all the races of men should be blessed.

After God had spoken in this way, Abraham looked around, and beheld a ram that had been sent to take the place of Isaac. And he seized and killed it and laid it on the altar as a burnt-offering. Then father and son with much rejoicing returned to where the two young men were waiting for them, and they all proceeded homeward together.

Not long afterwards, Sarah, who was one hundred and twenty-seven years of age, fell sick and died, and Abraham buried her in the land of Hebron.

CHAPTER III.

REBEKAH.

In those days, when men lived so much longer than they do now, they did not marry at so early an age. It was not, therefore, until Isaac was nearly forty years old that Abraham thought of obtaining a wife for him. Now the women who lived in the land of Canaan were worshippers of false gods, and Abraham did not wish his son to marry among them. He wanted him instead to have a wife from the land in which he had formerly lived, and where he had relations who feared God.

So he chose the oldest of his servants, and intrusted to him a number of valuable presents which he was to give to the chief men in that country, and he told him that he was to bring home with him a maiden called Rebekah, the grand-daughter of his own brother Nahor, and that this maiden was to be a wife for Isaac. The servant promised to perform his mission faithfully, and he set out on his journey. After travelling many days, he came in sight of the town of Haran. Here he saw a number of maidens coming out of the town to fill their pitchers with water at the well. He dismounted from his camel and waited for the maidens to come up to him. And while they were approaching he prayed that God would give him a sign so that he might know which was Rebekah, in case it were the will of God that Rebekah should marry Isaac. The sign he asked for was this, that while all the others should deny him water to drink, she might give it to him.

Then, when the maidens were at the well, he went up to

them and asked for some water to drink. But, while the others refused, pretending that they needed it all at home and could spare none for him, one of the company rebuked them for their rude behavior to a stranger, and, turning to him, offered her pitcher in a kind and obliging manner. So the servant guessed that this must be Rebekah; but, in order to be certain, he praised her for her generosity and good nature in giving to a stranger the water which it cost her so much pains to draw, and asked who were her parents, that he might give them joy in the possession of such a daughter. And she did not disdain to answer his inquiries, but told him her family.

"My name," she said, "is Rebekah, and my father's name was Bethuel, the son of Nahor. But my father is dead, and I live with my mother and my brother Laban."

When the servant heard this, he was very glad at what had happened and what was told him, for he now plainly saw that God had directed his journey and had answered his prayer. He took out some bracelets and other ornaments and gave them to her as a reward for her kindness. And when she had thanked him, she asked him to come and lodge with her family, as night was approaching and he would not be able to proceed any farther on his journey until morning. The servant accepted her invitation, saying that from such as she had shown herself to be he might guess how good and kind were the mother and the brother who had brought her up, and he knew that they would welcome him to their house. Moreover, he said, he would not be burdensome, but would pay for his entertainment. To which she replied that he was right in what he said about her relations, for they were good and hospitable people, but complained that he should think they would accept money for their hospitality. He must come to the house as a guest. But first, she said, she would inform her brother Laban, and when he had given her leave, she would conduct him in.

Having obtained this permission, she invited the stranger into the house, and his camels were taken care of by Laban's servants, and Laban himself brought him in to supper. And after he had eaten and drunk, the servant of Abraham told Laban and Rebekah's mother who he was, and why he had come there. He explained to them that Abraham was a wealthy and a good man, and that Isaac was his heir. Abraham, he said, might, indeed, have chosen any of the women that dwelt in his neighborhood as a wife for his son, but he preferred a maiden of his own tribe. And this also seemed to be the will of God, who had directed the servant's journey and answered his prayer when he asked that Rebekah should be pointed out to him. Therefore the servant begged that they would give their consent to the marriage.

When Laban and his mother had heard all these things, they saw indeed that the finger of God had directed the whole matter, and they freely gave their consent. And Abraham's servant brought Rebekah back with him, and she was married to Isaac.

A little while after this, Abraham died, at the age of one hundred and seventy-five, and he was buried in Hebron, by the side of his wife Sarah. And Isaac succeeded to all his possessions.

CHAPTER IV.

JACOB AND ESAU.

God blessed Isaac and Rebekah, and gave them two sons, who were twins. Just before their birth God told Isaac that He would give him these sons, and that they should both be the founders of great nations, but that the younger should

excel the other. And when they were born, Isaac called
the elder Esau, which means rough or hairy, because the
child was born with hair all over his body, and the younger
he called Jacob. Esau was the favorite son of Isaac, but
Jacob was his mother's favorite. When these sons had
grown up to be men, and Isaac was very old and feeble, and
also blind, he called to his favorite son Esau and explained
to him that, being himself now unfitted for offering up the
sacrifices to God, he was anxious that his son should be
his worthy successor. He therefore bade him go out into
the woods and kill as much venison as he could, and prepare him a supper. After the supper was over, Isaac said,
he would bless his son and pray to God for him, and God
would let him know what his future life would be. So
Esau went out hunting. But Rebekah had overheard what
Isaac said, and she was anxious that Jacob also should receive the blessing of his father and have his future revealed
to him. She therefore bade Jacob kill some young goats
and prepare a supper. Jacob obeyed his mother, and when
the supper was ready he took a goat's skin and laid it
upon his arm. He thought that his blind father, feeling
the hair of the goat, would mistake him for his brother
Esau. And it happened indeed as he had expected. For,
when he brought the supper to his father, Isaac, hearing his
voice, recognized it as the voice of Jacob, and bade him approach. But when he took hold of Jacob's hand, which was
covered with the skin of the goat, he said, " Thy voice is like
the voice of Jacob, yet because of the thickness of thy hair
thou must be Esau."

So, suspecting no deceit, he ate of the supper, and then
poured out his prayers to God, and said, " O Lord of all ages,
and Creator of all substance; for it was Thou that didst propose to my father great plenty of good things, and hast
vouchsafed to bestow on me what I have; and hast promised
to my posterity to be their kind supporter, and to bestow on

them still greater blessings; do Thou therefore confirm these
Thy promises, and do not overlook me because of my present
weak condition. Be gracious to this my son; and preserve
and keep him from everything that is evil. Give him a happy
life, and the possession of as many good things as Thy power
is able to bestow. Make him terrible to his enemies, and
honorable and beloved among his friends."

Such was Isaac's prayer, and he had just finished when
Esau came in from hunting. Esau was grieved and angry
when he found what his brother had done, and he prayed
his father to give him the same blessing that he had given to
Jacob. But Isaac, though he too lamented the mistake, could
not now remedy it, because all his prayers had been spent
upon Jacob. However, when Esau burst out weeping, the
father strove to comfort him, and predicted that he should
excel in hunting and strength of body and bravery, and
should obtain glory forever on those accounts, he and his descendants after him, but nevertheless that he should always
serve his brother.

CHAPTER V.

JACOB FLIES FROM ESAU.

REBEKAH was afraid that Esau might inflict some punishment upon Jacob because of the deceit he had practised upon
him, and she therefore besought her husband to choose a wife
for Jacob from among her own kindred. And Isaac having consented that Jacob should marry Rachel, the daughter
of her brother Laban, the young man was sent to visit her
in her native country. On his journey through the land of
Canaan, Jacob, because he knew the people who dwelt there
were idolaters, refused all their offers of hospitality and pre-

ferred rather to take up his lodgings in the open air. At night-time he gathered up a heap of stones to serve as a pillow. And once as he was sleeping thus he beheld a wonderful vision. He seemed to see a ladder that reached from the earth unto heaven, and angels were going up and down upon it, and at last God himself stood above it and was plainly visible to him. And God, calling him by name, told him that because he was the son of so good a father, and because he was the descendant of Abraham, He would watch over him and bless him. And the marriage which he contemplated would be a happy one, and he would have a great multitude of descendants, to whom the land of Canaan would be given.

"Fear no danger, therefore," said the Lord, "and be not disheartened because of the many hardships thou must undergo, for I will watch over thee and direct what thou art to do in the time present, and still more in the time to come."

Jacob rose from his sleep refreshed and strengthened. And because of the great promise that had been made to him in that place, he poured oil upon the stones, and promised that if he lived and returned safe he would offer sacrifices upon them, and that of all the flocks and herds and silver and gold which God should give him, he would give a tenth part to the Lord. That is to say, he would build altars and offer sacrifices and do good to the poor.

So he proceeded on his journey, and at length came to Haran. Meeting a number of shepherds in the suburbs of the town, he questioned them whether they knew a man named Laban, and whether he was still alive. And they answered that they knew him well, for he was an important man in the town, and that his daughter Rachel fed her father's flock together with them. They wondered, indeed, that she was not now among them, for it was the usual time for her appearance. And even as they spoke, the maiden came out of the city and came near to where they were. Then the other shepherds pointed Jacob out to her, and told her that he was a stranger who came to inquire about her father's affairs. And she, being pleased with his appearance, spoke kindly to him, and asked him who he was and what he wanted, and hoped it might be in their power to supply his wants.

Jacob was surprised at the beauty and grace of the maiden, which were greater than that of any one he had ever seen. And he hastened to tell her who he was, that he was the son of Isaac and Rebekah, and the nephew of her father Laban.

"And now," he continued, "I have come to salute you and your family, and to renew those friendly feelings which are proper between us."

The maiden gladly welcomed him to their country, and having embraced him, she bade him follow her, as she led the way to her father's house. She assured him that his visit would give Laban the greatest pleasure, for he was always thinking of Rebekah and talking of her. And it was, indeed, as she had said. For when Laban heard who Jacob was, he threw his arms round him and kissed him, and eagerly welcomed him into the house. After they had conversed together for some time, Laban asked Jacob why it was that he had left his aged father and mother to come on so long a journey, and assured him that if he stood in need of any assistance he would gladly give it to him. Then Jacob opened his heart to Laban, and told him that he had left his father's roof because of his fear of Esau, and also because his mother did not wish him to marry any of the Canaanitish women, but to choose a wife from her own tribe.

Laban promised that he would treat Jacob with great kindness, and make him head-shepherd of his flock, and when he should have a mind to return to his parents he would send him back loaded with presents. Jacob replied that he would gladly work for his uncle and would serve him faithfully, but as the reward of his labors he asked only that Laban would give him his daughter Rachel to wife. Laban was well pleased with this arrangement, and said he would give her to Jacob provided he would agree to stay with him for some time, for he was not yet prepared to part with her. And Jacob consented to stay seven years, for his love for Rachel was so great that this seemed a small sacrifice. But when the seven years were ended, Laban refused to give Rachel to Jacob, and in her place he gave him his elder daughter, Leah. For he said it was not right that the younger sister should be married before the elder. However, he told Jacob that if he would work another seven years he might have Rachel also as his wife. So Jacob remained with Laban and worked seven more years for him, and at the end of that time he had both Leah and Rachel for his wives. And they bore him sons and daughters.

For six years longer Jacob and his wives and children dwelt in the land of Chaldea. Then, having been full twenty years absent from his own land, he desired leave of his father-in-law to take his wives and go home. But, as Laban would not give him leave, he decided that he would go secretly. Calling his wives to him, he asked them what they thought of this journey. And he found that they approved of it and were willing to go. Therefore, one day when Laban was away from home, shearing his sheep, Jacob gathered together all his flocks and his other possessions, put his wives and his children upon camels, and set out on his journey towards the land of Canaan. But Laban, after one day's time, learning of Jacob's departure, was much troubled, and pursued him, leading a band of men with him. On the seventh day he overtook the fugitives, and found them resting on a hill. It was evening, and Laban determined not to disturb them then, but to wait until next morning. But in the night-time God stood by him in a dream and warned him to treat his son-in-law and his daughters in a peaceable manner, and not to venture upon anything rashly or in anger, but to make a league with Jacob. And God told him that if he despised their small number and attacked them in a hostile manner, He would Himself assist them.   Laban, being warned in this manner by God, next day called Jacob to him and asked him why he had gone away secretly, and had carried Rachel and Leah and their children with him without letting him know.   Jacob answered that he had gone in secret because Laban would not let him go in any other way.

" I am not," said Jacob, " the only person to whom God has given a love for his own country.   He has made it natural to all men, and therefore it was but reasonable that after so long a time I should wish to go back to my home.   And as to thy daughters, I did not force them to come away with me, but they were willing to do so, from that just affection which wives naturally bear to their husbands.   They follow, therefore, not so much myself as their own children."

And after more conversation of the same nature, Laban was obliged to acknowledge that Jacob was in the right.   So he made a promise, and bound it by oaths, that he would bear him no malice on account of what had happened, and Jacob made the same promise, and swore also that he would always love and cherish Laban's daughters.   And in memory of these promises they raised a pillar in the form of an altar upon the mount where they were standing ; whence that mount was called Mount Gilead, which means the mount of testimony, and the land was known as the land of Gilead ever after.   Now when they had feasted after the making of the league, Laban returned home.

CHAPTER VI.

THE MEETING OF JACOB AND ESAU.

As Jacob was travelling homeward he was much disturbed in his mind, because he remembered the sin he had been guilty of towards his brother Esau, and he was afraid that Esau had not forgiven him. Being desirous, therefore, of knowing what his brother's intentions were, he sent some servants before him, who were charged to go to Esau with this message : "Thy brother Jacob is returning to his native land, and he hopes that during the many years that have expired the enmity between him and you has been laid at rest. He brings with him his wives and his children and all his possessions, and he will deem it his greatest happiness to share with his brother what God hath bestowed upon him."

And when they had delivered this message Esau was very glad, and went to meet his brother with four hundred men. But Jacob, hearing that he was coming with such a number of men, was greatly afraid, for he did not know how Esau felt towards him. However, he committed himself into the hands of God and awaited his brother's arrival. In case the men attacked him, he determined to defend himself and his family as well as he could. He therefore distributed his company into parts; some he sent before the rest, and the others he ordered to come close behind, so that if the first were over-powered, they might have those that followed as a refuge to fly to. And when he had put his company into this order, he sent some of them to carry presents to his brother; the presents consisted of cattle and other four-footed animals, some of which were very rare and very valuable. But he did not send all these together : he made several droves, or flocks,

of them.   Then when Esau met the first drove and asked
whose cattle they were, the men were to answer that they
belonged to Jacob, who was sending them as a present to his
brother Esau.   And when he met the second drove and asked
the same question he was to be answered in the same way, and
so with the other droves, until he had seen them all.   Jacob did
this in order that Esau might be softened in case he were still
angry.

It took Jacob a whole day to make all these arrangements.
Then, as night came on, he sent his company across a river
which lay before them, and he himself remained behind.   And
there came an angel of God, who wrestled with him.   Jacob
did not know at first that he was an angel.   All night long
they wrestled, and when the morning light shone in the sky
the angel had not prevailed against him.   Then the angel informed him who he was, and told him to be pleased with his
victory, for it meant that the race of which he was to be the
founder would be great and victorious.   The angel also told
Jacob to take the name of Israel, which means in the Hebrew
language, " One that hath fought with an angel," and he then
disappeared.

During the struggle Jacob had hurt his thigh, and on this
account he never afterwards ate that part of an animal, and his
descendants have never eaten it either.

Full of peace and comfort, Jacob, or Israel, as he was now
called, went to join his wives and his companions.   And soon
Esau and his men came in sight, and when he had approached
so near that Jacob could see his face, he perceived that there
was no anger in it.   So Jacob ran forward to meet him, and
bowed down before him.   Esau raised him up and embraced
him.   And after the brothers had conversed together, Esau
offered to go with Jacob to their father, Isaac.   But Jacob
thanked him, and said that his wives and children were tired
with their long journey and needed rest.   So Esau left him
and returned to his own country.

Jacob went on in his journey a little way to a place called Succoth, where he stopped to rest. After a little while he went to Bethel, where he had seen the vision of the angels and the ladder, and he offered sacrifices there. And Jacob left Bethel and came near to Bethlehem, and God gave him another son, whose name was Benjamin. But Rachel, the boy's mother, died before they came to Bethlehem, and they buried her on the way.

At last he arrived at Hebron, in the land of Canaan, where his father, Isaac, was still dwelling, in extreme old age. He found that his mother, Rebekah, was dead. And only a few years after the return of Jacob Isaac himself died, at the age of one hundred and eighty-five. Esau and Jacob buried him by the side of Rebekah, in Hebron, in the cave where Abraham and Sarah were also buried.

CHAPTER VII.

JOSEPH AND HIS BRETHREN.

AFTER the death of Isaac, Jacob grew richer and more prosperous, and in time he came to be looked upon as the most highly blessed by God of all the men in that country. He had twelve sons, who were strong and handsome young men, capable of doing much work in the fields. Jacob was very proud of these sons, and was fond of them all. But he was especially fond of Joseph, who, next to Benjamin, was the youngest of all, for Joseph was not only the handsomest of the young men, but he was also the kindest and the most obedient.

Now this affection of the father excited the envy and hatred of his brethren, and the hatred was increased when Joseph told

them of two dreams of his, which, when interpreted, foretold that his future happiness would be greater than that of
any of the others.

The first of his dreams was as follows: He thought that in
harvest-time he and his brothers were binding up sheaves of
grain, and his sheaf stood still in the place where he set it, but
their sheaves ran to bow down to it, as servants bow down to
their masters. And the brothers were angry when they heard
this dream, because it seemed to mean that they would bow
down to Joseph. They did not let Joseph know the meaning
they put upon it, but only prayed in secret that what they
feared might not come to pass.

The second dream was even more wonderful than the first.
It seemed to Joseph that the sun and the moon came down
from heaven with eleven stars and bowed down to him. He
told this vision to his father in the presence of his brethren,
and begged him to interpret it. Jacob was secretly pleased
with this dream, for it seemed to promise great things to his
favorite son, and he guessed that this was its meaning: the
sun and the moon signified the father and mother of Joseph,
and the eleven stars were his brethren, and the time would
come when Joseph, by the blessing of God, should be honored and deemed worthy of worship by his parents and his
brethren. The second dream made the brothers still more
angry than the first.

A short time after this, Joseph's brethren went down to
a country called Shechem, which was famous for its pasturage, and there they fed their flocks. But as they had not
told their father of their removal he became very anxious,
and sent Joseph out to see if he could not learn any news
about them. The brethren rejoiced when they saw Joseph
coming towards them, for they had resolved to kill him.
Reuben, the eldest, was less hardened in his heart than the
others, and he began to reason with them, telling them that it
was a great crime to kill a brother, even if he had done a

serious wrong, and Joseph had done no wrong. But when he saw that his words were of no avail, he begged of them at least not to kill their brother with their own hands, but to cast him into the pit that was hard by, and so let him die, and at least they would not then have defiled their hands with his blood. To this the young men agreed. Reuben took the lad and tied a cord around him and let him down gently into the pit. And then he went his way to seek for such pasturage as was fit for feeding the flocks.

After Reuben was gone, Judah, who was another of the brethren, saw a company of merchants, called Ishmaelites, who were carrying spices and Syrian wares out of the land of Gilead to sell to the Egyptians. Then he advised the others to draw Joseph out of the pit and sell him to these merchants, for in this way they would be rid of him without the guilt of murder. They all agreed to this; and Joseph was drawn up out of the pit and sold to the merchants for twenty pieces of silver.

In the night-time Reuben came back to the pit with the intention of secretly saving Joseph. And when he called to him and received no answer he was much distressed, fearing they had destroyed him after he was gone. But when he went to his brethren and complained to them they told him what they had done, and he was satisfied.

The brethren then considered among themselves what they should tell their father. They had taken away from Joseph the coat which he had on when he came to them,—a beautiful coat of many colors given to him by Isaac,—so they decided to tear that coat to pieces, and to dip it into goat's blood, and then to carry it and show it to their father, that he might believe Joseph had been destroyed by wild beasts. And when they had so done, they came to the old man, and he recognized the coat as the one he had given to Joseph, and, believing that his favorite son had been slain, he lamented sorely and could not be comforted.

CHAPTER VIII.

JOSEPH IS SOLD INTO BONDAGE.

THE Ishmaelite merchants took Joseph with them into Egypt. The king of that country was named Pharaoh, and one of the chief officers in his army was named Potiphar. Potiphar bought Joseph from the merchants to be his slave. And he found him to be so good and trustworthy that he gave him charge of the whole house, and taught him the learning that became a free man, and gave him leave to eat at his own table instead of the table of the other servants.

But after a while the wife of Potiphar persuaded her husband that Joseph was a wicked man, and Potiphar was angry and threw him into prison.

Even in the prison, however, God raised up friends for Joseph. The keeper of the prison, himself, was moved kindly to him, because he found that Joseph was careful and faithful in everything that he asked him to do, and he therefore set him over the other prisoners, as Potiphar had set him over the other servants, and allowed him also better food than was given to the rest. Nor were the other prisoners jealous of him, for they also learned to like him and respect him. Often after the hard labors of the day were over they gathered together to discourse among themselves, and to inquire one of the other what was the reason of their being condemned to a prison. Among these prisoners were two of the king's servants who had offended him; one was his cup-bearer, who carried his wine-cup to him when he wanted to drink, and the other was his chief baker. And these men were under the care of Joseph, and were friendly to him.

One day the cup-bearer told Joseph of a dream he had had, and asked him to interpret it. He saw in his sleep a vine with three branches, and on each branch was a cluster of grapes, large already and ripe for gathering. And he squeezed the juice of these grapes into a cup and gave this cup to the king to drink, and the king received it from him with a pleasant countenance. Then Joseph told him to be of good cheer, for that the three branches he had seen in his dream meant three days, and within three days Pharaoh would send for him to be taken out of prison, and he should wait on the king and give the cup into his hand as he had been accustomed to do. Then Joseph told him he should remember his friends when this good fortune arrived, and should speak to the king concerning himself, who had been unjustly put into prison.

Now when the chief baker had heard Joseph's interpretation of the cup-bearer's dream he was glad. For he, too, had dreamed a dream, and he hoped that it had an equally pleasant meaning. So he told it to Joseph.

"I thought," he said, "that I was carrying three baskets on my head, one on top of the other. Two were full of loaves, and the third contained sweetmeats and other eatables such as are prepared for kings. But the birds of the air came flying and ate them all up, though I tried to drive them away."

When Joseph heard this dream he felt grieved for his friend. And he told him that the baskets meant three days, and that on the third day he should be crucified and devoured by fowls, while he was not able to help himself.

It came to pass exactly as Joseph had foretold. On the third day after this conversation was the king's birthday, when he made a feast to all his servants. And he sent to the prison and freed the cup-bearer from his bonds and restored him to his former position. But he had the chief baker taken out and crucified.

For two years longer Joseph remained in prison, as the

cup-bearer forgot all about him in his good fortune, and did not speak to the king as he had promised. But at the end of that time the cup-bearer was reminded of his friend in the following manner. Pharaoh one night dreamed two dreams which troubled him exceedingly, for they seemed to predict evil. And he called together all the wise men of the country, but when they could give him no interpretation of his dreams he was still more troubled. And now it was that the memory of Joseph and his skill in dreams came into the mind of the cup-bearer. So he went to the king and told him how when he and the chief baker were in prison together they each of them had a dream, and the dream was interpreted to them by a young man who was their companion in prison, and what the young man told them came true.

Then the king commanded that Joseph should be taken out of prison and brought to him. When the young man appeared, Pharaoh told him that he had heard of his skill in interpreting dreams, and that he had dreamed two dreams whose meaning he wished to know. And then he told him his dreams.

"I thought," said the king, "that as I stood by the river seven cows came up out of the water. They were large and fat, and they went into the marshes near by. And seven other cows, who were lean and ill-favored, came up to meet them out of the marshes, and they ate up the fat cows, yet they remained as lean and ill-favored as before. And then I awoke. And I fell asleep again, and saw another dream, much more wonderful than the other, which disturbed me still more. I saw seven ears of corn growing up out of one root. They were all good and filled with grain. And near these I saw seven other ears of corn, and they were spoiled and bad and had no good grain in them. And the seven bad ears ate up the seven good ones."

Then Joseph told the king that both his dreams signified one and the same thing. The seven fat cows and the seven good ears meant seven years of plenty and fruitfulness, while the seven lean cows and the seven bad ears meant seven years of famine and distress. And the meaning of the dreams was that there would come seven good years in Egypt, when the wheat would grow well and there would be plenty for the people to eat. But after those seven good years would come seven years of famine, when the grain would not grow well and the people would want for bread.

Then Joseph advised Pharaoh what he should do in order to provide against this famine. He told him that during the seven good years he should see that the Egyptians were not wasteful of the grain, but were made to reserve what they would have spent in luxury and beyond their necessity for the time of want. And the best way to do this, he said, would be to take the grain away from the husbandmen as soon as it was ripe, and allow them only so much as would be sufficient for their wants. The king consented to do as he was told, and he said that as Joseph had shown so much wisdom in explaining his dreams and in advising him what to do, he would intrust him with the duty of saving up the grain, and give him power to do what he thought would be for the benefit of the people of Egypt and of the king.

So instead of being sent back to prison Joseph was made one of the great men in the court of Pharaoh. And he was clothed with purple, which only the greatest men were allowed to wear, and he drove in his chariot through all the land of Egypt, and took the grain from the husbandmen, allowing them only so much as was necessary for food and for seed. But he did not tell any of them the reason why he did so. The grain he took in this manner he put away in storehouses, that it might be kept safe until the seven years of famine began.

CHAPTER IX.

HOW JOSEPH, WHEN HE HAD BECOME FAMOUS IN EGYPT, HAD
HIS BRETHREN IN SUBJECTION.

JOSEPH was now thirty years of age. The king, who held
him in high honor, gave him to wife a virgin named Asenath,
who was the daughter of one of the great men of his court.
And two sons were born to Joseph, whose names were Manasseh and Ephraim.

After Egypt had happily passed through seven years of
plenty the famine came upon them in the eighth year, as
Joseph had foretold. When the people came running to
the king's gates, crying for bread, he told them to go to
Joseph, who would relieve them. Joseph opened his great
storehouses and sold the grain to them. Nor did he open
this market for the people of Egypt only, for there was
a famine in the surrounding countries, and Joseph gave liberty to strangers to buy also, believing that all men should
have assistance from those who lived in happiness.

Now the people in Canaan suffered grievously from the
famine. Therefore, when Jacob learned of the great storehouses of grain that were in Egypt, and how strangers were
welcomed, he determined to send his sons there to purchase
grain. He retained only Benjamin, who was the youngest
of all, and the ten others he sent into Egypt.

So the sons of Jacob came to Joseph to buy corn of him.
Joseph knew them at once, but they did not know him. For
he was only a boy of seventeen when they sold him into
slavery, and he was now a man of thirty. They did not even
know whether he was still alive, and of course they could

know nothing of his wonderful good fortune in a strange
land. Joseph's heart warmed to them as soon as he saw
them, for his was a kind and loving nature. But he determined before he discovered himself to them to try them, and
see whether they were as wicked as ever, or whether they
had repented of their cruelty to him. So he put on a very
stern expression of face and asked them whence they came
and who they were. And when they told him that they came
from Canaan and were brothers, he pretended that he did not
believe them.

"It is impossible," he said, "that a private man could bring
up ten sons to be so strong and vigorous and handsome, such
an education of so many children being not easily obtained
by kings themselves." And he accused them of being spies,
and said that they came from several countries, and joined
themselves together, and only pretended to be of kin. Now
Joseph said this in order that they might tell all about themselves and give him news of his father and of Benjamin, who,
he saw, was not among them. For he feared that they might
have done some wicked deed against Benjamin also, and
either made away with him or sold him into slavery.

The brethren were much distressed at what Joseph said,
and feared that very great danger hung over them. But
Reuben, the elder, spoke up and assured Joseph that they
were true and faithful men, and not spies, and that they were
all children of one father.

"Our father's name," he said, "is Jacob, a Hebrew man,
who had twelve of us for his sons, and while we were all alive
we were a happy family; but when one of our brethren,
whose name was Joseph, died, our affairs changed for the
worse, for our father made a long lamentation for him, and
we are in affliction, both on account of our brother's death
and of the sorrow of our aged father. We are now come to
buy corn, having intrusted the care of our father to Benjamin, our youngest brother, and if thou sendest to our house,

thou mayest judge if we are guilty of the least falsehood in what we say."

But still Joseph seemed not to believe them. And he put them in prison for three days, so that he might think what to do to them. On the third day he sent for them to be brought before him, and told them that in order to satisfy him of the truth of what they said they must bring their youngest brother with them the next time they came to Egypt. And, as a pledge that they would do this, one of their company was to remain behind until they returned.

When the brethren heard this decision they were greatly troubled. They wept among themselves, and they told one another that God was now punishing them for their wickedness to Joseph. Reuben reminded them that he had sought to dissuade them from their cruel purpose, and he earnestly exhorted them to bear in patience the just punishment of God. They spoke all these things in their own language, not knowing that Joseph understood them. But Joseph, seeing their distress, had to go away from them, that they might not see him, for what they said made him weep. Soon he returned, and took Simeon, one of his brothers, and said that he should remain with him as a pledge that the others would return. Then he bade them take the grain they had bought, and go their way. He also told his steward to put back secretly into their sacks the money that each one had paid.

When they had come into the land of Canaan they told their father what had occurred to them, and he was much grieved. And when they opened their sacks of grain before him, and each man found the sum of money he had paid put back into his sack, they were all surprised and afraid, not knowing how it had happened. For a long time Jacob refused to allow them to return with Benjamin, in spite of all their entreaties. But at last the corn they had brought was exhausted. And when Jacob saw that his children and his grandchildren were starving for want of bread to eat, he was obliged to relent. So he gave Benjamin to the brothers, and bade them go to Egypt to buy more grain. And he lamented sorely at their departure, and they also shed many bitter tears.

As soon as they came into Egypt they were brought down to Joseph's house. Here no small fear disturbed them, lest they should be accused about the price of the corn as if they had cheated Joseph. They made a long apology to Joseph's steward, telling him that when they arrived home they found the money in their sacks, and now they had brought it back with them. He said he did not know what they meant, so they were delivered from that fear.

Then Simeon was released and allowed to join them, and they were all taken into the presence of Joseph. And the brethren offered him presents of fruit and honey and turpentine, which their father had sent. Then he asked how their father was, and they answered he was well. Pointing to Benjamin, he asked if this was the youngest son they had spoken of, and they told him that it was. Joseph laid his hands on Benjamin's head and prayed that God would bless him. But when his affection to him made him weep, Joseph retired, not wishing that his tears should be seen by his brethren. Then Joseph took them to supper, and they were set down in the order in which they used to sit at their father's table. And although Joseph treated them all kindly, yet he sent to Benjamin double what the rest of the guests had for their share.

After supper, when they had composed themselves to sleep, Joseph commanded his steward to give them their measures of grain, and to hide its price again in their sacks. He also told him to put his golden cup into Benjamin's sack. This he did in order to make trial of his brethren, whether they would stand by Benjamin when he should be accused of having stolen the cup and should appear to be in danger, or whether they would leave him, and, depending on their own innocence, go to their father without him.

Early next morning the men started on their journey back to Canaan, greatly rejoicing at their good fortune because they had been so kindly treated and were returning home with both Simeon and Benjamin. But they had not gone far when they were overtaken by a troop of horsemen, who surrounded them. Among the horsemen was the steward who had placed the cup in Benjamin's sack. And when the brethren asked in surprise what was the reason of this sudden attack upon men whom a little while before their lord had thought worthy of an honorable and hospitable reception, the steward replied by calling them wicked wretches, who had forgotten Joseph's kindness and hospitality, and had carried off the cup out of which he had in so friendly a manner drunk to them. Then the brethren protested that they were innocent, and they asked that a search should be made, and that if the cup were found upon any of them, they should all be punished. But the steward answered that he alone who was guilty of the theft should be punished, and the rest should not be blamed. So the brethren opened their sacks one after the other for the steward to make his search, until at last it came to Benjamin's turn, and in his sack the cup was found. Then they lamented, and rent their garments, and wept for the punishment which their brother was to undergo; and they all returned with him into the city.

When they came before Joseph he upbraided them, and said,—

"How came you, vile wretches that you are, to make so evil a return for my kindness to you?"

But when the steward told him it was Benjamin alone that was guilty, Joseph said he would release the others, who might return to their father in safety, and he would make Benjamin his slave. The brothers were filled with sorrow and amazement when they heard this. And Judah spoke up

for them, and told Joseph that Benjamin was the best beloved
of their father and that none of them would go home without
him.   He begged, therefore, that Joseph would take him in
the place of Benjamin, and punish him instead.   All the other
brethren also cast themselves at the feet of Joseph and offered
to deliver themselves up for the preservation of Benjamin.

Then Joseph could contain himself no longer.   He sent
all the servants out of the room, and when they were gone
he made himself known to his brethren.   And because after
the first moment of surprise they were afraid, thinking of
the evil they had done to him, he assured them that he had
entirely forgiven them.   He told them also that all he had
done was to try them and their love to their brother, and he
was rejoiced to find them so kind and good and loving.

"So," he continued, "I believe you were not wicked by
nature in what you did in my case, but that all has happened
according to God's will, and instead of bearing you a grudge
I return you my thanks, that you have concurred with the
intentions of God to bring things to their present state."

When Joseph had said this he embraced his brethren, who
were all in tears.   Then he ordered a banquet to be served
before them, and there was great feasting and rejoicing.   And
when Pharaoh heard the story he also was glad at Joseph's
good fortune in finding his brethren, and he sent them wagons
full of grain and gold and silver as presents for their father.
Joseph also gave them many valuable gifts to bear to Jacob.
He told them to invite Jacob to come down to Egypt with all
his goods and possessions, for he would be made welcome
there, and would be given some of the best lands to live on.
Then he embraced them again, and bade them adieu.

When Jacob saw his sons returning to him, and Benjamin
among them, he was rejoiced.   And when they told him their
story and he learned that Joseph was not dead, but was living
in great splendor in Egypt, it seemed at first too wonderful
to be true, and he could hardly believe them.   But when at

last he was convinced of the truth, he determined to lose no
time in setting out to visit his son.

So he departed from the land of Canaan, with his sons and
all belonging to them.   There were seventy in the family by
this time, including the wives and the children of his sons.
When they reached Beersheba, where Isaac, his father, had
built an altar many years before, Jacob offered sacrifices upon
it.   But his mind was not at rest, for there were many things
that troubled him.   He feared lest the happiness there was
in Egypt might tempt his children and their descendants to
fall in love with it and settle in it, and no more think of
returning to the land of Canaan, whose possession God had
promised to them; he feared also that if this descent into
Egypt were made without the will of God his family might
be destroyed there, and he doubted if he was strong enough
to bear the journey and if he would live to see Joseph after
all.

With these doubts in his mind he fell asleep.   But God
appeared to him in a dream and assured him that the journey
was in accordance with His wishes.

"I come now," said the Lord, "as a guide to thee in this
journey, and foretell to thee that thou shalt die in the arms
of Joseph, and I inform thee that thy descendants shall be
many ages in authority and glory, and that I will settle them
in the land which I have promised them."

Jacob, encouraged by this dream, went on more cheerfully
towards Egypt.   When Joseph understood that his father
was approaching, he went out to welcome him, and they
met at a place called Heroopolis.   Jacob almost fainted away
at this unexpected and great joy, and Joseph was much affected.   When they had embraced and wept over each other,
Joseph advised his father to continue his journey slowly,
and he himself hastened before with five of his brethren,
to let the king know that Jacob and his family had come.
Pharaoh rejoiced to hear this.   He asked Joseph what sort

of life his brethren loved to lead, that he might give them
leave to follow the same, and, being answered that they were
shepherds and had followed this calling all their lives, he said
they should be employed in this way in Egypt also.

Then Joseph, when Jacob arrived, brought him before the
king, and Jacob blessed Pharaoh. Pharaoh asked Jacob how
old he was, and marvelled greatly when told that he was one
hundred and thirty years old. And he gave him leave to live
with his children in Heroopolis; for near that city the king's
shepherds pastured their flocks.

When Jacob, or Israel, had lived seventeen years in Egypt,
he fell sick and died. On his death-bed he offered up prayers
for his sons, and foretold to them that their descendants would
possess the land of Canaan, and he commanded his own sons
to admit Ephraim and Manasseh, the sons of Joseph, into
their number, so that their descendants also might enjoy the
promises of God. When he was dead, Joseph, by the king's
permission, carried his father's dead body to Hebron, and
there buried it at a great expense. His brethren were at first
afraid to return to Egypt, because they feared that since the
death of his father, for whose sake he had been so merciful to
them, Joseph might be tempted to punish them for their former
wickedness. But he persuaded them to fear no harm and to
entertain no suspicions. So he brought them back with him,
and gave them great possessions, and never left off watching
over them and their children. They all dwelt together in
peace and unity, and their children grew up and had children
of their own, and at last when Joseph was one hundred and
ten years of age he died.

CHAPTER X.

THE SUFFERINGS OF THE CHILDREN OF ISRAEL.

AFTER the death of Joseph and his brethren, the Israelites, or children of Israel, as their descendants were now called, continued to live in Egypt. Pharaoh died, and his descendants ruled after him, and then the kingdom passed into another family of Pharaohs. Meanwhile the Egyptians, forgetful of the benefits which they had received from Joseph, began to look with envy upon the prosperity and happiness of the children of Israel. So they became very cruel in their treatment of them. They obliged them to do hard work, to cut a great number of channels for the river, to build walls round their cities, and also to build the pyramids.

Four hundred years they spent under these afflictions. At last a still greater cruelty was practised against them. For it happened that one of the Egyptian wise men, who was able to foretell what would happen in the future, told Pharaoh the king that about this time there would be born a child to the Israelites who, if he were suffered to live, would bring the Egyptian dominion low and would raise the Israelites, that he would excel all men in virtue, and would obtain a glory that should be remembered through all ages. Then the king commanded that every male child born to the Israelites should be cast into the river, and that if any parents should disobey him and let their little boys live, they and their families should be destroyed. This law caused great mourning and weeping among the children of Israel, for they knew that if it were carried out their race would soon be at an end. There was a man among the Israelites named Amram, who was a leader among them. He too was greatly troubled because of this law, and he went out and prayed to God. And God answered his prayer. He stood by him in his sleep and exhorted him not to despair. He reminded him of what He had done for the Israelites in the past, and He told him He would continue His favors in the future.

"Know, therefore," said the Lord, "that I shall provide for you all in common what is for your good, and particularly for thyself what shall make thee famous; for that child, out of dread of whose nativity the Egyptians have doomed the Israelite children to destruction, shall be a child of thine, and shall be concealed from those who watch to destroy him; and he shall deliver the Hebrew nation from the distress they are under from the Egyptians. His memory shall be famous while the world lasts; and this not only among the Hebrews, but among other nations also."

When the vision had informed him of these things, Amram awoke and told it to Jochebed, who was his wife. And shortly after God gave a male child to this couple, whose birth was kept a secret from the Egyptians. They nourished the child at home secretly for three months, but after that time Amram, fearing it might be discovered and slain, determined to intrust the care of the infant to God. So he and his wife made a cradle of bulrushes, or long weeds that grew by the river, and daubed it over with pitch so as to keep out the water. Putting the infant into the cradle, they set it afloat upon the river, and left its preservation to God. But Miriam, the child's sister, watched by the river bank to see what became of the cradle.

King Pharaoh had a daughter named Thermuthis, who had come down that day to bathe in the river. Seeing a cradle borne along by the current, she sent out some of her maidens that could swim to get it and bring it to her. When they returned with the cradle and she saw the little child, she felt a

4

great love for it on account of its beauty. Miriam now came
to where the princess was standing, and asked if she might
not go and call one of the Hebrew women to nurse the child.
The princess told her she might do so. Therefore she went,
and returned with her mother, who was known to nobody
there. And the princess intrusted the nursing of the child to
its own mother.

When the boy was a few years old she sent for him, as she
had determined to bring him up as her own son. And she
named him Moses, which means, in the Egyptian language,
drawn out of the water. He grew up tall and beautiful, and
showed great quickness at his studies. The princess, finding
that he was likely to prove a remarkable man, took him one
day to her father, and said to him,—

" I have brought up a child who is of a divine form and of
a generous mind; and as I have received him from the bounty
of the river, in a wonderful manner, I thought proper to adopt
him for my son and the heir of my kingdom."

And when she had said this, she put the infant into her
father's hands. He took him, and kissed him, and playfully
put his crown upon the child's head; but Moses threw it down
to the ground and trod upon it with his feet. And when the
sacred scribe saw this (he was the same person who had foretold that a child would be born to the Hebrews who would
bring the dominion of Egypt low) he made a violent attempt
to kill him, and cried out,—

" This, O king! this child is he of whom God foretold, that
if we kill him we shall be in no danger; he himself shows it
by his treading upon thy crown. Take him, therefore, out
of the way, and deliver the Egyptians from the fear they are
in about him; and deprive the Hebrews of the hope they have
of being encouraged by him."

But Thermuthis prevented him, and snatched the child
away. The king would not listen to the scribe and allowed
Moses to live. He was, therefore, educated with great care.

So the Hebrews depended upon him, and were of good hopes that great things would be done by him; but the Egyptians were suspicious of him. Yet because, if Moses had been slain, there was no one else that would be likely to rule wisely over Egypt, they were afraid to kill him.

CHAPTER XI.

THE BRAVERY OF MOSES.*

WHEN Moses had grown to be a man, a war broke out between the Egyptians and their neighbors the Ethiopians. A great battle was fought, in which the Ethiopians were successful. Being puffed up by this victory, they determined to conquer the whole land of Egypt. And they gathered together their armies and invaded Egypt. Now the Egyptians were in great terror, and they asked their priests and their wise men to pray to God and find out what they should do. Then the same wise man who had foretold the birth of Moses advised them to seek the assistance of Moses and make him the general of their armies. So Pharaoh commanded his daughter to produce him. Upon which, when she had made him swear he would do him no harm, she delivered him to the king. But she reproached the wise man who had before advised the Egyptians to kill him, and was not ashamed now to own their want of his help.

Then Moses went out at the head of a great army, and he surprised the enemy and attacked them before they knew he was coming. For they expected he would come against them

---

* The story told in this chapter is not contained in the Bible, and Josephus probably derived it from traditionary sources.

by water, as the land was difficult to be passed over in many places, owing to the vast number of poisonous snakes that infested it. But Moses showed his wisdom in a wonderful manner. He took with him a number of birds called ibises, a sort of stork, who devour serpents and are their greatest enemies, so much so that the serpents are afraid of them, and glide away when they know they are coming. As soon, therefore, as Moses was come to the land which was the breeder of these serpents, he let loose the ibises, and by that means drove them away. And being thus enabled to come upon the Ethiopians before they were aware, and when they were not prepared for him, he attacked and beat them with great slaughter. And the Ethiopian army fled out of Egypt, and were pursued by Moses into their own country and defeated again, insomuch that they were in danger of being reduced to slavery and all sorts of destruction. And at length they retired to Saba, which was a royal city of Ethiopia. This place was very difficult to besiege, for it was built on an island in the river Nile, and was surrounded by a great wall. While Moses was uneasy at the army's lying idle on the banks of the river, for it seemed like madness to attempt crossing it when the enemy could fight against them from behind their fortifications and hurl their darts and javelins without any danger to themselves, it happened that the daughter of the king of the Ethiopians saw Moses in the distance, and fell in love with him on account of his beauty and his bravery. Therefore she sent to him the most faithful of all her servants to propose marriage. He accepted the offer, provided she would deliver up the city to him. No sooner was the agreement made than it took effect immediately; and when Moses had cut off the Ethiopians, he gave thanks to God, and celebrated his marriage. Then he led the Egyptians back to their own land.

CHAPTER XII.

HOW MOSES FLED OUT OF EGYPT TO MIDIAN.

THE Egyptians, instead of being grateful to Moses for his success, hated him still more, partly because they were envious and partly because they were afraid he might take advantage of his good fortune and try to destroy their government. The king, also, was afraid of him, because of what the scribe had predicted. Moses, learning that there were plots against him to kill him, secretly made his escape. And when he came to a city called Midian, which lay near the Red Sea, he sat down by a certain well, and rested himself there after his long journey. Now water was very scarce in that country, and this well had been seized by some shepherds, who would not let any one else use it, for fear there would not be enough left for their own flocks. While Moses was resting, there came to the well seven sisters, daughters of a priest named Jethro, who wished to draw water there, but the shepherds drove them away. Then Moses rose and attacked the men and drove them away, and when he had done this he helped the flocks of the maidens to water. The sisters went home and told their father of the assistance a stranger had given them, and entreated that he would not let this generous action go without a reward. The father was well pleased with the gratitude of his daughters, and bade them bring Moses into his presence. And when Moses came, he thanked him for his kindness, and adopted him as his son, and gave him one of his daughters in marriage, and appointed him to be the guardian and superintendent over his cattle.

One day Moses, going out to feed Jethro's flocks, took them up a mountain called Sinai. This was the highest of all the mountains there, and the best for pasturage, but the shepherds were afraid of ascending it because of the opinion men had that God dwelt there. And a wonderful prodigy happened to Moses. For a fire sprang up out of a thorn-bush, yet the green leaves and the flowers were not consumed by it. Moses was affrighted at this strange sight, and still more when a voice out of the fire called to him by name. The voice, however, bade him be of good cheer, and directed him to set out for Egypt, where he would be made the commander and conductor of the Hebrews.

"For," said the Lord, "they shall inhabit the happy land which your forefather Abraham inhabited, and shall have the enjoyment of all good things, and thou by thy prudence shalt guide them to those good things."

Then Moses, astonished, asked, "How shall I, a private man and of no abilities, persuade my countrymen to leave the land in which they dwell and follow me, or, if they should be persuaded, how can I force Pharaoh to permit them to depart?"

But God exhorted him to be courageous, and promised to be with him, and to assist him in his words when he was to persuade men, and in his deeds when he was to perform wonders. And as a sign that what He said was true, He bade him throw his rod upon the ground. And the rod became a serpent and rolled itself round in its folds, and erected its head as if to dart at any one that might attack. Then it became a rod again. After this God bade Moses put his right hand into his bosom, and when he took it out again it was white as chalk, but afterwards it returned to its natural color. Moses also, at God's command, took some of the water that was near him and poured it upon the ground, and the color was that of blood. Then God assured him that He would be a support to him, and bade him make use of those wonders in order to obtain belief among men that he was sent by God and did everything according to His commands.

So Moses returned to Jethro, and obtained leave to go to Egypt for the benefit of his own people. He took with him his wife and his children, and when he came near the borders of Egypt, Aaron, his brother, met him. He told Aaron what had happened on the mountain, and of the commands of God. And soon after, reaching the place where the Israelites lived, he also told the chief men of these commands, and when they doubted, he showed them the signs that God had taught him. So they took courage and believed that the day of their deliverance was at hand.

Now the Pharaoh was dead in whose reign Moses had fled away into Egypt, and a new Pharaoh reigned in his place. Moses went at once to his palace, and reminded him of what he had done for the Egyptians in their war against the Ethiopians, and how he had received no reward for it. And he told the king what things had happened to him on Mount Sinai, and when the king denied him he made him see the signs. Then the king was angry, and called him a bad man, who had formerly escaped from his Egyptian slavery, and now came back with deceitful tricks and wonders and magical arts to astonish him. And when he had said this, he commanded the priests to let him see the same wonderful sights, knowing that the Egyptians were skilful in magic and cunning, and he told him he was not the only person who knew them and pretended them to be divine; but that he would only be believed by the unlearned. Now when the priests threw down their rods, they became serpents. But Moses was not daunted at it, and said,—

"O king, I do not myself despise the wisdom of the Egyptians, but I say that what I do is as much superior to what these do by magic arts and tricks as divine power exceeds the power of man. But I will show that what I do is not done by craft or deceit, but that these signs appear by the providence and power of God."

And when he had said this, he cast his rod down upon the ground, and commanded it to turn itself into a serpent. It obeyed him, and went all round, and devoured the rods of the Egyptians, until it had consumed them all. It then returned to its own form, and Moses took it into his hand again.

However, the king was no more moved than before; and becoming very angry, he told Moses that he should gain nothing by this his cunning and shrewdness against the Egyptians. And he commanded him that was the chief task-master over the Hebrews to give them no rest from their labors, but to compel them to submit to greater oppressions than before. And though he had allowed them straw before for making their bricks, he would allow it them no longer; but he made them work hard at brick-making in the day-time and gather straw in the night. Now when their labor was thus doubled upon them, they laid the blame upon Moses, and complained bitterly that he had done them no good, but only harm. Yet Moses did not let his courage sink for the king's threatenings, nor did he abate his zeal on account of the Hebrews' complaints, but he nerved himself, and set his soul resolutely against them both, and used his utmost diligence to procure liberty to his countrymen. So he went to the king, and besought him to let the Hebrews go. He warned him not to oppose the designs of God, for if he did he would bring down grievous punishments upon himself and his people, and he further told him that the Israelites would go out of the country even against the will of Pharaoh.

CHAPTER XIII.

THE TEN PLAGUES OF EGYPT.

THE king despised the words of Moses, and would not listen to them, and great plagues were sent by the Lord upon the Egyptians.

First the river ran with bloody water, and the Egyptians that ventured to drink of it were visited with great pains and torment. There was no other water to drink, for all the springs were dried up. But to the Israelites the river was sweet and fit for drinking, and noway different from what it used to be. Then the king, being in great fear and not knowing what else to do, gave the Israelites leave to go. But when the plague ceased, he changed his mind and would not suffer them to go.

God, seeing he was proud and wicked, sent a second plague upon the Egyptians. A great number of frogs overspread the land; the river also was full of them. And the frogs crept into their houses, and spoiled the vessels that they used, and were found in what they ate and what they drank, and came in great numbers upon their beds. Pharaoh again grew afraid, and ordered Moses to take the Israelites with him and be gone. Upon which the whole multitude of frogs vanished. But as soon as Pharaoh saw the land freed from this plague, he forbade the departure of the Israelites.

God punished him with a third plague. An innumerable quantity of lice appeared upon the bodies of the Egyptians and upon their cattle, and there was no way of destroying the vermin. Then Pharaoh gave leave to the Israelites to depart.

But when the plague ceased, he said they must leave their
children and wives behind them, as pledges that they would
return. Whereat God was provoked, and sent another plague.
He filled the country with a number of small flies, of a kind
that had never been seen there before, and whose bite was
poisonous to both man and beast. But when Pharaoh refused
to yield to this plague, and would only allow the Israelites
and their wives to go if they would leave their children
behind them, God visited the land with still more grievous
calamities. The bodies of the Egyptians broke out into terrible sores, and a great many of them perished. Their cattle
also were afflicted and perished. Then hail was sent down
from heaven, and the hailstones were larger than any that
had ever been seen in that country, and they broke down
the boughs laden with fruit and did other damage. After
this a tribe of locusts consumed the seed which was not hurt
by the hail, so that all hope of fruit of any kind was destroyed.
Yet Pharaoh still contested with God, and would only let
Moses take away the Israelites with their wives and children
if they would leave their cattle behind them. Then a thick
darkness arose and covered the land of the Egyptians,
whereby their sight was obstructed and their breathing hindered, and it lasted for three days and three nights. And this
was the ninth plague.

Then God told Moses that with one more plague He would
compel the Egyptians to let the Israelites go. Moses told
his people to get ready for the journey. In every household
he commanded that a lamb should be killed as a sacrifice,
and its blood sprinkled on the door-post. Then the lamb
should be roasted and eaten, and whatever portion of it was
left should be burnt.

That night God went through the land of Egypt, and the
first-born in every Egyptian house was stricken dead. But
God passed over every house that was marked with blood-
stains, so that none of the Israelites died.

In commemoration of this event the children of Israel ever afterwards celebrated a yearly feast called the Passover, because God had passed over their households while visiting the tenth plague upon the Egyptians.

In every Egyptian house, in the royal palace as well as in the meanest hut, there arose a great sound of moaning and lamentation when it was found that the oldest child had been slain. And the people came to Pharaoh and begged him to let the Israelites go. Pharaoh himself was now anxious to be rid of them. So he called Moses to him, and said,—

"Go away out of the land, you and your people, and take your flocks and herds with you."

CHAPTER XIV.

THE CROSSING OF THE RED SEA.

In this way the Israelites went out of Egypt. The number of all of them, including the women and children, is not known with certainty, but of those that were able to bear arms there were six hundred thousand.

They left Egypt just two hundred and fifteen years after Jacob had removed there with his sons. But the Egyptians soon repented of having allowed the Israelites to go. Pharaoh also was sorry, and he gathered together his soldiers and his horses and chariots and started off in pursuit of the fugitives. After three days he came in sight of them, just as they had reached the banks of a sea, called the Red Sea, which separates Asia from Africa. Great was the terror of the Israelites when they saw these armed men coming towards them. They were themselves unarmed, and could not fight. They were shut in by the mountains on the right hand and the left, and the Red Sea was in front of them, so they could not flee. In despair they gathered round Moses, and he calmed them and comforted them, telling them that God would not forsake them in their extremity. Then he led the Israelites to the sea. And he took his rod, and having prayed to God, he smote the sea with his rod, and the waters parted and rolled back on each side and left the ground dry. And he went down upon the dry ground, and bade the Israelites follow him upon that divine road.

Now when the Egyptians from a distance saw the Israelites go down into the sea, they thought at first they were distracted, and were going rashly to certain destruction. But when they saw that they were gone a great way without any harm, and that no obstacle or difficulty fell in their journey, they wondered greatly, and made haste to pursue them. By the time they had reached the shore of the sea the last of the Israelites had safely crossed over to the other side. Then Pharaoh with his chariots and horsemen and foot-soldiers went down into the sea in pursuit of them. For the Egyptians were not aware that they went into a road made for the Israelites only; for the deliverance of those in danger, not for those who followed to destroy them. As soon, therefore, as their whole army was in the sea, the waters came together again and covered them. Showers of rain also came down from the sky, and dreadful thunders and lightning and flashes of fire. And thus did all these men perish, so that there was no one left to be a messenger of this calamity to the rest of the Egyptians.

The Israelites were not able to contain themselves for joy at their wonderful deliverance and the destruction of their enemies, so that all the night long they were employed in singing hymns and in mirth. Moses also composed a song unto God, containing His praises and a thanksgiving for His kindness.

CHAPTER XV.

THE FALL OF MANNA.

IT was not long before the rejoicing of the Israelites was turned again into moaning and sorrow. For the country into which they had come was a desert or wilderness, and there was nothing for them to eat or to drink. They had indeed brought some water along with them, but this was soon exhausted; and when this was spent, they had to dig deep wells with much toil and pain, and the water they found in this way was bitter and not fit for drinking, and this in small quantities also. And late one evening they came to a place called Marah, which was so called from the badness of its water, for Mar means bitterness. Now here there was a well in which there was a great deal of water, and they had been told that it was the only well for many hundred miles around. Yet was this water bitter, and not fit for men to drink, and not only so, but it was intolerable even to the cattle.

Moses grieved greatly to see the people so cast down. For they all of them ran to him and begged of him, the men begging for the women, and the women for the infants and children, that he would find some way of delivering them from their terrible thirst. He therefore betook himself to prayer to God, that He would change the water from its present badness and make it fit for drinking. And when God had granted him that favor, he took a stick that lay at his feet and divided it in the middle. He then let it down in the well, and told the Israelites that God had listened to his prayer, and would sweeten the waters in case they did what he enjoined upon them. And when they had asked him what they were to do, he bade the strongest men among them that stood there to draw up water, and told them that when the greater part was drawn up, the remainder would be fit to drink. So they labored at it till the water came up sweet and pure.

And they journeyed and came to Elim. This place looked well from a distance, for there was a grove of palm-trees there; but when they came near, the palm-trees were found to be feeble and ill-grown for want of moisture. Here the Israelites, having exhausted their provisions, suffered grievously from hunger, and complained bitterly, and laid the blame upon Moses. But he came into the midst of them even while they clamored against him and had stones in their hands to kill him. And he spoke kindly to them, and reminded them of the wonderful ways in which God had helped them in the past, and told them that He would assist them also in the future. By this means he pacified the people and restrained them from stoning him, and brought them to repent of what they were going to do.

Then he went up a mountain and prayed to God for assistance, and God promised to hear him. Accordingly, a little time after there came a vast quantity of quails, and hovered over them, till, weary of their flight, they fell down upon the Israelites, who caught them and satisfied their hunger with them. And Moses thanked God for this assistance.

But presently after this first supply of food He sent them a second, for as Moses was lifting up his hands in prayer a white dew fell down from heaven. Moses, when he found it stick to his hands, guessed that this also was food sent by God, and he tasted it and found it was indeed so. Seeing the people knew not what it was, but thought it snowed, he told them this dew did not fall from heaven after the manner they supposed, but was sent them for food. They tasted it and were pleased with the food, for it was like honey in sweetness and pleasant flavor, but in bigness equal to coriander-seed. And very eager they were in gathering it up. But they were told to gather up only so much as was necessary for themselves and their families for one day, because every day there would be more on the ground for them. Some, distrusting this promise, gathered up more than was necessary, but next day they found it was spoiled and had worms in it. This food supplied the want of all other foods to those that fed on it. The Israelites called it manna, which means, what is this? for they knew not what it was.

They journeyed on and came to a place called Rephidim. Here they again suffered for want of water, and again they turned their anger against Moses. He at first avoided the fury of the multitude, and then betook himself to prayer to God, beseeching Him that as He had given them food when they were in want of it, so He would give them drink now. And God did not long delay to give it to them, but promised Moses He would procure them a fountain and plenty of water, from a place whence they could not expect any. He commanded him to smite a rock that lay in front of him with his rod, and when he did so, water burst out in abundance, and it was very sweet and pure. And all the Israelites were astonished at this wonderful thing, and when they had satisfied their thirst, they gave thanks to God.

CHAPTER XVI.

THE VICTORY OVER THE AMALEKITES.

Now there were a people called the Amalekites in that neighborhood, who, when they heard of the coming of the Israelites, determined to fight with them and conquer them.

Moses exhorted his people to be brave and to resist these enemies. There was a brave and good man among them, named Joshua, whom Moses chose to be the captain of the Israelites, to command them in the battle. When the Amalekites arrived, Joshua went out with his men and attacked them, and both sides fought long and bravely. But Moses, with his brother Aaron and another man named Hur, had gone up a high mountain to pray for his people that they might be successful. So long as he stretched out his hands towards heaven, the Israelites were too hard for the Amalekites, but when he was tired and lowered them, the Amalekites prevailed. Therefore Aaron and Hur stood on each side of him, and assisted him and held up his hands. When this was done the Israelites conquered the Amalekites, and they would have killed them all if darkness had not come on and put a stop to the bloodshed.

This victory was of great use to the Israelites, for it terrified all their enemies so that they durst no more attack them. Moreover, they acquired a vast quantity of riches, for a great deal of silver and gold was left in the enemy's camp, as well as brazen vessels and other things that served for use in the family and for the furniture of their tents. And the Israelites now began to pride themselves upon their courage and strength, and to take exercise for the purpose of inuring themselves to fatigue and danger. Such were the consequences of this battle.

On the next day Moses stripped the dead bodies of their enemies, and gathered together the armor of those who had fled and left it behind them. He also gave presents to those who had distinguished themselves in the battle, and he highly commended Joshua, whom all the army praised on account of the great actions he had done. He also foretold that the Amalekites should be utterly destroyed hereafter, because they fought against the Israelites when they were in distress in the wilderness. Moreover, he refreshed the army with feasting, and allowed them to rest for a few days. Then, going slowly on, he came to Mount Sinai, where the vision of the bush and other wonderful things had happened to him.

CHAPTER XVII.

HOW MOSES ENTERTAINED HIS FATHER-IN-LAW, JETHRO.

WHEN Jethro, the father-in-law of Moses, who, you will remember, lived in the neighborhood of Mount Sinai, heard of the deeds of Moses and the Israelites, and how they had defeated the Amalekites in a great battle, he was very glad. He came to visit Moses, and Moses welcomed him and made a great feast for him, near the place where he had seen the vision of the burning bush, and all the multitude of the Israelites partook of the feast. Then they sang hymns of thankfulness, and Jethro made a speech in which he praised the Israelites, and especially their leader, Moses.

Next day Jethro saw Moses in the midst of a great crowd of men, settling their disputes. For whenever they differed about anything they came to Moses, believing that he would do justice between them, and they always accepted his decision. But because of the great number of men that were under him Moses was kept very busy. When the day's work was over Jethro took him aside, and said to him that he ought to leave the trouble of lesser disputes to others and himself take care only of the greater ones and of the safety of the Israelites; for many others might be found who were fit to decide disputes, but only Moses could take care of the safety of so many thousands of men.

"Make use of this method," said Jethro. "Take a review of the army, and appoint chosen rulers over tens of thousands, and then over thousands; then divide the thousands into five hundreds; and again into hundreds, and into fifties; and set rulers over each of them, who may distinguish them into thirties, and keep them in order; and at last number them by twenties and by tens. And let there be one commander over each number, to be chosen from the number of those over whom they are rulers, but such as the whole multitude have tried, and do approve of, being good and righteous men ; and let these rulers decide the controversies the people under them may have one with another. But if any great cause arise, let them refer it to the rulers of a higher dignity; and if any arise that is too hard for even their determination, let them send it to thee. By these means two advantages will be gained,—that the Hebrews will have justice done them ; and thou wilt be able to attend constantly on God, and procure Him to be more favorable to the people."

This was the advice of Jethro; and Moses received it very kindly, and acted according to his suggestion. Nor did he conceal the invention of this method, or pretend to it himself, but informed the multitude who it was that invented it. Nay, he has named Jethro in the books he wrote as the person who invented this ordering of the people, thinking it right to give a true testimony to worthy persons, although he might have got reputation by ascribing to himself the inventions of other men. Whence we may learn the virtuous disposition of Moses.

CHAPTER XVIII.

MOSES ASCENDS MOUNT SINAI, AND RECEIVES LAWS FROM GOD.

Now Moses called the people together, and told them that he was going from them unto Mount Sinai, to converse with God; to receive from Him and to bring back with him a certain oracle.   And he enjoined them to pitch their tents near the mountain.   When he had said this, he went up to Mount Sinai, which is very difficult to be ascended by men, not only on account of its height, but because of its precipices also.   And besides this, it was terrible on account of the belief that God dwelt there.   The Israelites moved their tents, as Moses had bidden them, and took possession of the lowest parts of the mountain, and were glad to think that Moses would return from God with promises of the good things he had proposed to them.   So they feasted, and put on themselves and on their wives and children their best raiment, and waited for their conductor.   And they prayed to God that He would favorably receive Moses, and let him know what His will was, so that they might live in the way that was pleasing to Him.

In this manner they passed two days; but on the third day, before the sun was up, a cloud spread itself over the whole camp of the Hebrews, such as none had before seen, and encompassed the place where they had pitched their tents.   And while all the rest of the air was clear, there came strong winds, that raised up showers of rain, which became a mighty tempest.   There was also terrible lightning and thunder.   This sight, and the amazing sound that came to their ears, greatly disturbed the Hebrews, for they were not such as they were accustomed to; and then the rumor that was spread abroad, how God frequented that mountain, made them more alarmed, so they sorrowfully stayed within their tents, fearing that Moses had been destroyed by the divine wrath, and expecting the like destruction for themselves.

While they were under these fears, Moses appeared coming down the mountain.   And his face was joyful and greatly exalted.   When they saw him, they were freed from their fear.   The air also became clear and pure and the storm passed away.   Then Moses called together all the people, and when they were gathered in a great multitude, he stood on an eminence, whence they might all hear him, and said,—

"God has received me graciously, O Israelites, as He has formerly done; and has suggested a happy method of living for you, and an order of government. And He is now present in the camp. I therefore charge you, for His sake, and the sake of His works, and what we have done by His means, that you do not put a low value on what I am going to say, because the commands do not come from me, Moses, the son of Amram and Jochebed, but from Him who obliged the Nile to run bloody for your sakes, and tamed the haughtiness of the Egyptians by various sorts of judgments; who provided a way through the sea for us; who contrived a method of sending us food from heaven, when we were distressed for want of it; who made the water to issue out of a rock, when we had very little of it before; by whose means Adam was made to partake of the fruits both of the land and of the sea; by whose means Noah escaped the deluge; by whose means our forefather Abraham, of a wandering pilgrim, was made the heir of the land of Canaan; by whose means Isaac was born of parents who were very old; by whose means Jacob was adorned with twelve virtuous sons; by whose means Joseph became a potent lord over the Egyptians: He it is who conveys these instructions to you by me as His interpreter. And let them be held by you in great respect; for if you will follow them, you will lead a happy life: the land will be fruitful, and the sea calm; you will be also terrible to your enemies; for I have been admitted into the presence of God, and been made a hearer of His incorruptible voice; so great is His concern for your nation and its duration."

When he had said this, he brought the people, with their wives and children, so near the mountain that they might hear God Himself speaking to them about the rules which they were to practise. And they all heard a voice that came from above, and spoke ten commandments.

The first commandment teaches us that there is but one God, and that we ought to worship Him only. The second commands us not to make the image of any living creature to worship it. The third, that we must not swear by God in a false matter. The fourth, that we must keep the seventh day, by resting from all sort of work. The fifth, that we must honor our parents. The sixth, that we must abstain from murder. The seventh, that we must not commit adultery. The eighth, that we must not be guilty of theft. The ninth, that we must not bear false witness. The tenth, that we must not admit of the desire of anything that is another's.

Now when the multitude had heard God Himself giving these precepts they rejoiced at what was said, and the congregation was dissolved. But on the following days they came to Moses's tent, and desired him to bring them other laws from God. Accordingly, he appointed such laws, and afterwards informed them in what manner they should act in all cases.

When matters were brought to this state, Moses went up again to Mount Sinai. He made his ascent in their sight, and stayed there so long a time (for he was absent from them forty days) that fear seized upon the Hebrews, lest Moses should have come to any harm; nor was there anything else so sad, and that so much troubled them, as this belief that Moses was perished. Now there was a variety of opinion about it: some saying that he was fallen among wild beasts, and others that he was departed and gone to God; but the wiser sort were quiet and waited, though they grieved sorely. And the camp durst not remove all this while, because Moses had bidden them to stay there.

But when the forty days and as many nights were over, Moses came down. He had tasted no food during all that time. His appearance filled the army with gladness, and he declared to them what care God had of them, and in what way they might live happily. He also informed them that during the days of his absence God had told him to build a tabernacle for Him. And God had said that He would descend into this tabernacle and be present at the prayers of the Israelites, and they should carry it about with them, and there would no longer be any occasion for Moses to go up to Mount Sinai. When he had said this, he showed them two tables of stone with the ten commandments engraven upon them, five upon each table; and the writing was by the hand of God.*

CHAPTER XIX.

THE BUILDING OF THE TABERNACLE.

THE people rejoiced at what Moses told them, and they brought him silver, and gold, and brass, and woods of all kinds, in order that he might build the tabernacle. When all these things were brought together, Moses appointed architects, and he gave them the plans of the building, which he had drawn from directions given by God Himself.

The tabernacle was a large tent, where the worship of God was conducted by the priests. It could be taken down and put up again, like the other tents, for the Israelites had to carry it about with them in all their wanderings. The tabernacle when it was set up was sixty feet long and twenty feet broad. It was divided into two rooms. Into the first room the priests were admitted to perform the sacrifices, but the second no one could enter except the high-priest, and he

---

* The Bible tells us that when Moses was away on Mount Sinai the Israelites took advantage of his absence to erect an idol similar to those they had seen in Egypt. They made this idol out of gold and worshipped it. It was on account of this sin that God condemned the Israelites to wander for forty years in the wilderness. Josephus does not mention this, however.

was allowed to enter only once a year, on the day when a great feast, called the Feast of the Atonement, was celebrated. The first room was called the Holy Place; the second was called the Holy of Holies. In the Holy of Holies was placed the ark of the covenant. This was a chest, or box, made of a precious wood called shittim-wood, and covered all over with pure gold. On its top were the figures of two angels made of gold. Inside the ark were placed the tables of stone upon which God had written the Ten Commandments. The tabernacle stood in a large court, which was surrounded by a wall made of poles and curtains. To this court all the people were admitted. At the entrance was the large altar upon which animals that had been killed were burned as sacrifices, and between this altar and the entrance to the tabernacle was the laver, or fountain, made of brass, where the priests washed their hands and feet while they were about the service of God.

The tribe of Levi was set apart to furnish the priests for all the Israelites, and no man could be a priest who was not a Levite; that is, a member of the tribe of Levi. This was the tribe to which Moses and Aaron belonged. Aaron was appointed high-priest, for God had so commanded. And Moses caused beautiful garments to be made for him, which he was to wear when he performed his sacred duties.

CHAPTER XX.

MOSES REMOVES FROM MOUNT SINAI, AND CONDUCTS THE PEOPLE
TO THE BORDERS OF CANAAN.

AND now the time was come for the Israelites to leave Mount Sinai. After travelling for a long time, they came to a place called Hazeroth. Here, because they were suffering again from thirst, they became rebellious and complained against Moses, blaming him because he had brought them out of the land of Egypt and made false promises to them. They also cried that they wanted flesh meat and were not satisfied with the manna which came from heaven. Moses spoke kindly to them, and promised he would procure for them a great quantity of flesh meat, and that not for a few days only, but for many days. This they were not willing to believe, and when one of them asked whence he could obtain such a plenty of food, he replied,—

"Neither God nor I, O ye Israelites, although we hear so many murmurs and complaints from you, will leave off our labors for you, and you shall soon see that I speak the truth."

And, indeed, he had barely left off speaking, when the whole camp was filled with great numbers of quails. There were so many of them that they covered all the ground. And the people went out and gathered them, and satisfied their hunger. But it was not long before God punished the Israelites for the words they had spoken in anger, and a great many of them sickened and died.

From Hazeroth Moses led the Israelites to a place called Paran, which was near the borders of Canaan. Here he gathered the people together, and, standing in the midst of them, he said,—

"Two things has God promised to bestow upon us, liberty and the possession of a happy land. The first you now enjoy, and the other you will quickly obtain. For we now have our abode near the borders of Canaan, which is the land that God promised us, and which no human strength can prevent our taking. Let us, therefore, prepare ourselves for the work, for the Canaanites will not give up their land without fighting, and it must be wrested from them by great struggles in war. We must first send spies, who may take a view of the goodness of the land, and of the strength of its defenders. But, above all things, let us be of one mind, and let us honor God, who is our helper and assister."

When Moses had spoken, the multitude shouted in approval. Twelve men were chosen, one out of each tribe, who were to be sent out as spies. And they went over into the land of Canaan, and travelled through it for forty days, and then came back again. They brought with them some of the fruits that grew in the land, and gave an account of the great quantities of good things the land afforded. Then the multitude were pleased, and wished to go to war at once to obtain these good things. But the spies went on to tell them of the great difficulty there would be in obtaining the land; that the rivers were so large and deep that they could not be crossed, the mountains were so high that they could not be passed over, and the cities were strong, with walls and firm fortifications around them.

So the Israelites imagined, from what they had heard, that it was impossible to get possession of the country. And they and their wives and children set up a great lamentation, as if God would not indeed assist them, but had only made false promises. They also again blamed Moses, and made a clamor against him, and against his brother Aaron, the high-priest. And they passed that night in murmuring, and in the morning they got together, intending to stone Moses and Aaron and return into Egypt.

But there were two of the spies who were good and faithful men: their names were Joshua and Caleb. They went into the midst of the multitude, and stilled them, and desired them to be of good courage, and neither to condemn God, as having told them lies, nor to hearken to those who had affrighted them. And they encouraged them to hope for good success, and told them they should gain possession of the happiness promised them, because neither the height of mountains nor the depth of rivers could deter men of true courage, especially when God would take care of them and assist them.

"Let us then go," said they, "against our enemies, and

have no suspicion of ill success, trusting in God to conduct us, and following those that are to be our leaders."

Thus did these two exhort them, and endeavor to pacify the rage they were in. But Moses and Aaron fell on the ground, and besought God, not for their own deliverance, but that He would put a stop to what the people were unwarily doing, and would bring their minds, which were now disordered by passion, into a quiet temper. The cloud also did now appear, and stood over the tabernacle, and declared to them the presence of God to be there.

Moses came now boldly to the multitude, and informed them that God was moved at their abuse of Him, and would inflict punishment upon them, not indeed such as they deserved for their sins, but such as parents inflict on their children, in order to their correction. "For," he said, "when I was in the tabernacle, and was bewailing with tears that destruction which was coming upon you, God put me in mind what things He had done for you, and yet how ungrateful you had been to Him, so that you could be induced by the timorousness of the spies to think that their words were truer than His own promise to you. Therefore, though He would not indeed destroy you all, nor utterly exterminate your nation, which He had honored more than any other part of mankind, yet He would not permit you to take possession of the land of Canaan, or to enjoy its happiness, but would make you wander in the wilderness, and live without a fixed habi ation, and without a city, for forty years together, as a punishment for this your transgression; but He hath promised to give that land to our children, and He will make them the possessors of those good things which, by your ungoverned passions, you have deprived yourselves of."

The multitude were calmed down by this discourse of Moses, and they grieved and were in affliction. And they besought Moses to procure their reconciliation to God, so that He would no longer allow them to wander in the wilderness, but w uld bestow cities on them. Moses told them that he could not do this, that God had not determined lightly or rashly, and that this punishment could not be remitted.

CHAPTER XXI.

THE CHILDREN OF ISRAEL MURMUR AGAINST MOSES.

THE life which the Israelites led in the wilderness was so disagreeable and troublesome to them, and they were so uneasy at it, that although God had forbidden them to meddle with the Canaanites, they could not be persuaded to be obedient to the words of Moses, and to be quiet. Believing they would be able to beat their enemies, even without his approbation, they accused him of wishing to keep them in a distressed condition, in order that they might always stand in need of his assistance. They therefore resolved to fight with the Canaanites, saying that God watched over them not out of regard to the prayers of Moses, but on account of their fore fathers, whose affairs He took under His own conduct. And they also said that it was because of their own virtue that He had formerly procured them their liberty, and that He would continue His assistance now they were willing to take pains for it. They declared that they were of themselves strong and brave enough for the conquest of their enemies. But even if Moses could alienate God from them, it was best for them to be their own masters, and bear no longer with the tyranny of Moses over them.

When, therefore, they had come to this resolution, as being best for them, they went against their enemies. But those enemies were not dismayed either at the attack itself, or at the great multitude that made it, and received them with great courage. Many of the Hebrews were slain; and the remainder of the army, being thrown into confusion, fled in a shameful manner and were pursued to their camp. This unexpected misfortune filled them with despair; as they now understood that this affliction came from the wrath of God, because they rashly went out to war without His approbation.

Moses saw how deeply they were affected by this defeat, and being afraid lest the enemy should grow insolent upon this victory and should attack them with the desire of gaining still greater glory, he resolved to withdraw the army into the wilderness to a farther distance from the Canaanites. So the multitude gave themselves up again to his guidance, for they saw that without his care for them their affairs could not be in a good condition. And he caused the host to remove, and went farther into the wilderness.

It is usually the case with great armies, especially after ill success, that they are hard to be pleased and are governed with difficulty. And so it now befell the Jews, for they being in number six hundred thousand, and by reason of their great multitude not readily subject to their governors, even in prosperity, were more than usually angry, both against one another and against their leader, because of the distress they were in, and the calamities they endured. And a sedition broke out, by which they were in danger of being all destroyed, but were notwithstanding saved by Moses, who would not remember that he had been almost stoned to death by them. The manner in which the sedition broke out was as follows:

There was a man among them named Korah, who held a high position because of his wealth and of his family. He was of the same tribe as Moses, and akin to him, which made him all the more jealous, because he thought that, being his equal in birth and of far greater riches, it was not fair that Moses should be so far above him in dignity. But especially was he angry because Aaron, the brother of Moses, had been appointed high-priest, as he coveted that position for himself.

So, gathering around him two hundred and fifty of his friends, he raised a great clamor against Moses, saying it was not right in Moses to confer the priesthood upon his own brother, when there were so many other men better fitted for the office. Now, Korah was one who was able to speak well and who could easily persuade men by his speeches. And others also conspired with him, who coveted the priesthood for themselves, and their words provoked the people to be seditious, so that they gathered together in great confusion and disorder. And they clamored against Moses, saying that God did not choose Aaron for the priesthood, because He never would have passed over so many superior persons for one who was inferior, or, even if He did choose Aaron, He meant the honor to be bestowed upon him by the people, and not by his own brother.

Moses was not affrighted by this sedition, for he knew that he had always acted right. So he came to where the people were gathered, and, raising his voice so that they might all hear him, he told Korah that on the morrow he and all the others who wished to be appointed to the office of high-priest should come to the tabernacle, holding in their hands a censer full of burning incense. And Aaron should do the like, and the Lord would give them a sign to show which was the man He chose to be high-priest.

The multitude were pleased with what Moses said, and left off their turbulent behavior. The next day they gathered together at the tabernacle in order to be present at the sacrifice, and at the decision that was to be made between the candidates for the priesthood. Korah and a number of the others came also, as they had agreed, with censers in their hands. But Abiram and Dathan, two of the men who had desired the priesthood, refused to be present at the decision, though Moses sent for them to come. Then Moses himself went out to where their tents were, and bade the heads of the people to follow him. And he cried out with a loud voice to the Lord, asking Him to give a sign of His displeasure. Whereupon the ground was moved of a sudden, and the agitation that set it in motion was like that which the wind produces in the waves of the sea. The people were all greatly affrighted at the sight. Then suddenly the ground that was under the tents of these wicked men gave way with a great noise, and they, and all that belonged to them, sunk down and were swallowed up, and perished so entirely that there was not the least appearance that any men had ever been seen there. For the earth that had opened under them closed again and became entire as it was before.

And now Moses called for those that contended about the priesthood, that trial might be made who should be priest, and that he whose sacrifice God was best pleased with might be ordained to that function. There attended two hundred and fifty men, all of whom were honored by the people. Aaron also, and Korah, came forth, and they all offered incense in the censers which they brought with them, before the tabernacle. Hereupon so great a fire shone out as no one ever saw before; it was very bright and had a terrible flame, such as is kindled at the command of God alone, by whose eruption on them all the company, and Korah himself, were destroyed, and this so entirely that their very bodies left no remains behind them. Aaron alone was preserved, because it was God that sent the fire to burn those only who ought to be burned.

But Moses found that the people were not yet satisfied, and still complained about the priesthood. Therefore he called the multitude together and patiently heard what they had to say for themselves, without opposing them. He only desired that the heads of the tribes should bring each a rod to him having inscribed upon it the name of the tribe to which each belonged, and that he in whose rod God should give a sign should receive the priesthood. This was agreed to. So the rest brought their rods, as did Aaron also, and Aaron had

written upon his rod " Levi, " the name of the tribe to which
he belonged. These rods Moses laid up in the tabernacle of
God. On the next day he brought out the rods before the
multitude, and while those of the other eleven men were the
same exactly as when they were laid away, the rod of Aaron
had blossomed, and had branches and buds and ripe almonds,
—the rod having been cut from an almond-tree. The people
were so amazed at this strange sight that they laid aside their
hatred to Moses and Aaron and began to admire the judgment of God concerning them, so that thereafter they
applauded what God had decreed, and permitted Aaron to
enjoy the priesthood peaceably, and his children after him.

Shortly after this Miriam, the sister of Moses and Aaron,
died. And in the same year, when the Israelites had come
upon a place called Petra, in Arabia, Aaron, having been
warned by Moses that the time had come for him to die, went
up a high mountain, in the sight of them all, and, having
reached the top, he put off his pontifical garments and
delivered them to Eleazar, one of his sons, to whom the high-
priesthood belonged because he was the eldest. Then, while
the multitude looked upon him, he died.

CHAPTER XXII.

THE ISRAELITES DEFEAT KING SIHON AND KING OG.

THE people mourned for Aaron thirty days, and when this
mourning was over, Moses removed the army from that place
and came to the river Arnon. On the other side of this river
was the land of the Amorites. This land was fruitful, and
could maintain a great many men with the good things it
produced. Moses sent messengers to Sihon, the king of this

country, asking that he would grant his army a passage, and promising to do no harm to the country or to its inhabitants. But Sihon refused his demand, and put his army in battle-array and prepared to hinder the Israelites from crossing the river.

Then Moses inquired of God whether He would give him leave to fight, and God answered yes, and that He would give him the victory. So the Israelites joyfully put on their armor and went to meet the enemy, who, though they had seemed brave enough before the battle commenced, were then found to be cowardly, so that they could not sustain the first onset, but fled away, and were pursued with great slaughter. Sihon, their king, was also killed, and the Israelites took possession of their land, which was full of abundance of fruit. Such was the destruction which overtook the Amorites, who were neither wise in council nor brave in action.

While matters were in this state, Og, the king of Gilead and Gaulanitis, fell upon the Israelites. He was a friend of king Sihon, and had gathered an army in haste to come to his assistance. Finding him already slain, he determined to revenge him by defeating the Hebrews. But after a great battle he was himself defeated and slain. Now Og was a great king, and he ruled over sixty cities, all of which fell into the hands of the Israelites. He was a giant, twice the size of an ordinary man, and the iron bedstead in which he slept measured four cubits, or eight feet, in breadth, and nine cubits in length.

CHAPTER XXIII.

THE PROPHET BALAAM.

THE Israelites journeyed on, and came to the land of the Moabites. The king of that country was named Balak, and when he saw how great the Israelites were grown, he was afraid for himself and for his kingdom. He did not know that the Israelites would not meddle with any other country, but were to be contented with the possession of the land of Canaan, God having forbidden them to go any farther. So he determined to make an attempt upon them. But he did not judge it prudent to fight them after they had met with such great successes, and he sent ambassadors to the neighboring country of the Midianites to consult with them what he should do. Now these Midianites, knowing that there was a great prophet of the name of Balaam, who lived on the Euphrates River, sent some of their princes along with the ambassadors of Balak, to entreat the prophet to come and curse the Israelites. For they believed that the curse of Balaam would bring down the wrath of God upon the Israelites. Balaam received the ambassadors very kindly, and told them that he was willing to comply with their request, but that God was opposed to his wishes, for that this army which they entreated him to come and curse was in the favor of God. And he advised them to go home again, and not to persist in their enmity against the Israelites; and when he had given this answer he dismissed the ambassadors.

But the Midianites, at the earnest entreaty of Balak, sent other ambassadors to Balaam, and at last he consented to go

against the Israelites.   He saddled his ass and started on
his journey.   But a divine angel met him on the way, when
he was in a narrow passage and hedged in with a wall on
both sides.   Balaam could not see the angel, but the ass did,
and backed against one of the walls, without regard to the
stripes which Balaam, when he was hurt by the wall, gave
her.   But when the angel continued to distress the ass, and
Balaam redoubled his stripes, it fell down upon the ground,
and by the will of God made use of the voice of a man, and
complained of Balaam's injustice in whipping it when she
was hindered in going on by God Himself.   And when he
was disturbed by reason of the voice of the ass, the angel
became visible to him, and blamed him for his cruelty, and
told him the brute creature was not in fault,—for he himself
had come to oppose his journey by the command of God.
Upon which Balaam was afraid, and would have turned back
again, but the angel told him to go on, but that he should
speak nothing save what the Lord should suggest to his
mind.

Balak received the prophet joyfully, and when he had entertained him in a magnificent manner, he desired him to go to
one of the mountains to take a view of the state of the camp
of the Israelites.   And Balak and his attendants went up the
mountain with him.   When they had all reached the top,
Balaam desired the king to build him seven altars, and to
bring him as many bulls and rams.   And the king did so, and
Balaam slew the sacrifices and offered them as burnt-offerings,
and began to prophesy.   But though Balaam would gladly
have pleased the king by cursing the Israelites, the Lord took
possession of him, so that he could only prophesy good
things concerning them.   He said that the Israelites were a
happy people, because the Lord was with them, and that
they should excel all nations in virtue and fill the earth with
their glory.   And they should take possession of the land
which God had appointed for them, and they should be

sufficiently numerous to supply the world and every region of it with inhabitants out of their stock. Many more things he said in praise of them.

Now Balak was displeased with this, and said Balaam had broken his contract with him, and that he would give him none of the great presents he had promised, because instead of cursing his enemies he had praised them. But Balaam answered that he could not help it, for the Lord put such words as He pleased in the mouths of the prophets when they prophesied, and the Lord's words were always true.

"But now," he continued, "since it is my desire to oblige thee as well as the Midianites, let us rear other altars, and offer the like sacrifices again, that I may see whether I can persuade God to permit me to bind these men with curses."

When Balak had agreed to this, God again prevented Balaam from cursing the Israelites. Then Balaam fell on his face and foretold a number of calamities that would befall the great cities of the earth. And what Balaam said came true afterwards. Balak was very angry, and sent the prophet away without any of the presents he had promised him. But before Balaam went home he told Balak and the Midianites of a plan by which they might obtain the destruction of the Israelites, which was to endeavor to make them forsake the true God and worship the false idols of the Midianites. In order to do this he advised that the Midianite maidens should seek to make the young men of the Israelites fall in love with them and marry them, and then they would bring their husbands with them to the feasts which were held to the idols. And many of the Midianite maidens did marry with the Israelites, and persuaded them to come and eat at their feasts and bow down to their idols. Then the Lord was angry, and sent a great plague, which destroyed many thousands of these men, and the rest repented of their wickedness.

But because of what the Midianites had done Moses sent an army against their land. And the Midianites were defeated in a great battle, in which their five kings were slain, and the army of the Israelites returned rejoicing, with a great number of oxen and sheep and asses which they had captured, as well as quantities of gold and silver and other precious things.

About this time two of the tribes of Israel, the tribes of Gad and of Reuben, came to Moses and asked him that he would give them the land of Gilead, which had been captured from the Amorites, in order that they might live there. Moses at first was angry, believing that they wanted to stay there because they were afraid of fighting against the Canaanites. He said to them, "Shall you rest here while your brethren go to war?" But they answered that when they had built cities wherein they might leave their wives and children and possessions, they would go along with the rest of the army and fight against the Canaanites. Moses was pleased with what they said. So he called for Eleazar the high-priest, and for Joshua and the heads of the other tribes, and it was agreed by all of them that the land of Gilead should be given to these two tribes upon condition that they should join in all the wars until the Israelites were settled in the land of Canaan. And half of the tribe of Manasseh also asked and received permission to remain in Gilead.

CHAPTER XXIV.

THE DEATH OF MOSES.

WHEN the forty years of wandering which God had foretold had almost come to an end, so that there were only thirty days left, Moses felt that it was time for him to die.*

---

* The Bible tells us that Moses was condemned to die before the Israelites entered the promised land, because he allowed himself to fall into a passion

And he appointed Joshua to be his successor, both as the leader of the armies of the Israelites and as a prophet to receive the messages of the Lord, for God had signified to him that this was the man of His choice. Then Moses called together the multitude of the Israelites, and he spoke many words of wisdom to them, and gave them laws for their government. And when he had spoken he read them a song he had composed, which contained predictions of what was to come to pass afterwards. And all things happened as Moses predicted, so that this song proved a testimony to all generations of the truth of the words of Moses. He delivered all the books which he had written, and which are the first five books of the Bible, to the priests, and he gave them also the ark, in which were placed the ten commandments written on tablets of stone. He told the priests to take care of the tabernacle. And he exhorted the Israelites that when they had conquered the land of Canaan they should destroy all the people and overturn their idols. And they should not forget the injuries of the Amalekites, but should make war against them and inflict punishment upon them for what they had done to them when they were in distress in the wilderness. And Moses pronounced blessings upon those who were diligent in the worship of God and in the observance of the laws, and who did not reject what Moses had said to them, but he uttered curses upon those who should transgress the laws. He wrote down these blessings and these curses, that they might never be forgotten, and he also inscribed them on each side of the altar.

Again, on the next day, he called the people together, all the men and the women and the children, and even the slaves, that they might all solemnly swear to observe the laws which he had given them and to take vengeance on all who

---

when they murmured against him. But Josephus was a great admirer of Moses, and he did not like to say anything to his discredit.

disobeyed them. And the multitude bound themselves by a solemn oath. And Moses warned them that if they broke this oath God had declared to him that they should experience great misfortunes.

"Your lands," he said, "shall be overrun by your enemies, and your cities and your temples overthrown, and you shall be sold as slaves to hard masters, and you will repent when repentance will be too late."

Having said these words, Moses further informed the multitude that the time had come when he must leave them, for this was the day appointed for his death. He bade them farewell, and blessed them again, and commended them to God. And the multitude fell into tears,—even the women and the children lamented and beat their breasts,—and though Moses knew that he ought not to be cast down at the approach of death, yet what the people did so overcame him that he wept himself. Now as he went thence to the place where he was to vanish from their sight, they all followed after him weeping. But Moses beckoned with his hand to those that were afar off, and bade them stay behind in quiet, while he spoke to those that were near him and exhorted them not to make his departure so sorrowful. So they restrained their tears, or sobbed only in silence, and let him depart as he desired. Only the rulers of the tribes, with Eleazar and Joshua, followed him. But when he had come to the mountain called Abarim, or Nebo, which is near the city of Jericho, and affords to such as are upon it a view of the greater part of the land of Canaan, he dismissed the rulers. And as he was going to embrace Eleazar and Joshua, and was still discoursing with them, a cloud stood over him on a sudden, and he disappeared.

Moses was one hundred and twenty years old at the time of his death, and he had ruled over the Israelites for forty years. The people mourned for him thirty days. Nor did ever any grief so deeply affect them as did this upon the death of Moses.

CHAPTER XXV.

JOSHUA, THE COMMANDER OF THE HEBREWS, MAKES WAR WITH THE CANAANITES.

WHEN Moses was taken away from among men, in the manner already described, and when the mourning for him was over, Joshua commanded the multitude to get themselves ready for an expedition, for they would soon cross over Jordan. He also sent spies to Jericho, to discover what forces they had, and what were their intentions. And calling to him the rulers of the tribes of Reuben and Gad and the half tribe of Manasseh, who had been permitted to take up their habitation in the country of the Amorites, he put them in mind what they had promised Moses, and told them to prepare themselves to perform what they promised. So fifty thousand of them accompanied him, and he marched from Abila to Jordan.

Now when he had pitched his camp, the spies came to him immediately. And they were well acquainted with the whole state of the Canaanites, for they had been able to take a full view of the city of Jericho without disturbance, and saw which parts of the walls were strong, and which parts were insecure, and which of the gates were so weak that they might afford an entrance to their army. At first those that met them took no notice of them, supposing they were only strangers. But at night they retired to a certain inn that was near the wall, which was kept by a woman named Rahab. And here, having eaten their supper, they were considering how to get away, when information was given to the king that there were

some persons come from the Hebrews' camp to view the city
as spies, and that they were in Rahab's inn. So he sent
some men to take them and bring them to him, that he
might put them to torture and learn what their business was
there. But Rahab hid the spies under a heap of flax which
had been laid to dry on the top of her house, and said to
the king's messengers that certain unknown strangers had
supped with her a little before sunset, and had just gone
away, but might easily be overtaken. So these messengers set
off at once in pursuit along those roads which they thought
the spies had taken, but could hear no tidings of them.
When the tumult was over, Rahab brought the men down,
and desired them, when their brethren should have obtained possession of the land of Canaan, to remember what
danger she had undergone for their sakes. And she made
them swear to preserve her and her family. The spies acknowledged that they owed her gratitude for what she had
done, and swore to requite her kindness. They told her
when she should perceive that the city was about to be taken,
to put her goods and all her family, by way of security, in
her inn, and hang out scarlet threads before her doors or
windows, that the commander of the Hebrews might know
her house and take care to do her no harm. Then they let
themselves down by a rope from the wall, and escaped, and
came and told their own people what they had done in
their journey to the city. Joshua also told Eleazar the high-
priest and the senate what the spies had sworn to Rahab,
who confirmed what had been sworn.

Now while Joshua was debating how the army should cross
the river, for there were no bridges, and they had no boats,
God spoke to him, and promised that He would so dispose of the river that they could pass over it. So on the
third day thereafter Joshua told the people to make themselves ready. And he made the priests go down to the river,
first of all, with the ark upon their shoulders. Then went

the Levites, bearing the tabernacle and the sacred vessels that were used in the sacrifices. After them the entire multitude followed according to their tribes, each tribe having their wives and children in the midst of them. As soon as the priests had entered the river, the water ceased to flow, and dry land appeared. And the priests stood still until the whole multitude had crossed. Then they passed over also, and as soon as they had come out of the river the water flowed as before.

So the Israelites pitched their camp at the distance of ten furlongs from Jericho. The heads of the tribes had been commanded by Joshua to take each a large stone from the bed of the river while they were crossing it, and Joshua now took these stones and built an altar. This altar was to remain as a memorial of the miracle that had been performed there. They celebrated the feast of the passover here, and they reaped the corn that grew in the land, and parched and ate it. And on the morrow the manna, which for forty years had sustained them, ceased any longer to come. For now they were in the land of Canaan, where there was plenty of food for them. Then Joshua, whom the Lord had instructed what to do, called the priests to him, and told them that they should go all round the walls of the city, bearing the ark on their shoulders and blowing on their seven trumpets, with the senate following them. And when they had done this for six days, on the seventh Joshua gathered the armed men and all the people together, and told them that the city should now be taken, for God would make the walls fall down of their own accord. And he charged them to kill every one in the city, even the women and the children, and to destroy all the animals, and to take nothing for themselves. All the gold and silver in the city should be brought together to be consecrated to the Lord. But he reminded them to spare Rahab and her kindred and their possessions.

When he had said this and had set his army in order, he led it against the city. And they all went round the

walls, following the priests with the ark, and when they had
gone round it seven times, and had stood still a little, the
walls fell down, though no instruments of war or other force
had been applied to them by the Israelites.

So they rushed into Jericho, and slew all the men that were
therein, while they were still affrighted at the surprising overthrow of the walls and were unable to defend themselves.
And not only the men, but the women and the children were
all slain, and the city was filled with dead bodies. Rahab
and her family alone were saved, and when she was brought
to Joshua he thanked her for what she had done, and he gave
her lands to live on, and held her ever after in great esteem.

There was an immense quantity of gold and silver, and of
brass also, that the Israelites took from out of the houses and
heaped together, which spoils Joshua delivered to the priests
to be laid up among their treasures. But a man named
Achar, of the tribe of Judah, finding a royal garment woven
entirely of gold, and a large piece of gold, thought it very
hard that he must give away what it had cost him so much
trouble to obtain, and he therefore dug a ditch in his own
tent and concealed them there.

A few days after the capture of Jericho, Joshua sent three
thousand armed men to take Ai, a city situated at a little
distance off. But these men were defeated by the people of
Ai and driven back, with a loss of thirty-six of their number.
Then the Israelites were in great distress, for they feared that
the Lord had forgotten His promises to them. And Joshua
cried out to the Lord, and the Lord answered him, and said
that this defeat had come upon the Israelites because there
was sin among them; for one of their number had stolen
things that were consecrated to Him, and they must search
out and punish the offender.

This Joshua told the people; and calling for Eleazar the
high-priest, and the men in authority, he cast lots tribe by
tribe, and man by man, until at last the lot fell to Achar.

He confessed the theft and produced what he had taken, whereupon he was immediately put to death and buried at night, as became a public malefactor.

When Joshua had thus purified the host, he led them against Ai. And at night he hid a number of his soldiers near the walls. The rest attacked the city, and when the inhabitants, who were made bold by their former victory, marched out against them, they pretended to flee. By that means he drew the army away from the city, and, having done so, he suddenly ordered his forces to turn round again and attack the enemy. At the same time he gave a signal which had been agreed upon, and the men who had been hidden rushed into the city, the gates of which were wide open, and slew all that they met with. Then Joshua pressed hard against those that had come against him, and forced them to a close fight, and defeated them, so that they ran away. And when they had been driven back to the city they were surprised and afraid, seeing that it was taken, and they scattered about the fields in a disorderly manner, and were noway able to defend themselves. So they were all slain. And the Israelites plundered the city, and brought away herds of cattle and a great deal of gold and silver, for this was a rich country. And Joshua allowed them to keep all these things for their own.

CHAPTER XXVI.

THE PEOPLE OF GIBEON.

THERE were a people called the Gibeonites living near the city of Jerusalem, who were a very cunning people. They saw the destruction that had come upon the inhabitants of Jericho and of Ai, and they feared the like miseries for them-

selves. So they sent ambassadors to Joshua to make a league
of friendship with him. Now these ambassadors thought it
would be dangerous to confess that they were Canaanites,
because they knew that Joshua had been commanded to destroy the nations of Canaan. So they decided to deceive him
by a stratagem. They put on old and torn garments, and
came to Joshua, and, standing in the midst of the people, they
said that they had come a long distance to see him, so that
their clothes, which were new when they started out, were now
greatly worn by the length of time they had been on their
journey. And they said they were sent by the people of
Gibeon, who dwelt outside of the land of Canaan, to make a
league of friendship with the Israelites, for the Gibeonites had
rejoiced to hear that by the favor of God the Israelites were
to possess the land of Canaan, and desired to be admitted
into the number of their citizens. Then Joshua and the people of Israel, believing what these men told them, that they
were not of the nations of the Canaanites, swore that they
would be friends with them, and the men departed well
pleased. But when Joshua led his army to the country at
the bottom of the mountains in this part of Canaan, he
learned that the Gibeonites dwelled near there, and that they
were of the stock of the Canaanites. So he sent for their
governors, and reproached them with the cheat they had put
upon him. They answered that they were afraid for their
lives, and saw no other way to save themselves. And, as the
children of Israel had sworn to let these people live, they
determined to make them public servants and use them in
cutting the wood and drawing the water needed at the tabernacle.

But the king of the city of Jerusalem was angry that the
Gibeonites had gone over to Joshua. So he called upon the
kings of the neighboring nations to join together and make
war upon them. Then the Gibeonites sent in great distress
to Joshua to come and help them. And Joshua made haste

with his whole army to assist them, and, marching day and
night, he fell upon the enemy as they were going up to
the siege, and defeated them, and pursued them down the
descent of the hills.   And God lengthened the day, that the
night might not come on too soon and hinder the Israelites
in pursuing their enemies.   And Joshua captured the king of
Jerusalem and the four other kings who assisted him, as they
were hiding in a cave, and he put them all to death.

And now there went a great fame abroad of the courage of
the Israelites, and those that heard how they had defeated all
their enemies were affrighted.   So a number of the Canaanite
kings gathered together all their people into one great army.
The number of this army was three hundred thousand armed
footmen and ten thousand horsemen and twenty thousand
chariots, so that because of the multitude of their enemies
Joshua and the Israelites were greatly affrighted and lost all
their hope of success.   But God reproved them for their cowardice and bade them put their trust in Him, for He would
help them.   So Joshua regained his courage, and he went out
against the enemy, and after five days' march he came upon
them and gave battle.   There was a terrible fight, in which
great numbers of the Canaanites were slain.   When they fled
Joshua pursued them and cut them down.   Their kings also
were all slain.   And the Israelites passed over all their country without opposition, no one daring to meet them in battle,
and they besieged their cities and took them and slew all the
inhabitants.   But there were still a number of cities left belonging to other Canaanite kings, and these were situated in
places where they were difficult to be besieged, and were surrounded with strong walls.

Joshua had now grown old, and he felt he could no longer
lead the armies of the Israelites as he used to do.   So he
brought all the people to the city of Shiloh, and there he
placed the tabernacle, for that seemed a fit place for it, because of the beauty of its situation.   Then he went on to the

city of Shechem, where Moses had told him he was to build
an altar for all the tribes of Israel, that they might sacrifice
there. And he built the altar in the way Moses had instructed him, and when they had sacrificed, and pronounced
the blessings and the curses that Moses had taught, and had
left them engraved on the side of the altar, they returned to
Shiloh.

Then Joshua spoke to all the people, and he asked them to
choose men from out their tribes who were skilful at exam-
ining and measuring land. Each tribe accordingly chose a
man, and the men so chosen were sent out over the land of
Canaan, to measure it and to estimate the fertility of the
different parts, and they wrote the description of all the land
in a book which they carried with them, and after they had
been gone seven months they returned to Joshua in the city
of Shiloh. Joshua made an equal division of the land according to the description they made of it, and cast lots among the
nine tribes and the half tribe of Manasseh who had not yet
had any land portioned out to them, so that the Lord might
show what part of the land each tribe should have. And
after the Lord had shown them this, Joshua told the men of
Israel to go and take possession of their shares, and each
tribe was to drive out any heathen nation that was found on
their land. But as the tribes of Reuben and Gad and the
half tribe of Manasseh had already been peacefully settled in
the land of the Amorites beyond the Jordan, Joshua called to
him the fifty thousand men from those tribes who had followed him during all his wars, and told them he would no
longer need their services, and that they might go home to
their wives and children. But first he enjoined upon them to
respect the laws which Moses had given them, and to love
and serve the Lord their God, and to remember their kinship
to the other tribes of Israel.

Then the men of these tribes bade farewell to their brethren
of the other tribes, and shed many tears. When they had

passed over the river Jordan, they built an altar on the banks, as a monument to future generations, and a sign of their relation to those that lived in the lands on the other side. But when those on the other side heard of the building of this altar, and knew not with what intention it was built, they thought it was done because these tribes wished to leave off the worship of the true God and to introduce strange gods. And they cried out in anger, and armed themselves to go out in war against them and punish them for their disobedience to the laws of their country. But Joshua, and Eleazar the high-priest, and the senate restrained them, and persuaded them first to send messengers to their brethren to question them concerning their intentions in raising strange altars, and if they found their intentions were evil they might then go to war with them. Accordingly, Phineas, the son of the high-priest, and ten more men who were held in high esteem among the Israelites, were sent across the river to question the other tribes and to learn why they had built another altar.

"For," said the ambassadors, "we do not like to believe that you intend to forget God, and leave the ark and the altar that is common to all of us, in order to introduce strange gods and the wicked practices of the Canaanites. But if it be true that you intend to do this, we will esteem you as no better than the Canaanites, and will collect our armies and come over the Jordan and destroy you in like manner as we have destroyed them."

Then the chief men of the other tribes rose and explained that they had not abandoned their God, that they still intended to come to the altar of the tabernacle to offer their sacrifices with the rest of the Israelites, and that the new altar had not been built for worship, but to serve as a memorial to their children forever, and to remind them of their relationship to the other tribes who dwelt across the Jordan.

This answer pleased Phineas and the other ambassadors, who accordingly returned to Joshua and reported before an assembly of the people what answer they had received. Joshua also was pleased to find that he was under no necessity for leading a part of the Israelites against the rest and making them shed one another's blood. So he offered up sacrifices of thanksgiving to God, and dismissed the assembly.

In the twentieth year after this, when he was very old, he sent for those of the greatest dignity in the several cities, and for the rulers, and for as many of the common people as could be present; and when they were come, he put them in mind of all the benefits God had bestowed on them; how from a low estate He had raised them to so great a degree of glory and plenty. And he exhorted them to take notice of the intentions of God, which had been so gracious towards them; and told them that the Deity would only continue their friend in case they persevered in their piety; and that it was proper for him, now he was about to depart out of this life, to leave such an admonition to them, and he desired that they would keep in memory this his advice to them.

Joshua, after he had thus discoursed to them, died, in the hundred and tenth year of his age. About the same time died Eleazar the high-priest, leaving the high-priesthood to his son Phineas.

CHAPTER XXVII.

THE DESTRUCTION OF THE BENJAMITES.

After the death of Joshua and of Eleazar, Phineas informed the people that it was the will of God they should commit the government to the rulers of the tribe of Judah, and that this tribe should destroy the race of the Canaanites.

Now there was a king in Canaan called Adonibezek, who, believing that when Joshua was dead he could easily defeat the men of Israel, called together his armies to fight them. The Israelites came out and gave them battle, and slew above ten thousand of them, and put the rest to flight. And in the pursuit they took Adonibezek, whose fingers and toes they cut off. And Adonibezek acknowledged that this was a just judgment of God, for he had not been ashamed to do the like to seventy-two kings whom he had conquered. He was then taken to Jerusalem and put to death.

The Israelites went on conquering the heathen nations as God had commanded, and took most of their cities. Yet they did not persevere until they had driven them all out of the land, but permitted many of them to live in peace, on condition that they would pay them a tribute. And being tired of fighting, the Israelites applied themselves to the cultivation of the land, which produced them great plenty and riches. Whereupon God was provoked to anger, and told them that as, contrary to His directions, they had spared some of the Canaanites, those Canaanites would in time to come tempt them to sin and cause them great trouble. And though the Israelites were distressed at what God told them, yet were they still unwilling to go to war, preferring to live in peace and luxury. And God was not pleased with them, and withdrew His protection from them for a time, so that their government did not prosper, and at last they fell to fighting among themselves. And the way of it was this.

A certain man of the tribe of Ephraim was travelling with his wife through the land which belonged to the Benjamites. Having stopped to rest in a city of that land called Gibeah, his wife was there cruelly slain. On reaching home he sent word to all the other tribes what had happened to him. And the people were greatly angered, and they gathered together in large numbers at Shiloh, and determined to take up arms against the citizens of Gibeah unless the murderers were given up to them. Ambassadors were therefore sent to the Benjamites, demanding that these men should be delivered up for punishment. But the Benjamites refused, and said they would go to war first.

When the ambassadors returned with this answer, the people of the other tribes were still more angry. They took an oath that no one of them would ever give his daughter in marriage to a Benjamite, and that they would make war with greater fury against that tribe than their forefathers made war against the Canaanites. So they sent out against the city of Gibeah an army of four hundred thousand men. Now the army of the Benjamites was only twenty-five thousand and six hundred, but they had among them five hundred men who excelled in slinging stones, and with their help the Benjamites beat the Israelites when they first joined battle. Of the Israelites there fell two thousand men; and probably more would have been destroyed had not the night come on, and broken off the fight. So the Benjamites returned to the city with joy, and the Israelites returned to their camp in a great fright at what had happened. On the next day, when they fought again, the Benjamites beat them again, and eighteen thousand of the Israelites were slain, and the rest deserted their camp out of fear of a great slaughter. And coming to Bethel, a city that was near their camp, they fasted on the next day, and besought God through Phineas the high-priest, that His wrath against them might cease, and that He would be satisfied with these two defeats, and give them the victory and power over their enemies. Accordingly, God promised that He would do so.

The Israelites then divided the army into two parts. One half of them hid in ambush about the city of Gibeah by night. The other half attacked the Benjamites next morning, and then slowly retired before them, being very anxious to draw all the men out of the city. And indeed even the old men and young men that were left in the city, as too weak to fight, came running out now to join in the pursuit. However, when they were a great way from the city the Israelites ran away no longer, but turned back to fight them. And lifting up the signal they had agreed on, those that lay in ambush rose up, and with a great noise fell upon the enemy. Now when the Benjamites saw they had been deceived, they knew not what to do, and when they were driven into a certain hollow place which was in a valley, they were shot at by those that encompassed them, till they were all destroyed, except six hundred, who, forming themselves into a close body of men, forced their passage through the midst of their enemies, and fled to the neighboring mountains, and remained there. Then the Israelites burned Gibeah, and slew the women, and the males that were under age; and did the same also to the other cities of the Benjamites. And indeed they were so enraged that they sent twelve thousand men out of the army and gave them orders to destroy the city of Jabesh-Gilead, because it did not join with them in fighting against the Benjamites. Accordingly, those that were sent slew the men of war, with the children and wives, except four hundred virgins. To such a degree had they proceeded in their anger, because they not only had the suffering of the Levite's wife to avenge, but the slaughter of their own soldiers.

However, they afterward were sorry for the calamity they had brought upon the Benjamites, although still believing those men had suffered justly for their offence against the laws, and they appointed a fast on that account, and recalled by their ambassadors those six hundred who had escaped.

The ambassadors found these men on a rock called Rimmon, which was in the wilderness. They told them the Israelites lamented the disaster that had befallen the Benjamites, and had determined they would not let the whole race perish, but would allow these few survivors to return to their home.

"We give you leave," said the Israelites, "to take the whole land of Benjamin to yourselves, and as much cattle and gold and silver as you are able to carry away with you."

5463

And the Israelites also gave them the four hundred virgins of Jabesh-Gilead for wives. But there were still two hundred of the Benjamites that had no wives, and the Israelites deliberated how they might get wives for them. For they had sworn before the war began that no one would give his daughter to wife to any of that tribe, and the oath could not be broken. Then, while they were debating, a man rose out of the assembly and said he could show them a way whereby they might procure the Benjamites wives enough and yet keep their oaths. And when they asked how that could be, he answered,—

" Three times a year, when we meet in Shiloh, having our wives and our children with us, let the Benjamites be allowed to steal away and to marry such maidens as they can, while we neither encourage nor forbid them. And if any of the parents take it ill, we will tell them that they ought to have better guarded their daughters."

The Israelites were pleased with this advice, and determined to follow it. So, when the festival was going on, these two hundred Benjamites scattered themselves along the roads near the city of Shiloh, and hid by twos and threes in the vineyards and other places, and waited for the coming of the virgins. And as the virgins walked along in an unguarded manner, the men rushed out upon them, and carried them off and married them.

In this way all the Benjamites got themselves wives. And they flourished, and soon increased to be a multitude, and recovered their former happy state.

CHAPTER XXVIII.

DEBORAH AND BARAK.

THE Israelites continued, however, to be indolent and fond of pleasure. Forgetting what God had said to them, they made friends with the Canaanites, and married among them, the men of Israel taking wives from among the heathens, and the daughters of Israel marrying heathen men. Some even forsook their own forms of worship and sacrificed to the heathen idols, and assisted in other evil doings that were common among the Canaanites. God therefore was angry with them, and He allowed Chushan, the king of the Assyrians, to conquer them and take their cities and make them his servants. For eight years they lived in bondage, and then God took pity on their prayers. There was a man among the Israelites called Othniel, who was strong and courageous, and God told him that the time had now come when He would deliver the Israelites from bondage. So, with a few other brave men, he attacked one of the garrisons that the king of the Assyrians had set over the people, and slew them. And when the Israelites saw that he had been successful in his first attempt, they flocked around him in great numbers, and soon defeated all the armies of the Assyrians and drove them out of the country. Thereupon Othniel was chosen the ruler of the people, with the name of Judge, and he ruled them for forty years.

But after the death of Othniel the affairs of the Israelites again fell into disorder. They neither paid to God the honor that was due to Him nor obeyed the laws, and they were therefore conquered again by Eglon, the king of the Moabites. He built himself a royal palace at Jericho, and did all he could to oppress the people, so that for eighteen years they were reduced to poverty. And again the Israelites repented of their sins and returned to God, and God forgave them.

There was a young man of the tribe of Benjamin whose name was Ehud, and God appointed him to be the liberator of his race. This man became familiar with the king of the Moabites, and was beloved not only by him but by all his attendants. One day Ehud took a dagger and hid it under his garments. He went to the house of the king, carrying presents to him, as he had often done before. Being admitted into the private chamber of Eglon, the king bade his servants that attended him to leave them, because he had a mind to talk with Ehud. He was sitting on his throne, and fear seized upon Ehud lest he should miss his stroke and not give him a deadly wound. So he raised himself up and said he had a dream to impart to the king by the command of God. And when the king leaped off his throne to hear the dream, Ehud smote him to the heart. Then, leaving his dagger in the body, he went out and shut the door after him. Now the attendants of Eglon, hearing no sound in his room, thought he was sleeping, and durst not disturb him. But towards evening, fearing some uncommon accident had happened, they entered the room. When they found the king dead, they were in great disorder and knew not what to do. Before the guards could be got together, an army of Israelites, whom Ehud had collected, attacked the palace and slew a great number of the Moabites, and the rest made their escape across the Jordan. So the Israelites were freed from their persecutors, and they appointed Ehud their judge. And when he died, a man named Shamgar was made judge in his place, but he ruled only a short time.

Again the Israelites sinned, and the Lord punished them.

Jabin, the king of the Canaanites, came against them with an army of three hundred thousand men, and he had with him a great captain, named Sisera. The Israelites were sorely beaten and condemned to slavery. For twenty years they endured great hardships. And when at length they had become penitent and were so wise as to learn that their misfortunes arose from their contempt of the laws, they went to a prophetess named Deborah and besought her to pray to God that He would take pity on them. And God listened to the prayers of Deborah, and told her that the people of Israel were to take for their general a man named Barak, who was of the tribe of Naphthali.

So Deborah sent for Barak, and bade him choose out ten thousand young men to go against the enemy, for God had said that that number was sufficient, and He would give them the victory. But Barak was afraid, and said he would not go as a general unless Deborah would also go as a general with him. Then she was angry, and replied,—

"Thou, Barak, dost meanly deliver up that authority which God hath given thee into the hands of a woman ; and I do not reject it. But thou shalt lose all the glory thou mightest have won, for a woman also shall kill Sisera."

And Barak and Deborah collected together ten thousand men and went out against Sisera. But when Sisera came to meet them, the number of his army affrighted the Israelites, and Barak with them, so that they were ready to flee before them. But Deborah withheld them, and commanded them to fight that very day, for God had assured them the victory.

So the battle began. And when they had come to a close fight there arose a great storm of rain and hail. And the wind blew the rain in the face of the Canaanites, and so blinded them that their arrows and slings were of no advantage, and they found it difficult even to use their swords. But the storm incommoded the Israelites very little, for it blew on their backs. Moreover, they took courage, believing that God was assisting them, and fought the more bravely. And, after a great number of the Canaanites had been slain, the rest, seeing they were beaten, began to flee. And Sisera fled also, and came to the tent of a woman called Jael, who was a friend to the children of Israel. He asked her to conceal him, and she let him come into her tent. And when he asked for something to drink she gave him sour milk, of which he drank so immoderately that he fell asleep. When he was asleep Jael took an iron nail, and drove it through his temples, with a hammer, into the floor. And when Barak came a little while afterwards she showed him Sisera, nailed to the floor. And thus was Sisera killed by the hand of a woman, as Deborah had foretold. Barak was made judge, and ruled over Israel for forty years.

CHAPTER XXIX.

GIDEON.

Barak and Deborah died about the same time. After their death the Midianites called to their assistance the Amalekites and the Arabians, and made war against the Israelites, and defeated them, and drove them from their cities and from their houses, so that they lived in caves in the mountains. The Midianites also carried off their grain and their cattle, and there was great danger of a famine.

Then the Israelites cried to the Lord for assistance. There was a man among them named Gideon. One day he was secretly threshing some wheat in his wine-press, for he was too fearful of the enemy to thresh it openly on the threshing-floor. And God appeared to him in the form of an angel, and said to him that he was a happy man and beloved of God.

To this Gideon answered, laughing scornfully, " Is this an indication of God's favor to me, that I am forced to use this wine-press instead of a threshing-floor?" But the angel exhorted him to be of good courage, and told him that he should make an attempt to recover liberty for his people.

" Nay," said Gideon, " it is impossible for me to do that, for the tribe to which I belong is a small one, and I myself am young and not fit for great actions."

But the angel answered that God would supply what he was deficient in, and would afford the Israelites victory under his guidance.

Gideon told this story to other young men, and they believed him, and immediately there was an army of ten thousand young men got ready for fighting. And Gideon was chosen their captain.

At night, as Gideon slept, God appeared to him in a dream, and said that He wished the Israelites to acknowledge that victory came from Him and not from the greatness of their army, and therefore all this number of men would not be necessary. So He told him to bring his army, about noon, in the violence of the heat, to the river, and those men that bent down on their knees and drank calmly he should look upon as brave men, while those who hurriedly scooped up the water with their hands were cowardly and in dread of their enemies.

And when Gideon had done as God commanded, there were found to be three hundred who drank water hurriedly from their hands. God told him to choose out this number, for with only three hundred cowardly men under him He would give him the victory. But, as Gideon himself was in great fear, God wished to reassure him, and He told him to take one of his soldiers and go near to the tents of the Midianites at night-time, for that he should have his courage raised by what he saw and heard. So he obeyed, and went, taking his servant Phurah with him; and as he came near to one of the tents he discovered that those who were in it were awake, and that one of them was telling his fellow-soldier a dream of his own. And Gideon could hear every word he said. The dream was this : He thought he saw a barley-cake, such a one as could hardly be eaten by men, it was so vile, rolling through the camp, and overthrowing the royal tent, and the tents of all the soldiers. Now the other soldier explained this vision to mean the destruction of the army.

" For," said he, " the seed called *barley* is allowed to be the vilest sort of seed, and the Israelites are known to be the vilest of all the people of Asia, and since thou sayest thou didst see the cake overturning our tents, I am afraid God hath granted the victory over us to Gideon."

When Gideon had heard this, hope and courage came upon him. Commanding his soldiers to arm themselves, he told them of this vision of their enemies. They also took courage, and were ready to perform what he should enjoin them. So Gideon divided his army into three parts, each part containing a hundred men : they all bore empty pitchers and lighted lamps in their hands. Each of them also had a ram's horn in his right hand, which he used instead of a trumpet. And at dead of night they stealthily crept into the enemy's camp, and on the signal given sounded with the rams' horns, and broke their pitchers, and lit their lamps, and shouted, and cried, " Victory to Gideon, by God's assistance." Whereupon a disorder and a fright seized upon the Midianites while they were half asleep, so that a few of them were slain by their enemies, but the greatest part by their own soldiers, on account of the diversity of their language, and when they were once put into disorder, they killed all that they met with, thinking them to be enemies also. As the report of Gideon's victory came to the other Israelites, they took their weapons and pursued their enemies, and overtook them in a certain valley, and slew them all, with their kings. And Gideon was made judge over Israel, and ruled forty years.

CHAPTER XXX.

CONCERNING ABIMELECH AND THE OTHER JUDGES WHO SUC-CEEDED GIDEON.

GIDEON had more than seventy sons, for he was married to many wives. Among them was one named Abimelech, who was cruel and wicked. Now he was anxious to be ruler over the Israelites, so he went to his mother's relations in the city of Shechem and persuaded them to help him, and he came with them to his father's house and slew all his brothers except the youngest, Jotham, who had the good fortune to escape. Abimelech did this in order that none of them might be elected rulers over Israel.

After Abimelech had governed for three years, the people grew tired of him, for he was harsh and tyrannical, and the Shechemites drove him away both from their city and their tribe. But he gathered an army and fought with the Shechemites, and defeated them, and took their city and razed it to the ground. He put to death the inhabitants, and only a small number escaped out of the city. These fled to a strong rock not far from the city, where they settled and prepared to build a wall for their protection. When Abimelech learned their intentions, he came upon them with his forces. He laid fagots of dry wood around the rock until it was entirely surrounded, and then he set them on fire and threw in whatsoever burned most easily, so that a mighty flame was raised, and nobody could fly away from the rock, but every man perished.

After Abimelech had destroyed Shechem, he marched

against a rebellious city named Thebes, and fought against
it and took it. There was a great tower in the middle of
the city, whither all the inhabitants fled. Then Abimelech
came near the tower to besiege it. But a woman who was
on the tower threw down a piece of millstone, which struck
him on the head and felled him to 'the ground. He knew
that he was dying, but he did not want it to be said that
he had been killed by a woman, so he told one of his
attendants to draw his sword and put him to death, and the
attendant did so.

Abimelech was succeeded in the government of the country
of the Israelites first by Tola, who ruled for twenty-three
years, and then by Jair, who ruled twenty-two years. They
were wise rulers, and the people prospered under them.

After the death of Jair, however, the people began to sin
again, and to despise God and their laws. Then the Ammonites and the Philistines laid waste their country with a great
army. And the people called out again to the Lord, confessing their sins, and He had mercy on them and resolved to assist them. But by this time the enemy held the greater part
of the country in slavery, and had penetrated to the land beyond the Jordan where the two and a half tribes lived. The
inhabitants of the country went out to meet them, but they
wanted a commander. Now there was a man among them
named Jephthah, who was a great captain. Yet his fellow-
citizens had been unkind to him, and had allowed him to be
despoiled of his rightful inheritance by his brethren. So he
was angry and would not at first yield to their entreaties.
But when the Israelites entreated him further, and promised
that if he would lead them out to battle they would grant
him the government over them all his life, he at last consented.
He encamped his army at a place called Mizpah. Here he
prayed for victory, and vowed, if he came home in safety, to
offer in sacrifice the first living creature that met him on his
return. Then he joined battle with the enemy and defeated

them with great slaughter. And he pursued them to their own land, and overthrew many of their cities, and took a great quantity of cattle and gold and silver. But, as he came back, a great sorrow overtook him. For the first living thing he met on his return was his daughter. She was his only child, and when he saw her he lamented and rent his clothes, and told her of his vow. But she told him that he might do with her as he had vowed, that she was glad to die on the occasion of her father's victory and the liberty of her fellow-citizens. She only desired Jephthah to give her leave for two months to bewail her youth with her companions, and she would then give herself up to him. Accordingly, when that time was up he sacrificed his daughter as he had promised,—offering such an oblation as was not conformable to the laws or acceptable to God.

After Jephthah had ruled for six years he died. And three other judges, named Ibzan, Helon, and Abdon, ruled after him in succession, but nothing remarkable happened in all the years that they ruled.

CHAPTER XXXI.

CONCERNING SAMSON, AND WHAT MISCHIEFS HE WROUGHT UPON THE PHILISTINES.

AFTER the death of Abdon the Philistines conquered the Israelites and held them in slavery for forty years.

There was at that time among the Israelites a man named Manoah, who was held in great honor on account of his many virtues. He had a wife who also feared the Lord, but the couple were not blessed with any children, though they continually prayed to God for them. One day an angel of God appeared to the wife as she was alone and brought her the good news that she should have a son, who should be of great strength, and by whom, when he was grown up to man's estate, the Philistines should be afflicted. And the angel told her that he was never to drink wine, and that his hair should never be cut. Then the angel departed.

The woman told her husband, when he returned, of the angel's visit, and of his message to them. But he would not believe it was an angel, so the wife entreated God to send the angel again, that he might be seen by her husband. The angel appeared to her again when she was alone. She asked the angel to stay until she could go and call her husband, and that request being granted, she went for Manoah. But though he saw the angel he was still doubtful. He asked him who he was, so that when the child was born they might return him thanks and make him a present. The angel replied that he wanted no present. But at the earnest request of Manoah he agreed to stay long enough to let them prepare him a meal. So Manoah slew a kid and bade his wife boil it. When all was ready, the angel told them to set the bread and meat upon a rock. Touching them with a rod he held in his hand, a bright flame sprang up and consumed them. And as they looked the angel ascended up to heaven by means of the smoke, as by a vehicle. Now Manoah was afraid that some danger would come to them from this sight of God, but his wife bade him be of good courage, for that God had appeared to them for their benefit.

In due time the child was born, and was called Samson, which means a strong man. And as he grew up his parents were careful to follow the commands of the angel, letting his hair grow long and giving him no wine to drink.

When Samson was a young man, he went with his parents to Timnath, a city of the Philistines, where there was a great festival. Here he met a maid of that country, with whom he was so much pleased that he asked his parents to let him marry her. But they would not consent at first, because she was a daughter of the Philistines, who were the enemies of the Israelites. At last, however, finding that Samson had made up his mind and could not be persuaded to forget her, they withdrew their objection.

Once as Samson was going to Timnath to visit the maiden a lion met him, and though the youth was without sword or spear he was not afraid, but waited for the lion to spring on him, and then strangled it with his hands.

Soon after he passed along the same road, on his way to the maiden, and turning aside to see the carcass of the lion, he found that a swarm of bees had gone into it and made honey there. He took some of the honey, and gave it, with other presents, to the maiden.

At last the day appointed for the marriage arrived. A great wedding-feast was held in Timnath. And among those that came to it were thirty young men of the Philistines, who had been given to Samson under pretence of being his companions, but in reality to watch over him and see that he attempted no disturbance. The feast lasted seven days, and on the first day Samson said to his companions,—

"Come, now, if I propose you a riddle, and you can guess it within these seven days, I will give every one of you a linen shirt and a garment as a reward of your wisdom."

The young men were very anxious to try if they could guess the riddle, and they asked him to tell it. Then Samson said,—

"A great devourer produced sweet food out of itself, though itself were very disagreeable."

For three days his companions thought over this riddle and could not guess it. Then they came to Samson's wife, and asked her to find out the answer from her husband and to let them know it, threatening to burn her if she could not find out.

So she asked Samson to tell her, and when he refused she

wept, saying that he did not love her, until at last he could refuse no longer. He told her, therefore, how he had killed a lion and found bees afterwards in its breast, and how he had brought honey away from it. And next morning she told this to the Philistine young men. And on the seventh day they came to Samson and said,—

"Nothing is more disagreeable than a lion to those that meet one, and nothing is sweeter than honey to those that eat it."

Then Samson knew that his wife had betrayed him, and he answered,—

"Nothing is so deceitful as a woman, for such was the person who told you this secret."

Then Samson went out, and meeting with some Philistines who dwelt in a town named Askelon, he slew thirty of them, and took their clothing, which he gave to his companions, as he had promised. But he was angry with his wife, and divorced her, and she, despising his anger, soon after married one of the Philistine youth. At this Samson became still angrier, and he resolved to punish all the Philistines as well as her. It was then summer-time, and the crops were almost ripe for reaping. Samson caught three hundred foxes, and tying pieces of blazing wood to their tails, he let them loose in the fields of the Philistines, so that the wheat and other grain was burned up and destroyed. When the Philistines knew this was Samson's doing, and learned the reason, they sent their rulers to Timnath, and burned his wife and her relations as the cause of their misfortunes.

Samson fought with all the Philistines whom he met anywhere, and slew a great many of them. Afterwards he went to live on the top of a rock named Elam. And the Philistines gathered up a number of men to capture him and to punish those who harbored him. The Israelites were afraid, and some of them came to Elam and told Samson that the Philistines would treat them cruelly so long as they allowed him to remain in their country. Then Samson asked them what they wished with him. They answered that they wished to bind him and give him over to the Philistines. He only made them swear they would not kill him, but would deliver him over alive to the Philistines. And when they had sworn he came down from the rock, and they bound him with two cords and took him to the camp of the Philistines. The Philistines shouted with joy when they saw him, thinking they would now be revenged. But when they had surrounded him, Samson burst his bonds, and, catching up the jawbone of an ass that happened to lie at his feet, he fell upon his enemies and slew a thousand of them, and put the rest to flight.

Samson was very proud of this victory, and he rejoiced greatly, saying that it did not come from the assistance of God, but from his own strength and courage. But a great thirst came upon him, and he grew so weak that he was glad to cry to God for help. And God was moved with his entreaties, and opened a spring in that place, and when he had drunk of its waters his strength came to him again.

Samson had so little fear of the Philistines after this victory that he went in broad daylight to one of their chief cities, named Gaza, and took up his lodging in an inn. When the rulers of Gaza heard that he had come, they set guards at all the gates to prevent his going out again. But Samson got up in the middle of the night and came to the gates, and when he found them shut, he pulled the doors off their hinges and carried them on his shoulders to the top of a hill. There was a woman among the Philistines named Delilah, to whose house Samson often went. When the rulers of the Philistines knew this, they came to her and promised her a great deal of gold and silver if she would find out from Samson what made him so strong. So the next time he came to the house, she first pretended to praise him for all his great actions, and at last she asked him how it was he was so much stronger than all other men. Samson guessed why she asked him this, and in order to deceive her he said,—

"If I am bound with seven green withes I shall be as weak as other men."

Withes were ropes made out of twigs or green branches of trees, and were very tough.

Delilah believed him, and told the lords of the Philistines. So one day when Samson was asleep, a number of soldiers came and bound him in the way he had told her. Then Delilah awoke him, saying that some people had come to attack him. And Samson, starting up, broke the withes as easily as if they had been thread. Then Delilah said that she was only trying him, to see if he had told the truth, and she wept a good deal and pretended to be very sad because he would not trust in her. And again she asked him to tell her about his strength.

Samson again deceived her, and said,—

"If you bind me with seven new ropes I will lose my strength."

But when Delilah had bound him with the ropes, he broke them as easily as he had broken the withes. Then he told her that if she could weave or plait his long hair in a way which he showed her, he would become weak. But when Delilah did this, he rose as strong as ever. At last Samson allowed himself to be moved by her tears and reproaches, and he told her the truth.

"My hair," he said, "has never been cut since I was born, God having ordered me to let it grow long. If you cut off my hair I shall be as weak as other men."

One day, as Samson was sleeping, the wicked Delilah cut off all his hair, and then called to the Philistines to come and take him. And he was no longer able to resist them. So they bound him and put out both his eyes and threw him into prison.

Not long afterwards there was a festival in Gaza, among

the Philistines, and all the chief people had gathered in a
great hall, whither they ordered Samson to be brought, that
they might make sport of him. Now Samson's hair had
grown long again while he was in prison, and his strength
had returned to him. But the Philistines did not know this,
and Samson, to deceive them, pretended to be very weak, and
asked the youth who guided his steps to let him rest on the
pillars that supported the house. When the boy had done
this, Samson took hold of the pillars and shook them so
fiercely that he overthrew them. And the house fell down
upon the Philistines, crushing to death more than three thousand of them, and Samson himself died with them.

CHAPTER XXXII.

THE STORY OF RUTH.

AFTER the death of Samson, Eli the high-priest ruled
over Israel, and in his time there was a famine in Canaan.
There was a man of the Israelites named Elimelech, who lived
in the city of Bethlehem. Being unable to obtain food for
his family, which consisted of his wife Naomi and two sons,
he took them with him to the land of Moab. He prospered
there, and married his sons to women of Moab. After ten
years he died, and his sons soon after died also, and the
mother, Naomi, was left alone with her daughters-in-law.

Naomi, full of grief, resolved to return to her own country,
for she had learned that the famine was over there. Her
daughters-in-law wished to go with her, but Naomi told them
they had better remain and marry men of their own nation,
and she prayed God that they would be happier in a second
marriage than they had been in their first. And one of her

daughters-in-law, whose name was Orpah, did as Naomi desired, and remained behind, but the other, whose name was Ruth, would not leave her.

They came into Canaan, to the city of Bethlehem, where Naomi used to live. To all those who called Naomi by name she would answer, "Do not call me Naomi, for that means pleasant; call me rather Marah, which means bitter."

At Bethlehem there was a man named Boaz, a near relation of Naomi's husband Elimelech. He was a rich man, and owned a great deal of land. It was the harvest-time, and Ruth went out into the fields to glean, that is, to pick up the ears of corn that had been left by the reapers. She strayed into the fields that were owned by Boaz, and Boaz, seeing her, asked his chief servant, "What woman is this?" And the servant told him who she was.

When Boaz learned that this was the woman who had accompanied Naomi from the land of Moab, he praised her greatly for her goodness and her kindness to her mother-in-law, and he told his servants that she might not only glean, but might reap the grain and carry away all she was able. And he also said that the servants were to give her to eat and to drink when they served out the meals.

So Ruth gleaned in the fields all day. And when she had come home, she told Naomi of what had happened to her. Naomi informed her who Boaz was, that he was a kinsman of Elimelech, her former husband, and that according to the law of Moses he ought to marry Ruth, because she was the widow of one of his nearest relations.

"Wash thyself, therefore," said she, "and anoint thee, and put on thy best garments, and go down to the place where he is threshing his barley, but let the man not see thee till after he has done eating and drinking. Lay thyself down at his feet when he sleeps, and when he wakes he will tell thee what he will do."

So Ruth did as she was told. And after Boaz had eaten

and drunk, and had fallen asleep, she placed herself at his feet. When he woke, he asked her who she was and what she wanted. And she answered, "I am Ruth, thy servant; suffer me to remain here."

Then Boaz knew who she was, and remembered also that she was the widow of his kinsman. So he bade her gather up all the barley she could and take it to Naomi. And he said to her,—

"If the man who is nearest of kin to thy dead husband wishes to marry thee, thou shalt follow him. But if he refuse, I will marry thee according to law."

Ruth returned to Naomi, and they rejoiced together at these words of Boaz, for now they knew he would not desert them in their poverty. And Boaz went down to the city at noon, and made Ruth come before an assembly of all the rulers. He also summoned the nearest kinsman of her dead husband, to whom he said,—

"Do you not possess the property of Elimelech and his sons?"

"Yes," answered the other, "I possess it, for the law gives it to me as their nearest kinsman."

"Nay," returned Boaz, "it is not sufficient to perform only a part of the law, for the wife of Mahlon is come hither, whom thou must marry, according to the laws, if thou wouldst retain the fields which belonged to her husband."

Then the man answered that, as he was already married and had children, he would forego his right, and give up the widow and the inheritance to Boaz.

Boaz accepted the offer, and took Ruth for his wife. And within a year they had a son, whose name was Obed. Obed was the grandfather of David, who was the greatest king that ever ruled over Israel.

CHAPTER XXXIII.

THE BOY SAMUEL.

WHEN Eli the high-priest was judge in Israel, there was a man named Elkanah, who went every year from the city of Ramath, where he lived, to offer up a sacrifice at the tabernacle at Shiloh. He had a wife named Hannah, whom he loved very much, but she was not happy, because God had not given her any children. In her sorrow she came to the tabernacle and prayed, and made a vow that if God would give her a son she would consecrate him to the service of God all his life, and he should assist the high-priest in the sacrifices.

As she was praying and weeping, Eli the high-priest thought she had drunk too much wine, and he reproached her for it.

"Nay," said Hannah, "I have not drunk wine, but I am in great sorrow because I have no child, and I pray God to give me one."

Then Eli spoke kindly to her, and said that God would surely hear her prayer and give her a son.

And indeed not long after a son was born to her, and she called his name Samuel, which means, Asked of God. She did not forget her promise, for when he was old enough she brought him to the tabernacle to serve the Lord there. And God afterwards gave her other children, sons and daughters.

Eli had two sons, Hophni and Phinehas, who were priests, but were very wicked men. All the people cried out against them, and Eli also mourned over their wickedness, and feared greatly that some punishment would be inflicted on them by the Lord.

One night Samuel, who was then twelve years of age, heard the voice of God calling him by name as he slept. And he woke up and ran to Eli, thinking it was he who had called him. But Eli said,—

"I did not call; lie down again."

Twice more did the voice call to Samuel, and each time the boy rose and went to Eli. The third time Eli said to him,—

"Indeed, my son, I was silent now as before; it is God who is calling to thee. Go, therefore, lie down, and if He call thee again, say, Speak, Lord, Thy servant heareth."

And the voice did call him again, and Samuel answered as Eli had bidden. Then the Lord spoke, and said that a great misfortune would happen to the Israelites, that they would be defeated by their enemies, and that the two sons of Eli would be killed, because they were wicked and their father had not punished them as they had deserved.

Samuel was very sad when he heard this, and he would not have told it to Eli, but that Eli obliged him to do so. Then the father knew that his sons must die, and that the Lord was displeased with him also; and he was much grieved.

Shortly afterwards the Philistines made war upon the Israelites, and defeated them in a great battle. Four thousand were slain, and the rest retreated to the camp in disorder. The Israelites thought that if they sent for the ark, and took it with them the next time they fought, they would be victorious. So the ark was sent to the camp, and Hophni and Phinehas accompanied it, because their father was too old to come. Before they set out, Eli told them that if the ark was taken, and they came back without it, he would not receive them. The arrival of the ark gave great joy to the Israelites, and the Philistines were afraid when they heard of it. But both sides found they were mistaken, one in its joy and the other in its fear. For in the next battle the Philistines conquered again. They slew thirty thousand of the Israelites, among whom were the sons of Eli, and the ark itself fell into their hands.

A man of the tribe of Benjamin, who had escaped with difficulty from the field of battle, brought to Shiloh the news of this great defeat, and of the loss of the ark. The whole city was full of lamentations. Eli the high-priest, who was sitting on a high throne at one of the gates, heard these cries and knew that some great calamity had happened. He sent for the messenger to come to him. And when he learned of the defeat of the Israelites he was not surprised, though he grieved greatly, because the Lord had prepared him to expect these things. But when he was told of the loss of the ark, he fell off from his seat to the ground and died, for his grief was greater than he could bear. He was ninety-eight years of age, and had ruled forty years.

CHAPTER XXXIV.

THE RETURN OF THE ARK.

THE Philistines bore the ark in triumph to their city of Ashdod, and put it into the temple of Dagon, their god, with the other spoils that they had taken. Next morning, when they came to worship this false god, they were alarmed to find that their idol had fallen upon its face on the ground before the ark. They put it back in its place, but again and again they found it in the morning on the ground. God also sent a great sickness upon the people of Ashdod, so that many of them died. And a multitude of rats rose up out of the ground and ate up all the fruits and plants, so that there was danger of a famine. Then the citizens, believing that the ark was the cause of their troubles, resolved to send it to another city, called Askelon, whose inhabitants were willing to receive it. But the plagues visited this city also, and when the ark was removed to other places, it carried with it the scourge of God upon the inhabitants. The whole country was now alarmed, and the inhabitants of the principal cities met together to decide what they should do. And as they were not all agreed that their troubles came upon them because of the ark, some wise men proposed a plan by which they might decide if this were so. They told the Philistines to build a new cart, or wagon, upon which to place the ark, and to this cart should be yoked two cows that had young calves, and that had never drawn a cart before. The cart should be brought to a place where three roads met, and be left there without a driver. " And if," said the wise men, " the cows do not return to their calves, but of their accord choose the road that leads to the land of the Israelites, we shall know that the ark has been the cause of all our evils; but if they take another road, then we shall think that our troubles have come by chance to us, and that God did not send them."

Every one approved of this advice, and it was determined that the plan should be carried out.

The cows chose the road that led straight on to the Israelites, and the Philistines followed at a distance, to see what would happen. When the cows had come to a village called Bethshemesh, they stopped, although there was a grassy plain in front of them. The people were reaping their wheat when they saw it come, and their delight was very great. But in the midst of their joy they forgot the reverence due to God, and they dared to open and look into the ark. Now the ark, as we have seen, was kept in the Holy of Holies, where only the priests might enter. Even a Levite might not touch the ark, under pain of death. Therefore God showed His displeasure at the sin of these men, and seventy of them died on the spot. Then the others knew they were not worthy to have the ark in their midst, and they sent to the senate of the Israelites, informing them that the ark had been restored by the Philistines.

Then the ark was taken to the city of Kirjath-jearim, where it was placed in the house of a good man, named Abinadab, who was a Levite. Here it remained for twenty years. During all this time the Israelites lived very piously, and God blessed them in many ways. And Samuel, who after Eli's death had become judge over the people, seeing that their hearts were softened, thought this would be a good time to exhort them to recover their liberty from the Philistines.

So he called together the multitude and made a speech to them. He showed them the wickedness of their past conduct, and spoke of the evils that had followed from it, praised them for their repentance, and told them that if they continued in the right path God would certainly look down upon them with favor and deliver them from their enemies.

The Israelites were pleased with his words, and replied that they were willing to do whatever the Lord commanded. Samuel ordered them to come together again in the city of Mizpah, which means a watch-tower. There they sacrificed and fasted and offered up public prayers. The Philistines, learning of this gathering, came against them with a large army. And they rushed upon the city while the people were sacrificing, thinking they would surprise them and easily defeat them. But suddenly the earth began to tremble and shake under their feet, then it opened with a loud roar as of thunder, and swallowed up a great number of the Philistines. The rest threw away their arms and fled in the greatest confusion. The Israelites pursued and gained a complete victory. After that they gained other victories, and recovered all the towns they had lost, and they drove the Philistines out of the land of Canaan.

When Samuel was grown old and could no longer attend to all the affairs of the government, he gave a portion of his authority to his two sons ; but the sons had no share of their father's virtues. For they took bribes from those who came before them to have their disputes settled, and decided not according to the justice of the case, but according to which side gave them the most money. Besides this, they disobeyed many other of the commands of God. So the Israelites came to Samuel at Ramah, and told him that as he was now too old to govern them, and as his sons behaved so wickedly, they would like to be like the other nations around them, and have a king to rule them. Samuel was very sad when he heard this, and, thinking their desire for a change of government rose from some dislike against himself, he made his complaint to God.

And God said to Samuel,—

"It is not with thee, but with me that they are dissatisfied. For they do not want me to rule any longer over them. They will repent when it is too late, and will be sorry for their ingratitude to me and to you. But I command you to give them as their king the man whom I will point out to you, though first you must point out to them the rights and great power of a king and all the evils that may follow from having one."

So Samuel got the people together, and told them that the king they wished for would often be a cruel master to them, and they would have to give him much of their money and their goods to keep up his grandeur, and he would take their children, whether they liked it or not, to be his soldiers and servants. But the multitude still said, "We want a king like the other nations, to rule over us and to go out to battle at the head of our armies."

Then Samuel dismissed the assembly, telling them that when the time was come he would announce to them who had been chosen for their king.

CHAPTER XXXV.

SAUL IS CHOSEN KING.

THERE was a man of the tribe of Benjamin whose name was Kish. He had a son named Saul, who was a tall and handsome man. One day some of the asses that belonged to Kish strayed away from his fields and were lost. And Kish told Saul to go in search of them. Saul wandered for some time about the country from place to place without learning anything about the asses. Fearing his father might grow uneasy at his stay, he thought of returning home, when his servant advised him to go to Samuel the prophet, and perhaps he could tell them where they should look. Saul was pleased with the advice, and he went to the city of Ramah and asked the way to the prophet's house. Some maidens pointed it out to him, and told him at the same time that he must make haste, for the prophet was just about to sit down to a great feast. Now the fact was that Samuel was giving this feast in honor of Saul. For the day before, when he was praying, God told him that on the morrow, at that very hour, he would send to him the man who was to be king of Israel. And Samuel was now expecting the visitor,—for the hour named had almost arrived. And when Saul appeared, Samuel knew him to be the man, and rose and invited him in to the feast. And he made him and his servant sit down above all the other guests, who were seventy in number, and he gave orders that the best of everything was to be set before Saul. When the time for going to bed had come, the others left, but Saul remained with the prophet and slept with him.

Early next morning Samuel woke Saul from his sleep, and accompanied him part of the way home. When they were out of the city, he asked Saul to send his servant before him, as he had something he wished to say to him only. Samuel then took out a small vial of oil, and pouring it upon the head of Saul, he saluted him, and said,—

" God hath appointed you king over His people, to avenge them against the Philistines. And as a sign that what I say is true, you will meet at a short distance from here three men, who will salute you and speak kindly to you, and offer you bread and wine. And a little farther on you will meet two men, who will inform you that the asses are found. And afterwards you will meet a company of prophets coming down from the hill, and the Spirit of the Lord shall seize you, and you will begin to prophesy with them and be changed into another man."

And everything happened as Samuel had said.

Then Samuel called all the tribes together at Mizpeh, and informed them that since they had rejected God, and chosen to have a king instead, they must throw lots to find out who the person was. The lot first fell upon the tribe of Benjamin, then upon the family of Metri, and lastly upon the person of Saul himself.

But Saul was not in the assembly, for he knew beforehand that the lot would fall upon him, and he did not want to seem anxious to be king. Messengers were sent to fetch him, and when he arrived Samuel presented him to the people. And when they saw how tall and strong and handsome he was they were well pleased, and cried out, " God save the king !" But there were some who murmured and did not like this new king.

CHAPTER XXXVI.

THE DEFEAT OF THE AMMONITES.

At this time the Ammonites were waging war with the Israelites. Nahash, their king, at the head of a great and warlike army, had made an expedition against those tribes which lived beyond Jordan, and taken many of their cities, and, to make it impossible for them to regain their liberty, he put out the right eye of every man who fell into his hands. For this made the men useless in war, as warriors held their shields with their left hand, and therefore in front of the left side of their face, while they looked at their enemy with the right eye. Then Nahash marched on into the land of Gilead, and encamped before the city of Jabesh. And he sent ambassadors to the people, commanding them to give themselves up and let their right eyes be plucked out, or else to suffer a siege and have their city entirely overthrown. He thus gave them their choice, whether they would lose a small member of their body or perish altogether. The citizens of Jabesh were so frightened that they could not make up their minds what to do, and they asked Nahash to give them seven days to seek for help from the rest of the Israelites, saying they would fight if they received this assistance, but would surrender themselves in case it did not arrive. And Nahash despised the Israelites so much that he allowed them to seek for all the assistance they wished.

When the messengers came to Saul he was seized with a divine fury, and sent them back to Jabesh with word that he would gather up his army and be with them on the third day, and would attack the enemy and defeat them before sunrise. And he did as he said, and on the third day before sunrise he fell on the Ammonites. They were taken by surprise, and though they fought bravely they were defeated, and their king was slain. Saul pursued them to their own country, and laid it waste, and took much gold and silver and other booty.

In the second year of Saul's reign he raised an army of three thousand men. Two thousand of these he kept as a royal guard, the other thousand he placed under the command of his son Jonathan and sent him to Gilboa. Now the Israelites of that country were still under the dominion of the Philistines, who treated them very cruelly. Jonathan attacked some of the Philistine soldiers who were stationed near Gilgal, and defeated them. Then the Philistines sent a great army into the land of Israel. Saul went to Gilgal, and called upon the inhabitants to arm and defend themselves. But many were so afraid at the numbers of their enemies that they fled to the mountains and hid themselves in caves, others crossed over the Jordan to the land of Gilead, and only a few remained with Saul.

Then Saul sent word to Samuel the prophet to come and advise him what to do. And Samuel replied that he would be with the king at the end of seven days, and they would offer up sacrifices together. But as Samuel did not come till the evening of the seventh day, Saul grew impatient and offered up the sacrifices alone. As soon as he had done it Samuel came, and Saul went out to meet him. Samuel reproached Saul for what he had done and would accept no excuses, and told him that God was angry with him, and would take the kingdom away from him and put another man in his place. Then Samuel returned home.

Saul and Jonathan counted the men around them and found there were only six hundred, and the most of these had no arms. For the Philistines had not allowed the people they conquered to have spears or swords, and had taken all their iron away, and had sent out of the country all the workmen who made those weapons. Therefore Saul was much disturbed in his mind, and knew not what to do.

His son Jonathan, however, was a bold and daring youth, and had determined upon a plan of his own. The Philistines had now come in sight of the Israelites, and were encamped near them on a mountain, just above a steep precipice. Jonathan told his plan only to one soldier, who was his armorbearer. The Philistines did not believe that any one could climb up the precipice, and therefore they did not take care to guard it.

" Now," said Jonathan, " if you and I creep up the precipice at night and fall upon the enemy as they sleep, they will be put into great confusion and will not know what to do. But first let us ask the Lord for a sign whether it is pleasing to Him that we should do this. Let us go out of our camp in the daylight and show ourselves to the enemy, and if they mock us and bid us climb up to them, then we shall believe that God favors our plan; but if they say nothing, we shall know that we can do nothing."

So the two went out of the city towards the camp of the Philistines. And when they had come within speaking distance, they heard the Philistines laughing among themselves and saying, "See! the Israelites are crawling out of their dens and caves;" and then some of the enemy cried out to Jonathan,—

" Come on, ascend up to us, that we may inflict a just punishment upon you for your rashness."

Then Jonathan knew that the Lord would give him the victory. So he and the armor-bearer withdrew, and at nighttime they climbed up the precipice and fell upon the enemy. They slew twenty men, and the whole camp was wakened out of its sleep in great disorder, and as there were many different tribes in the army, they did not know one another in the darkness, but every tribe thought the other was a band of Israelites.

So they fought one against another, and many were slain in this way, while many others in seeking to flee fell headlong down the precipice.

Saul was told by his watchmen that there was a strange tumult in the camp of the enemy. So he called his men together, and they went out after the Philistines, and set upon them as they were slaying one another. Many also of those who had fled to dens and caves, hearing that Saul was gaining a great victory, now came rushing out to join him, and he soon found himself at the head of an army of ten thousand men. The Philistines were now scattered all over the country, fleeing away in terror, and Saul set out in pursuit. But first he bound himself and his whole army by an oath not to eat the least thing before evening, till they had been revenged on their enemies. Whoever broke the oath was to be put to death. Now Jonathan knew nothing of this oath. Being in hot pursuit of a band of the enemy, he came to a forest where there were many honey-bees, and breaking off a piece of honey-comb, he ate part of it. But the Israelites around him told him what had been sworn by the army, and Jonathan threw the honey-comb away.

At evening the army was ordered to halt, that they might rest and eat. And Saul told the priests to offer sacrifices and pray to God to know whether he would continue to be successful. But the priests told him they could receive no answer.

"Surely," said Saul, "there must be some cause for God's silence, and there is some sin against Him that we know not of. Now I swear that though he that hath committed this sin shall prove to be my own son Jonathan, I will slay him, and so appease the anger of God against us."

The multitude applauded his decision. Lots were ordered to be cast, and the offence fell upon Jonathan. Saul asked him what he had done.

"Oh, father," answered the youth, "the only sin I know of is

9

that yesterday, when I knew not of the oath you had sworn, I tasted of a honey-comb before evening."

Saul said he would keep his oath and slay Jonathan. And Jonathan said he was ready to die if his father so willed it. But the multitude were so pleased with this noble self-sacrifice, as well as so grateful for the bravery which had won them a great victory, that they all swore another oath, and bound themselves not to let Jonathan be put to death. In this way they saved him from the king his father, and at the same time they offered up prayers to God to pardon the fault he had committed.

CHAPTER XXXVII.

THE SIN OF SAUL.

AFTER his great victory over the Philistines, Saul turned his arms against the Moabites, the Ammonites, and the kings of Edom and Soba, and defeated them all. Then Samuel came to him and told him that God remembered the wickedness of the Amalekites, in attacking the children of Israel while they were passing through the wilderness, and that the time had now come for the destruction of that cruel and bloody race. So he commanded him to go out against them, and kill them all, together with their cattle and their asses. And all the valuable things that belonged to them were to be burnt as a sacrifice, and Saul was to keep nothing for his own use.

In obedience to this order, Saul put himself at the head of two thousand men and marched against the Amalekites. He defeated them in battle, and took their cities, and slew men, women, and children. But when he had taken captive Agag, their king, he admired his beauty so much that he persuaded himself he ought to be spared. And his soldiers also disregarded the commands of God, and they did not kill all the herds and the flocks, but kept the best of them and returned with them to their own country.

Then the Lord appeared to Samuel, and told him what Saul and the people had done, adding that He now repented of having made Saul king. So Samuel next morning came to Saul with a heavy heart. The king ran out to meet him, and said,—

"I return thanks to God, who hath given me the victory; for I have performed everything He hath commanded me."

To which Samuel replied,—

"How is it, then, that I hear the bleating of sheep and the lowing of cattle in the camp?"

"The people," said Saul, "have reserved these for sacrifices, but the Amalekites are all destroyed. No one of them remains alive except their king, and him have I brought with me in order that I may consult with you what to do with him."

But the prophet said that God was not pleased with sacrifices when they are made in disobedience to His commands, and he told Saul again that because he had offended God his kingdom would be taken away from him and given to a man who was more worthy of it. Then was Saul grieved, and he confessed that he had acted wrongly. But he said that if he were forgiven this time he would never sin again. And he prayed the prophet to stay a little while and offer sacrifices to God, that His wrath might be appeased. But Samuel knew that what God had determined could not be altered, and he turned to go. Then Saul hastily caught hold of the prophet's cloak to stop him, and the cloak was torn in his hands.

"Even so," said Samuel, "shall your kingdom be torn from you and given to another."

Saul again confessed that he had sinned, and prayed that the prophet would at least stay and worship God with him in the presence of all the people. Samuel granted him that favor, and went with him and worshipped God. Then he ordered that King Agag should be brought before him. And when Agag lamented, and said death was very bitter, Samuel said to him,—

"As thou hast made many Jewish mothers in Israel to lament and bewail their children, so shalt thou, by thy death, cause thy mother to lament also."

And, having given orders that the king should be killed, Samuel returned to his home.

Saul was very sorrowful on account of what Samuel had told him, and because he knew that God was his enemy. He went up to his royal palace at Gibeah, and after that day he came no more into the presence of the prophet. When Samuel mourned for him, God told him to leave off mourning, and to take the sacred oil and go to the city of Bethlehem, to a man named Jesse, and to anoint one of his sons who should be pointed out to him. Samuel went as he was commanded. At Bethlehem he made ready a sacrifice, and invited Jesse and his sons to come to it. Jesse came with his eldest son, who was so tall and strong and handsome that the prophet felt sure this must be the chosen one. But God told him no, that it was not the outside of man He considered in making His selection, but rather the heart and the spirit. The prophet asked Jesse to send for his other sons. Five others came, all as handsome and strong as the first, but none of these was selected. Then Samuel asked Jesse if he had not other sons.

"Only one more," answered Jesse, "a shepherd who takes care of our flocks. His name is David."

"Let him come also," said the prophet.

So David was sent for, and came. He was a very young man, but he, too, was handsome, and there was something brave and warlike in his appearance.

As soon as the prophet saw him, he knew he was the chosen of the Lord. And he took the oil and poured it on his head and anointed him before all his brethren. From that moment the Spirit of God departed from Saul and rested upon David.

Meanwhile, Saul, being abandoned by God, became very sad and gloomy, so much so that at times he was driven almost to frenzy. The physicians advised him to look out for some skilful musician who would play sacred hymns to him and soothe his soul to peace. Then one of Saul's servants told him that in the city of Bethlehem he had seen a son of Jesse, who was not more than a child in years, but who was skilled in music and the singing of hymns, and was also a manly and warlike lad. It was David of whom he spoke, for David played very well upon the harp. And Saul sent messengers to Jesse, asking that David be made to come to his palace. So Jesse sent his son and gave him presents to carry to the king. And Saul was pleased with the lad, and also with his music, for when David played upon his harp the sad spirit of the king went away, and he was well again.

CHAPTER XXXVIII.

DAVID AND GOLIATH.

A FRESH war broke out between the Israelites and the Philistines. The two armies encamped upon two neighboring hills with a narrow valley between them. There came a man out of the camp of the Philistines who was called Goliath. He was a giant, being nearly ten feet in height. He stood in the valley between the two armies, and cried out in a loud voice to the Israelites,—

" I will fight any man in your army whom you may choose to send me. And if he fights me and kills me, then the Philistines will agree to be your servants; but if I kill him, then you must be our servants. For is it not better to place one man in danger than to place a whole army in danger?"

No one among the Israelites durst answer him, and he returned to his own camp. Next day he came out and used the same words. And every morning for forty days he came out and defied the men of Israel.

Three of Jesse's sons were in Saul's army. David used sometimes to come and bring them provisions and other presents from his father. On one of these visits he heard the boasting words of Goliath. He was filled with anger, and said to his brethren,—

" I am willing to fight in single combat with this giant."

But his elder brother reproved him, and told him he talked foolishly, and bade him return to the flocks. David did not answer his brother, because of the respect he felt for his age, but on his way out of the camp he told some of the soldiers that he was willing to fight the giant. And when Saul was told what the young man had said, he sent for him, and asked him if it was true that he desired to fight with the giant.

" Yes, O king," said David, " for I do not fear this Philistine, but will go down and fight with and conquer him, big and fierce as he is, and you and your army will gain great glory when he shall be slain by one who has little experience in war, but who looks like a child, and in years is almost a child."

Saul wondered at the boldness of the youth, but he told him that he was too young for so great an enterprise.

" Nay," said David, " for I know that the Lord will assist me and give me the victory. For once I slew a lion that had stolen a lamb from my father's flock, and afterwards I slew a bear which had come up to attack me. And I will slay this Philistine as I slew the lion and the bear."

And Saul said to David, " Go thy way to the fight, and may the Lord be with thee."

Then Saul gave David his own armor to wear. But David when he had put it on found it too heavy, and said, "I cannot go with this." So he laid it aside, and took a staff in one hand and a sling in the other, and he chose five smooth stones out of the brook, which he put into his shepherd's sack, and in this manner he started out to meet Goliath.

When the giant saw him coming he began to jeer at him, because he was so young and carried no warlike weapons.

"Dost thou take me for a dog," he asked, "that thou comest to me with stones?"

"I take you," said David, "for something less than a dog."

The giant became very angry at these words, and he cursed David and told him he would "tear his body into a thousand pieces, and give them to be eaten by the birds and the beasts."

"Nay," said David, "thou comest to me with a sword and with a spear and a breastplate, but I have God for my armor, who will destroy thee by my hands, and I will this day cut off thy head and cast the other parts of thy body to the dogs."

Then David fitted one of the stones into his sling, and he ran forward and slung it against the Philistine. The stone hit Goliath in the forehead and sank into his brain, and he fell dead upon the ground, and David stood over him and cut off his head with the giant's own sword.

Upon the fall of Goliath, the Philistines all fled. The Israelites pursued them with loud cries of joy to the borders of Gath and to the gates of Askelon, and there were slain of the Philistines thirty thousand, while twice as many were wounded.

As Saul returned in triumph, a number of women and girls came out to meet the army with songs and dances, and praised them for their victory. And especially they praised Saul and David, but David more than Saul. For they said, "Saul hath killed his thousands, and David hath killed his tens of thousands." The king was angry when he heard these songs, and was jealous of David. He was afraid of him also, because he saw that God was with the youth, and he knew God no longer looked kindly on himself.

So he thought he would rid himself of David by making him captain of a thousand men and always sending him on the most dangerous expeditions. But David always returned safely, and his great bravery won him the applause of all. Michal, the king's daughter, heard so much about him that she fell in love with him, and told her father she wished to marry him. This put a new plan into Saul's head. He told David that if he would bring to him the heads of six hundred Philistines he would give him his daughter Michal in marriage. Saul said this because he hoped David would be slain himself before he could kill so many men. But David went out and fought with the Philistines and killed a great number of them, and brought six hundred of their heads to Saul. Then the king was obliged to give Michal to him for his wife. But he hated and feared him more than ever. So he resolved to have David slain, and he commanded his son Jonathan and his most faithful servants to kill him. Now Jonathan loved David, and wondered greatly at what his father commanded, but instead of obeying he told David of the secret charge that had been given him, and advised him to be absent the next day.

"I will talk to my father," said he, "if I find him well and in a good humor, and will show him what a wicked thing it is that he wants me to do."

Next day it happened that Saul was much better than usual; Jonathan spoke to him, and told him that it would be very unwise, as well as a great crime, to kill David, who had been so useful in delivering them from their enemies, and whose help they might need at any time. And Saul saw that Jonathan was right, and he suffered David to live.

CHAPTER XXXIX.

SAUL AGAIN PERSECUTES DAVID.

Soon after this the Philistines made war again with the Israelites, and David was sent against them with an army. He won the victory and returned in triumph, and the people received him with shouts of joy and praise. Again Saul was angry and jealous. And the evil spirit returned and tormented him to fury. Saul commanded David to come to his bedside and sing and play to him on his harp. The king held a javelin in his hand, and while David was playing he flung the javelin at him with great force, but David saw it coming and avoided it. Then he fled to his own house and remained there all day.

But at night the king sent officers to the house, who were to watch it and see that he did not escape. For he intended to bring David to trial and have him put to death. Michal guessed what her father's intentions were, and she came in great distress to David, her husband, and said,—

" Let not the sun find thee here when it rises, for if it do that will be the last time it will see thee ; fly away, then, in the night-time, for know this, that if my father find thee, thou art a dead man."

So she let him down by a cord out of the window where Saul's men could not see him, and he escaped.

After she had done this, she arranged the bed so as to make it look as if a sick man were lying in it, and put under the bedclothes the liver of a goat that had been freshly killed. At daybreak Saul's messengers knocked at the door.

Michal told them that David had been sick during the night, and she drew the curtains of the bed, and the liver, which was still warm and throbbing, caused the bedclothes to move up and down, so that the men believed David was breathing like one that had the asthma. They went to the king with this story, but Saul ordered that David should be brought into his presence, no matter how sick he might be. And when the men returned and lifted up the bedclothes, they saw that the princess had deceived them. And Saul was angry with his daughter for what she had done.

David fled to the prophet Samuel, at Ramah, and told him of all Saul had done. Samuel took him to a place called Naioth, where he lived for some time with the prophet. Afterwards David went to the place where Jonathan was, and complained to him that though he had done no evil, yet Saul was anxious to have him killed. But Jonathan sought to comfort him, and told him he was mistaken, that the king did not wish him to be killed.

"My father," said Jonathan, "always consults me before he does anything, and asks my advice, and as he has said nothing to me about wishing your death, I do not believe what you imagine can be true."

But David swore to him that so it was. And he said to Jonathan, "To-morrow is a feast-day, when I have been accustomed to sit down with the king at supper. I am afraid to go there, and if the king asks thee why I am absent, tell him that you gave me permission to go to Bethlehem to keep a festival with my own tribe. If he say, 'It is well that he went,' then you may assure yourself that he bears no enmity to me. But if he answer otherwise, that will be a sure sign that he hath some design against me. And you will let me know what was the king's answer."

Jonathan swore he would do as David requested. And when David asked, "Who shall tell me what thy father's answer is?" Jonathan replied,—

" As soon as I know my father's mind, I shall go out into the plain where I am accustomed to practise shooting with the bow. If I shoot three arrows at a mark and then bid my servant run and get the arrows, for they are in front of him, then thou mayest know there is no mischief to be feared from the king, but if thou hearest me say something else, then expect evil from the king."

The young men then embraced and bade each other farewell. When Saul sat down at the feast and saw that David's seat was empty, he inquired of Jonathan why the son of Jesse was not present. Jonathan answered,—

" He asked leave of me to go to Bethlehem to celebrate the festival with his own tribe."

Then it was that Jonathan understood how great was his father's hatred for David. Saul could not restrain his anger, he heaped abuses upon Jonathan, and called him a traitor and a wicked and unnatural son. He ordered him to go and fetch David, that he might be punished as he deserved.

But Jonathan spoke gently, and asked,—

" What sin hath David done, that thou wouldst punish him ?"

Saul became still more angry with his son, and he no longer contented himself with bare words, but snatched up his spear and leaped upon Jonathan, and would have killed him if he had not been prevented by his officers.

Then the king's son rose hastily from supper, for he was too much grieved to be able to eat anything. All that night he wept, because he knew now that David's death was decided upon. As soon as it was day he went out into the plain where he practised with his bow, and having shot three arrows, he dismissed his servant without telling him to pick them up. David had been hiding near the plain, and he now came out and fell at Jonathan's feet. Jonathan lifted him up, and they embraced each other and wept. Then David bade Jonathan farewell, and they parted.

CHAPTER XL.

DAVID FLEES FROM SAUL.

DAVID fled first to the city of Nob, where the high-priest Ahimelech sheltered him, and afterwards to the land of the Philistines. When he came to the city of Gath, he was recognized by the servants of the king, whose name was Achish, and they said, "This is David who hath killed many tens of thousands of the Philistines." And they took him and brought him before Achish. But David, fearing the anger of the king, pretended to be mad, and foamed at the mouth, and acted so strangely that Achish said, "You see the man is mad; why do you bring him to me? have I need of such a fellow as this?" So they let him go.

David then fled to a cave which was near the city of Adullam, and he lived there. When his brethren found out where he was they came to him, and others also came to him who were discontented with the way in which Saul governed, until at last David found he had four hundred men around him. He took courage, now such a force was come to him, and went to the land of the Moabites, and asked their king to let his followers live in Moab until their affairs were in better condition. The king granted him this request. But a prophet came to David and told him to go and live in the land of Judah. So he went to the city of Hareth, and remained there. When Saul heard that David had been seen with a great many men around him, he was much troubled. He called his officers around him and spoke to them about David, and asked them if they knew what his plans were, but none of them

could tell him.   Then a man named Doeg said to Saul that
he had seen David in the city of Nob, where he was harbored
by the high-priest Ahimelech.   Saul, therefore, sent for the
priest and for all his kindred.   And he asked him,—

"Have I ever done thee any evil, that thou hast received
the son of Jesse, and hast bestowed upon him both food and
weapons, when he is plotting to get the kingdom away from
me?"

The high-priest said he did not know that David was an
enemy of the king's, for was he not his son-in-law, and a captain in his army, and a faithful servant?

Saul would not believe him.   He commanded the armed
men that stood about him to kill the high-priest and all his
relations.   But they durst not do this.   Then Saul turned to
Doeg and told him to slay them.   Doeg went and collected
other men as wicked as himself, and they slew Ahimelech and
his relations.   And Saul sent these men to Nob, where they
slew all the inhabitants, sparing neither women nor children.
The only person that escaped was Abiathar, a son of Ahimelech, who went to David and told him what Saul had done.
David grieved greatly, blaming himself for having brought
this misfortune upon the high-priest and his family.

CHAPTER XLI.

SAUL'S ADVENTURE IN THE CAVE.

ABOUT this time David heard that the Philistines had
marched into the land of Judah and were laying waste the
fields around the city of Keilah, for it was now harvest-time.
He and his followers went against them and defeated them,
and they stayed with the people of Keilah until they had

securely gathered all their grain and fruits. The fame of this exploit reached Saul's ears, and he was glad to know that David was in Keilah, and said, " God hath now put him into my hands, since He hath obliged him to come into a city that hath walls and gates and bars."

So he commanded his army to set upon Keilah suddenly, and when they had besieged and taken it to kill David. But God revealed to David that he would be slain if he remained in that city, for the people of Keilah would give him up in order to make their peace with Saul. So he took his four hundred men and retired into a desert near the city, called Engedi. When Saul heard that David had fled, he did not go to Keilah after him. From the desert David went to the land of the Ziphites, where he lived in a wood. Here Jonathan came to him and spoke kindly to him, and told him to be hopeful of the future. And David and Jonathan made a solemn covenant of friendship, promising never to harm each other, after which Jonathan returned to his own home.

Now the men of Ziph, to please Saul, informed him that David was with them, and said they would help the king to capture him. But David learned of their evil designs, and he fled to a great rock which was in a wilderness near the city of Maon, and after that he removed to a cave in the country of Engedi.

Saul took three thousand men and went to Engedi in search of him. And Saul came to the cave in which David and his men were hidden, but he did not know they were there. It was very long and broad, and a good many men could hide in it. Saul went alone into the cave. While he was there, David's men wanted him to rise and slay him. But David would not do this, but he went up softly behind Saul, and cut off a piece of his robe. When Saul rose and left the cave, David followed and called to him by name.

Saul recognized the voice, and turned round.

Then David bowed down to the ground, and asked Saul

why he had listened to the wicked men who told lies about him, and who said that it was his desire to slay the king.

"For if I wished to kill thee," said David, "I could easily have done so just now, for when I cut off the skirt of thy garment, I could as easily have done the same to thy head." And David held up the piece he had cut from Saul's robe. Saul then knew the danger he had been in, and was so touched by the generosity of David that he wept. And he said, "Thou hast shown this day that thou art a righteous man. And now I know well that some day the Lord will make thee king of Israel. Promise me, therefore, that thou wilt not destroy my family after I am dead, but wilt forgive the injuries I have done thee." And David promised that he would not, and Saul went back to his own kingdom.

Shortly after, Samuel died, and all the children of Israel came to Ramah to see him buried, and they wept for him a great number of days.

CHAPTER XLII.

THE WIFE OF NABAL.

DAVID and his followers went back to the wilderness of Maon. There was a rich man in that neighborhood, named Nabal, who had a great many sheep and goats. David and his followers looked after Nabal's flocks, and would not allow any one to come near them, or to molest his shepherds. When shearing-time was come, David sent ten messengers to Nabal, telling him of the good care he had taken of his sheep, and asking him for food as a small return for all he had done. But Nabal was a foolish and ill-natured man, and he asked, "Who is David?" When they answered, he was the son of Jesse, Nabal cried that there were many servants that had run away from their masters as David had done, but he would not give such people any assistance.

When the messengers returned to David with these words, he was very angry, and he swore that he would that night destroy the house and all the possessions of Nabal. By this time he had six hundred men under his command. He told four hundred to arm themselves and come with him.

Nabal had a very wise and prudent wife, whose name was Abigail. She had learned from the young men of David's message, and of how it had been received, and she was grieved at it. When her husband, who had become drunk with wine, was fast asleep, she saddled her asses and loaded them with all sorts of presents and went in search of David. She met him as he was coming down a hill at the head of his four hundred men. And she got down from the ass and bowed down before him with her face to the ground, and entreated him not to mind the words of Nabal. Then she asked him to accept the presents she brought with her. David's anger was calmed by what the woman said, and he took her presents and spoke kindly to her, and suffered her to return home in peace.

Now when Nabal recovered from his drunkenness, his wife told him of the danger he had been in. He was greatly frightened by her story, so that all the strength went out of his body, and he sickened and died within ten days. When David learned that Nabal was dead, he said that he had only received his proper punishment, but for himself he rejoiced that God had preserved him from going down to Nabal's house in his anger and staining his hands with blood.

And David loved Abigail, and invited her to come and live with him and be his wife. She said to his messengers that she was not worthy of so great an honor, but she would do as David said. So she came with all her servants, and was married to him.

CHAPTER XLIII.

SAUL AGAIN PURSUES DAVID.

AFTER Saul had returned to his palace, his old anger against David rose again within him, and he was sorry that he had not attacked him in the cave. Learning from some of the men of Ziph that David was in the wilderness of Maon, he took three thousand men and went in search of him.

David heard of his coming, and sent out spies, who returned and told him that Saul had made his camp in a place called Hachilah. Then David took with him his nephew Abishai, and at night-time, when all Saul's army was asleep, they entered the camp. They went into Saul's tent, and when Abishai would have slain the king, David prevented him. He took only the spear and the cruse (or bottle) of water that stood by Saul's bed, and then he and his nephew stole silently out of the camp without having been seen or heard by any one.

When David had reached the top of a neighboring hill, he cried out in a loud voice and awaked the soldiers out of their sleep.

And Abner, the commander, asked who it was that called.

"It is I," said David, "the son of Jesse, whom thou seekest to capture. But what is the matter with thee, that being a man favored by the king and the commander of his armies, thou dost take so little care of thy master's body? If thou wilt look for the king's spear and his cruse of water, thou wilt learn what a mighty misfortune was ready to overtake thee in thy very camp without thy knowing anything about it."

Now when Saul knew David's voice, and understood what had happened, he confessed that David had done a very noble thing. And he said that he would no longer molest David or seek to injure him, but that he might go back in safety to his family. When the day broke, Saul led his army homeward.

CHAPTER XLIV.

THE WITCH OF ENDOR.

DAVID was still afraid of Saul, for he knew that he was not to be depended upon. So he thought it better to go and abide in the land of the Philistines. With his six hundred men he went to Achish, the king of Gath, and Achish received him kindly, and gave him the town of Ziklag for himself and his followers to live in. Soon after war broke out anew between the Philistines and the Israelites, and Achish asked David to go with him to battle and bring his six hundred armed men. David went with him as he was requested.

The Philistines made their camp near a city called Shunen, and Saul and his army made their camp on the mountain of Gilboa, where they could overlook the enemy's forces. Saul was terrified when he saw the numbers of the Philistines, and he inquired of God by the prophets whether he would win the victory; but God made him no answer. Then in his terror Saul determined to consult a witch. Witches were evil women who were thought to raise the souls of the dead and make them foretell what was going to happen. Now Saul had made laws against these witches, as the Lord had commanded him to do, and he had banished them from the country whenever he learned where they were. The few that were left practised their wicked arts in secret. Saul was told of one of these who lived at Endor. He put off his regal robes, and disguised himself, and took two men with him and went to the woman by night. He told her she must raise up the ghost of Samuel. She did not know her visitor was Saul, but she refused to obey him till he had made a solemn promise that no harm should befall her. Then the woman called up the soul of Samuel, and he came and stood before her; but Saul could not see him. Samuel told the woman who her visitor was, and she said to him,—

" Art thou not King Saul ?"

The king answered, " I am," and then he asked her what she saw.

" I see a noble person," she answered, " who in form is like a god."

Saul bade her tell him what age he was, in what habit he appeared, and what he looked like. She answered,—

" He is an old man, very handsome, dressed in a priest's mantle."

Then Saul knew it was Samuel, and he bowed himself down to the ground. And the soul of Samuel asked him, " Why hast thou disturbed me to bring me up ?"

Saul replied, " I am sore distressed, and forsaken of God, and can obtain no knowledge of the future either by prophets or by dreams, and these are the reasons for which I have recourse to thee."

Samuel said, " It is wrong for thee to seek me when God hath forsaken thee. However, hear what I have to say. David is chosen king in thy place, and will finish the war with success, but thou shalt lose thy dominion and thy life, because thou hast not kept the commandments of the Lord. The Israelites will be defeated to-morrow by the Philistines, and both thou and thy sons will fall in battle."

When Saul had heard this, he fell down on the floor through grief. The witch raised him up and gave him to eat, and dismissed him as soon as he had strength to go.

CHAPTER XLV.

THE DEATH OF SAUL.

MEANWHILE, David and his six hundred men were causing a great deal of uneasiness to the Philistines. For when the commanders saw him they came to Achish and said, "Is not this David, the Israelite who hath slain so many of our brethren?" And when the king answered that it was, they advised him not to let him join in the battle, for he might turn against them and befriend the people of his own nation. "Make him go back," they said, "to his habitation in Ziklag." So Achish called David and told him that he had better return with his six hundred men, for that the lords of the Philistines were afraid of him. And David gladly did as he was told. Now it happened that while he was away a party of Amalekites had fallen upon the defenceless town of Ziklag and burned the houses, and carried away all the women and children as slaves.

Then David and his companions rent their clothes and wept aloud. And the men were angry with him, blaming him for their misfortunes, and they talked of stoning him. But he took counsel from God, and told them he would lead them against the enemy. They had not gone far when they came upon a man who was sick alone in a field. And they gave him food, which strengthened him, for he had not eaten for three days. Then he told them he was an Egyptian, a servant of one of the Amalekites, and that his master had left him three days ago when he fell sick. So David made use of him as a guide to conduct him to the place where the Amalekites could be found.

The Amalekites were at this time feasting and drinking or lying upon the ground in a drunken slumber, as they did not fear any attack. David and the Israelites fell upon them in this condition, and slew them, so that none of them escaped, except four hundred young men who were mounted on camels. And the men of Israel got back their wives and children, and all the spoil that the Amalekites had taken, not only from them but from other nations.

The Philistines, after David had gone, went out and fought against the men of Israel and won a great victory. Saul and his sons fought very bravely, knowing that they had nothing to hope for except an honorable death. They therefore brought upon themselves the whole power of the enemy, till they were encompassed round and the sons were all slain. Then the army of the Israelites was put to flight, and all was disorder and confusion and slaughter. Saul himself was forced to fly with a strong body of soldiers around him, but the archers of the Philistines threw their arrows and destroyed his soldiers, so that he was left almost alone. Then he turned and fought, and when he had received so many wounds that he was not able to bear up any longer, he said to his armor-bearer, "Draw thy sword and kill me, lest the enemy take me alive." But his armor-bearer was afraid, and would not. Then Saul drew his own sword and fell upon it, but he could not make it pass through him, and calling to one who was by him, who was an Amalekite, he desired him to force the sword through his breast. This the Amalekite did, and, taking the royal crown from Saul's head and the jewels and bracelets from his arms, he fled from the field. And when the armor-bearer saw that Saul was slain, he killed himself.

On the next day, when the Philistines came to strip the bodies of the slain, they found Saul and his sons lying dead on Mount Gilboa. They cut off their heads, and hung their bodies on crosses at the walls of the city Bethshan. But this barbarity came to the ears of the Israelites who lived in Jabesh-Gilead, and all the brave men in that city arose, and by journeying all night they came to the city of Bethshan next morning. They took down the bodies of Saul and his sons and carried them to Jabesh, where they buried them. For the enemy were either not able, or not bold enough, to hinder them, on account of their great courage.

CHAPTER XLVI.

DAVID IS MADE KING OF ISRAEL.

DAVID was still at Ziklag. He had not heard of the great victory of the Philistines, or of the destruction of the Israelites. But on the third day after the fight there came to Ziklag the man who slew Saul at his bidding. His clothes were rent, and ashes were upon his head. David asked him whence he came. And the man told him that he had fled from the battle, that the Israelites were defeated and many thousands of them had been killed, and that Saul and his sons were among the slain. To prove that what he said was true he produced the crown and the bracelets and gave them to David. David rent his garments, and continued all that day in weeping and lamentation. His grief was increased by the thought that Jonathan, his dearest friend, had been slain.

When David had paid these honors to the king, he inquired of God by the prophet where he should go to dwell. God answered that he was to go to Hebron, in the land of Judah. Then David left Ziklag and came with his followers to Hebron, and the people of the tribe of Judah chose him for their king.

But Abner, who was the general of Saul's army and a very

active and brave man, learning of what had happened in
Judah, went to the camp and brought away a fourth son of
Saul, named Ishbosheth, and passed over to the land beyond
Jordan and ordained him king over all the Israelites except
the tribe of Judah, and he was angry with the tribe of Judah
for choosing David king, and declared war against them.
David appointed Joab, his nephew, to be general of his army,
and sent him out to fight Abner. The two armies met near
the city of Gibeon and prepared for battle. Abner proposed
that, in order to see which were the best warriors, twelve of
the bravest men should be picked out from each side and
should fight together. This was done, and the twenty-four
men drew their swords and rushed at each other, and fought
so desperately that every one of them perished. When these
were fallen down dead, the armies came to a sore battle, and
Abner's men were beaten. From this time, therefore, there
was civil war in Israel, which lasted a great while, and in which
the followers of David grew stronger, while the servants and
subjects of Saul's son grew weaker and weaker every day.
When Ishbosheth had ruled for seven years, two of his captains plotted against him, thinking that if they should slay
him they would receive large presents from David and be
made commanders by him. One hot day they came at noon
into Ishbosheth's house, and found him alone and asleep in
an upper room, with none of his guards around him. And
they killed him, and cut off his head, and brought it to David
at Hebron. But David was not pleased at what they had
done, and he told them that they were wicked men and should
be punished as they deserved. He had them put to death,
but the head of Ishbosheth he buried with great honor.

Then the chief men among the Israelites, learning of the
death of Ishbosheth, came to David in Hebron and told him
that they wished him to be their king. So at last David ruled
over all the tribes of Israel. He called a great meeting of all
the men who were able to bear arms, and they came to Hebron

in warlike array, and brought with them great quantities of wine and grain and fruits, and presented them to David. And when the people had rejoiced for three days in Hebron, David went out with his army against the city of Jerusalem.

Up to this time the men of Israel had been unable to conquer the city of Jerusalem from the Canaanites, who had held it against all their attacks from the time of Joshua, a period of five hundred and fifteen years. When they saw David coming, they laughed him to scorn. Shutting their gates, they placed upon the walls all the lame and the blind and the sick among them, and cried out to him that these poor wretches would be sufficient to defend the city against the Israelites.

David was angry at their insolence, and he besieged Jerusalem, and soon took the lower part of the city. Then the inhabitants retreated into a great citadel, or fortress, which was on a hill called Zion. David, knowing that the citadel was a very strong one and would be difficult to take, thought it well to offer some reward to his soldiers. He announced that whoever should first cross over the ditches that were beneath the citadel, and should ascend the citadel itself and take it, should have the command of the entire army given to him. All the Israelites rushed forward very eagerly and crossed the ditches and climbed up the walls of the citadel. But Joab was ahead of the rest, and as soon as he had reached the top of the citadel he cried out to the king and claimed the chief command. The Canaanites could not resist the force of this attack, and they were all slain.

David rebuilt the whole of Jerusalem, and called it the city of David, and he lived there all the time of his reign. There was a king named Hiram who lived in the town of Tyre, and he made a league of friendship with David. The men of Tyre were skilful workers in wood and stone. And Hiram sent builders and carpenters to David, and they built him a royal palace at Jerusalem.

CHAPTER XLVII.

THE REMOVAL OF THE ARK.

FOR more than seventy years the ark had remained in the town of Kirjath-Jearim, at the house of Aminadab. But David thought that now it would be proper to bring it out of that city and carry it to Jerusalem, and there to keep it and offer before it those sacrifices and other honors with which God was well pleased. He called together all the priests, and the Levites, and the captains of the army, and the young men and maidens, and they went in solemn procession to the city of Kirjath-Jearim. And they took the ark and laid it upon a new cart drawn by oxen. Before it went the king, playing on his harp, and the multitude followed singing, some of them with trumpets and cymbals and other musical instruments, and so they brought the ark to Jerusalem. Now the ark, it will be remembered, could be touched only by the priests. It happened that, as the procession was nearing the city, the ark was jolted, and nearly fell from the cart. One of the drivers, whose name was Uzzah, stretched out his hand and took hold of it. And the Lord was angry at him, because he was not a priest and yet touched the ark, and struck him dead.

Then David was afraid that if he received the ark into his house he might suffer as Uzzah had suffered. So he stopped on the way and left it in the house of a righteous man named Obededom, who was a Levite. Here the ark remained for three months, and the Lord blessed Obededom while it remained there, so that he who had been a poor man became

rich and prosperous, and the object of envy to all. Then
David was encouraged to believe that the Lord would bless
him also if the ark was in his house, so he called together
the priests, and with seven companies of singers they went to
the house of Obededom and took away the ark and put it in
the tabernacle which David had built for it in his garden.
David was with them while they moved the ark, and he
played on his harp and sang and danced with the multitude.
Then, when the ark had been placed in the tabernacle, he
offered costly sacrifices, and blessed all the people, and gave
to each one of them a loaf of bread and a cake, together with
a portion of the sacrifices.

Michal, David's wife, had seen him dancing before the
ark, and she despised him for it, and reproved him when he
entered the palace, saying that so great a king ought not to
be seen dancing with the common people. But he answered
that he was not ashamed to do what was pleasing to God.

When the king looked around his palace and saw how
beautiful it was and how comfortable and convenient, he
thought within himself that it was not right to keep the ark
of God in a tabernacle while he was in the enjoyment of all
these good things. He consulted with a prophet named
Nathan, whether he might not build a splendid temple in
which the ark could be placed. Nathan at first told him he
might do as he chose. But in the night-time God appeared
to the prophet and bade him tell David not to build the
temple. "For David," said God, "has fought in a great
many wars, and his hands are defiled with the blood of his
enemies. But after his death there shall be a temple built by
a son of his, who shall be called Solomon, and who will be a
man of peace and have no blood on his hands." Therefore
David did not go on to build the temple, but he rejoiced to
learn that he should have a son who would reign after him,
and he gave thanks to God.

CHAPTER XLVIII.

THE SIN OF DAVID.

MANY nations made war against David, but by the help of God he triumphed over them all. Among his chief enemies were the Ammonites, who had joined their forces with the king of Syria and invaded the land of Israel. David went out against them at the head of his army and defeated them with great slaughter. Then he returned home to Jerusalem, but he sent Joab with the army into the land of the Ammonites to lay waste the country and besiege their cities.

One evening David went, as was his custom, to walk on the roof of the palace. A little way off he saw a woman of great beauty, and on inquiring her name he learned she was called Bathsheba, and was the wife of a man named Uriah, who was in the army under Joab. David fell in love with Bathsheba on account of her beauty, and he determined he would make her his wife. He sent for Uriah to come to the palace. And David spoke kindly to him, and inquired about the army and about the siege. But at the end of three days he sent him back with a letter to Joab. In this letter he told Joab that Uriah had offended him, and he wished to have him punished. Therefore he directed that in the next battle Uriah should be placed in some position of great danger, and when the enemy approached all the other soldiers were to fly and leave him to be slain.

Joab did as he was told. He set Uriah in the front of the battle, and when the Ammonites made a sally out of the city, all the soldiers that were near Uriah fled away. Uriah received the enemy alone, and, though he fought bravely and slew many of them, he was himself soon overpowered and slain.

When David learned from Joab that Uriah was slain, he made Bathsheba his wife. But the Lord was angry at what David had done. And He sent Nathan the prophet to upbraid the king for his wickedness.

Nathan came and said, "O king, I wish to ask thy advice in a certain matter. There were two men living in the same city, one of whom was rich and the other was poor. The rich man had many flocks of cattle and sheep, but the poor man had only one ewe lamb. This he brought up with his children and let her eat her food with them, and loved her as if she were one of his daughters. A stranger came to visit the rich man, and instead of killing one of his own flock in order to feast him, he sent for the poor man's lamb and took her away by force, and killed her for the stranger's feast."

David was angry at this, and said "that the rich man was a wicked man for doing this, and he should be made to give to the poor man four lambs for the one he had taken away, and he should be punished with death also."

Then Nathan answered, "Thou art the man of whom I speak. For the Lord made thee king over Israel, and made thee rich and great, and gave thee wives and children, yet hast thou caused Uriah, who was a poor man, to be slain in order that thou mightest marry his wife, whom he loved. Know, then, that God will punish thee for thy wickedness, and one of thy own sons shall rise up against thee and drive thee from the kingdom."

David bowed down his head to the ground and confessed with tears that he had sinned. Nathan, touched by his sorrow, told him that if he truly repented the Lord would forgive him at last and give him back his kingdom. Having said these words, he departed.

God gave a son to David and Bathsheba, whom David

greatly loved. But a sickness came upon the child, and David was so troubled that he refused any food for seven days, and lay upon the floor and wept. On the seventh day the child died, and the servants were afraid to tell David. "For," they said, "if he grieved so much while the child was sick, how much greater will be his grief when he learns that it is dead!" But when David looked at them and saw them whispering together, he knew what had happened. And he said, "Is the child dead?" and one of the servants answered that he was. David rose and washed himself, and took a white garment, and went into the tabernacle and prayed. Then he came out and sat down to eat. His kindred and his servants were much surprised at this, and one of them asked him how it was that he who had grieved so much while his child was sick, grieved no longer now he was dead. David answered, "While the child was alive I fasted and wept, thinking in this way that God might allow it to live, but now the child is dead, there is no longer any occasion for grief, which would now be useless."

When he had said this, they commended the king's wisdom and understanding.

Afterwards God gave to David and Bathsheba another son, who, by the command of Nathan, was called Solomon.

CHAPTER XLIX.

THE REBELLION OF ABSALOM.

DAVID had a great many children, and among them was a son named Absalom, whom he loved more than all the others. He was tall and handsome, and he had very long and beautiful hair, which hung down his back. But he was a wicked man, and when one of his brothers, named Ammon, sinned against him, he killed him and fled away to another country. At first David was very angry with Absalom, but after three years his anger died away, and he sent for him to return to Jerusalem. Still he refused to see him, and commanded him to remain in his own house, and not to come to the royal palace.

For two years Absalom lived in Jerusalem without seeing his father. One day he sent for Joab, because he wanted Joab to go on a message to the king. But Joab would not come to him. Then Absalom called some of his servants, and bade them go and set fire to Joab's grain. When Joab heard who had done this he was angry, and came to Absalom and asked him why he had ordered his grain to be burnt. Absalom replied that it was because he wanted him to come and take a message to the king. "For," he said, "I am much distressed on account of my father's anger, and I beg of thee to pacify him, since, if I cannot see the king, I might as well have remained in a foreign country."

Joab was touched by the young man's sorrow, and he agreed to carry his message to the king. David loved his son so much that he easily allowed himself to be persuaded, and he sent for Absalom to come to him. Absalom came, and cast himself down on the ground and begged for forgiveness. And the king raised him up and forgave him, and promised to forget what he had done.

Absalom was only pretending to be sorry, for he really did not love the king his father, but only wished to be a great man among the Israelites. He procured a great many horses and chariots, and had fifty armed men to go before him whenever he rode out. He also used to rise early in the morning and go every day to the king's palace, and speak kindly to the men who came there to ask for favors or to have their quarrels decided. And those against whom judgment had been rendered he took aside, and said to them that if he had been king he would have decided in a different manner. In this way he made himself very popular with the people. When at last he thought the time had come to set up a rebellion, he asked leave of his father to go to Hebron and make sacrifices to God, for, he said, he had sworn to do this when he fled out of the country.

When Absalom had reached Hebron, he sent out word to the people of Israel that he was going to make himself king in place of his father. And a great multitude of men came to Hebron to help him, for they preferred him to David. Among those that came was one named Ahitophel, a very wise man, who was David's counsellor or adviser.

David was much troubled when he heard of Absalom's rebellion. As many of his bravest men had left him, he was afraid to remain in Jerusalem, and resolved to fly to the lands beyond Jordan. Collecting the few faithful friends who still remained to him, he went out of the city. The priests and Levites would have followed with the ark, but David advised them to stay behind. The king went out of the city weeping and bareheaded, and when he had reached the Mount of Olives, there came one who told him that Ahitophel had gone over to Absalom. This distressed him more than anything, for he knew that Ahitophel was a prudent and wise man, and that Absalom would receive much benefit from his counsels; and he prayed to God that He would make Absalom distrust the counsels of Ahitophel and refuse to take them. At the top of the mountain David was met by a faithful friend of his, named Hushai. Hushai wished to go with him, but David asked him to remain in Jerusalem as a spy, and to send him word of everything that happened there. He also told him to pretend that he was a friend of Absalom's, and to contradict all the counsels given by Ahitophel, for in this manner, said David, Hushai could do a great deal of harm to the rebels.

A little farther on, at a place called Bahurim, there came

out to meet him a kinsman of Saul's, whose name was Shimei, and he threw stones at David, and cursed him and called him evil names. When Abishai, David's nephew, would have attacked the man, David withheld him, for he said that the Lord was allowing Shimei to curse him, and it was part of the punishment He was sending upon him. So he went on his way without taking any notice of Shimei, who ran along the other side of the mountain, and continued to curse him.

Meanwhile, Absalom had come to Jerusalem with his counsellor, Ahitophel, and all his army. And David's friend, Hushai, went to Absalom and bowed down before him, and offered him his services. Absalom was glad to receive him, for he knew he was a wise and prudent man.

Absalom asked Ahitophel to advise him what he should do in the war against his father. Ahitophel said that if he would let him have ten thousand men, he would go out against David and slay him, and bring the soldiers back again in safety. Absalom was pleased with this advice, and he sent for Hushai, and, informing him of what Ahitophel had said, he asked for his opinion also. Now Hushai feared that if the advice of Ahitophel were followed, David would be taken and slain, for he had not yet had time to raise an army to defend himself. He therefore advised Absalom not to send out so small a body of men, but to wait until he could raise a large army, and then he would surely defeat the king. And God made Absalom prefer the advice of Hushai to that of Ahitophel.

Then Hushai went to the priests, who were the friends of David, and told them what had been decided upon, and they sent a messenger to David. But when Ahitophel learned that his advice was rejected, he saddled his ass and rode away to his own country. Calling his family together, he told them that Absalom would not follow his advice, and that he would surely be defeated by David. "Therefore," he said,

" I do not wish to live any longer, and fall into the hands of David, who will certainly punish me for having given my assistance to Absalom."

When he had spoken thus, he went into another room and hanged himself.

CHAPTER L.

THE DEATH OF ABSALOM.

DAVID passed over Jordan and came to Mahanaim, a very fine and strong city. All the chief men of the country received him with pleasure, and furnished him with plenty of provisions for himself and his followers.

By this time Absalom had gathered together his army, and he came after his father. Then David counted the men who were with him, and found there were four thousand ; and he set captains over them, and made Joab chief captain. He would himself have led them out to battle, but his friends would not let him, for they said the enemy would care more to kill him than to kill the whole army of his followers. So David remained in the city. When his army was ready to march out to meet Absalom, he spoke to the commanders, and exhorted them to be brave and faithful, but prayed them to spare his son Absalom for his sake.

Now, although David's army was so small, they were superior to the others in strength and skill in war. After a hard fight they won the victory. And they pursued the enemy and slew many thousands of them. Absalom himself fought long and bravely. But when he found that there was no more hope, he jumped on the back of a mule and fled away. The mule ran under the thick branches of a great oak, and

Absalom's long hair was caught among the branches, so that he was pulled off the back of the mule, which ran away without him.

And one of David's army came to Joab and said, "I saw Absalom hanging from an oak-tree."

Joab answered, "If thou hadst shot at and killed Absalom, I would have given thee fifty shekels."

But the man said, "I would not have killed my master's son for a thousand shekels. Did he not desire in the hearing of us all that the young man should be spared?"

Joab asked him where he saw Absalom; and when the man told him, he went to the place and found him still hanging from the oak. He shot him with an arrow and killed him. Then he took the dead body down from the tree and cast it into a great chasm and piled stones upon it. After he had done this he blew his trumpet as a signal that the army was to stop any further pursuit and return to the city.

Then Ahimaaz, who was one of the priest's sons, came to Joab and asked leave to go and tell David of this victory. But Joab answered, "Thou hast always been the messenger of good news to the king, and it would not be well for thee to go and acquaint him that his son is dead."

He then called a man named Cushi, and told him to run to the king and tell him all he saw.

But again Ahimaaz besought Joab to let him go as a messenger, and assured him that he would only speak about the victory. Joab let him go. And Ahimaaz took a nearer road to the city than Cushi did, and arrived before him.

King David was sitting near the gate of the city waiting for tidings of the battle. One of the watchmen told him he saw a man coming who was running very fast. David said, "He brings news of the battle." A little while after the watchman reported that another messenger was following him, and David said, "He too brings news." By this time Ahimaaz had come so near that the watchman recognized

him, and told David who he was. David was very glad, and
said,—

"Ahimaaz is a messenger of good tidings, and he brings
such news from the battle as we shall be glad to hear."

Even while the king was speaking, Ahimaaz appeared at
the gate and fell down on his face before him. When David
asked him of the battle, he answered,—

"I bring good news of a great victory and of the restoration of thy kingdom."

Then David asked him what had become of Absalom.

But Ahimaaz answered,—

"I came away on the sudden as soon as the enemy was defeated, but I heard a great noise of those that pursued Absalom, and could learn no more because of the haste I was in."

When Cushi had arrived and told David again of the victory, David asked him how Absalom had fared, and Cushi
answered,—

"May as great a misfortune befall all thy enemies as hath
befallen Absalom!"

Then David knew that his son was dead. And he was in
great distress, and went up to a chamber that was over the
gate of the city, and wept, and beat his breast, and tore his
hair, and cried, "Oh, Absalom, my son, would that I had died
and ended my days with thee!"

When the army and Joab learned how the king mourned
for his son, they were sorry and ashamed, and they did not
like to enter the city in the habit of conquerors, but came in
with their heads drooping and shedding tears as if they had
been beaten. Joab, however, plucked up courage and went
into the chamber where David was, and comforted him, and
told him that he ought not to mourn so over Absalom, who
would not have mourned, but would have rejoiced, at David's
death.

"Thou seemest," said Joab, "to hate those that love thee
and undergo dangers for thee; nay, to hate thyself and to

love only those that are thy bitter enemies; for if Absalom had gotten the victory, there had been none of us left alive, but all, beginning with thyself and thy children, would have miserably perished. Leave off, therefore, thy unreasonable grief, and come and show thyself to thy soldiers and return them thanks for the great deeds they have done this day."

David saw that Joab was right, and he left off mourning, and came out and sat in the gate of the city, where all the people ran to him and saluted him.

CHAPTER LI.

DAVID IS RESTORED TO HIS KINGDOM.

AFTER the death of Absalom, the inhabitants of Jerusalem, including all those who had sided with the rebels, sent to David to come back again to his kingdom. And the other tribes also sent messages to David. So David returned with his followers. When he reached the river Jordan, a number of the principal men of Israel came out to meet him, and laid a bridge of boats across the river, that the king might pass over with ease. Among these men came Shimei, who had cursed David when he was leaving Jerusalem. Shimei came upon the bridge and fell at David's feet, and besought him to forgive him, for he knew that he had sinned. Then Abishai, David's nephew, said,—

" Shall not this man die, because he cursed the king whom the Lord hath set over us?"

But David answered that he intended to forgive all men their sins against him, and he bade Shimei rise up and be of good courage, for he should be allowed to live.

Then David went on to Jerusalem and entered his royal

palace. There was a man, however, named Sheba, of the tribe of Benjamin, who refused to submit to David, and he stirred up a sedition and proclaimed himself king. Joab was sent out against him, and finding Sheba had fled to a strong city named Abel-beth-maachah, Joab went thither and besieged it.

Then a woman who lived in the town, and who was wise and prudent, appeared upon the walls and called for Joab. When he appeared, she said,—

" God ordained kings and generals of armies in order that they might cut off the enemies of the Israelites, but now thou art endeavoring to overthrow a town belonging to thy own people, which hath never done thee any harm."

Joab answered that he did not wish to kill any of the Israelites or destroy their cities, and if the citizens would deliver up Sheba, who had rebelled against the king, he would be glad to withdraw his army. Then the woman went down to the citizens, and said,—

" Are you willing to perish miserably for the sake of a vile fellow whom nobody knows? And will you have him for your king instead of David, who hath been your benefactor, and oppose your single city to his mighty armies?"

So she prevailed with them, and they cut off Sheba's head and threw it into Joab's army. When this was done the king's general sounded a retreat, and raised the siege.

CHAPTER LII.

GOD SENDS A PESTILENCE UPON THE ISRAELITES.

WHEN peace had been established over all his dominions, King David was anxious to know how many people he ruled over. Therefore he told Joab to go out and number the people. Joab took with him the heads of the tribes and the scribes, and went over the country of the Israelites and inquired at every household. At the end of nine months and twenty days he returned to the king, and told him that he had numbered all the tribes except those of Levi and of Benjamin, and there were among them one million three hundred thousand men who were able to bear arms and go to war.

There was a law given to Moses, that if the multitude were numbered, a half-shekel should be paid to God for every head. David did not comply with this law, and the prophet came and told him that God was angry with him. David felt that he had sinned, and he prostrated himself before God and begged Him to be merciful and to forgive him. But God sent Nathan the prophet to tell him that He intended to punish him and his people for their crime. And He said he might choose which of these three punishments he would prefer:

"Would he have a famine come upon the country for seven years? Or would he have his enemies conquer and rule over the land for three months? Or would he have three days of pestilence among the people?"

David was in great trouble to know which he should choose, but he considered within himself, and answered Nathan that it was better to fall into the hands of God than into those of his enemies. He meant that he chose the three days of pestilence.

So God sent an angel that brought a great pestilence down upon the children of Israel, and in one morning seventy thousand of them had died. David had put on sackcloth, and he lay on the ground praying to God and begging that the pestilence might now cease, and that He would be satisfied with those that had already perished. Looking up into the air, he saw the angel floating over Jerusalem with his sword drawn. Then David prayed the Lord to punish him and spare his people.

God heard his prayers, and caused the pestilence to cease. And He sent a prophet named Gad, who commanded David to go up at once to the threshing-floor of a man named Araunah, and build an altar there, and offer sacrifices.

Araunah lived on a hill named Moriah, which was within the city of Jerusalem. He was threshing his wheat when David and the rulers appeared before him. And he ran to the king and bowed, and said,—

" Wherefore is my lord come to his servant ?"

David said that he had come to buy of him his threshing floor, that he might build an altar there and offer sacrifices to God.

Then Araunah said he would let him have the threshing-floor as a gift, and he would also give him his oxen for a burnt-offering. But David thanked him, and said that he desired to pay for everything, as it was not just to offer a sacrifice that cost nothing. So he bought the threshing-floor for fifty shekels, and offered sacrifices, and God was pacified and became gracious again. Now this was the same place where Abraham had formerly sacrificed a ram instead of his son Isaac. And when David saw that God was pleased with his sacrifices, he called that place the altar of all the people, and he chose it as the place on which the temple should be built.

CHAPTER LIII.

THE DEATH OF DAVID.

DAVID, who was now very old, began to make ready stones and timber and iron for the building of the temple. And he set many masons to shaping the stones, and carpenters to cutting beams out of the cedar-trees, for he said that as his son Solomon was young and inexperienced, he would prepare for him the materials for building the temple.

He called Solomon to him, and told him that God had chosen him as his successor to the kingdom of Israel, and had foretold that he would build a temple for the ark. He bade Solomon also take notice of the preparations he had made for this purpose, and informed him that he had laid by in his treasury a great deal of gold and silver to pay the workmen and those who furnished the materials.

But another of David's sons, whose name was Adonijah, wished to be king in place of Solomon. And because his father was now weak and old, he determined not to wait for his death, but to displace him at once and rule in his stead. Therefore he made a great feast for his friends, and persuaded them to name him king. When David heard this, he said that on account of what Adonijah had done he would make Solomon king at once. And he ordered his servants to saddle his mule and to place Solomon upon it, and take him to a fountain named Gihon, where they were to anoint him king. Then they were to blow trumpets and cry aloud, " Long live King Solomon !" so that all the people might know he had been made king by his father.

This was done, and afterwards Solomon went to the royal palace and sat upon the throne. And the people came, and shouted and rejoiced with dancing and singing.

Adonijah and his guests were still sitting at their feast when they heard the sound of trumpets and rejoicing. And when they were wondering what it might mean, a messenger ran in and told them of the anointing of Solomon. Thereupon all the guests dispersed and went to their own homes, leaving Adonijah alone. Adonijah was greatly troubled, and he prayed to God, confessing his sin. But when Solomon was told that Adonijah was sorry for what he had done and was afraid lest he should be killed, he said that if Adonijah proved himself a good man no harm should be done to him, and he commanded him to go to his own house.

David called together all the chief men among the Israelites, and told them that he had chosen Solomon to rule over them, because the Lord had pointed him out as the proper person. He also told them about the temple which he had wished to build, how God had prevented him from doing so, because he was a man of war, whose hands had been stained with blood, and how Solomon had been appointed to carry out the work.

Then David, in the sight of them all, gave the descriptions and the plans of the building to Solomon. He asked the people to help Solomon in the work, for he was a young man who had had little experience; and he showed them that the work would be easy because of the great preparations he had made for it himself, and the large sums of money that he had saved up for the purpose.

When David had ceased speaking, many of the chief men came forward and said they would help Solomon, and give him quantities of gold and silver and brass, and other things that would be useful.

David ordered that solemn sacrifices should be offered up, and that a great festival should be celebrated. And he himself ate and feasted with the multitude.

Shortly afterwards David died, at the age of seventy, having ruled for forty years. He was buried in Jerusalem with great magnificence.

CHAPTER LIV.

THE REIGN OF SOLOMON.

ONE of Solomon's first cares was to go to Hebron and sacrifice to God on the brazen altar that was built by Moses. He offered up there one thousand sheep and oxen as a burnt-offering. God was pleased with his piety, and appeared to the king in his sleep and offered him anything that he desired to have. Solomon did not ask for gold or silver or other riches, as many young men would have done, but he said,—

"Give me, O Lord, a sound mind and a good understanding, so that I may speak and judge the people according to truth and righteousness."

With this answer God was well pleased, and He said He would give Solomon wisdom greater than that of any other mortal who had ever lived, and He would add to this gift all those things which Solomon had not asked for, such as riches, glory, and victory over his enemies. God also said that He would preserve the kingdom to Solomon's descendants if he continued righteous and obedient to Him, and imitated the virtues of his father.

Solomon soon had an opportunity of showing his wisdom. For there came before him at his royal palace in Jerusalem two women. One of them said to him,—

"O king, I and this other woman dwell together in one room, and we each of us had a little son. And this woman, by accident, smothered her child in the night so that it died, and while I was sleeping she put her dead child in my arms, and took from me my child, which was alive, and laid it in her bed. And when I rose in the morning to feed my child, I found in its place this dead body, and I saw my child in the arms of the woman, and she refused to give it back to me."

When this woman had done speaking, Solomon turned to the other and asked her what she had to say. She replied that the child was hers, and that the other woman had not told the truth. Every one present was puzzled and knew not which of the women to believe. Then the king bade them bring in both the dead child and the living child. And he sent for one of his guards, and commanded him to draw his sword and cut both the children into two pieces, that each of the women might have half the living and half the dead child. All the people present laughed secretly at the king, thinking he was but a boy and that the decision was a very silly one. But they soon changed their minds and were forced to admire his wisdom. For she that was the real mother of the living child cried out that he should not do so.

"Rather than see my son die," she said, "I would have you give it to the other woman and believe it is hers, for then I should be able at least to see it again."

But the other woman was willing to see the child divided, and even mocked at the sorrow of her neighbor.

Then the king knew which was the true mother. And he gave the child to her that had cried out to save it, and condemned the other as a wicked woman, who had not only killed her own child through carelessness, but was willing to see her friend's child killed also.

The people looked upon this judgment as a sign of great wisdom, and they ever after accepted all the king's decisions as being just and wise.

In the fourth year of his reign Solomon began to build the temple. Before this time he had been engaged in continuing the preparations made by David, and in gathering together timber and stone and iron. Hiram, king of Tyre, who had been David's friend, made a league of friendship with Solomon also, and let Solomon have many of his most skilful workmen, and Solomon in return sent him corn and oil and wine. And Hiram's servants and Solomon's servants hewed down the cedar-trees on Mount Lebanon, and split them up into beams, and went to the quarries and cut out large stones, and shaped them so that they would fit together, and other workmen carried the timber and the stones into Jerusalem.

The temple was built according to the plans left by David. The foundations were made of great stones, buried deep in the ground. The body of the building was of white stone, and was two stories high. In the front part was a porch, the top of which was built up in the form of a steeple or tower above the rest of the building, and was about two hundred feet high. The roof was made of cedar, and the walls also were covered on the inside with boards of cedar, that were carved in the shape of flowers, and inlaid with gold.

The interior of the temple was divided into two chambers. The innermost of these, which was called the Most Holy Place, was for the ark; and across the door-way, between these two chambers, there hung a veil of blue and purple and scarlet, and the brightest and softest linen. Two angels, carved out of gold, and about fifteen feet high, stood in the Most Holy Place, with their wings spread out, so that the right wing of one touched the wall at one side, and the left wing of the other touched the wall at the other side, and the other wings just touched each other, and were a covering to the ark, which was placed beneath the figures.

In the other chamber stood the altar of incense, which was made of cedar covered with gold, and ten thousand candle-sticks, of which one was always kept lighted. There were, moreover, in this room a great many tables, one of which was large and made of gold, and upon this were set the loaves that were given to God, but the others were smaller, and contained vessels of gold and silver, many thousand in number.

In the court before the temple stood the brazen altar upon

which sacrifices were offered. And there was a great basin here, so large that it was called a sea of brass, that rested on the backs of twelve brass oxen. This was to hold water for the priests to wash their hands and their feet in before they offered the sacrifices. There were ten lavers also, which were set upon wheels, and could be moved about from place to place, and these were used for washing the dead bodies of the animals that were to be sacrificed.

At the entrance to the temple stood two great pillars of brass, one at the right hand and the other at the left, and one of these pillars was called Jachin, and the other Boaz. It took seven years to build the temple. When it was finished, Solomon ordered all the Israelites to gather together at Jerusalem, both to see the temple he had built and to remove the ark into it. And all the people came, and they celebrated a great feast, and the priests took up the ark and carried it into the temple. When the ark had been put into the Most Holy Place, under the wings of the angels, and the priests had left it, there came down a cloud from heaven and spread itself in a gentle manner through the temple, sprinkling everywhere a mild and pleasant dew. Then everybody knew that God had descended into the house that had been built for Him, to show that He was well pleased. Solomon kneeled down before the temple and prayed God to watch over the children of Israel, and to accept the sacrifices and listen to the prayers that were offered up in the temple.

Then Solomon rose and addressed the people, exhorting them to serve God and obey the laws that Moses had given them. After having spoken many words of wisdom, he brought sacrifices to the altar. And there came a fire running out of the air, and it rushed upon the altar in the sight of all, and consumed the victims that were laid upon it. The people marvelled greatly, and knew that the Lord accepted the sacrifices.

The king offered up other sacrifices also,—in all, twenty-two thousand oxen and a hundred and twenty thousand sheep. He celebrated a great feast at the same time, which lasted for fourteen days, and all the people of Israel were invited to it, and they came and feasted on the flesh of the peace-offerings that he had made. After this the people were dismissed to their own homes, and they went with joyful hearts, thankful to the king for all the great works he had done for them, and praying to God to preserve him as their king for a long time.

In the night-time God again appeared to Solomon, and told him that He had heard his prayers and would abide in the temple and watch over the people of Israel. When they sinned He would punish them, but when they repented and came to the temple and prayed for pardon He would pardon them. And He promised again that if Solomon would obey Him and worship Him, he should have a long life and his descendants should reign after him. But if he fell away and abandoned the true God and worshipped idols, then He would cut him off in his youth; and if the people fell away, they should be cast out of the land which God had given to their fathers, and be scattered over strange lands, and their temple should be destroyed by the enemy, and their cities overthrown.

CHAPTER LV.

THE QUEEN OF SHEBA.

AFTER the temple had been finished and dedicated, Solomon began building a palace for himself. It took him thirteen years to finish this palace, for he did not have as many workmen to help as there were on the temple. The palace was a large and magnificent building, and, like the temple, it was made of white stone, and adorned with cedar wood and gold and silver. It contained two great halls, one of which was the dining-room, for feasting and drinking, in which all the vessels were of gold, and the other the hall of judgment, where people came to have their disputes settled. There was also a great number of smaller rooms, and they were all ornamented in a very costly manner.

Solomon built walls around the city of Jerusalem, so as to fortify it more strongly against all enemies, and he also built a number of new cities, which in due time waxed strong and great.

The fame of all that Solomon had done, and of his power and riches and great wisdom, filled all the neighboring countries. Among others, the queen of a far-off country called Sheba, who was a great lover of wisdom, heard so much about him that she determined to come and see him, in order that she might converse with him and learn wisdom from his lips. So she came to Jerusalem with great splendor, and brought with her camels laden with gold and precious stones and spices.

Solomon received her kindly, and showed her over his palace and over the temple. She talked with Solomon, and asked him hard questions about things which she wished to know, and wondered at the wisdom of his answers. She wondered also at the magnificence of everything she saw,—at the temple and the royal palace, at the costly food which was placed upon the table, at the number of the servants and the skilful manner of their attendance, as also at the daily sacrifices that were offered up in the temple, and the careful management which the priests and Levites used about them. She confessed that she had not believed half of the wonderful reports that had reached her ears concerning the power and glory of Solomon, but now she saw that they fell far short of the truth. And she gave to Solomon presents of the things she had brought with her, and he in return gave her costly presents. Then with her servants she returned to her own land.

CHAPTER LVI.

THE SIN OF SOLOMON.

ALTHOUGH God had blessed Solomon in so many ways, and made him one of the richest and most powerful of kings, yet he did not remain mindful of the benefits that had been bestowed upon him, and he fell into grievous sins. He took for his wives a great number of heathen women, though God had forbidden any of the Israelites to marry them; and when Solomon was old and weak, his wives persuaded him to worship their idols and to forsake the true God. Then the Lord was very angry with him, and He sent a prophet to tell him that because of his wickedness his kingdom should be divided, and his sons should rule over only a small part of it.

There was a young man among the Israelites whose name was Jeroboam. He was a brave man and a skilful general. A prophet one day came to him and saluted him, and taking him aside to a place where there was no other person present, he rent his garment into twelve pieces and bade Jeroboam take ten of them.

"For this is the will of God," said the prophet; "He will part the dominions of Solomon. Only two of the tribes will be left to his sons to rule over, and He will give ten tribes to thee, because Solomon hath sinned against Him." When Solomon heard what the prophet had said, he tried to kill Jeroboam, but the young man fled from the country and sought the protection of Shishak, king of Egypt.

Not long after Solomon died. He was ninety-four years of age, and had ruled eighty years.

CHAPTER LVII.

THE FOLLY OF REHOBOAM.

ON the death of Solomon his son Rehoboam declared himself king in his place. Many of the rulers, however, sent for Jeroboam to return from Egypt and meet them at Shechem, where they might consider the matter of the succession. Hither Rehoboam came also. And Jeroboam and the rulers met him, and asked him whether he intended to rule over them gently and mildly, or to imitate the injustice and severity into which his father had fallen. Rehoboam told them he would give them an answer in three days. So they left him.

After they had gone, Rehoboam asked advice of his father's old counsellors. They told him to speak kindly to the rulers and assure them that he would be a mild and just king. But Rehoboam was not satisfied with this advice, and he consulted with the young men about him who were his friends. They told him that it did not befit him, who was the son of a great king, and should be a great king himself, to answer these men as they wished to be answered.

Rehoboam took their advice, and when the rulers and the people returned to him, he said,—

" My little finger shall be thicker than my father's loins, and if ye have met with hard usage from my father, ye shall meet with rougher treatment from me ; and if he chastised you with whips, ye must expect that I will do it with scorpions."

These were the words that the young men had told him to use. When the people heard them, they were angry, and

12

cried out that they would not have Rehoboam for their king. So ten of the tribes chose Jeroboam to rule over them. But the tribes of Judah and of Benjamin remained faithful to Rehoboam. Rehoboam was making ready a great army to proceed against Jeroboam and his people, but God sent a prophet named Shemaiah to forbid this, saying it was not just that brethren of the same country should fight one against another. So the expedition was abandoned.

Jeroboam built himself a palace in the city Shechem and dwelt there. He did not want his people to go to Jerusalem and worship there with the other two tribes, fearing that they might be tempted to return to their first king. So he made two golden calves and built temples for them, one in the city of Bethel and the other in Dan. When the feast of the tabernacles was near at hand, he called the people together, and told them that it would no longer be necessary for them to go to Jerusalem, which was an enemy's city, to worship God.

"I have made two golden calves," said Jeroboam, "one in the city of Bethel and the other in Dan, so that you may go to whichever city is most convenient and worship God there. And I will ordain for you priests and Levites from among yourselves, that you may not need the sons of Aaron."

Then Jeroboam ordained himself high-priest, and with other priests of his own appointing he prepared to offer up sacrifices at the temple in Bethel. But when everything was ready, and just as he had ascended the steps of the altar in sight of all the people, a prophet came to him from Jerusalem. This prophet was named Jadon. He was sent by God, who was angry with Jeroboam. And he stood in the midst of the people and within hearing of the king, and said,—

"God bids me tell you that a king named Josiah shall be born of the family of David, who shall slay all these false priests that are living in his time, and shall burn the bones of those that are dead, because they are deceivers of the people,

and teach them false worship. And to show that what I say
is true, a sign will be given you to-day, and this altar shall be
broken to pieces, and all the fat of the sacrifices shall be
poured upon the ground."

When the prophet had said this, Jeroboam fell into a passion, and stretched out his arm, ordering the people to lay
hold of Jadon. But the arm instantly became shrunk and
withered, so that he could not draw it back again. At the
same moment the altar was shattered, and all that was upon it
was poured out upon the ground. Then Jeroboam was afraid,
seeing that God was with the prophet, and he asked him to
pray that his right arm might be made well. And the
prophet prayed for him, and his arm was made well. Jeroboam invited Jadon to come in and sup with him, but Jadon
answered,—

"God hath forbidden me to taste of bread or water in this
city, and hath also told me to return on a different road from
that on which I came."

Jadon turned to go back by another way to the land of
Judah. There was living in Bethel a certain wicked old man,
who was a false prophet. He was held in great esteem by
Jeroboam, and when his sons came and told him about the
prophet from Judah and of all he had done, he was troubled.
For he said to himself, "This stranger will be held in great
honor by the king, who will forget me." So he ordered his
sons to saddle his ass, and he followed after Jadon. He found
him resting under a large oak-tree, and he complained of
him, because he had not come into his house and eaten with
him. But Jadon answered that God had forbidden him to eat
or to drink in the city of Bethel.

"Nay," said the old man, "surely God did not forbid thee
to eat and drink with me, for I am a prophet as thou art, and
worship God in the same manner that thou dost, and it is by
His order that I now come to thee, to bring thee to my house
and make thee my guest."

Jadon believed this lying prophet, and went back with him. But while they were feasting and making merry, God appeared to Jadon, and said that he should be punished for transgressing His commands.

"On thy way home," said the Lord, "thou shalt meet a lion, who will tear thee in pieces, and thy body shall not be buried in the sepulchre of thy fathers."

Everything happened as the Lord had said. And some travellers came and told the false prophet that they had seen the body of Jadon lying in the road, while a lion stood beside it. The old man sent his sons to bring the body to Bethel, where it was buried. And he said to his sons, "When I am dead, bury me in the same sepulchre with this prophet, for the words that he spoke shall surely come true." Then he went to Jeroboam, and said,—

"Wherefore art thou disturbed at the words of this silly fellow?"

Jeroboam told him the wonders that Jadon had performed. But the old man laughed at these things, and said,—

"Thy arm was enfeebled by the labor it had undergone in preparing the sacrifices, and a little rest soon brought it back to its former state. And as to the altar, it was new, and could not bear the weight of so many sacrifices, therefore it fell apart."

Then he told Jeroboam of the death of the prophet, and said that surely God had punished him for delivering false prophecies. And the king allowed himself to be persuaded, and continued in his wicked courses.

All the priests and the Levites, together with many good and righteous men among the subjects of Jeroboam, left him and went to dwell in the kingdom of Rehoboam, for they were not willing to be forced to worship the golden calves. But as his prosperity increased, Rehoboam also became forgetful of the true God, and despised His worship and sacrificed to idols. Many of the people followed his example,

until God was angry with them, and determined to punish
them. He therefore allowed Shishak, king of Egypt, to
conquer their cities, and Shishak despoiled the temple and
the palace of the king, and carried off all the gold and silver
and other treasures, and he then returned to Egypt. Not
long afterwards Rehoboam died, and was succeeded by his
son Abijah.

CHAPTER LVIII.

HOW JEROBOAM WAS PUNISHED BY GOD.

MEANWHILE, Jeroboam also had drawn down upon himself
the punishment of God. A son of his whom he dearly
loved fell sick. And Jeroboam told his wife to lay off her
robes and disguise herself so that no one might know her,
and go to the prophet Abijah, at Shiloh. This was the
prophet who had foretold that Jeroboam should be king.

"And when thou art come to him," said Jeroboam, "speak
to him as a private person, and ask him if thy son who is ill
will get well."

Now when Jeroboam's wife was near the prophet's house,
God appeared to Abijah and informed him who she was and
what answer he was to give her. So the prophet cried out
to her,—

"Come in, O thou wife of Jeroboam. Why dost thou
conceal thyself? Thou art not concealed from God, who
hath appeared to me and informed me thou wast coming, and
hath told me what to say to thee. Return, then, to thy husband, and repeat to him these words as coming from God:
'I made thee a great man when thou wast a man of little
account, and divided with thee the kingdom of David, and
because thou hast forgotten all these things and hast forsaken

me and worshipped strange gods, I will cast thee down again, and will destroy all thy family, and make them food for the dogs and for the fowls of the air, and thy people shall be punished with thee.' But do thou, O woman, make haste back to thy husband, for when thou reachest the city thy child will be dead. And all the people shall mourn for him and bury him; but he is the only one of Jeroboam's sons who shall be buried in the grave."

Then Jeroboam's wife returned to her husband, and she wept on the way, mourning at what the prophet had said. And she found the child was dead, as had been foretold.

CHAPTER LIX.

THE SUCCESSORS OF REHOBOAM.

WHEN Abijah succeeded his father Rehoboam, Jeroboam gathered together a great army to make war upon him. But though the army of Abijah was a much smaller one, God gave him a wonderful victory. The army of Jeroboam was put to flight, and five hundred thousand were slain. This was a larger number than had ever before been slain in any battle recorded in history. Abijah marched against the cities of the ten tribes and took many of them, and brought away great quantities of treasures.

Abijah ruled only three years, and he died, and was succeeded by his son Asa. Jeroboam also died after he had been king for twenty-two years, and was succeeded by his son Nadab, in the second year of the reign of Asa.

Nadab resembled his father in wickedness. After he had governed for two years, a man named Baasha rebelled against him and slew him, and made himself king in his place. Baasha put all the family of Jeroboam to death, and the words of the prophet came true, for their bodies were not buried, but were devoured by the dogs and the fowls of the air. Baasha ruled for twenty-two years, and he died, and Elah, his son, succeeded him.

Elah reigned for only two years, and he was then slain, as he was feasting in the house of one of his friends, by Zimri, a captain in the army. Zimri proclaimed himself king in his place. Now the men of Israel were at that time besieging a city of the Philistines named Gibbethon. They did not want Zimri for their king, but they chose instead Omri, their general. Omri led them against Tirzah, where Zimri was, and besieged it. When Zimri saw that the city had no one to defend it, he fled into the inmost part of the palace and set it on fire and burnt himself with it. Omri reigned over the ten tribes for twelve years. He built a city called Samaria for his royal residence, and lived there. And the kings of the ten tribes of Israel continued to live there as long as their kingdom lasted,—for nearly two hundred years.

CHAPTER LX.

ASA, KING OF JUDAH.

WHEN Omri died, he was succeeded by his son Ahab. Now during all these years Asa, the son of Abijah, and grandson of Jeroboam, had been reigning in Jerusalem. He did not imitate the vices of his fathers, but was just and righteous in all his actions, and he feared God and worshipped Him. He destroyed all the idols and purified the kingdom from the wicked practices of the heathen. God blessed him, and gave him a long and prosperous reign, and made him triumph over his enemies. A great king named Zerah, who ruled over Ethiopia, was the first to declare war against him. He brought with him an army of one million men, one hundred thousand of whom were mounted on horses. Asa met him at Mareshah, a city belonging to the tribe of Judah, and when he saw the multitude of the enemy he cried out and besought God to give him the victory, for without His aid it were madness to attack such a large army. God heard his prayer, and told him He would be with him in the coming battle. Then Asa joyfully rushed against the enemy, and after a long and bloody fight he defeated them and pursued them as far as their own country, and took a great booty. When Asa and his army were returning in triumph to Jerusalem they were stopped on the way by a prophet, who spoke to them, and said,—

" The reason, O men of Judah, that you have obtained this victory from God is that ye have shown yourselves good and religious men, and if ye persevere in virtue God will ever grant you victory over your enemies; but if ye fall away and return to your idols, ye shall be visited by heavy afflictions, and the time will come wherein no true prophet will be left in your whole multitude, nor a priest who shall deliver you a true answer from the sacrifices, but your cities shall be overthrown and your nation scattered over the whole earth, and ye shall live the lives of strangers and wanderers."

Therefore Asa and his subjects determined to live in the practice of virtue, and God blessed them accordingly. And after Asa had reigned happily and prosperously for forty-one years he died, and his son Jehoshaphat succeeded him.

CHAPTER LXI.

AHAB, KING OF ISRAEL

AHAB, the son of Omri, was a very wicked king, worse even than those who had governed the ten tribes of Israel before him. He worshipped the calves which Jeroboam had made, and imitated all the wicked practices of the heathen. He was encouraged in this course by his wife, who was named Jezebel, and was the daughter of the king of Tyre. This woman was active and bold, and she not only taught her husband to worship her gods, but she built a great temple to the principal god among them, whose name was Baal, and appointed priests and false prophets to offer up sacrifices to him and to deliver oracles.

There was a prophet of God named Elijah, who came to Ahab and told him,—

" God will not send any more rain into this country until I return to you."

Then Elijah departed from the king and went out into the desert, and took up his abode by a stream of water. Every day his food was brought to him by ravens. There was a great drought in all the land, so that all the moisture was dried up, and the stream of water ceased to flow. Then God told Elijah to go to a city called Zarephath, where he should find a woman who was a widow, who would give him food and lodging.

At a short distance from the city he met a poor woman gathering up sticks. This was the person God had pointed out to him. Elijah spoke to her, and desired her to bring him some water to drink. As she was going to fetch it he called her back, and asked her to bring him a loaf of bread also. But the woman said that she had at home nothing more than a handful of flour and a little oil, and that she was now gathering a few sticks to make a fire, that she might bake the flour for herself and for her son, after which, she said, they must both perish of famine, as they had nothing for themselves any longer.

Elijah said to her, " Be of good courage, and do not despair. First of all, make me a little cake, for I promise you that your vessel shall never be empty of flour, nor your cruse of oil, until God sends rain from heaven."

The woman obeyed, and neither she, nor her son, nor the prophet was in want during the whole of the famine, for God made the flour and the oil to last all that time.

One day the widow's son sickened and died. Then she came to the prophet, weeping and beating her breast, and complained that he had been sent because God wished to punish her for her sins, and therefore it was her son had died. But he bade her take comfort and give him her son's body, for he would bring him to life again. He carried the body into his own room, and laid it on the bed, and cried to God, and said,—

" O Lord, hast thou brought evil upon the woman who hath sheltered me? I beseech thee, O Lord, let the child's soul come into him again."

And God heard Elijah's prayer, and sent the soul of the child into him again.

CHAPTER LXII.

THE MIRACLES OF ELIJAH.

Now the famine grew to be so severe that not only men, but horses and other animals, found it difficult to live. For there was hardly any moisture in the land at all, and neither grasses nor vegetables would grow. So the king called for Obadiah, his steward, and bade him go to the rivers and the fountains, and if any grasses grew near them, he was to cut them down, and bring them to feed his horses and cattle. Ahab and Obadiah went out to search all through the land, and Obadiah took one road and the king another. Obadiah was a just and good man. Not long before, Jezebel, in her rage, had ordered that all the prophets of the true God should be killed, but Obadiah had saved one hundred of them alive, and hidden them in caves, where he had fed them on bread and water. He had not travelled very far when he met Elijah, for God had told the prophet that it was now time to go to Ahab and inform him that rain was coming.

Obadiah spoke to Elijah and asked him who he was, and when he had been told, he fell on his face before him. Then Elijah said, " Go to the king, and tell him I am here ready to wait on him."

But Obadiah answered, " What harm have I done thee that thou seekest my death ? For knowest thou not that Ahab hath sought thee everywhere in order to kill thee ? And if I go to him with thy message, the Lord will surely protect thee and carry thee away while I am gone, and the king, when he finds thou art no longer here, will surely put me to death."

Elijah bade him fear nothing, and solemnly promised that day to appear before Ahab.

Obadiah went and gave the prophet's message to the king. And Ahab came to Elijah, and said, in great anger,—

" Art thou the man that afflicts the people of Israel, and causes famines and droughts ?"

" Nay," answered Elijah, " thou art that man, for it is the wickedness of thyself and thy family which hath excited the wrath of God, and brought these calamities upon the country."

Then Elijah told Ahab to assemble all the people on Mount Carmel, and to bring thither all the priests and prophets of Baal, about four hundred in number. So the priests and the people came, and Elijah stood in the midst of the multitude and addressed them, saying,—

" How long, O men of Israel, will you waver in your opinions and remain undecided whether to serve the God of your fathers, or this Baal whom Ahab hath set over you ? For if you believe our God to be the one true God, then obey His commandments; but if you do not believe in Him, and believe these strange gods are the true gods, then follow them and obey them only."

The people heard what Elijah said, but they made no answer.

Then the prophet continued,—

" Let us make a trial of the power of our God and of the power of these strange gods. I am the only prophet of our God here present, and there are four hundred priests of Baal. Now I will take a bullock and kill it as a sacrifice, and place it upon pieces of wood without kindling any fire, and let these priests of Baal do the same thing. And I will pray to my God, and they shall pray to their god, to send down fire from heaven to consume the sacrifices. And in this way you will learn which is the true God."

The people were pleased with this proposal, and cried out that it should be as Elijah had said.

Then the prophets of Baal killed a bullock, and laid it on pieces of wood, and cried to their god to send down fire to burn it. But no fire came at their prayer. Then Elijah mocked them, and told them to call louder, for perhaps their god was asleep, or on a journey. And they did so, and leaped about the altar and cut themselves with swords and lances, for this was their manner of worshipping. But still no answer came to their prayer.

Then Elijah bade the prophets go away, but asked the people to come close up to him to see that he did not hide any fire among the wood. And he took twelve stones and built an altar, and dug a trench or ditch around it. He laid pieces of wood upon the altar, and placed a bullock on the wood. Then he ordered the people to fill four barrels with water, and pour the water over the altar, so that the bullock and the wood were both soaked, and the ditch was filled up with water.

When this had been done, Elijah prayed to God and asked Him to make manifest His power to a people that had remained so long in the blindness of error. And a fire came down from heaven in the sight of the multitude, and fell upon the altar and consumed the sacrifice, till the very water was set on fire and the place was become dry.

When the Israelites saw this, they fell down and worshipped God, and called Him the one true God, and said all other gods were false. And at Elijah's bidding they seized the false prophets and slew them.

Then Elijah spoke to the king, and told him that now he might go home and eat and drink, for the rain was coming and the famine would soon be at an end. So Ahab went his way. But Elijah went up to the highest point of Mount Carmel, and sat on the ground, and leaned his head upon his knees. The sky was still entirely clear, and after a little time

Elijah told a servant who was with him to go and look towards the sea and let him know if he saw a cloud rising anywhere. Six times the man went and came back with the answer that he saw nothing. But the seventh time he said he saw a small black thing in the sky not larger than a man's foot. When Elijah heard that, he sent to Ahab, telling him he had better make haste to the nearest city before the rain came down. Ahab rode in his chariot towards the city of Jezreel. In a little time the sky was all covered with clouds, and a brisk wind sprang up, and there was a very great rain. Ahab reached Jezreel just as the storm burst, and the Lord gave Elijah strength to run before the chariot, so that he came to the gate of the city ahead of Ahab.

When Jezebel, the wife of Ahab, heard of all the wonders that Elijah had wrought, and how he had slain her prophets, she was very angry, and sent messengers to him, threatening him with death. Elijah was frightened, and fled to the city of Beersheba. There he left his servant and went away into the desert. Being very sorrowful, he prayed that he might die. Then he lay down and slept under a tree. On waking in the morning he found food and water set by him. When he had eaten and drunk he felt much refreshed, and he walked on till he came to Mount Sinai, and, finding a cave there, he took up his abode in it. One day, while he was in the cave, he heard a voice calling to him, but he knew not whence it came. The voice asked, " Why hast thou left the city and come hither ?"

Elijah answered, " The king's wife seeks to punish me, because I slew the prophets of the false gods and persuaded the people that He only whom they had worshipped from the beginning was God. Therefore have I fled from the city."

Then Elijah heard another voice telling him that he should come out on the next day into the open air, and should then learn what he was to do. When Elijah came out accordingly, a bright flame leaped out of the earth, and the earth itself

shook and trembled, and he heard a divine voice ordering
him to return home, and to ordain Jehu king of Israel and
Hazael of Damascus king of Syria, and that these two kings
would punish all the wicked men that had rebelled against
God. The voice also told him to ordain as prophet, to succeed himself, a man named Elisha, who lived in the city of
Abel. So Elijah departed from Sinai, and on his way he
came across Elisha, who was ploughing in the fields. Elijah
threw his mantle over Elisha, who at once left off ploughing
and began to prophesy. And having first obtained permission
to take farewell of his parents, the new prophet followed Elijah,
and became his disciple and servant all the days of his life.

CHAPTER LXIII.

NABOTH'S VINEYARD.

THERE was a man named Naboth, who had a field near the
city of Jezreel. Now this field was next to a field that
belonged to the king. And the king wanted to buy Naboth's field, in order that he might make one farm out of
the two properties. But Naboth refused all his offers, saying
that the land had come down to him from his fathers, and he
did not wish to part with it.

Ahab was greatly grieved at this, and Jezebel, noticing his
affliction, asked him the cause of it, and he told her. Then
Jezebel told him he need not distress himself, for she would
have Naboth punished. She sent word to the rulers of Jezreel, commanding them to call together an assembly of the
people, at which three bold men should rise and accuse Naboth of having blasphemed God and the king, after which he
was to be taken out and stoned to death. All was done as

the queen had commanded, and then the rulers of Jezreel
wrote to Ahab, asking him to take the farm of Naboth as a
gift.   Ahab was glad, and rose at once from his bed and went
to see the farm.   But God was very angry, and He sent Elijah
to meet him there.   And Elijah said to Ahab,—

"Because thou hast done this unjust thing, the Lord will
punish thee.   Thy blood and the blood of thy wife shall be
shed in the place where Naboth was stoned to death, and the
dogs will come and lick it up.   And thy family will be
destroyed from off the face of the earth."

CHAPTER LXIV.

HOW BENHADAD, KING OF DAMASCUS AND SYRIA, MADE TWO EXPEDITIONS AGAINST AHAB.

BENHADAD, the king of Damascus and Syria, declared war
against Ahab.   Thirty-two other kings assisted Benhadad,
and they invaded the kingdom of Israel with a mighty army.
Ahab retreated into the city of Samaria, and shut himself up
in it with all his men.   And Benhadad sent messengers to
Ahab, who said,—

"Thy riches and thy children and thy wives are Benhadad's, and if thou wilt give him leave to take of these all
he may want, Benhadad will withdraw his army and leave off
the siege."

Ahab was afraid, and he bade the messengers go back and
say that Benhadad might take all those things.

But Benhadad was not satisfied, and again he sent messengers to Ahab, who said,—

"Since thou dost admit that all thou hast is Benhadad's, he
will to-morrow send his servants to search through thy house

and the houses of all thy people, and they shall take whatever they find to be valuable and good of its kind."

Then Ahab gathered together the people and told them what Benhadad had said. And the people declared that Ahab should not consent to this, but should fight against Benhadad.

When the messengers returned with this answer, Benhadad sent word to Ahab that he would besiege the city, and that his army was so large that if every man took only a handful of earth, they would raise a bank higher than the walls of Samaria, to which Ahab trusted. But Ahab replied that he should not boast until he had won the victory. Benhadad was feasting with the thirty-two kings when this answer reached him. He was very angry, and bade his army prepare for battle. Ahab, meanwhile, was in great fear on account of the multitude of the enemy. But the Lord sent a prophet to Ahab, who told him not to fear, for he would win the victory. While Benhadad and the other kings were drinking themselves drunk in their tents, Ahab and a few thousand of the Israelites fell upon the Syrian army and put them to flight. Benhadad himself escaped from the field with difficulty.

The prophet spoke a second time to Ahab, warning him that Benhadad would return again next year. Ahab kept himself in readiness, and when Benhadad came again at the head of another large army, he went out to meet him; and though his army was a very small one, God gave him the victory again. More than one hundred thousand of the Syrians were slain in this battle, and the rest fled away to a city called Aphek, but just as they had reached it the walls around the city fell down with a great noise, and buried twenty-seven thousand of the fugitives in the ruins.

Benhadad, with some of his faithful servants, fled into the city and hid himself in a cellar. Then Benhadad's servants spoke to him, and said that the kings of Israel were merciful men, and that if they went out to Ahab and humbled themselves before him, he would spare the life of Benhadad. Benhadad allowed them to go, and Ahab received them kindly, and bade them bring Benhadad to him. And Ahab took that wicked king into his chariot, and because he promised to give him some cities he spared his life and sent him back into his own country.

But a prophet called Micaiah came to one of the Israelites and said, "Smite me on the head, for by so doing you will please God." When the Israelite refused, Micaiah foretold that, because he had disobeyed God, he should meet a lion who would destroy him. And it happened as the prophet had said. Then Micaiah came to another Israelite and repeated his command, and this Israelite smote him and wounded him in the skull. Micaiah bound up the wound with a handkerchief, so that his face was partly hidden, and he came before Ahab and said,—

"O king, I am a soldier in thy army, and a prisoner was committed to my care by an officer, and I suffered the prisoner to escape. Wherefore I am in great fear of death, for the officer threatens to slay me."

Ahab answered sternly that he deserved death for his disobedience. Then Micaiah uncovered himself, and Ahab recognized him. And Micaiah said,—

"Because thou hast suffered Benhadad to escape, whom the Lord meant thee to destroy, thou shalt be punished, and the Lord will so bring it about that thou wilt die by means of Benhadad, and thy army shall be defeated by his army."

Upon which Ahab was angry with the prophet, and commanded that he should be thrown into prison.

CHAPTER LXV.

THE DEATH OF AHAB.

FOR three years there was peace between Ahab and Benhadad. But because Benhadad had not given up Ramoth, one of the cities which Benhadad's father had conquered from the Israelites, Ahab determined to make war upon him. Jehoshaphat was at this time king of Jerusalem. He had married Ahab's daughter, and was friendly to him; therefore Ahab asked him to join in an expedition against the Syrians. Jehoshaphat was a good man, who feared the Lord. He told Ahab first to inquire of the prophets of God whether He would bless the expedition.

Ahab called together the false prophets of Baal and asked them if he would be victorious if he went against Benhadad.

The prophets answered that he would defeat the king of Syria as he had defeated him before.

But Jehoshaphat would not believe these men, and he said, " Is there not a prophet of the true God in this country whom we may consult ?"

Ahab answered, " There is one named Micaiah, but I hate him, for he hath prophesied that I shall be defeated and slain by the king of Syria. On which account I have thrown him into prison, where he now is."

Jehoshaphat said, " Bring him forth."

Micaiah was brought into the presence of the kings. And being questioned as to the future, he answered,—

" God hath shown me the children of Israel dispersed and

fleeing away from the Syrians, as a flock of sheep is dispersed when their shepherd is slain. And I interpret this to mean that the Israelites shall flee alive to their homes, and only their king shall perish."

But one of the false prophets, whose name was Zedekiah, besought Ahab not to listen to Micaiah. "For Elijah," he said, "was a greater prophet than Micaiah, and Elijah predicted that the blood of the king would be licked up by dogs near the city of Jezreel in Israel. Therefore Micaiah speaks falsely when he says thou wilt be slain in Syria. And if thou wantest a further sign that he is no true prophet, I will smite him, and let him then wither up my hand as the hand of Jeroboam was once withered up by the prophet Jadon."

Then Zedekiah smote Micaiah, and because no evil consequence followed to Zedekiah, Ahab took courage and led his army against the Syrians, and Jehoshaphat went with him. The king of Syria brought out his army to oppose him, and made his camp not far from Ramoth.

Ahab and Jehoshaphat had agreed that, in order to prevent the prophecy of Micaiah from being fulfilled, Ahab should dress himself as a common soldier, and give his robes and his armor to Jehoshaphat, so that the enemy should mistake Jehoshaphat for Ahab. This was done accordingly. Before the battle commenced, Benhadad had told his soldiers to kill no one but Ahab. When they saw Jehoshaphat dressed in the royal robes, they all rushed at him, but when they came closer they recognized that it was not Ahab, and fell back again. But a man in Benhadad's army shot an arrow into the air, not knowing where it would land or whom it would hit, and the Lord made it strike Ahab and pierce through his armor. Then Ahab knew that he was wounded unto death, and he told the driver of his chariot to carry him out of the host a little way. And he made some of his servants hold him up in his chariot and let him see the battle and give orders to the soldiers, for he did not want any one to know he was dying.

But towards sunset he fell down dead, and the Israelites all fled to their own homes.

The body of Ahab was carried to Samaria to be buried. But as the driver stopped by a fountain near the city of Jezreel to wash his chariot, which was full of blood, the dogs came out and licked up the blood of Ahab, as Elijah had prophesied that they would. The prophecy of Micaiah was also fulfilled, for Ahab had died at Ramoth.

Ahab was succeeded in the kingdom of Israel by his son Ahaziah.

CHAPTER LXVI.

JEHOSHAPHAT, KING OF JUDAH.

WHEN Jehoshaphat returned to Jerusalem from the battle with Benhadad, he was met by the prophet Jehu, who reproved him for having assisted so wicked a king as Ahab. The Lord, said Jehu, was angry with Jehoshaphat for this, but had delivered him from the enemy, because this was the first time he had sinned against Him.

Then Jehoshaphat humbled himself before God and offered sacrifices to appease His anger. And he went through the land of Judah commanding the people to put away their idols. He appointed judges over them also, whom he chose from the priests and the Levites and the chief men in each city, and he told these judges to fear God and see that justice was administered.

Soon after, the Moabites and the Ammonites made war against Jehoshaphat, and, marching into the land of Judah, they pitched their camp near the city of Engedi. Jehoshaphat sent word to his people to come to the temple at Jerusalem, and when they were assembled there, he prayed aloud to God, and the whole multitude, including women and children, joined him in his prayers. Then a prophet stood up and told them that God had heard their prayers and would fight against their enemies. And he informed the king that next day he was to bring his army out against the enemy, though he should not fight against them, but only stand still and see how God would destroy them.

Next morning the king marched out at the head of his army, but they brought no weapons with them. The priests blew on their trumpets, and the Levites and others sang hymns and sacred songs.

Then God caused a sudden terror and commotion to fall upon the Ammonites and the Moabites, so that they took one another for enemies and fought together, and not one man out of the great army escaped. When Jehoshaphat looked upon that valley where his enemies had been encamped and saw it full of dead bodies, he gave thanks to God. He gave his army leave to go down and take gold and silver and jewels from the bodies of the slain, and they were three days in gathering the spoil.

After this the heathen nations feared to attack Jehoshaphat, and he lived in peace and splendor.

CHAPTER LXVII.

AHAZIAH, KING OF ISRAEL.

AHAZIAH, the son of Ahab, was as wicked as his father, and encouraged his people in the worship of false gods. One day he fell down-stairs, and was badly hurt. And he sent messengers to Baal-zebub, the god of Ekron, to inquire if he would get well. But Elijah was sent by God to meet the messengers while they were on their way. He stopped them, and asked,—

"Have not the people of Israel a God of their own, that ye have to consult strange gods? Return ye, therefore, and inform your master that he will not recover."

The messengers returned to the king with this message. When the king learned, from the description they gave, that the man who had given the message was Elijah, he was very angry. So he sent a captain with fifty soldiers to seize the prophet and bring him to the palace.

The captain found Elijah sitting on a hill, and he commanded him to come with him to the king's presence.

"If thou dost not come peaceably, O prophet," said the captain, "we will carry thee by force."

Elijah answered, "In order that thou mayst know I am a true prophet, I will pray that fire may fall from heaven and destroy both thy soldiers and thyself."

And fire came down from heaven and burned the captain and his men.

Then the king sent another captain with fifty men, who came to Elijah and said,—

"Thou prophet, come down quickly, or I will carry thee down by force."

"If I be a prophet," answered Elijah, "let fire come down from heaven and burn thee and thy men."

And the fire came down and destroyed the captain and his men.

Then the king sent out a third captain, with the same number of men. This captain was wise and prudent. When he had come to where Elijah was, he spoke civilly to him, and said, "O prophet, I am sent by the king, and come not of my own accord. Therefore I pray you to have compassion on me and on my soldiers, and to accompany us into the presence of the king."

Elijah was pleased with these civil words, and he came

down from the mountain and followed the captain. When he had come to the king, he said,—

"Because thou hast despised the true God, and sent to the god of Ekron to ask about thy illness, thou shalt surely die."

And in truth Ahaziah died a short time afterwards. As he had no sons, he was succeeded by his brother Jehoram, who was a wicked man also. It was in the reign of Jehoram that Elijah disappeared from among men,* and Elisha became prophet of Israel in his stead.

CHAPTER LXVIII.

JEHORAM, KING OF ISRAEL.

JEHORAM, king of Israel, gathered up his armies to fight against the Moabites. And he sent to Jehoshaphat, the king of Judah, asking for his help. Jehoshaphat agreed to go to war with him, and the king of Edom also collected an army to assist him. So the three kings joined their forces and set out together. After they had journeyed for seven days, they were in distress for want of water for the men and the beasts. Then Jehoram cried out that God had forsaken them, and intended to deliver them into the hands of the enemy. But Jehoshaphat encouraged him, and bade him send to the camp and learn if any prophet of God had come along with the army. One of the soldiers said he had seen there Elisha, who was the servant of Elijah. So the three kings went to Elisha's tent and asked him, "What will become of the army?"

Elisha, seeing Jehoram, said to him,—

----

* According to the Bible, Elijah was taken up alive into heaven.

"Why dost thou come to me? Go to the prophets of thy father and thy mother, and let them assist thee."

But Jehoram still begged that the prophet would answer him.

Elisha said, "As surely as the Lord liveth, I would not answer thee were it not for the respect I bear to Jehoshaphat, who is a holy and a righteous man. But bring me hither a musician."

A musician came, and as he began to play the prophet became inspired. And he told the kings to dig many ditches in the valley.

"For," said he, "though there appear neither cloud, nor wind, nor storm of rain, ye shall see these trenches full of water, and the army and the cattle shall be saved by drinking of it, and, moreover, the Lord will deliver your enemies into your hands."

The words of the prophet came true, for next morning the Lord caused water to flow into the valley, so that the trenches were filled with it.

When the Moabites learned that the three kings had come against them, they gathered up their army and came to meet the Israelites. The sun had just risen, and its rays made the water in the ditches look red as blood. The Moabites falsely supposed that their enemies had been fighting with one another, and that this was their blood. They asked their king to let them go and gather the spoil from the camp, and then rushed in disorder towards the place. But they found themselves surrounded on all sides by their enemies, who killed a great many and put the rest to flight. The three kings pursued them into their own country, and took their cities, and overthrew their walls, and destroyed their harvests. They besieged the king of Moab in his royal city, but when the king found that he could not cut his way out or escape, he did a thing that showed despair and the utmost distress, for he took his eldest son, who was to reign after him, and lifting him up on the wall, where he might be visible to all the Israelites, he offered him up as a sacrifice to his god. When the kings saw this, they were so much affected by pity that they raised the siege, and every one returned to his own house.

Jehoshaphat died a short time after this expedition, having reigned twenty-five years. His son Jehoram, who, having married a daughter of Ahab, was a brother-in-law of his namesake, Jehoram, king of Israel, succeeded Jehoshaphat as king of Jerusalem.

CHAPTER LXIX.

THE MIRACLES OF ELISHA.

WHEN Jehoram, king of Israel, returned out of the land of Moab to Samaria, he had with him Elisha the prophet, who performed many miracles that are mentioned in the Bible.

It is related that the widow of Obadiah, Ahab's steward, came to him and said that her husband had fallen into debt, in order that he might be able to provide sustenance for the hundred prophets whom he had hidden from the wrath of Jezebel, and that when he died she and her children had been carried away to be made slaves by the creditors. So she besought Elisha to have pity on her condition. When he asked her what she had in the house, she replied, " Nothing but a little oil in a cruse."

The prophet told her to go and borrow a great many empty vessels from her neighbors. Then she was to go in her chamber and shut the door, and pour the oil into them all, for God would fill them. She did as she was told, and all this number of vessels was filled from the little cruse of oil. The prophet told her to sell the oil, to use a part of the price to pay her debts, and to keep the rest for herself and for her children. The woman did so, and was delivered from her husband's creditors.

Another of this prophet's miracles was wrought when Benhadad, king of Syria, declared war against Jehoram of Israel. Benhadad commanded his soldiers to go to a certain place where Jehoram was hunting, and capture him; but Elisha warned the king not to go hunting that day. Benhadad thought some of his own servants had betrayed his plan of capturing Jehoram, and he accused them of it, and swore he would put them to death. But one who was present told him that it was certainly Elisha who had warned the king, for Elisha knew all the most secret counsels of the enemy.

Then Benhadad asked in what town Elisha was living, and when he learned it was Dothan, he sent an army of soldiers with horses and chariots to Dothan, and they came by night and surrounded the city. In the early morning Elisha's servant came running to tell him of the multitude of enemies that had come to seize him. But Elisha told him to fear nothing, and he besought the Lord to make manifest to the servant His power and presence. God heard Elisha's prayer, and made the servant see a multitude of chariots and horses encompassing Elisha, till his courage revived, and he laid aside his fear at the sight of these things. After this Elisha further asked of God that He would dim the eyes of the enemy, and cast a mist upon them, so that they might not know him when they saw him. And the Lord did so, and Elisha walked into the midst of the enemy and asked them who it was they came to seek. They replied, " The prophet Elisha." Elisha said, " If you will follow after me I will deliver him to you."

Then he led them to the city of Samaria, where the king of Israel lived. He ordered Jehoram to shut the gates, and to place his own army round about them, and prayed God to clear the eyes of the Syrians. Accordingly, when they were

freed from the darkness they had been in, they saw themselves in the midst of their enemies, and were strangely
amazed and distressed. Jehoram would have slain them all,
but Elisha made him spare them and send them back to Benhadad, their master.

Benhadad also was greatly surprised when the men returned and told him their experience. He saw that he could
do nothing against the Israelites by stealth or cunning, so
he determined to trust to the superior strength of his army
and attack them openly. He moved his army against the
city of Samaria and besieged it, surrounding it so thoroughly
that no bread could be brought to the men of Israel from
outside, and soon there was a terrible famine in the city. One
day the king of Israel was walking among his soldiers, when a
woman came up to him and cried, " Have pity on me, O king !"

Jehoram, thinking she meant to ask him for something to
eat, told her hastily that he had nothing to give her, and bade
her begone.

But the woman clung to him, and said she only wished
him to hear her story and have justice done. The king told
her to speak; that he would listen. The woman said that
she and another woman, with whom she lived, had each a
son. And, because of their distress for want of food, both
had agreed to kill their children and eat them.

"So I killed my son first," continued the woman; "and
when we had finished eating him, the other woman broke her
agreement and would not give up her son, but hid him out
of my reach."

When King Jehoram heard this he rent his garments and
grieved greatly to know that his people were driven by famine
to such horrible practices. And he cursed Elisha the prophet
because he had not prayed to God to relieve them, and in his
anger he hastily sent a man to slay him.

Elisha was sitting in his house with his disciples. He
knew the evil designs of the king, and, turning to those about

him, he told them that Jehoram had sent one to cut off his
head.

" But," said he, " when the man arrives, take care that you
do not let him in, but press the door against him and hold it
fast, for the king himself will speedily follow him, having
changed his mind."

The man came, and was shut out of the house; and immediately thereafter the king arrived, for he had repented of his
wrath. Elisha told Jehoram that the very next day they
should have plenty of barley and fine flour. Then the king
rejoiced, but one of his captains who was with him laughed
scornfully, and said,—

" Thou speakest foolishly, O prophet, for it is not possible
that God will rain torrents of barley and fine flour into this
town."

To which the prophet replied,—

" Nevertheless, thou shalt see these things come to pass,
but thou shalt not be in the least a partaker of them."

Now, there were four lepers sitting by the gate of the city,
for there was a law that no person afflicted with leprosy should
be allowed within the walls of Samaria. And they said one
to another that if they remained there they would perish of
hunger, and even if they could go into the city, the famine
was there, and they would perish there too, so they resolved
to give themselves up to the enemy, thinking it were an easier
death to die by the sword than by starvation.

It was night when they came to this resolution, and they
set off at once. Now, God had begun to affright and disturb
the Syrians, and to bring the noise of chariots and armor to
their ears, so that they thought a great army was marching
against them and was coming nearer and nearer. And they
rushed in disorder out of their tents, and came before Benhadad and cried that Jehoram had sent for the king of Egypt
and the king of the Islands to come to his assistance, and the
armies of these kings were now on their way. Benhadad

believed what they said, for the same noise came to his ears, and he and his army left their tents and their horses and everything that was in their camps, and fled for their lives.

When the lepers arrived at the enemy's camp, therefore, there was no one there. And when they had crept cautiously from one tent to another and found them all deserted, they went back to Samaria, and called to the watchmen on the walls, and told them what they had seen. Now, the king, when he was told the story of the lepers, thought at first that the Syrians were laying a snare for his people, and had only retired a little way and hidden themselves, so that when the Israelites came into the camp they might fall upon them and kill them. He therefore sent out horsemen to ride over the country and discover if the Syrians were hidden anywhere. The horsemen went as far as the river Jordan, and could not find them. But the road was strewn with weapons and garments that the Syrians had thrown away in their haste.

When the king heard this he told the people to go and take the spoils of the camp. And they found a great quantity of gold and silver and herds of cattle, together with many thousand measures of wheat and barley. The king sent that officer who would not believe in the words of Elisha to stand at the gate and keep the people in order. But the crowd was so great that they pressed against him and suffocated him, so that he died.

When Benhadad, who had fled to Damascus, learned that it was God Himself who had cast his army into disorder, and that there had been no one marching against them, he was troubled to think that God was his enemy, and fell very sick. About this time Elisha came to Damascus, and Benhadad, hearing of his arrival, sent Hazael, one of his officers, to meet him and carry him presents and inquire of him whether the king would recover from his sickness.

The prophet said that the king would die, though his disease was not a fatal one. And looking at Hazael, Elisha wept. When Hazael inquired the reason of his tears, Elisha answered,—

"I weep out of pity for the people of Israel, and the terrible miseries they will suffer from thee, for thou wilt slay the strongest of them, and wilt burn their cities and destroy their wives and children."

Hazael asked, "How can it be that I shall have power to do all these things?"

Elisha answered,—

"God hath informed me that thou shalt be king of Syria."

Then Hazael returned to Benhadad and told him the prophet had said his disease was not a fatal one. But next day he spread a wet cloth over the king's face, so that he was suffocated. Hazael took the kingdom in his place.

CHAPTER LXX.

CONCERNING JEHORAM, KING OF JUDAH.

THE other Jehoram, who was king of Judah, was not a good man, in spite of the example left to him by his father Jehoshaphat. For his wife, Athaliah, the daughter of Ahab, taught him to worship strange gods, and he made all the people of Judah sin in the same way. And there came a letter to him from Elisha the prophet, saying that the Lord would punish him for his wickedness, and would allow his wives and children to be slain, and would send on him a terrible sickness.

Not long after this an army of Philistines and Arabians fell upon the city of Jerusalem, and took it, and slew the king's children, so that only one of his sons, named Ahaziah, escaped, and many of his wives, and carried away quantities of treasure from the city. Jehoram fell sick of a grievous illness and died, and his son Ahaziah was appointed king of Israel in his place.

CHAPTER LXXI.

DEATH OF JEHORAM, KING OF ISRAEL.

AFTER the death of Benhadad, Jehoram, king of Israel, besieged the city of Ramoth, and took it from the Syrians. But while the siege was in progress he was wounded by an arrow, and he returned to Jezreel to have the wound healed, leaving the army and the captured city in charge of Jehu, his general. Elisha the prophet then sent one of his disciples to Ramoth, and the disciple took Jehu into a private chamber and anointed him king of Israel, saying,—

"The Lord hath ordained thee king of Israel, that thou mayest destroy the house of Ahab, and avenge the blood of the prophets slain by Jezebel."

Then the disciple fled.

When Jehu came out again, the officers, who had seen him go in with the disciple, asked him what that young man wanted with him, and was he not a madman?

"Verily," answered Jehu, "the words he spoke were those of a madman."

And when they pressed him to know what those words were, Jehu said,—

"He chose me to be king over Israel."

Then the soldiers all rose and blew their trumpets, and cried,—

"Jehu is king of Israel!"

Jehu put himself at the head of the army, and marched

towards Jezreel. But when they were at some distance from
the city Jehu made his army halt, for he wished to take Jehoram by surprise. So he rode forward in his chariot, accompanied only by a few of his horsemen.

Jehoram was in his chamber, where Ahaziah, the king of
Judah, who was his sister's son, had come to visit him. A
watchman came into the chamber and reported that he saw a
troop of horsemen coming towards the city. Jehoram ordered
that a horseman should be sent out to meet them and inquire
what they wanted. But when the horseman met Jehu and
questioned him, Jehu bade him not meddle with such matters,
but to follow him. The watchman saw this, and reported to
Jehoram that the horseman had mingled himself among the
company, and was coming along with them. When the king
sent a second messenger, Jehu commanded him to do as the
former had done. When the watchman told this to Jehoram,
he at last got on his chariot himself, together with Ahaziah, and drove out to meet the horsemen. The two kings
came up to Jehu near the field of Naboth, and Jehoram
asked,—

"Are all things well in the camp?"

But Jehu answered, "How can all things be well when the
sins of thy wicked mother, Jezebel, have not been avenged?"

Then Jehoram was afraid, and turned his horses' heads,
and said to Ahaziah, "We are fought against by deceit and
treachery."

But Jehu drew his bow and shot an arrow, which pierced
the heart of Jehoram and killed him. And he shot another
arrow, which wounded Ahaziah; and though that king jumped
on a horse and fled away to his own kingdom, he nevertheless
died of his wound a few days after, and was buried in
Jerusalem.

Jehu rode on into Jezreel. And Jezebel, hearing what he
had done, came out and stood upon a tower on the wall of
the city, and said,—

14

"Thou art a fine servant, to kill thine own master!"

When he saw her he asked who she was, and commanded her to come down to him. But, as she would not do this, he bade some of her servants cast her down. They obeyed him, and the wall was besprinkled with her blood, and her body was trodden under foot by the horses, and so she died. Jehu came to the royal palace with his friends and sat down to dinner. First, however, he told his servants to go and take up the body of Jezebel and bury it, for she was a queen. But his servants could find only her skull and her hands and her feet: all the rest of her body had been eaten by dogs.

Jehu caused the family of Ahab to be put to death, and in this way the prophecies of Elijah were all fulfilled. He also destroyed the false prophets of Baal, and overturned the idols of that god. But he suffered the golden calves to remain, and allowed the Israelites to worship them. For Jehu was not a good man, and he soon forgot all the benefits the Lord had bestowed upon him.

CHAPTER LXXII.

JEHOASH IS MADE KING OF JUDAH.

WHEN Athaliah heard of the death of her brother Jehoram and of her son Ahaziah and of all the royal family of Ahab, she determined that she would put an end to the family of David also, though among them were her own grandchildren, the sons and daughters of Ahaziah. But in spite of her cruel resolution one of the sons of Ahaziah, named Jehoash, was preserved, in the following manner. Athaliah had a sister, named Jehosheba, who was married to the high-priest Jehoiada. She came into the royal palace after the slaughter of Ahaziah's kindred, and found Jehoash, who was only a year old, alive among the slain, and she took him with her and hid him, and she and her husband brought him up secretly.

Athaliah made herself queen of Judah, and ruled for six years. At the end of that time Jehoiada showed the boy whom he had brought up to the priests and Levites, and they decided to make him king. There were in the temple a number of spears and shields that had belonged to King David, and these the priests distributed among the Levites. On the appointed day the Levites came to the temple, and kept guard over it, to see that no armed men were allowed to enter. Jehoiada brought the child Jehoash out of the chamber in which he had been hidden, and told the people who he was, and anointed him king, and placed the crown upon his head. And all the people shouted with joy, for they were tired of the tyranny of Athaliah.

Athaliah heard the shouts, and came in alarm to the temple with her guards. The Levites allowed her to pass in, but they excluded her guards. When she saw the child standing with the crown upon his head, she rent her garments and cried out to the people to kill him, but Jehoiada caused her to be seized and taken out of the temple and slain.

Then Jehoiada made the people swear to be loyal to Jehoash, and take care of his safety and of that of his government. And Jehoash swore that he would observe the laws of Moses. The people then ran to the temple of Baal, which Athaliah had built, and demolished it, and slew the priests of Baal. Afterwards Jehoiada took Jehoash out of the temple into the royal palace, and when he had set him on the throne the people shouted for joy and feasted for many days.

Jehoash was seven years old when he took the kingdom. During his youth, and all the time that Jehoiada lived, he was careful to observe the commandments and was zealous in the worship of God. Being anxious to repair and rebuild the temple of God, which had been brought to decay by Jehoram and Athaliah and their sons, he took a wooden chest and made a hole in the lid, and set it up in the temple beside the altar. He desired the people to cast into the box through the hole whatever they wished to give towards the repair of the temple. So they strove with one another to see which would give the most, and large quantities of silver and gold were every day put into the box. Every day the priests counted over the money that had been given in the presence of the king, and it was turned into the treasury and the box was replaced. When a large sum had been collected in this way, the king and Jehoiada the high-priest set carpenters and masons to work, and they restored the temple to its former condition. As long as Jehoiada lived, the altar was every day heaped up with sacrifices.

But when Jehoiada died, the king fell away from God and neglected His worship. The people also went back to their idols. Zechariah, the son of Jehoiada, stood up in the temple and denounced the king and the people for their wickedness, and prophesied that God would punish them. Then Jehoash was angry, and ordered that Zechariah should be stoned to death where he stood, and the people obeyed him.

It was not long before God avenged the death of His priest. For Hazael, king of Syria, made an expedition against the country, and overthrew many of the cities, and would have taken Jerusalem but that Jehoash sent him all his treasures and all the treasures that were in the temple, and so bought him off. Afterwards Jehoash fell into a dangerous illness, and was killed in his bed by the friends of Zechariah.

CHAPTER LXXIII.

THE DEATH OF ELISHA.

MEANWHILE, the king of Syria had turned his victorious arms against Israel, which at this time was governed by Jehoahaz, who had succeeded his father, Jehu. Now, Jehoahaz was a very wicked man, and God allowed Hazael to defeat his armies, and take away from him his great cities, and reduce his people to slavery.

Jehoahaz died after he had reigned seventeen years, and was succeeded by his son Jehoash. As this was in the lifetime of Jehoash, king of Judah, there were now two kings of this name, as before there had been two Jehorams. It was during the reign of Jehoash of Israel that the prophet Elisha died. He was a very old man. On his death-bed he was visited by the king, who shed tears over him. But Elisha comforted him, and commanded a bow and some arrows to be brought to him, and he bade the king shoot the bow. The king shot three arrows and stopped. Then Elisha said,—

"If thou hadst shot more arrows, thou hadst utterly destroyed the kingdom of Syria, and swept it from the earth; but since thou hast been satisfied with shooting three times only, thou shalt fight and beat the Syrians no more times than three, and shalt only recover from them those cities which they cut off from thy kingdom in the reign of thy father."

When the king had departed, Elisha died, and he was buried in a magnificent manner. And it happened, shortly afterwards, that some robbers slew a traveller and threw his body into the grave of Elisha, and the murdered man came to life again.

Jehoash made war against Adad, the king of Syria, who had succeeded his father Hazael, and defeated him in three great battles, and took from him all that country and all those cities which had belonged to the kingdom of Israel. He also defeated Amaziah, king of Judah, as will be related in the next chapter. And having done these things, he died, leaving the throne of Israel to his son Jeroboam.

CHAPTER LXXIV.

AMAZIAH, KING OF JUDAH.

AFTER the death of Jehoash, king of Judah, his son Amaziah succeeded to the kingdom. Amaziah was a warlike prince, and he gathered together an army of three hundred thousand armed men of his own people, in order to lead them against the Amalekites and Edomites and Gebalites. He also sent to the king of Israel and hired one hundred thousand of his men for a hundred talents of silver. But as he was making ready to start, a prophet warned him that he should dismiss the Israelites, for they were bad men, and God would not bless him if he made use of such allies. Though Amaziah thought it was hard that he should be obliged to dismiss the Israelites after paying their hire, yet he obeyed the prophet. Then he marched with his own army against the enemy, and defeated them in many battles, and returned with a great booty.

Amaziah began to be puffed up with pride on account of his great victories, and he forgot that God had helped him, and even went so far as to worship the idols he had brought out of the country of the Amalekites. When a prophet was sent to upbraid him, Amaziah angrily told him to hold his peace and begone. The prophet answered that he would indeed hold his peace in future, but that God would surely punish the king.

Then Amaziah wrote an insolent letter to Jehoash, king of Israel, and commanded that he and his people should submit to him, even as the Israelites had formerly submitted to David and to Solomon, his ancestors.

"And if thou wilt not do this," wrote Amaziah, "thou wilt have to fight for thy dominion."

To which message Jehoash returned this answer in writing:

"King Jehoash to King Amaziah: There was once a tall cypress-tree in Mount Lebanon, and a thistle that grew beside it. The thistle spoke to the cypress, asking that the daughter of the cypress be given in marriage to the son of the thistle. But while the thistle was speaking there came a wild beast and trod it down. And this may be a lesson to thee, not to be so ambitious, and to have a care lest thou growest too proud on account of thy success over the Amalekites, and bringest dangers upon thyself and upon thy kingdom."

When Amaziah had read this letter he was very angry, and he gathered up an army to chastise King Jehoash and reduce him to subjection. But just as the men of Judah were marching out to give battle to the Israelites, a strange terror came down upon them from God, and they dispersed in confusion and fled from the field, leaving Amaziah alone and undefended. The Israelites took him captive, and Jehoash threatened to kill him unless he would persuade the people of Jerusalem to open their gates to him and receive him and his army into the city. Amaziah, being in terror for his life, did as he was told. Jehoash threw down a part of the wall and drove into the city through the breach, and became master of Jerusalem. He took away all the treasure he could find in the temple and in the royal palace and in the houses of the citizens, and returned to Samaria, leaving Amaziah behind him. After this some of the men of Jerusalem conspired against Amaziah and slew him, and he was succeeded by his son Uzziah.

CHAPTER LXXV.

THE PROPHET JONAH.

JEROBOAM the second, who succeeded his father, Jehoash, as king of Israel, was a very wicked prince, and was the cause of many misfortunes to his people. In spite of his wickedness, God was willing to make use of him to chastise the Syrians, who were also a very wicked people. He sent a prophet named Jonah to tell him that he should make war with the kingdom of Syria and destroy their towns, and Jeroboam did as he was told, and the Lord gave him the victory.

God had also told Jonah that he should go to a city named Nineveh and warn the citizens that a great punishment was in store for them. But out of fear he disobeyed God, and fled to the city of Joppa, and, finding a ship there, he embarked on it to go to Tarsus. On the passage a terrible storm arose, and the ship was in danger of sinking. Then the captain and his men began to pray to God, but Jonah did not join in their prayers, for he knew that it was on his account that the storm had been sent. The tempest increased, and the sailors began to think there was some one on board who was pursued by the anger of God. They threw lots to determine who this was, and the lot fell upon Jonah.

They asked him, " Who art thou, and what wicked thing hast thou done?"

Jonah answered, " I am an Israelite by birth, and a prophet of God, and if you wish to escape the danger you are in, cast me overboard, for I am the occasion of this storm."

At first they durst not do this, but finally they suffered Jonah to persuade them, and threw him overboard, as he had told them to do. The sea all at once became calm. And a great whale caught Jonah in his mouth and swallowed him alive. Jonah remained for three days in the whale's belly, and was then cast out upon the dry land. Jonah confessed his sin, and was forgiven by God; he then went to Nineveh to speak the words the Lord had intrusted to him.

Jeroboam the Second ruled for forty years, and then died, and his son Zechariah took the kingdom.

CHAPTER LXXVI.

UZZIAH, KING OF JUDAH.

UZZIAH was sixteen years old when he was made king of Judah in place of his father, Amaziah, who had been slain. At first he did what was right, and God blessed him, so that he prospered, and the kingdom flourished under him. But this success made him proud, and he forgot that it was God to whom he owed it. One day, on the occasion of a great festival, he put on the holy garment of the priests and went into the temple to offer up incense to God on the golden altar. The priests sought to dissuade him from his purpose, telling him it was not lawful for any but the descendants of Aaron to sacrifice at that altar. Then the king was angry, and threatened to kill them unless they held their peace. No sooner were these words uttered than the earth began to shake and tremble, the roof of the temple was rent, and the rays of the sun shone through and fell full upon the king's face, which at the same moment was covered all over with leprosy. A mountain that was near the city was split asunder by the earthquake, and half of it broke off from the rest and rolled four furlongs, till the roads, as well as the king's gardens, were spoiled by the obstruction.

As soon as the priests saw that the king's face was covered with leprosy, they ordered him out of the temple and out of the city, for there was a law that no leper should be allowed within the city walls. The king was so frightened and distressed at this strange calamity that he did what was commanded, and took up his abode outside the walls, and lived a private life, while his son Jotham took the government.

And he soon died, and Jotham was crowned king of Judah.

CHAPTER LXXVII.

ZECHARIAH, MENAHEM, PEKAHIAH, AND PEKAH, KINGS OF ISRAEL.

ZECHARIAH, the son of Jeroboam, reigned over Israel only six months, and was then treacherously slain by one of his servants, named Shallum, who proclaimed himself king. But Menahem, the general of the army, hearing of what Shallum had done, came against him and slew him, and made himself king. Menahem ruled for ten years with great cruelty, slaying those who did not wish him to be king, and destroying their towns. When he died, his son Pekahiah succeeded him. He was a wicked man also, and after a reign of two years he was treacherously put to death by one of his generals, named Pekah. Pekah made himself king, and reigned for twenty years, and he too was a cruel and sinful man.

CHAPTER LXXVIII.

AHAZ, KING OF JUDAH.

IN the mean while, Jotham, the son of Uzziah, had been ruling with wisdom and justice in Judah, and after he had been king for sixteen years he died, and was succeeded by his son Ahaz.

Ahaz proved an impious man and a transgressor against the laws of his country. He imitated the kings of Israel, and raised altars in Jerusalem to false gods, and taught his people to worship them. He even offered up human sacrifices, as the Canaanites did, and allowed his own son to be burnt on an altar.

While he was going on in these wicked courses, Pekah, king of Israel, made an alliance with the king of Syria and Damascus, and the two kings joined their forces and invaded the land of Judah. The Syrian king took several cities and slew their inhabitants and peopled them with his own subjects, and then returned to Syria. When Ahaz, who had shut himself up in the city of Jerusalem, learned that the Syrians had departed, he believed he would be more than a match for the king of Israel. So he sallied out with his army. But the Israelites defeated him with great slaughter and drove him back into Jerusalem. They laid waste all the country round about Jerusalem, and took captive the women and children of the tribe of Benjamin, and returned with them to Samaria.

Now there was one Obed, who was a prophet at that time

in Samaria. He met the army before the city walls, and cried out to them in a loud voice, and said,—

"Know, ye men of Israel, that ye have gotten this victory over the people of Judah not by reason of your own strength, but because God is angered against King Ahaz. And ye should have been satisfied with this success, and should not have made captives of your own kinsmen. Therefore I tell you to let these captives return home, and to do them no harm, for otherwise the Lord will punish you."

So the people consulted together, and decided to return the captives whom they had taken.

After this, King Ahaz sent to a king of the Assyrians, named Tiglath-Pileser, and sued for his assistance against the Israelites and the Syrians, promising to pay him large sums of money. So Tiglath-Pileser came to assist Ahaz, and made war upon the Syrians, and defeated them, and captured many of their towns, and afterwards he invaded Israel and took many captives. Ahaz took all the gold and silver that was in his treasury and in the temple of God and gave it to the king of Assyria. Now, Ahaz had been worshipping the gods of the Syrians, though that nation was his enemy; but when the Syrians were defeated, he lost faith in those gods and worshipped the gods of the Assyrians. For he was always ready to worship strange gods and to turn away from the true God, the God of his own nation, whose anger was the cause of his many defeats. He even shut up the temple and forbade the priests to offer sacrifices in it, and committed many other indignities.

When he had reigned sixteen years he died, and his son Hezekiah succeeded to the kingdom. Hezekiah was a very different man from his father. He was righteous and religious, and his first care was to restore the worship of the true God. So he called together the people and the priests and the Levites, and announced to them his intention. And he said to the people,—

"You know that because my father transgressed the law of God, and offered up worship to false gods, and persuaded you to do the like, you have suffered many and grievous punishments. Therefore I pray you who have been taught by these sad experiences to give up your idolatries, and to purify your souls, and to open the temple to these priests and Levites, and cleanse it with the customary sacrifices, for by these means we may render God favorable, and He will remit His anger towards us."

When the king had finished speaking, the priests opened the temple. And when they had set in order the vessels of God and cast out what was impure, they laid the sacrifices upon the altar according to the custom of their ancestors.

The king also sent out messengers to all his people, and to the people of the ten tribes of Israel, telling them that the worship of the true God had been restored in Jerusalem, and asking them all to come and celebrate the feast of the Pass-over, for it was now many years since the people had kept that feast as God commanded them to keep it. The people of Judah gladly accepted the invitation, but most of the Israelites laughed the ambassadors to scorn and treated them as fools; and when some of the prophets among them foretold that they would suffer great misfortunes if they refused this opportunity of returning to the worship of God, they took these prophets and slew them. Not all of the Israelites, however, were so blind and foolish, for some of them listened to the words of the prophets, and returned to the worship of God. And all these came running to Jerusalem.

When the time had come, Hezekiah and the priests and the rulers and all the people went up to the temple and offered up solemn sacrifices. And then they feasted for seven days, and there was everywhere great rejoicing. After the festival was ended, the people went out through the country and destroyed the idols everywhere and overthrew their altars. The king also gave orders that the daily sacrifices should be offered up according to law and at his own expense, and appointed that the tenth part of all the ground produced should be given to the priests and Levites. And thus did the tribes of Judah and Benjamin return to their old form of worship.

CHAPTER LXXIX.

THE DESTRUCTION OF THE KINGDOM OF ISRAEL.

AFTER Pekah, king of Israel, had ruled for twenty years, he was treacherously slain by one of his most trusted servants, named Hosea, and Hosea made himself king. He was a wicked man, and despised the worship of God. Shalmaneser, king of Assyria, invaded his kingdom and defeated him, and ordered Hosea to pay him a large sum of money every year. Hosea found it burdensome to pay this money, so he called upon the king of Egypt to assist him in casting off the yoke of the Assyrians. Shalmaneser heard of this, and he raised an army and marched into Israel, and in three years he had entirely conquered the country and taken all the cities, and their armies and their king he made prisoners. And he determined to put an end forever to the government of the Israelites; so he sent all the people away to the countries of Media and Persia, and he gave their country to a people called the Cutheans, who lived by a river called Cuthah. These people came and lived in the houses and towns of the Israelites; and because they took Samaria as their principal city they soon became known as Samaritans. Thus the kingdom of Israel came to an end two hundred and forty years after the ten tribes had revolted from Rehoboam; and no one knows what became of the tribes after this. And in this way were they punished for having despised the law of God and the voice of His prophets, who had so often warned them of what would happen if they persisted in their impiety.

When the Cutheans, or Samaritans, first came into their new country, they were worshippers of idols, and they brought their gods with them. But God sent upon them a grievous sickness, and many of them died; and when they found no cure for their miseries, they were informed by a prophet that if they worshipped God they would be relieved. So they sent ambassadors to the king of Assyria, asking him to send them some of those priests of the Israelites whom he had taken captive. And the priests came, and taught the Samaritans the worship of God, and the plague ceased immediately.

CHAPTER LXXX.

THE DESTRUCTION OF SENNACHERIB'S ARMY.

IN the fourteenth year of the reign of Hezekiah, king of Judah, the king of Assyria made war against him and took a great many of his cities. This was not the same king of Assyria who had destroyed the kingdom of Israel, but his successor, Sennacherib. When Sennacherib laid siege to Jerusalem, Hezekiah sent ambassadors promising him large presents if he would withdraw his army. Sennacherib took the presents, and then treacherously refused to raise the siege. He himself, indeed, crossed over to Egypt with a portion of his army to fight against the king of that country, but he left behind him a great number of men under his general, Rab-shakeh, commanding him to destroy Jerusalem.

Rabshakeh, with several of his captains, came close up to

the walls of Jerusalem, and commanded the people to give up their town to him if they did not wish his army to destroy it utterly.

The people were frightened at these words, and Hezekiah himself was much troubled. He rent his clothes and fell on his face, and besought God to assist him. He sent messengers also to a great prophet, whose name was Isaiah, asking him what he should do. And Isaiah returned answer, "God will destroy thy enemies, and they shall be beaten without fighting, and shall go home sorry and ashamed, and without that insolence they now show. And as for Sennacherib, he shall fail of his purpose against Egypt, and when he comes home he shall perish by the sword."

Everything happened as the prophet had foretold, for Sennacherib hastily retreated from Egypt on learning that a great army was coming to assist the king of that country, and when he joined his general, Rabshakeh, before Jerusalem, he found that on the very first night of the siege a grievous distemper had been sent down by God upon the Assyrians, so that one hundred and eighty-five thousand perished in one night.

So the king was in great fear, and fled with what remained of his forces to his own country and to his city, Nineveh. A little while after he was treacherously killed by his own son.

CHAPTER LXXXI.

MANASSEH AND AMON, KINGS OF JUDAH.

Hezekiah died after he had reigned twenty-nine years, and he was succeeded by his son Manasseh. But Manasseh, instead of following in the footsteps of Hezekiah, abandoned himself to all the wicked practices of those kings of Israel whom God had exterminated. Therefore God allowed the king of Babylon and Chaldea to invade Judea with a mighty army and lay waste the country. And Manasseh himself was brought captive to Babylon. Then it was that Manasseh repented of his sin and turned to God, praying Him to render his enemy humane and merciful. God heard his prayer, and granted him what he prayed for. For Manasseh was released by the king of Babylon and returned to Jerusalem.

He showed that his repentance was sincere, for he turned from all false worships, consecrated the temple anew, and re-established the sacrifices according to the law of Moses. But when he died, his son Amon, who succeeded to the throne, imitated only the youthful wickedness of his father, and it was not long before he reaped his reward. For he had reigned only two years when he was slain by a conspiracy of his own servants.

CHAPTER LXXXII.

JOSIAH, KING OF JUDAH.

THE people punished the murderers of Amon and gave the kingdom to his son Josiah, who was eight years old at the time. Josiah was a wise and good youth, and when only twelve years of age he exhorted the people to leave off the worship of idols and return to their own God. And he went about the country and threw down all the altars that were devoted to false gods, and destroyed the idols. He also caused the temple to be repaired, for during the reigns of his father and his grandfather it had been falling into decay. And while they were repairing the temple one of the priests came across the sacred books of Moses, that had been laid there and wellnigh forgotten by every one. He gave them to a scribe, named Shaphan, with orders to take them to the king. The king caused them to be read to him, and when he had heard what was said about those who transgressed the laws, he rent his clothes and was sore distressed, and sent messengers to a prophetess, named Huldah, begging that she would pray to God and appease His anger. "For," said the king, "on account of the sins of the kings who came before me, I fear that the race of the Jews has incurred the wrath of the Lord, and that He will punish us all and cast us out of our country."

And Huldah sent back word to the king that God had already delivered sentence against the Jews on account of the many sins they had committed, and it was too late now to change His purpose; but that on account of the virtue of Josiah He would not cast the Jews out while he was alive, but would wait for a later generation.

When this message was delivered to the king, he ordered all the people, including the women and the children, to come to Jerusalem. And he read them the holy books, and asked them all to take a solemn oath that they would worship God and keep the laws of Moses, and they all did so. Then the king slew all the false prophets that remained in the land, and he went into the country where the Israelites had lived, and, after burning the bones of the false prophets upon the altars built by Jeroboam, he destroyed those altars and all other buildings which the Israelites had raised in honor of strange gods. And in this way was fulfilled the prophecy of Jadon, given in the reign of Jeroboam. And when all the land had been purged, he called the people together to celebrate the feast of the Pass-over.

After Josiah had reigned prosperously for thirty-one years he was slain in a battle against Neco, king of Egypt. His son Jehoahaz then proclaimed himself king, but Neco made

him a prisoner, and caused a brother of his, whose name
he changed from Eliakim to Jehoiakim, to be installed king
in his place. Then Neco returned to his own country, carrying with him Jehoahaz, who died soon after.

CHAPTER LXXXIII.

THE INVASION OF NEBUCHADNEZZAR.

AFTER Jehoiakim had been king for four years, Nebuchadnezzar, the king of Babylon, marched against him with a great
army, and threatened to destroy the country unless Jehoiakim
would pay him a large sum of money every year. Jehoiakim
was frightened, and agreed to do this. But the third year
afterwards he heard that Nebuchadnezzar was about to fight
with the Egyptians, so he did not pay his tribute that year,
hoping the Egyptians would be victorious.

In vain did the prophet Jeremiah warn him against putting
his trust in the Egyptians, and foretell that Jerusalem would
be overthrown by the king of Babylon, who would take Jehoiakim captive. Jeremiah wrote down all his prophecies in
a book, and read them to the people in the temple. When
the rulers heard of this, they took the book from him and
brought it to the king. And the king ordered that it should
be read to him. But he was angry when he found what the
book contained, and tore it up and threw it into the fire.

Nebuchadnezzar came against the city, as the prophet had
foretold, and took it, and slew the king, Jehoiakim, and made
his son Jehoiachin king in his place. But afterwards Nebuchadnezzar repented of having put Jehoiachin on the throne,
fearing that he would endeavor to avenge his father's death,

so he displaced him and made Zedekiah king instead, having first made him promise that he would always be faithful to him. Zedekiah was a brother of Jehoiakim. He was not a bad man naturally, but was weak, and could easily be persuaded to do evil. He allowed his courtiers and his people to sin against the laws of Moses, and he worshipped false gods himself. Jeremiah came often to him and warned him that if he did not leave off his transgressions great calamities would fall upon him and his people, and the king of Babylon would destroy their cities and carry their people into bondage. And another prophet, named Ezekiel, also prophesied that God would punish him. Now, Zedekiah did not believe these prophets, because, although they agreed in all other points, they seemed to disagree in one thing, for Jeremiah said that Zedekiah " would be carried a captive to Babylon," while Ezekiel said that " he would not see Babylon." So Zedekiah flattered himself that neither prophet spoke the truth.

After Zedekiah had been king eight years he broke his promise to Nebuchadnezzar, and allied himself with the king of Egypt, who was fighting against Babylon. Nebuchadnezzar gathered up an army, and, having defeated the Egyptians, marched against Jerusalem.

The prophet Jeremiah had been thrown into prison by his enemies, but he did not cease to exhort the multitude to open their gates to the king of Babylon and trust to his mercy, for if they resisted the city would surely be taken, and they would suffer the worst at the hands of their conquerors. Then his enemies came to Zedekiah and accused the prophet of giving counsel to the people, and they persuaded the king to deliver him into their hands. And they came into the prison and took him and let him down into a pit full of mire, that he might be suffocated there. And he stood up to his neck in the mire, and would surely have perished if one of the king's servants had not obtained permission to draw him out again.

For the king was so weak and good-natured that it was easy to make him change his mind.

For eighteen months Nebuchadnezzar besieged Jerusalem, and then the city could no longer hold out against him. And when Zedekiah saw that all was lost, he took his wives and his children and his captains and his friends, and with them fled out of Jerusalem by night. But at daybreak the Babylonians overtook the fugitives near Jericho, and they seized the king and his wives and children, but let the rest escape. So Zedekiah was brought before Nebuchadnezzar. And Nebuchadnezzar reproached Zedekiah for having broken his promises to him who had made him ruler over Judea. Then he ordered the children of Zedekiah to be slain in the presence of their father, and he put out the eyes of Zedekiah, and bound him, and carried him to Babylon. Thus the prophecies both of Jeremiah and of Ezekiel were fulfilled, for the king of Judea was brought captive to Babylon, yet he did not see that city.

The general of Nebuchadnezzar's army was ordered to pillage the temple and the royal palace, and afterwards to set fire to them, and to overthrow the whole city to its foundations. And he did as he was told, so that not a stone remained in its place. He also carried away captive all the people of Jerusalem who were not slain, except a few of the poor of the land, who were left to work in the fields and vineyards. The gold and silver and all the treasures of the temple and the royal palace were taken to Babylon, and Nebuchadnezzar dedicated the holy vessels to the service of his own gods.

And thus the kingdom of Judah came to an end.

CHAPTER LXXXIV.

THE MURDER OF GEDALIAH.

NEBUCHADNEZZAR made a man named Gedaliah ruler over the handful of people who were left in Judea. He was a good man, and ruled justly. He took Jeremiah out of prison, and treated him kindly, and suffered him to live in the city of Mizpah, as he wished to do. Now, there were a certain number of the Jews who had fled from Jerusalem when it was taken. Hearing that the Babylonians had gone, they returned to their own country and submitted to the rule of Gedaliah. But there was among them a man named Ishmael, who was of the royal family of David, and he determined to wrest the government from Gedaliah. So he came with ten men to the house of Gedaliah, and Gedaliah, suspecting nothing, invited him and his men to dinner. But after they had eaten they rose up and slew the governor, and Ishmael fled to the land of the Ammonites.

The Jews were angry at what Ishmael had done, and were also greatly afraid, thinking the king of Babylon would avenge the death of his governor. They came in their distress to Jeremiah, and asked him what they should do. Jeremiah advised them to remain in Judea. But though they had asked his counsel, they would not accept it after he had given it, and they all removed into Egypt, carrying Jeremiah with them. So the land of Judah was left desolate and without any inhabitants.

CHAPTER LXXXV.

DANIEL.

NEBUCHADNEZZAR, king of Babylon, chose from among the captive Jews a number of young men who were strong and handsome and of good understandings. He handed them over to the care of tutors, and had them instructed in the language of the Babylonians and the Chaldeans, and in all the wisdom of the learned men of those nations. Among these youths were four princes of the house of Zedekiah, whose names were Daniel, Ananis, Misael, and Azarias, but Nebuchadnezzar changed their names, respectively, to Balthaser, Shadrach, Meshach, and Abednego. Daniel, however, is generally known by his Jewish name, while the others are mentioned in history by the names which Nebuchadnezzar gave them.

Daniel and his kinsmen disdained luxury, and determined to live only on fruit and vegetables. So they asked the servant who was over them to take for himself the meat and wine that was sent them from the king's table, and to leave them only the simple food. But the servant was afraid, saying that they would grow thin and pale, and the king would discover what he had done and be very angry with him.

"Nay," said the youths; "try us for ten days on the simple food, and if we then look less fat and healthy than the other young men, you may give us the meat and wine."

The servant agreed to this, and at the end of ten days the four youths looked fatter and heartier than the rest of the young men who were fed from the king's table. So the servant continued to keep for himself the meat and wine, and gave them only fruit and vegetables. And God was with them, so that they readily acquired all the learning of the Babylonians and the Chaldeans, as also of the Jews. Daniel was especially favored, so that God revealed to him the meaning of dreams and visions.

Now one night King Nebuchadnezzar dreamed a wonderful dream, and while he was still sleeping God explained the meaning of his dream to him. But when he awoke he forgot both the dream and its interpretation. He was much troubled, and sent for all the wise men and the prophets among the Chaldeans, and asked them to tell him his dream and its interpretation. The wise men told him that he asked what was impossible, but that if he would tell them the dream they would give him the interpretation. But Nebuchadnezzar threatened to put all the wise men to death, with their disciples and pupils, unless they could tell him both the dream and its meaning. When Daniel heard this, and that he and his kinsmen were in danger, he sent word to the king to put off the slaughter of the wise men for one night, for that he hoped within that time to obtain by prayer to God a knowledge both of the dream and of its meaning. And the king consented to this.

Daniel retired to his own house with his kinsmen, and prayed all that night to God. And God heard his prayer, and revealed to him the dream and its interpretation.

Early next morning the king sent for Daniel, who came joyfully into his presence. And he said,—

"O king, thou didst see in thy sleep a great image. Its head was of gold, its shoulders and arms of silver, its belly and thighs of brass, but the legs and the feet of iron. Then there fell a stone from the mountain upon this image and threw it down and broke it to pieces, so that the gold, the silver, the iron, and the brass were ground into powder, and the wind blew them away, no one could tell where. But the stone grew so large that the whole earth seemed to be filled with it. This was thy dream. The interpretation is as follows: The head of gold denotes thee and the kings of Babylon that have been before thee; the two hands and arms signify this, that thy kingdom shall be conquered by two kings, but the government of these kings shall also be destroyed by another king, who shall come from the west armed with brass, and another government that shall be like unto iron shall put an end to the power of the western king, and shall have dominion over all the earth, on account of the nature of iron, which is stronger than gold, or silver, or brass." *

When Nebuchadnezzar heard this and recollected that it was indeed his dream, he was astonished, and fell on his face before Daniel and saluted him as if he were a god. And he appointed Daniel and his kinsmen rulers under him of his whole kingdom.

But soon afterwards the three kinsmen of Daniel incurred the anger of Nebuchadnezzar. For that king made a great statue of gold and set it up on a plain in the province of Babylon. And he commanded all the principal men and the rulers in his dominions to come to the plain, and when the trumpet sounded they were to bow down and worship the statue. Those who refused to do this should be cast into a fiery furnace. The trumpet sounded, and every one obeyed the command of the king except Shadrach, Meshach, and Abednego,

---

* Josephus here adds, "Daniel did also declare the meaning of the stone to the king, but I do not think proper to relate it, since I have only undertaken to describe things past or things present, but not things that are future," and he refers any one that may be curious about the matter to the book of Daniel. Now Daniel explained the stone to mean that God would set up another kingdom which should destroy all other kingdoms that were before it, but should never be destroyed itself. Wise men are agreed that this is a reference to the kingdom of Christ. Josephus wrote his book for the Romans, and he feared to offend them if he foretold the destruction of their empire.

who said they could not offend in this way against the laws of their country. They were brought before the king, and he had them cast into the fiery furnace. But God saved them in a surprising manner, for the fire would not burn them. This great miracle recommended them still more to the king, who now saw that the blessing of God was upon them ; therefore he released them from the furnace, and they continued in great esteem with him.

Some time after this Nebuchadnezzar dreamed another dream, which meant that he should be despoiled of his kingdom and should pass seven years in the desert with wild beasts, after which he would return to his kingdom. No one of the wise men could tell him what the dream meant, except Daniel, and Daniel's interpretation came true.

After Nebuchadnezzar had reigned for forty-three years, he died, and was succeeded by Evil-Merodach, his son.

CHAPTER LXXXVI.

BELSHAZZAR'S FEAST.

ONE of the successors of Nebuchadnezzar in the kingdom of Babylon was named Belshazzar. He was the great-great-grandson of Nebuchadnezzar. After he had ruled for seventeen years, Cyrus, the king of Persia, and Darius, the king of Media, made war against him.

Belshazzar made a great feast in his palace, to which he invited all his lords. And he commanded his servants to bring in the holy vessels which Nebuchadnezzar had taken from the temple of Jerusalem, and to place them on the table, so that he and his lords and his wives might drink out of them. And while all the company were drinking and praising their own idols, they saw a hand come out of the wall, and it wrote certain words upon the wall. But no one could read the words or understand what they meant, though the king called for all the prophets and wise men to come to the palace. Then Belshazzar was greatly disturbed, and he caused it to be proclaimed throughout the country that if any one could read the writing on the wall and explain its meaning, the king would give him a chain of gold and clothe him in purple, which was the royal color, and give him a third of all his dominions. And many wise men were tempted by these offers, but when they came and saw the writing they could not read it.

The king's grandmother saw how greatly distressed he was, and she came to him and said that there was an old man among the Jews whose name was Daniel, who was of great sagacity, and had explained to Nebuchadnezzar many things that were known to no other man. Belshazzar sent for Daniel to come to him, and he repeated his promises to him if he would interpret the writing on the wall. But Daniel told him to keep his gifts, for he would explain the writing without requiring any reward. And Daniel said the words were Greek, and were as follows: Maneh, Thekel, Phares.

"Maneh," Daniel explained, "means a number, and it signifies that the number of years which God hath appointed for thy kingdom have nearly expired. Thekel means a weight, for God hath weighed thy kingdom in a balance and finds it going down already. Phares means a fragment, for God will break thy kingdom into pieces and divide it among the Medes and the Persians."

And what Daniel had foretold came true. For soon afterwards Babylon was taken by the Medes and the Persians, and Belshazzar himself was carried away into captivity.

CHAPTER LXXXVII.

DANIEL IN THE LIONS' DEN.

DARIUS treated Daniel with great respect, and brought him to Media, where he made him one of his chief rulers. But the other rulers were jealous of Daniel, and determined to rid themselves of him. They noticed that he prayed to God three times a day, so they came to the king, and said,—

"O king, the princes and governors of thy people have determined among themselves to pass a law that for the space of thirty days no one among them is to offer a petition or prayer either to the king or to the gods, and whoever disobeys this law shall be cast into a den of lions to be destroyed."

The king suspected no evil, and he agreed to this law and signed it. Every one obeyed except Daniel, who continued his daily prayers in the sight of all. Then the princes came to Darius and accused Daniel of having transgressed the law, and said that he ought to be cast into the den of lions. Though the king was much grieved, he could do nothing to save Daniel, for the laws of the Medes and Persians could not be altered. So he ordered his servants to cast Daniel into a den of lions, and a great stone was rolled over the entrance. Darius sealed up the stone with his own seal, so that no one could roll it away without breaking the seal, and he then returned to his palace in great distress, so that he could neither eat nor sleep. As soon as it was day, Darius rose and went to the cave. He found the stone in its place and the seal unbroken. Then he rolled away the stone and cried out in a loud voice to Daniel, asking him if he were still alive.

And Daniel answered that he was alive and had received no hurt from the wild beasts. And the king ordered him to come forth out of the den.

But the enemies of Daniel would not acknowledge that he had been saved by the hand of God, and they said that some one had given food to the lions, so that they were not hungry, and that was the reason Daniel had not been touched. Then the king said that he would prove if this were so or not. So he ordered a quantity of food to be thrown to the lions, and when they had eaten of it and had satisfied their hunger, he caused the enemies of Daniel to be cast into the den. And the lions fell upon these men and devoured them. So it appeared plain to Darius that it was God who had spared Daniel from their fury.

After this Daniel was held in greater honor than ever. The Lord also sent him visions and revelations of the future, and Daniel wrote these visions down and explained what they meant, and everything came to pass as Daniel had predicted.

CHAPTER LXXXVIII.

THE DELIVERY OF THE JEWS FROM BONDAGE.

Cyrus made himself king over Babylon, which he had conquered, in the seventieth year of the captivity of the Jews in that country. Now, Jeremiah the prophet had predicted that after the Jews had been held in bondage for seventy years they would be restored again to the land of their fathers and rebuild the temple. And more than two hundred years before this time Isaiah had mentioned Cyrus by name

as a mighty conqueror, to whom the Lord would give dominion over many nations, and who would cause a temple to be
built in Jerusalem to the Lord.

It happened one day that Cyrus was reading the book of
Isaiah, and he marvelled greatly at the prophecy, and an earnest desire seized upon him to fulfil what was so written. And
he wrote to all the people in Asia, and said,—

"Thus saith Cyrus the king: since God Almighty hath
appointed me to be king of all the earth, I believe that He is
that God which the nation of the Israelites worship, for, indeed, He foretold my name by the prophets, and that I
should build Him a house in Jerusalem, in the country of
Judea."

Then Cyrus called together all the principal men among
the Jews that were in Babylon, and told them that he gave
them leave to return to their own country and to rebuild
Jerusalem and their temple, and that he would be their assist-
ant, and would make the rulers and governors in the neighborhood of Judea contribute gold and silver for the building
of the temple.

Then the rulers of the Jews, and the priests and the Levites, and all the others who were willing to go, made ready
to start on their journey. Cyrus sent back to them the holy
vessels which Nebuchadnezzar had taken out of the temple
and carried to Babylon.

Now, the number of those that returned out of captivity
to Jerusalem was forty-two thousand four hundred and sixty-
two.

As soon as they reached Jerusalem they commenced rebuilding the temple. But their neighbors the Samaritans
were jealous and angry, for they feared the Jews would become a great nation again. And when Cyrus died, not long
afterwards, they wrote to his son Cambyses, and told him that
the Jews were a proud and rebellious race, and that if they
became powerful again they would not submit to the rule of

the Persians nor pay them tribute, but would strive to overthrow them. Cambyses believed what they said, and he made
the Jews stop their work on the temple. Cambyses reigned
for six years, and a few months after his death Darius was
elected to succeed him.

In the first year of his reign Darius made a great feast,
to which all the lords and rulers of his kingdom were invited. And after the king had eaten and drunk he went to
bed, but, being unable to sleep, he fell into conversation with
his three guards, and told them he wished to have a question
answered: "What were the strongest of these four things,
wine, kings, women, or truth?" He would give them all
night to think over what answer they should make.

"And whoever," he said, "shall speak most wisely and
truthfully in reply to this question, shall put on a purple
garment, and drink from cups of gold, and have a chariot
with bridles of gold, and a chain of gold about his neck,
and sit next to me and be called my cousin."

Then Darius went to sleep, but in the morning he sent for
his great men, the princes and the rulers of Persia and Media,
and gathered them round him in the room where he used
to give audience, and bade each of the guards to tell their
answers.

The first of the guards said that wine was the strongest of
all things, because it could intoxicate the mightiest king as
well as the meanest slave, and put both on the same level, so
that the king could no longer command, nor would the slave
obey; and it made men forget for a time all their greatest
sorrows and afflictions, and when they came out of their
drunkenness they forgot what they had done while they were
in that state.

Then the second of the guards spoke up and said that
kings were the mightiest of all things, for they rule over men,
and men are the most powerful of all living beings. Men
command all other animals and force them to obey them, but

men in their turn are forced to obey the commands of their kings. Therefore kings are the mightiest of all things.

Now the third guard was a Jew, whose name was Zorobabel. He was a grandson of Jehoiachin, the king of Judah, whom Nebuchadnezzar had brought captive to Babylon, and was, therefore, a prince of the house of David. When the second guard had stopped speaking, Zorobabel rose and said that wine and kings were mighty indeed, but women were mightier. For women were the mothers and wives of kings as well as of the men that planted vines, and therefore it was owing to women that there were kings and vines in the world. Moreover, the greatest kings were ruled by their wives and would do anything to please them.

"But, mighty as women are," continued Zorobabel, "both women themselves and the king himself are weaker than truth. For though the earth be large, and the heaven high, and the course of the sun swift, yet are all these moved according to the will of God, who is true and righteous. And all things else, however strong they may be, are mortal and short-lived, but truth is immortal and eternal."

The assembly cried aloud that Zorobabel had spoken the most wisely of the three. And the king himself was so much pleased with Zorobabel's answer that he commanded him to ask for something over and above what he had promised, for that he would give it to him on account of his wisdom. When he had said this, Zorobabel put him in mind of a vow he had made in case he should ever possess the kingdom. Now, this vow was to rebuild Jerusalem and to restore the temple of God.

"I only ask," said Zorobabel, "that you will keep this vow which you have sworn."

Darius was pleased with what he said, and rose and embraced him, and told him it should be as he wished. Then the king wrote to the rulers throughout his dominions, asking them to give free passage to Zorobabel and all those that were with him till they had reached Jerusalem. He sent letters also to the governors of Syria and Phœnicia, ordering them to make their subjects cut down the cedar-trees on Mount Lebanon and carry them to Jerusalem, and he proclaimed that all prisoners who were willing to go to that city to help in rebuilding the temple should be set at liberty. And the king made the Samaritans and other neighboring nations pay large sums of money to the Jews. And all that Cyrus intended to do before him relating to the restoration of Jerusalem Darius now ordained should be done.

So Zorobabel started out joyfully with a great number of the Jews that had not gone in the first journey to Jerusalem. The work on the temple was taken up again, and progressed very fast. Now, the Samaritans were a deceitful people, who pretended to be very friendly to the Jews when they saw them in prosperity, but were always enemies to them in their distress. So they came to Zorobabel and the rulers of the Jews, and said to them, " Let us help you in rebuilding the temple and be partners with you in its ownership, for we worship the same God that you do, and have offered sacrifices to Him ever since the king of Assyria gave us the land of Israel to live in."

When they had said this, Zorobabel and Joshua the highpriest and the rulers of the Jews answered that they could not let them be their partners in rebuilding the temple, but that when it was finished the Samaritans would have the same privilege as all other men to come and worship in the temple if they felt so disposed.

Then the Samaritans were angry, and they wrote to Darius as they had before written to Cambyses ; but Darius would not listen to them, and the building of the temple was allowed to proceed.

At the end of seven years it was completed, and solemn sacrifices were offered upon the altars. The time for celebrating the feast of the Passover was now at hand, and the

Jews came in great crowds to Jerusalem from all their villages and cities, and kept the feast for seven days with great joy.

CHAPTER LXXXIX.

ESDRAS.

WHEN Darius died, his son Xerxes took the kingdom. There was a Jew named Esdras, who was one of those that had remained in Babylon when his brethren returned to the city of their fathers. He was a priest, and very learned in the laws which God had given to Moses. Being anxious that his countrymen should live in accordance with these laws, he determined to go to Jerusalem to see that they were fully and firmly established. So, having asked and obtained permission from King Xerxes, he set out with a company of some six or seven thousand Jews who also wished to return to the holy city. It took them four months to cross the desert. Besides carrying with them a great many gold and silver vessels, Esdras and his friends had letters from the king ordering many of the governors of the countries near Judea to pay him sums of money.

On reaching Jerusalem, Esdras and his friends sacrificed to the Lord at the temple, and thanked Him for the care He had taken of them during their journey. Then some of the men of Jerusalem came to Esdras and told him that many of the people, including the rulers and the priests and the Levites, had offended against the law of Moses and taken heathen women for their wives. And they prayed Esdras to do all he could to enforce the laws, for otherwise God might be angry with all the people and punish them severely.

When Esdras heard this, he rent his garments and tore his

hair, and sat down in great distress. He feared that if he told the men to put away their heathen wives they would not obey him. And he knew very well that if they continued to live with these wives they would learn to worship idols and to commit sin as their fathers had done. All those who served God and respected the laws came to Esdras and grieved with him. And after a little while Esdras rose, and stretched out his arms to heaven, and prayed, saying,—

"I am ashamed, O Lord, to look up to heaven, because of the sins the people have committed, for they have forgot ten the punishments which Thou didst visit upon their fathers. But Thou, O Lord, who hast saved a remnant of Thy people out of captivity in Babylon, and hast restored them to Jeru- salem and to their own land, take pity on them, I beseech Thee, and forgive them what they have done."

After Esdras had said this he left off praying. And there came to him great numbers of men and women and children, weeping on account of the sins that had been done. Then one whose name was Jechonias, a principal man in Jerusalem, spoke to Esdras, and said,—

"We have sinned in marrying strange wives; therefore do thou order that all these wives be cast off, with the children that were born of them; and if any do not obey the law, let them be punished."

Esdras listened gladly to this advice, and he made the priests and the Levites and the heads of the people swear that they would put away those wives and children, according to the advice of Jechonias. And word was sent through all the land that the people should come to Jerusalem within three days, and if any man did not come, his property would be taken away from him. The people came together in this way, and Esdras told them they had sinned in taking strange wives, and that God would not forgive them unless these wives and the children that were born of them were put away. Then it was determined by the people that all who had married strange wives should come before the rulers of the towns in which they lived and renounce their wives. And within a month all the Jews had done as was determined. In order to appease God they offered sacrifices and slew rams as burnt-offerings.

A little while after, at one of the great feasts, the people all came to the temple and desired that Esdras should there read to them the laws of Moses. Accordingly, he stood in the midst of the multitude and read the laws from morning to noon. When the people heard the words of God, and remembered how many times they had offended against them, they were troubled, and wept. But Esdras bade them not weep, for it was a festival, when it was not lawful to lament, and he told them to go home and feast and rejoice, but to determine never again to fall into those sins.

And when Esdras had lived to a good old age he died, and was buried in Jerusalem.

CHAPTER XC.

NEHEMIAH THE CUP-BEARER.

THERE was a Jew, named Nehemiah, who lived in Susa, the capital of the Persian kingdom, and was cup-bearer to King Xerxes. As this man was one day out walking, he heard some strangers that were entering the city after a long journey speaking to each other in the Jewish language, so he went to them and asked them whence they came.

They told him, " From Judea."

Then he asked them in what state were the people and the city.

" They are in a bad state," answered the strangers, " for

the walls of the city have not yet been rebuilt, nor the gates set up, and the neighboring nations do the people a great deal of mischief."

Hereupon Nehemiah shed tears out of pity for the calamities of his countrymen; and, looking up to heaven, he said,—

"How long, O Lord, wilt thou overlook our nation while it suffers so great miseries, and while we are made the prey and the spoil of all men?"

And while he lamented thus, he was told that the king was going to sit down to supper; so he made haste, and went as he was, without washing himself, to minister to the king in his office of cup-bearer. But as the king was very pleasant after supper, and more cheerful than usual, he cast his eyes on Nehemiah, and, seeing him look sad, he asked him why he was sad. Nehemiah prayed to God to give him favor and afford him the power of persuading by his words, and said,—

"How can I, O king, appear otherwise than sad, when I hear that the walls of Jerusalem, the city in which my fathers are buried, are thrown down to the ground, and that its gates are consumed by fire? but do thou grant me the favor to go and build its walls, and to finish the building of the temple."

And the king granted him what he asked, and told him that he should carry an epistle to the governors, that they might pay him due honor, and afford him whatsoever assistance he wanted.

"Leave off thy sorrow, then," said the king, "and be cheerful in the performance of thy office hereafter."

So Nehemiah worshipped God, and gave the king thanks for his promise, and forgot his sorrow. Next day the king called for him, and gave him a letter to the governor of Syria and Phœnicia and Samaria, ordering him to pay due honor to Nehemiah, and to supply him with what he wanted for his building.

Nehemiah went to Babylon, and took with him many of his countrymen, and set out for Jerusalem, reaching it in the twenty-fifth year of the reign of Xerxes. He called together all the people to the city, and stood in the midst of the temple, and told them that he had come with the permission of the king of Persia to rebuild the wall of their city, and he exhorted them all to assist him. Then he gave orders that the rulers should measure the wall, and divide the work of it among the people, according to their ability. And when he had added this promise, that he himself, with his servants, would assist them, he dissolved the assembly. So the Jews prepared for the work.

But when the Ammonites, and Moabites, and Samaritans, and all who inhabited the neighboring countries, heard that the walls were going up again, they determined to do what they could to interfere with the builders. They attacked and slew many of them, and they frequently endeavored to kill Nehemiah himself. But Nehemiah took great care of his own safety, and set a number of men around himself as a guard to his body ; not that he feared death, but because he knew that if he were dead the walls of the city would never be raised. He also gave orders that the builders should have their armor on while they were building, and their swords by their sides. And at the distance of every five hundred feet trumpeters were placed, who were to give a signal whenever the enemy approached, so that the builders might be ready to receive them. In spite of all discouragements, therefore, the work went on apace, and in two years and four months the walls were finished. And when Nehemiah had done many other things which were worthy of commendation, he came to a great age, and then died.

CHAPTER XCI.

THE STORY OF ESTHER.

AFTER the death of Xerxes, the kingdom of Persia passed into the hands of his son, Artaxerxes. In the third year of his reign Artaxerxes made a costly feast for his friends and for the princes of his kingdom, which lasted for one hundred and eighty days. After this he made a feast for the rulers of other nations and for their ambassadors, which lasted seven days. The way in which this feast was celebrated was as follows: Artaxerxes caused a great tent to be pitched, which was supported by pillars of gold and silver, with curtains of linen and purple spread over them, and this tent was large enough for many ten thousands to sit down in. The cups out of which the guests drank were of gold adorned with precious stones; but Artaxerxes gave orders that, while the wine was to be given in such abundance that every one might drink all he wanted, no one was to be forced to drink, for it was the custom in Persia to oblige every one to drink to excess at a public feast.

Vashti, the queen, also made a feast for the women in the king's palace. Now, on the seventh day of the king's feast, being merry with wine, he was desirous of showing the queen to those that feasted with him, because he was proud of her beauty, which exceeded that of all other women. So he sent a messenger to command her to appear before him. The laws of Persia forbid any woman to be seen by strangers without a veil over her face, and Vashti, out of regard to these laws, refused to obey the king. Then Artaxerxes was

so angry that he broke up the entertainment, and he called
to him the wise men of his kingdom, and accused the queen
of disobedience, and asked how he should punish her.   One
of the wise men answered,—

"Vashti has done wrong not only to thee, O king, but to
all the Persians, for wives will no longer obey their husbands
when they learn that the queen has refused obedience to the
king."

So the wise man told Artaxerxes to punish his queen in
a severe manner, and, when he had done so, to announce the
fact publicly, so that it would be an example to all the people.
And the king decided that he would put away Vashti, and
take another queen in her place.

When Vashti had been put away, messengers were sent
over the land announcing the fact, and also ordering that all
the young and beautiful unmarried women should be sent to
Susa, in order that the king might choose the one he liked
best as his wife.   Among the maidens who came in this way
was a Jewess named Esther.   She was an orphan, and had
been brought up in Babylon by her uncle Mordecai, who was
the principal man among the Jews that had not returned to
their own land.   Now, of all the maidens Esther pleased the
king most; so he chose her out, and made a wedding-feast
for her, and placed a diadem on her head, and she came to
live at the royal palace as his queen.

As Mordecai loved Esther very much, he came from
Babylon to Susa, in order that he might be near her, and obtained employment in the palace.   But he did not let any one
know that he was the queen's uncle, and he advised Esther
not to tell the king that she was a Jewess.

Some time after this, two of the king's servants plotted together to kill Artaxerxes, but Mordecai discovered the plot,
and made it known to the king through Queen Esther.   The
king seized the servants and put them to death.   He gave no
reward to Mordecai at the time, but he bade the scribes set

down his name in the public records, where all the great events of the kingdom were written.

There was at the royal palace a man named Haman, an Amalekite by birth, who was in great favor with the king. All the other servants of the king bowed down to Haman when he appeared in their presence, but Mordecai would not bow down to him. When Haman observed this, he was angry, and he asked, "Who is that man?"

And he was answered, "It is Mordecai the Jew."

Then Haman was still more angry, for he said to himself, "The Persians, who are free men, bow down to me, but this man, who is no better than a slave, will not do so."

He made up his mind to punish Mordecai, and, being himself an Amalekite and an enemy of the Jews, he determined to ask the king to destroy the whole nation. So he came to Artaxerxes, and said,—

"O king, there is a certain wicked nation called the Jews, who are dispersed all over thy kingdom. The men of this nation are the proudest and most unsocial of all men; they will not mingle with other nations, nor worship their gods, and they have laws of their own which they obey, but they will not submit themselves to the laws of thy kingdom. Therefore they are dangerous men, and if thou wilt be a benefactor to thy subjects thou wilt give orders to destroy them utterly."

The king believed what Haman said to him, and told him he might do what he wished to the Jews. So Haman sent out a decree, and sealed it with the king's seal, and this decree ordered that all the Jews in the Persian empire should be put to death, with their wives and children, on a certain day named in the decree. When this decree was brought to the cities and countries over which Artaxerxes ruled, the governors everywhere prepared to carry it out, and everywhere there was great mourning and distress among the Jews.

Mordecai grieved with the rest; but he contrived to let Queen Esther know of the danger that threatened her nation, and he charged her to go to the king's palace and beseech him to save the Jews.

Now, the king had made a law that no one should come into his presence unless he was called, and men with axes in their hands stood around his throne to punish those that came without being summoned. But the king held in his hand a golden sceptre, and if he wished the offender to be spared, he held out his sceptre, and he who touched it was free from danger.

Esther prayed to God for assistance, and fasted for three days. Then she adorned herself as became a queen, and took two of her handmaids with her, and came thus into the presence of the king. But as she saw him sitting on his throne, in all the splendor of his royal robes, she trembled with fear, especially as he looked at her with a severe and angry frown ; her knees failed her, and she fell in a swoon in the arms of her maidens. But God touched the heart of the king, so that he forgot his anger and sprang from his throne and raised the queen, and placed the golden sceptre in her hand. Then he besought her to be of good cheer, for that no harm would befall her. And she, having revived under these soothing words, said to him,—

"My lord, it is not easy for me on the sudden to say what hath happened ; for as soon as I saw thee to be great and comely and terrible, my spirit departed from me, and I had no strength left."

It was with difficulty and in a low voice that the queen could say this, and the king, still anxious to console and support her, told her she might ask any boon of him, even to the half of his kingdom. Then Esther asked that he with his friend Haman should come to a banquet which she had prepared for him. He consented, and sent for Haman, and they went in together to the banquet. And while they were feasting, Artaxerxes asked Esther to let him know what she desired, saying again that he would part with one-half his kingdom for her sake. But she only asked him to come the next day to another banquet, and to bring Haman with him.

Haman went away that day in great joy, because he alone had had the honor of supping with the king at the queen's banquet. But as he passed out of the palace he saw Mordecai, who again refused to bow to him, and Haman was filled with anger. When he reached home, he called to him his wife and his friends, and told them what honor he had enjoyed, not only from the king, but from the queen also, and that he was invited to another banquet on the morrow.

"Yet," said he, "am I not pleased to see Mordecai the Jew in the palace."

Then Haman's wife advised him to give orders that a gallows should be made fifty cubits high, and that in the morning he should ask of the king that Mordecai might be hanged thereon. And Haman commended her advice, and ordered his servants to prepare the gallows in his own court.

That night God took away the king's sleep, and, as he wished to occupy his time with some useful matter, he called to his servant to read to him the book in which was kept the account of what things had happened during his reign. And after the servant had read about many great battles and how the victorious generals had been rewarded for their services, he came at last to the conspiracy which had been discovered by Mordecai. Here the king stopped him, and asked,—

"Is it not put down that Mordecai had a reward given him?"

But the servant answered that it was not so put down.

Then the king bade him leave off his reading, and, finding that it was nearly day, he gave orders that if any of his friends had already come to wait upon him and were standing in the court, the servants should tell him. Now, it happened that Haman was found there, for he had come earlier than usual to petition the king to have Mordecai put to death.

The king at once summoned Haman into his presence, and, when he was come in, he said to him,—

"Because I know thou art one of my best friends, I desire thee to give me advice how I may honor one whom I greatly love in a manner suitable to my magnificence."

Haman at once thought the king meant to honor him, and he answered,—

"If thou wouldst truly honor a man whom thou dost love, give orders that he may ride on horseback clothed in the royal robes and with a gold chain about his neck, and let one of thy intimate friends go before him and proclaim throughout the whole city that in this way doth the king honor those whom he loves."

The king was pleased with this answer, and he said to Haman, "Make haste and take the robes and the chain and the horse, and do to Mordecai the Jew as thou hast said. And because thou art one of my intimate friends and hast given me this advice, do thou go before the horse and make proclamation of the words thou hast advised."

At this unexpected order Haman was confounded, and at first knew not what to do. But he dared not disobey; so he took the king's robes and his horse and his chain, and went to Mordecai and told him what the king had said. Mordecai at first thought that Haman was mocking him, but when he was convinced of the truth of what he said, he put on the royal robes and got on horseback, and was led through the city by Haman. Then Mordecai returned to the palace, but Haman, full of grief and shame, went home and informed his wife and his friends of what had happened. And his wife told him that he would never be able to be revenged on Mordecai, for certainly God was with him.

Just then a servant came and summoned Haman to Esther's banquet. So he sat down with the king and the queen, and after they had all eaten and drunk, Artaxerxes asked Esther what was her request, for he would grant her anything she demanded. Then Esther confessed that she was a Jewess, and said that she and her nation were condemned to death, and besought the king to spare her and them.

The king asked, "Who hath condemned thy people to death?"

Esther answered, "Haman."

The king rose hastily from the table in anger and confusion and went out into the garden to compose himself. Then Haman threw himself down before the queen, begging her to spare his life. But when the king returned and saw him in this position, he was only angrier. Just then the servant who had been sent to summon Haman to the banquet came in and said that he had seen a high gallows in the court of Haman's house, and that when he had inquired who was to be hanged on it, he was answered, "Mordecai the Jew."

The king at once gave orders that Haman should be hanged on the very gallows he had prepared for Mordecai, and Haman was taken out and hanged accordingly.

Then the king told Esther to write letters in his name and to seal them with his seal, and these letters gave permission to the Jews on the day that had been mentioned in the former decree to arm themselves and resist all efforts that might be made for their slaughter, and to slay their enemies. Horsemen were sent all over the kingdom with these letters, and on the appointed day the Jews took down their armor and their weapons, and gathered themselves together in every city, and fought for their lives, and gained the victory over all who came against them. And for two days following they feasted and rejoiced, and the Jews have ever since held those days to be holy days, and celebrate upon them the feast they call Purim.

Mordecai became a great and illustrious person with the king, and assisted him in the government. He also lived with the queen, so that the affairs of the Jews were by their means better than they could ever have hoped for. And this was the state of the Jews during the reign of Artaxerxes.

CHAPTER XCII.

BAGOSES DEFILES THE TEMPLE.

FOR more than a hundred years after the death of Artaxerxes the Persian kings continued to hold dominion over Judea, though they treated the inhabitants kindly and allowed them to be governed by the priests of their own nation. The Jews flourished and grew wealthy and prosperous, but not much is known about them during this period until the reign of another Artaxerxes, called Artaxerxes Mnemon. At that time a man named John succeeded his father Judas as high-priest of Jerusalem. Now, John had a brother named Jesus, who was a friend of Bagoses, the general of the Persian army, and Bagoses had promised to procure the priesthood for Jesus. Jesus and John quarrelled together in the temple, and in his anger John slew Jesus.

God did not neglect to punish this unnatural crime. For when Bagoses heard of it he came to the Jews and said to them in anger,—

"Have you dared to perpetrate a murder in your own temple?"

And as Bagoses was going into the temple the people tried to stop him, saying it was forbidden for any but the priests to enter it. But Bagoses answered,—

" Am I not purer than the dead body of him that was slain in the temple?"

Therefore he pressed on into the sanctuary and defiled it. And he imposed tribute on the Jews, ordering them to pay fifty shekels out of the public treasury for every lamb that was offered in sacrifice during the next seven years.

CHAPTER XCIII.

MANASSEH.

WHEN John died, his son Jaddua succeeded to the high-priesthood. He had a brother whose name was Manasseh. Now there was one Sanballat, whom Darius, the last king of Persia, had sent into Samaria. He was a Cuthean by birth, and the Samaritans also came from the same stock. This man was anxious to live on friendly terms with the Jews, so he gladly gave his daughter in marriage to Manasseh.

But when Jaddua became high-priest the elders among the Jews became very uneasy that Manasseh, who was married to a foreigner, should be associated with him in any priestly duties. For they feared that this man's marriage would encourage others to transgress the law against taking strange wives. So they commanded Manasseh either to put away his wife or not to approach the altar. The high-priest himself joined with the people in their anger against his brother, and drove him away from the altar. Manasseh went to his father-in-law and told him that though he loved his wife he would be forced to give her up. But Sanballat told him that he might keep his wife, and be not only a priest but a high-priest, for that he would write to Darius and obtain from him permission to build another temple on Mount Gerizim, in Samaria, of which Manasseh should be high-priest.

Then Manasseh took up his abode with his father-in-law, and many other priests and Levites who had also offended against the law and married strange wives came and lived with him.

CHAPTER XCIV.

ALEXANDER THE GREAT.

JUST at this time Alexander the Great, king of Macedon, made an expedition into Persia with a great army in order to conquer all the country. Darius came down to meet him, and joined battle with him at a place called Isis, in Cilicia, which is not very far from Judea. All the people in Asia thought that Darius would easily defeat the invaders, whose numbers were comparatively small. Sanballat, therefore, promised his son-in-law that when Darius returned from his victory he would ask his permission to build the temple. But Darius was defeated with great slaughter, and fled back into Persia. Alexander marched forward and took many cities until he came to Tyre, which he besieged. From this place he sent a letter to the high-priest of the Jews asking him for troops and provisions, and calling upon him to transfer his allegiance from Darius to himself. The high-priest answered that he had given his oath to Darius not to bear arms against him, and that he would keep this oath so long as Darius remained in the land of the living.

Upon hearing this answer Alexander was very angry, and threatened that as soon as he had taken Tyre he would march against the Jewish high-priest, and through him teach all men to whom they must keep their oaths.

When Sanballat heard that Darius had been defeated he thought it would be best for him to join the cause of Alexander. So he came to Alexander with seven thousand of the Samaritan warriors, and gladly accepted him for his king in-

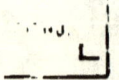

stead of Darius. The kind reception which Alexander gave him encouraged Sanballat to ask permission to build a temple in Samaria, and the permission was given. So the new temple was built, and Manasseh was made high-priest. But before it was finished Sanballat died.

Meanwhile, Alexander had conquered Tyre, after seven months' siege, and after two more months he had taken the city of Gaza also. Then he made haste to go up to Jerusalem to carry out his threat.

When Jaddua heard that Alexander was coming, he was greatly terrified. He ordered his people to join him in sacrifices and in prayers to God. And God appeared to him in a dream, and told him to take courage, and to adorn the city, and let the people clothe themselves in white, while all the priests were to put on the robes of their order, and with the high-priest at their head were to march out of the city to meet the king, for no harm would befall them.

Jaddua awoke rejoicing, and determined to do as he was told. And when he understood that Alexander was not far from the city, he went out in procession with the priests and the people.

Alexander saw the procession coming towards him, and when it had come so close that he could distinguish the features of the high-priest, he ran forward and bowed down before him, and adored the sacred name of God that was written upon his mitre. His generals wondered among themselves, thinking he had suddenly become insane. One of them, named Parmenio, went up to Alexander and asked him the meaning of what he did. Alexander answered,—

"When I was at Dios, in Macedonia, considering how I should conquer Persia, I fell asleep one day, and in a dream I saw this very person, clothed in these same garments, who exhorted me to make no delay, but boldly to pass over the sea, for that the God whom he worshipped would give me dominion over the Persians."

Alexander was escorted into Jerusalem by the high-priest and his attendants, and he went up into the temple and offered sacrifice to God according to the high-priest's directions. And the high-priest brought out the book of Daniel, and showed Alexander the prophecies which declared that the empire of Persia should be destroyed by one of the Greeks. Alexander, delighted with his reception, offered the Jews whatever they should desire. The high-priest asked that his countrymen might be allowed to obey the laws of their forefathers, and also be freed from the tribute which the Persians made them pay every seventh year. Alexander granted these requests, and when the Jews further asked that their brethren in Babylon and Media should be allowed to enjoy their own laws, he agreed to this also. And he said to the people that if any of them would enlist in his army, he would allow them still to continue under their own laws; and many were ready to accompany him in his wars.

Then Alexander left Jerusalem and overran Persia and conquered it. And ten years afterwards he died, and his kingdom was divided among his generals.

CHAPTER XCV.

PTOLEMY SOTOR.

When the empire of Alexander was divided, Egypt fell to the share of one of his generals, named Ptolemy, who was surnamed Sotor. Ptolemy determined to seize the whole of Syria. He advanced against Jerusalem, and cunningly delayed his attack until the Sabbath-day. He knew that all the inhabitants were at rest upon that day, and, moreover, they did not suspect him of being an enemy. So he marched into the city under pretence of wishing to sacrifice on the altars, and, when he once was within the walls, he took possession of it. None of the Jews dared to resist him, for it was against the law to fight on the Sabbath. The conqueror carried away with him a number of captives, whom he settled in Egypt, and, finding them to be good citizens and faithful to their word, he treated them so well that many others of the Jews were induced to come of their own accord to Egypt.

CHAPTER XCVI.

PTOLEMY PHILADELPHUS.

WHEN Ptolemy Sotor had ruled for forty years, he died, and was succeeded by Ptolemy Philadelphus. This king was a great patron of learning. He founded a library in Alexandria, which soon grew to be the most magnificent collection of books in the world. The librarian whom he placed over it was named Demetrius, and he made it his business to buy all the books he could find that were of any value or interest. One day Ptolemy called Demetrius to him and asked him how many ten thousands of books he had collected.

"I have already," answered Demetrius, "about twenty times ten thousand books in the library, but in a little time I shall have fifty times ten thousand."

Then Demetrius went on to say that he understood there were many books of laws among the Jews, which were of great value and would be worth adding to the king's library. "But these books," he said, "are written in the Jewish language and in strange letters, which makes it very difficult for the Greeks to read or understand them. Wherefore I think it would be a good plan to have all these books translated into the Greek language and placed in the library."

Ptolemy was pleased with what Demetrius proposed, and he counselled him to prepare a letter to the high-priest of the Jews about the matter.

Meanwhile, at the advice of one of his friends, named Aristeus, who was a wise and just man, Ptolemy set free the Jews who had been brought captive into Egypt by Ptolemy Sotor, and who now numbered one hundred and twenty thousand.

Then the king ordered a number of gold and silver vessels to be made as a present for the high-priest at Jerusalem, and with these presents he sent a letter telling the priest that he had set free all his countrymen who had formerly been in bondage, and that he only asked in return that he would assist him in having a translation made of the sacred books of the Jews, to be placed in the library at Alexandria.

"Thou wilt, therefore," continued the letter, "do well to choose out and send to me men of a good character, who are elders in age, six in number out of every tribe. And let these be learned men, skilled in the laws, and able to translate them into the Greek language. And when the translation shall be finished, I shall think that I have done a work glorious to myself."

The high-priest at this time was named Eleazar. He was pleased at the king's letter, and he gladly chose out and sent him seventy-two learned men out of the twelve tribes, who carried with them to Alexandria the sacred books of the Jews. When the king heard that the elders had reached the city, he dismissed all other visitors and ordered that they should be brought at once into his presence. And, as the old men came in, he treated them with great respect, and asked them many questions about their books. He also greatly admired the way in which they were written, for they were in letters of gold on thin sheets of parchment, and these sheets were joined together so perfectly that no one could tell where one sheet ended and the other began. He then said that he returned them thanks for coming to him, and still greater thanks to him that sent them, and, above all, to that God whose laws they appeared to be. Then did the elders and those that were with them cry out with one voice and wish all happiness to the king, at which he was so much affected that he wept for joy. And when he had bidden them deliver the books to those that were appointed to receive them, he asked the men to come in and sup with him.

Twelve days afterwards the elders began their translation. They worked in a house that Demetrius had prepared for them. It was built on an island near the sea-shore, and was a quiet place, where they could write and converse together without being interrupted. In seventy-two days all the books of the law were translated and written out in the Greek tongue. Then Demetrius the librarian called together all the Jews that were in Alexandria, and the elders read the translation to them, and they were satisfied with it.

The king rejoiced that the work had been brought to so happy an end, and he was greatly delighted when the laws were read to him, and was astonished at their deep meaning and wisdom. Turning to Demetrius, he asked,—

" How comes it to pass that these laws, which are so wise and wonderful, have never been mentioned by any of our poets or historians ?"

Demetrius answered, " No one has dared to make a description of these laws, because they are divine and venerable, and because some that have attempted it have been afflicted by God."

And then Demetrius spoke of one Theopompus, who had intended to write concerning these laws, but had been afflicted with madness for thirty days, and when he came to his senses, he was told in a vision that his madness fell upon him because he had indulged too great a curiosity about divine matters

and was desirous of publishing them among common men.
Whereupon he appeased God by prayer, and the madness
never visited him again.

"Moreover," continued Demetrius, "the tragic poet Theo-
dectes intended to make mention of things that were contained in the sacred books in one of his dramas, whereupon
he was afflicted with blindness, and, being conscious of the
reason of this disorder, he prayed to God, and was restored to
sight."

The king gave orders to Demetrius that great care should
be taken of the sacred books, so that nothing might ever be
added to or taken away from what was written in them. And
he sent the elders back to their own country with many
handsome presents.

CHAPTER XCVII.

PTOLEMY EUERGETES.

WHEN Ptolemy Philadelphus died, he was succeeded by his
son, Ptolemy Euergetes. During the reign of this monarch
the high-priest in Judea was named Onias. He was a great
lover of money, and he did not like to part with the twenty
talents which the king of Egypt exacted every year from the
high-priest. One year he neglected to pay this tribute. Then
Ptolemy was angry, and sent an ambassador to Jerusalem,
and, when Onias still refused to pay his taxes, the ambassador told the people that the king of Egypt would seize upon
their land and send soldiers to live upon it.

Onias had a nephew, named Joseph, who, though young in
years, was much respected in Jerusalem on account of his
wisdom and prudence. This young man went to Onias, and
reproved him for bringing the nation into danger, telling him

that if he was so great a lover of money as to be unwilling to part with it, he ought at least to go to the king and ask him to remit either the whole or a part of the sum demanded. But Onias answered that he was old and feeble, and did not care to go to the king. He added that he was willing, if necessary, to lay down the priesthood, as he did not care for the dignity any longer. Then Joseph asked his uncle to let him go and interview the king of Egypt in his stead. Onias consented. Joseph went into the temple and called the Jews together, and told them not to be disturbed at what his uncle had done, for that he himself would go to Egypt and explain matters to the king. The people were glad to hear this, and returned joyfully to their homes.

Joseph went down from the temple, and invited the ambassador to come to his house. He feasted him for many days, and gave him rich presents. Then he told him to return to the king, his master, and say that Joseph, the nephew of the high-priest, was coming to excuse the people. The ambassador was much pleased with the frank and generous nature of Joseph, and he promised that he would assist him in every way. On his return to Egypt he gave Ptolemy the message which Joseph had intrusted to him, and he praised the young man so highly that both the king and the queen felt well disposed to him before they had seen him.

Meanwhile, Joseph sent to his rich friends in Samaria and borrowed money from them to help him on his journey. Now, every year the king used to sell the right of collecting his taxes to such as offered the highest sum for the right. This was called farming out the taxes. The person who bought the right of collecting the taxes was entitled to keep for himself all that he could collect. Sometimes he was not able to collect as much money as he had paid for the right, and then, of course, he lost; but usually he collected more than he had paid. When Joseph set out on his journey for Egypt the time had come round for the annual farming of the taxes, and he met many merchants who were going to the court of Ptolemy to contest for the right of collecting the taxes. These men saw Joseph journeying on the way, and laughed at him for his poverty and mean clothing. On arriving at Alexandria, Joseph was told that King Ptolemy was at Memphis, and he hastened thither to meet him. The king happened to be in his chariot with his wife, and with his friend Athenion, the ambassador who had been sent to Onias at Jerusalem. Athenion at once recognized Joseph, and made known to the king who he was, and Ptolemy asked Joseph to come up into his chariot. And as Joseph sat there Ptolemy began to complain of the conduct of Onias. But Joseph answered,—

"Forgive him on account of his age, for thou knowest that old men are like children, and are foolish; but thou shalt have from us, who are young men, everything thou desirest, and shalt have no cause to complain."

The king was pleased with what the young man said; and when he had talked a little longer with him, and found him a sensible and pleasant companion, he invited him to come to the royal palace and stay with him as his guest. And the king returned with Joseph to Alexandria, where the great men of the place were much surprised at the favor bestowed on the young Jew.

On the day on which the taxes were to be farmed out, a great number of bidders came to the palace. The sums which they offered for the right of collecting taxes in the countries under Egyptian rule amounted in all to eight thousand talents. But Joseph stepped forward and said that this sum was too low, and that he would give twice as much. The king was pleased to hear this offer, and said he would sell the right to Joseph. But first he asked him if he had any sureties; that is, men of wealth and position, who would see that Joseph would carry out his promises, or would forfeit the money themselves if he did not do so.

Joseph answered in a firm and pleasant manner,—

" I will give you sureties who will be good and responsible persons, and whom you will have no reason to distrust."

" Who are they ?" asked the king.

" I will give thee," replied Joseph, " no other persons than King Ptolemy and his queen, Cleopatra."

Ptolemy laughed at Joseph's words, and was so well pleased with the jest that he granted him the farming of the taxes without any sureties. This was a sore grief to all the merchants who had come from a distance to bid for the taxes, and they returned crestfallen to their own countries.

Joseph took with him two thousand of the king's foot-soldiers and started out to collect the taxes. Coming to the town of Askelon, in Syria, he demanded that the citizens should pay him what was due. But the citizens refused, and even spoke insultingly to him. Upon which, Joseph seized twenty of the principal men and put them to death. And he took all their gold and silver and sent it to the king, and informed him what he had done. Ptolemy sent back word that he had acted rightly, and that he had his full permission to do as he deemed best in future. When the people of the other cities heard of what had happened in Askelon they were afraid, and they received Joseph with great honor, and paid their taxes to him.

CHAPTER XCVIII.

HYRCANUS, THE SON OF JOSEPH.

FOR twenty-two years Joseph continued to gather the taxes, and as the sum he gathered every year was larger than that which he paid to the king of Egypt, he grew very wealthy. He married and had eight sons, the youngest of whom was named Hyrcanus. Joseph loved Hyrcanus the best of all, for he was good and obedient. All the sons were sent to be taught by learned men who were skilled in training youth, but the only one who profited by this instruction was Hyrcanus, the others being too dull and lazy to learn anything. And once Joseph, to test the cleverness of Hyrcanus, gave him three hundred oxen, and bade him go into the wilderness and sow the land there. But without the lad's knowledge he took away the harness by which the oxen were bound to the ploughs. So when Hyrcanus came to the place which he was to plough he found he had no harness. The men who were with him advised him to send home to his father for the harness. But Hyrcanus told them this would be too great a waste of time. And he slew twenty of the oxen, whose flesh he gave to his men to eat, and used their hides to cut up into leather for the harness. When he had sowed as much land as his father had ordered he returned home. And Joseph received him very gladly, and praised him for what he had done.

This happened when Hyrcanus was about thirteen years of age. Now at this time Ptolemy Philopator, who was the son of Ptolemy Euergetes, was king of Egypt. Joseph was told that the king had a new son born to him, and that all the principal men in Syria and the other countries subject to Egypt were going to Alexandria to assist in celebrating a great feast in honor of the child's birth. Joseph felt that he was too old to make so long a journey himself, but he asked his sons if any of them wished to go. The elder all excused themselves, saying they were not educated, or able to make speeches in public, and that Hyrcanus had better be sent. Joseph gladly listened to their advice, and he called Hyrcanus and asked him if he would go. Hyrcanus said he would. Joseph then said that he would give him money for his journey, and also many handsome presents for the king. But Hyrcanus answered that he himself would need very little money for the journey, and as to the presents, he had better wait until he reached Alexandria, and he could buy the presents there. So he asked his father to give him a letter to one of his stewards, named Arion, who lived in Alexandria, commanding Arion to pay to Hyrcanus whatever sum the latter might require. Joseph agreed to this, and gave him the letter. Then Hyrcanus made haste to Alexandria.

Now, the brothers of Hyrcanus were all envious of him because he was their father's favorite son. So they wrote letters to many of the chief men in Egypt, asking them to put Hyrcanus to death.

The boy, however, arrived safely in Alexandria. He went first to the steward, Arion, and, presenting his father's letter, boldly asked for a thousand talents. This was such a large sum that Arion refused to give it to him. Hyrcanus then complained to the public officer that Arion refused to obey his master Hyrcanus, and had him thrown into prison. Now, the wife of Arion was a friend of Cleopatra, the wife of King Ptolemy, and she at once hastened to the queen, asking her to obtain liberty for Arion.

Cleopatra laid the matter before the king, who summoned Hyrcanus into his presence. When the boy appeared, the king wondered to see how young he was, and he said to him,—

"Since thou hast been sent to me by thy father, Joseph, why didst thou not come into my presence at once? And wherefore hast thou cast into prison thy father's steward, Arion?"

Hyrcanus answered, "I did not come into thy presence at once, O king, because I did not wish to appear there without such gifts as were becoming to thy dignity. And I cast the slave Arion into prison because he refused to obey my orders, for I am his master by my father's appointment, and it matters not whether a master be little or big, his orders should be obeyed. Unless such rebels as these are punished, thou thyself mayst expect to be disobeyed by thy subjects."

Upon hearing this answer the king fell to laughing, and wondered at the great soul of the child.   And he refused to release Arion from prison until he had obeyed Hyrcanus.

Arion, on learning this, gave Hyrcanus a thousand talents, and was let out of prison.   The king was so much pleased with the boy's ready wit that he invited him to dine at the royal palace with the principal men of the kingdom.   These men were jealous of the favor Ptolemy showed to the young Jew, and they endeavored to turn him into ridicule.   When they had eaten, they bade the servants take the bones they had left and place them in a heap in front of Hyrcanus. And they asked the king's jester, who was named Trypho, and whose business it was to make jests at public banquets, to call the king's attention to these bones.

So Trypho went and stood by the king, and said,—

"Dost thou see, my lord, the bones that lie by Hyrcanus? They are an emblem of the manner in which his father, Joseph, stripped all Syria, till it was as bare as Hyrcanus hath made these bones."

The king, laughing at what Trypho had said, turned to Hyrcanus and asked him how he came to have so many bones before him.

"Very rightfully, my lord," answered the boy, "for only dogs eat both flesh and bones, as these thy guests appear to have done ; but men eat the flesh and cast away the bones, as I have done."

The king laughed louder than ever, and he made all the guests join in applauding the jest, so greatly was he pleased with it.   So the men only succeeded in turning themselves into ridicule.

Next day Hyrcanus went to every one of the king's friends and the men who were powerful at court, and, having paid his respects to them, he inquired privately of their servants what presents they intended to make the king on his son's birthday.   Some said they would give twelve talents, and

others more ; but twenty talents was the highest sum named
by any of them. Hyrcanus pretended to every one of them
that he was grieved not to be able to give more than five
talents himself. The servants laughed at him for his poverty,
and they told their masters, who were pleased to think that
Hyrcanus would fall into disgrace with the king on account
of the meanness of his presents.

The day came at last, and all the great men of Egypt and
of the countries subject to Egypt made their appearance, and
gave their presents to the king. None of these amounted to
more than twenty talents in value. But Hyrcanus had secretly
purchased two hundred slaves, half of whom were boys and
half girls. He had dressed them magnificently, and placed a
talent in the hands of each. He now made them come forward, and he presented the boys to Ptolemy and the girls to
Cleopatra. Every one marvelled at the richness of these
gifts, and the king and the queen marvelled the most. Then
Ptolemy in his gratitude told Hyrcanus to ask for anything
he wished and it should be granted to him. Hyrcanus only
asked that the king would write to his father and his brethren
about him. He well knew that they would be angry with
him at what he had done, and he hoped that the king's letter
would protect him from their anger. And when the king
had paid him great respect, and given him very large gifts,
and written, as he had promised, to his father and his brethren, he dismissed him.

On the return of Hyrcanus to Judea his brethren went out
to meet him and kill him, for they were jealous of the favor he
had received from the king. And even his father, because
he was angry at the large sum he had drawn from the steward
Arion, was willing that he should be punished. But when
the brethren attacked Hyrcanus, he defended himself so well
that two of the brethren, with a great many of their men,
were slain, and the rest escaped to Jerusalem. Hyrcanus,
however, fearing for his safety, then withdrew beyond the

Jordan, and became collector for that district. Shortly after his father, Joseph, died. About the same time the high-priest, Onias, died also, and was succeeded by Simon. A contest now arose between the sons of Joseph for the division of their father's wealth, the elder sons refusing to allow Hyrcanus any share of it. The new high-priest sided against Hyrcanus, who again fled beyond the Jordan, to a place called Heshbon, and built himself a magnificent palace there. This was all of white marble, with animals of great size sculptured upon it, and around it ran a deep canal of water. The rocks near the palace were hewn out into chambers and halls for banquets and sleeping-rooms. But none of the doors anywhere were wide enough for more than one man to pass through, lest the master should be surprised by his enemies, his brothers. Here Hyrcanus ruled for seven years, and then, fearing he would fall into the hands of Antiochus Epiphanes, the king of Syria, he put himself to death.

CHAPTER XCIX.

ANTIOCHUS EPIPHANES.

ANTIOCHUS, the king of Syria, mentioned in the last chapter, was surnamed Epiphanes, or the Illustrious, though by some people he was called Epimanes, or the Madman. He succeeded his brother Seleucus on the throne of Syria. Seleucus had been a friend of Ptolemy Epiphanes, and during the reigns of these two monarchs the kingdoms of Syria and Egypt had been at peace with each other. But Ptolemy Epiphanes had died shortly before Seleucus, and his son, Ptolemy Philometor, who succeeded him, was only about twelve years of age. Antiochus thought that he would be able to conquer Egypt on account of the youth of its new king, and he made war against Ptolemy Philometor. He took several cities, and made haste to Alexandria, in hopes of taking it by siege and subduing Ptolemy, who reigned there. But the Romans, who were at this time a mighty nation, sent word to Antiochus that if he did not withdraw from Egypt they would raise a great army and come to the assistance of Ptolemy. And, as Antiochus was afraid of the Romans, he obeyed them at once, and retreated out of Egypt.

Now at this time the affairs of Jerusalem were in great confusion; for the high-priest, Onias III., had died, leaving a son who was too young to take the sacred office. Two of the brothers of Onias had fought among themselves for the high-priesthood. One of these brothers was named Jesus, a name which he had changed to Jason. The other had originally been called Onias also, but had changed his name to Menelaus. Some of the people had taken sides with Jason and others with Menelaus, but Jason had at last succeeded in driving his brother from the kingdom; so Menelaus with several of his friends had fled to Antiochus, and offered him their services if he would lead an army against the Jews. This happened while Antiochus was preparing for his expedition into Egypt; and when the Romans forced him to leave that country he at once marched against Jerusalem. He took it without difficulty, for the friends of Menelaus opened the gates to him; and he slew many of the opposite party, and plundered the city, after which he returned to Syria. Menelaus was allowed to remain high-priest, but two foreign officers were made governors of Judea and Samaria.

Two years afterwards Antiochus returned to Jerusalem with his army, and, having again been admitted within its walls, he treated the inhabitants with great cruelty, not even sparing those that had let him into the city. He killed a number of persons who were known to be friends of Ptolemy, and plundered their houses, as well as the houses of all the other wealthy men. He carried away the treasures in the temple, and put a stop to the sacrifices, and he placed an idol in the temple, and ordered the people to bow down to it and worship it. The altar he polluted by offering up swine on it, well knowing that these animals were considered unclean by the Jews, and that it was against the law of Moses even to eat of their flesh. He also obliged the Jews to do many other unlawful and wicked things, and those who refused to obey him were put to death in cruel ways.

CHAPTER C.

MATTATHIAS.

At this time there was a Jewish priest named Mattathias, who dwelt at a city called Modin. He had five sons, John, who was surnamed Gaddis, Simon, surnamed Mathes, Judas, surnamed Maccabeus, Eleazar, surnamed Auran, and Jonathan, surnamed Apphus. Mattathias lamented to his children the sad state of affairs in Judea, and the ravage of Jerusalem and of the temple, and he told them that it was better for them to die for the laws of their country than to live a shameful life of obedience to their conqueror.

Some of the officers of the king came to Modin to oblige the inhabitants to do what was commanded by him. And because Mattathias was a leading man among them, and the father of a large family, they desired him to begin the sacrifices to false gods. Mattathias said he would not do it, and even if all the others obeyed the commands of Antiochus, he would not obey them, nor would any of his sons obey them.

But another of the Jews came up and sacrificed as Antiochus had commanded. And Mattathias, in great anger, drew his sword and ran at the Jew and killed him. His sons also drew their swords and fell upon the king's soldiers and slew them. Mattathias overthrew the altar to the idol, and cried out in a loud voice,—

"If any one be zealous for the laws of his country and for the worship of God, let him follow me."

Then he and his sons fled to the desert, and a great number of Jews followed him, with their wives and children, and took up their dwelling in caves. The Syrian generals gathered up their forces and marched against them. They surprised one thousand of the Jews in a cave, and attacked them on the Sabbath-day, and, as the Jews would not fight on that day, they were put to death without any resistance. After this, Mattathias and his followers determined that although they would not attack an enemy on the Sabbath, they would hold it lawful, nevertheless, to defend themselves against an attack; since if they did not do this the enemy would always choose that day to fall upon them and kill them, and it would not be long before they were all destroyed.

Mattathias and his men lay hidden in their caves, and every now and then, as opportunity offered, they would come out and pour down upon the towns that were near them, kill the Syrian soldiers, overthrow the heathen altars, and oblige the wicked Jews who had obeyed their conquerors to return to the worship of the true God. The fame of the great deeds of Mattathias was carried all over the land, and men and women from all parts of Judea hastened to the desert to join him. So Mattathias got a great army about him, and after he had been their general for one year he died. With his dying breath he exhorted his sons to continue the good work he had begun, and he told them to choose as his successor his third son, Judas Maccabeus, because he was strong and brave and would lead the army to victory.

CHAPTER CI.

JUDAS MACCABEUS.

JUDAS MACCABEUS was, therefore, chosen general of the Jewish army in the desert. He soon showed that the choice was a wise one, for he won two great victories, first against an army of Samaritans, under a general named Apollonius, and next against an army of Syrians, led by the general Seron. In both these battles a great many of the enemy were slain, and, among others, the generals themselves fell.

A third army, under a general named Ptolemy, was sent against Judas by the Syrians. This army consisted of forty thousand foot-soldiers and seven thousand horsemen, and it was also joined by many of the wicked and cowardly Jews who had been afraid to follow their brethren into the desert. Judas heard that this great army was coming, and he called together his own men and exhorted them to be bold and fear not, and to put their trust in God. But if any among them were afraid, he told them they should leave the ranks, for only brave men were wanted. After counting all that were left, he found he had only three thousand men, most of whom were very poorly armed.

When Ptolemy had reached a city called Emmaus, which was close to the desert inhabited by the Jews, he made his camp there. He determined that he would surprise the rebels, so he sent a general named Gorgias with six thousand soldiers to fall upon the Jews by night. Some wicked Jews, who had deserted from the army of Judas, acted as guides to show Gorgias the way. Judas learned the plan of the

enemy, and he determined that he would secretly leave his
camp and march against the Syrian army at Emmaus and
surprise them.   So at night he stole out of his camp, leaving
the fires burning, and when Gorgias arrived on the spot, he
was much disappointed at finding no one there.   Meanwhile,
Judas about daybreak reached Emmaus with his three thousand men.   The Syrian soldiers had not yet awakened from
sleep.   Judas ordered the trumpets to be sounded, and rushed
down upon the foe.   They awoke in great confusion and disorder, and though a few tried to fight, the rest ran away and
were pursued by the Jews.   More than three thousand were
slain, and the Jews returned rejoicing to the enemy's camp
to seize upon the weapons and the silver and gold that had
been left behind.   And when Gorgias and his soldiers returned and saw from a distance that their camp was in the
hands of the Jews, they also were afraid, and retreated from
the country of Judea.

Still another army was sent against Judas, under a general
named Lysias.   This army consisted of sixty thousand men.
The army of the Jews had now increased to ten thousand.
When Judas saw the great number of his enemies, he prayed
to God to assist him.   Then he joined battle with the first of
the enemy that appeared, and beat them, and slew about five
thousand of them, so that the rest of the army was greatly
terrified.   Lysias himself was alarmed at the brave and desperate way in which the Jews fought, and he called off
his troops and retreated out of the country, determined to
gather together a still greater army and to return in a little
while.

Then Judas called all his people together, and told them
that after these many victories which God had given them
they ought to go up to Jerusalem and purify the temple and
offer sacrifices there.

The people agreed, and Judas led them to Jerusalem.
There were a number of Syrian soldiers in the city, who re-

treated to the citadel and intrenched themselves there. Judas ordered some of his soldiers to lay siege to the citadel. He himself, with the rest of his men, after purifying the temple, celebrated a great feast, which lasted for eight days.

Now the nations around Jerusalem were alarmed to see that the Jews were regaining their liberty and their power, and they rose in arms against them. But Judas and his brethren marched out and defeated them and laid waste their countries.

While he was gaining these victories outside of Jerusalem, Judas found it difficult to overcome the enemies that were in the city. The Syrians still held possession of the citadel, and, as this overlooked the temple, they would frequently rush out and destroy the Jews when they were engaged in the sacrifices. Therefore Judas pressed the siege of the citadel with great vigor. When it seemed as if the Syrians could hardly hold out much longer, some of them escaped by night and went to their own country to ask for assistance. Now, Antiochus Epiphanes had died a short time before, and had been succeeded by his son, who was called Antiochus Eupator. This Antiochus was little more than a boy. He was angry when he heard of all the great successes of the Jews under Judas, and he determined to subdue them. So an army was collected of about a hundred thousand footmen and twenty thousand horsemen and thirty-two elephants.

With this army Antiochus marched into Judea. Judas, at the head of his forces, went out to meet him. Just before the battle commenced, a brother of Judas, named Eleazar, seeing a man among the enemy who was mounted upon a richly-adorned elephant, thought that this must be King Antiochus. Running swiftly forward, far in advance of the Jewish army, he fought his way all alone to where the elephant was. He could not reach up to the man that rode upon it, and he therefore plunged his dagger into the breast of the animal. It fell dead, crushing Eleazar under its weight.

Now, although this was a very brave action, it was also a very foolish one. For the man on the elephant was not the king, but a private soldier; and even if he had been the king, Eleazar was not able to do him any harm, but, on the contrary, he escaped unhurt, while Eleazar himself was killed. The Jews, moreover, were disheartened by the ill success of Eleazar's attempt, and looked upon it as an ill omen. And in fact, in the battle that followed, they were not successful, though Judas was enabled to withdraw in good order to the temple of Jerusalem. Antiochus followed, and relieved the garrison in the citadel, and laid siege to the temple. But the Jews held out bravely; the Syrian army began to suffer from want of provisions, and word was brought to Antiochus that a rebellion had broken out against him in his absence. Anxious to return to his own country, Antiochus sent to Judas and to those that were besieged with him, and promised to give them peace and permit them to live according to the laws of their forefathers. They gladly received his proposals, and, having made Antiochus swear that he would keep his promises, they allowed him to come into the temple. But when Antiochus saw how strong the place was, he broke his oaths, and ordered his soldiers to pull the walls down. Then he returned to Syria, taking with him the high-priest Menelaus, for he believed him to be the cause of all the evils that had happened to the Syrians; for it was Menelaus who had wickedly advised Antiochus Epiphanes to compel the Jews to leave the religion of their fathers. So he put him to death at a place called Berea, and in his place he made one Alcimus high-priest of the Jews. Now, the rightful heir to the priesthood was Onias, the son of that Onias (brother of Menelaus) whom Menelaus had succeeded. When this Onias saw that the priesthood had been transferred from his family to another, and that his uncle had been slain, he fled to

Egypt. Here he was kindly received by King Ptolemy, and in course of time he built a new temple at a town called Heliopolis, where the Jews of Alexandria used to come to worship.

CHAPTER CII.

HOW JUDAS MACCABEUS WON TWO GREAT VICTORIES.

ANTIOCHUS returned home and put down the rebellion which had broken out. But shortly after a new rebellion was raised by a man named Demetrius, who claimed to be the lawful heir to the throne of Syria, and who was successful. Antiochus and his general, Lysias, were captured and put to death.

Shortly after Demetrius had been made king, Alcimus, the new high-priest of the Jews, came to him and complained that Judas and his brethren were his enemies and would not allow him to perform the duties of his office. Demetrius was angry at this, and he sent for his general, Bacchides, and told him to take a great army and accompany Alcimus to Jerusalem. And he gave him orders, also, to slay Judas and all those that refused to acknowledge the authority of Alcimus. In this way the Jews were forced to submit to the high-priest so long as Bacchides remained in the land. But Judas and his followers, who had escaped from Jerusalem at the approach of Bacchides, returned as soon as he went back to Syria, and Alcimus was again forced to fly to his royal master for protection.

Demetrius sent another army into Judea, commanded by a general named Nicanor. Judas met him at a place called Capharsalama and defeated him, killing five thousand of his soldiers. Nicanor retreated to Jerusalem, where, in revenge, he behaved very cruelly to the inhabitants, and threatened that if they did not find some way of delivering Judas into his hands, he would pull down their temple when he came again to the city. He departed from Jerusalem, leaving the priests and the people full of fear because of his threats. He pitched his camp at a village called Bethoron, and, having been joined here by another Syrian army, he again gave battle to Judas. Judas had no more than one thousand soldiers with him, but he boldly led them out to fight, and after a hard struggle he won a great victory. Nicanor himself fell in the battle.

After this Judea enjoyed peace for a little while. Alcimus the high-priest had died, stricken down suddenly by the hand of God, as he was endeavoring to pull down the wall of the sanctuary which had been there of old, and Judas entered Jerusalem and was elected high-priest. In order to secure for himself a powerful ally, Judas sent ambassadors to Rome to make a treaty with the people of that state. And the Jews and the Romans agreed to be friendly, and to assist each other in their wars as much as possible.

CHAPTER CIII.

DEATH OF JUDAS MACCABEUS.

IT was not long before Demetrius determined to punish the Jews for the death of his general, Nicanor. So he sent Bacchides at the head of an army into Judea. With about three thousand soldiers Judas pitched his camp at a place called Bethzetho. But when Bacchides approached and the Jews saw the great number of their enemies, they became afraid, and many of them ran away, leaving Judas with only eight hundred men. And when these eight hundred men would have persuaded Judas to retreat and wait until he had a larger army before attacking the enemy, his answer was,—

"Let not the sun ever see such a thing as that I should show my back to the enemy. Rather let me die in this battle than so tarnish my glory."

This bold speech inspired his men with fresh courage, and they determined to stand or fall with their brave commander.

Bacchides drew his soldiers out of the camp and put them in order of battle. Then he sounded his trumpets and rushed upon Judas. For a long time the victory seemed to be doubtful. Each side fought bravely. In spite of the small number of the Jews they would not give way. After some hours of fighting, Judas noticed that Bacchides with all his strongest men was fighting in the right wing of his army. Therefore he thought that if he could defeat this wing he would gain the victory. With his bravest warriors he rushed against the right wing, and broke their ranks and slew many of them, and forced the others back for a great distance. But meanwhile the left wing of the Syrian army, seeing what had happened, rushed off in pursuit of Judas, and came up behind him in such a way that he was hemmed in between the two wings of the army, surrounded on all sides by the enemy. Judas saw that the day was lost, and that nothing was left to him but to sell his life as dearly as possible. And after killing a number of the enemy, he himself fell, covered with wounds.

CHAPTER CIV.

JONATHAN.

AFTER his victory over Judas Maccabeus, Bacchides entered Jerusalem, and gathered around him all the wicked Jews
who were tired of living according to the law of Moses, and
he put them at the head of the government. And they delivered up into his hands many of those who had been friends
to Judas. Bacchides tortured these men cruelly and put them
to death. The good and faithful Jews greatly lamented this
state of things, and they came to Jonathan, the brother of
Judas, and begged him to be their general, and to lead them
against their enemies as his brother had done. Jonathan
gladly agreed to this, and, gathering together those that were
willing to join him, he pitched his camp in a wilderness near
the lakes of Jordan. He remained in this neighborhood for
about two years, though Bacchides frequently marched against
him and tried in vain to dislodge him. At last, losing heart
at these many failures, Bacchides made a treaty of peace with
Jonathan and returned to Syria, and after this departure he
never came to Judea again.

Jonathan then went to a city called Michmash, and established his government there. But Jerusalem and many of
the stronger towns were still held by Syrian soldiers and by
Jews who were enemies of Jonathan.

CHAPTER CV.

ALEXANDER BALA.

ABOUT seven years after Jonathan had been chosen general of the Jews, a great rebellion broke out in Syria against Demetrius. For a man named Alexander Bala said that he was a descendant of Antiochus Epiphanes, and the rightful heir to the throne. Many of the principal men of the country supported his claim, so that he was able to gather around him a great army and make war against Demetrius. Now this rebellion gave Jonathan new strength and importance, for both Demetrius and Alexander Bala were anxious to secure his help, and they made him great offers. Alexander sent him a purple robe and a gold crown and appointed him high-priest of Jerusalem, and promised that when he had secured the throne of Syria he would always live in friendship with the Jews and assist them in their wars. Demetrius also sent presents to Jonathan, and he withdrew his soldiers from the towns of Judea and allowed Jonathan to return to Jerusalem. But the citadel in Jerusalem was still held by wicked Jews and deserters, who refused to give it up.

Jonathan determined to befriend Alexander Bala. He probably did not put much faith in the promises of Demetrius, who had been his enemy for so long a time. Moreover, the Romans sided with Alexander, and Jonathan was anxious to be on friendly terms with that great people. The result showed the wisdom of his decision, for Alexander defeated and killed Demetrius in a great battle.

CHAPTER CVI.

DEFEAT AND DEATH OF ALEXANDER BALA.

ALEXANDER took the kingdom of Syria, and wrote to King Ptolemy, of Egypt, asking him for his daughter in marriage. Ptolemy was glad to secure a powerful ally in this way. The wedding was celebrated with great pomp and splendor. Jonathan was invited to attend it, and when he came he was received with the highest honors. King Alexander made him take off his garments and put on instead a purple robe, and sit with him on his own throne.

The reign of Alexander was not a long one. The son of Demetrius, who was called Demetrius also, claimed his father's throne, and made war against Alexander. Ptolemy led an army into Syria to assist his son-in-law. But that ungrateful and foolish prince treacherously conspired against the life of Ptolemy. The latter discovered the plot, and was so angry that he at once took his army over to the young Demetrius. Alexander was defeated and dethroned, and fled into Arabia. But it happened that in the battle Ptolemy's horse took fright at the bellowing of an elephant and threw his rider. Some of the soldiers of the enemy saw the accident, and rushing to where Ptolemy lay, they inflicted many dangerous wounds before they could be driven off by the Egyptians. Ptolemy was taken up mortally wounded, and died on the fifth day afterwards. Just before his death he received a present of the head of his enemy Alexander, sent him by an Arab chief to whom the defeated monarch had fled.

CHAPTER CVII.

DEMETRIUS NICATOR.

DEMETRIUS, who was surnamed Nicator, took the throne of Syria after the defeat of Alexander Bala. At this time Jonathan had laid siege to the citadel of Jerusalem, which was held by his enemies among the Jews who had denied the religion of their fathers. Finding themselves hard pressed and in danger of being overcome, some of these wicked men escaped by night and came to Demetrius and sought to obtain his assistance. Demetrius commanded Jonathan to come to him; and Jonathan, leaving his troops to press the siege, took with him the elders of the people, and the priests, and many presents of gold and silver, and came to Demetrius, and pacified him, and made him his friend. So Demetrius refused to assist the wicked Jews, and he made a treaty of peace with Jonathan on the same terms that Alexander Bala had granted.

Jonathan also chose out and sent three thousand of his soldiers to be a guard to Demetrius. And only a short time afterwards it happened that these soldiers saved the life of Demetrius; for that king was very unpopular in his capital city of Antioch, the people of which rose in rebellion against him. They laid siege to his palace, and would probably have taken it had not the Jewish soldiers mounted the roof and shot arrows at the crowd below. The roof was so high up that the Jews were out of reach of the weapons of the citizens, and thus they could shoot without being disturbed. They also shot at the houses that were near the palace, and, having driven the people out of them, they rushed down and set the houses on fire. The houses in the town were built close together, and the fire spread rapidly. The Jews, meanwhile, leaped from one roof to another, and kept up a continual shooting of arrows into the streets. Then the rest of the king's troops, seeing that because of the fires and the arrows of the Jews the citizens had been thrown into complete confusion, rushed out upon them and slew a great many; and the rest threw down their arms and gave themselves up to the king.

Demetrius gave public thanks to the Jews, and sent them home laden with presents. Yet, a short time afterwards, he forgot all the benefits they had rendered him, and broke his promises to Jonathan, demanding from him the tribute that the high-priests of Judea had formerly paid to the kings of Syria. When Jonathan refused to pay it, Demetrius threatened to make war upon him. And he would have carried out his threat had he not been prevented by new dangers that arose at home.

There was a general, named Trypho, who had fought under Alexander Bala. This man, taking advantage of the hatred felt towards Demetrius by many of his subjects, placed a crown upon the head of a young son of Alexander, named Antiochus, and proclaimed him king. A large army soon collected around the new king, and Trypho led them against Demetrius and defeated him with great slaughter. Demetrius fled away, and Antiochus mounted the throne. The young king sent letters to Jonathan asking him for his assistance and friendship, and promising his own friendship in return. Jonathan gladly listened to these offers, and made a treaty of peace with Antiochus, and agreed to help him in his war with Demetrius. And, in fact, he raised an army which defeated Demetrius in two great battles.

CHAPTER CVIII.

THE REVOLT OF TRYPHO.

TRYPHO, the general who had raised Antiochus to power, was a very ambitious man. Seeing that the new king was only a boy, he determined to displace him and usurp the throne of Syria for himself. But, as Jonathan was a friend of Antiochus, he thought it would be best to get him out of the way first. So he gathered up an army and went out to meet Jonathan at a place called Bethsan. As Jonathan had with him an army of forty thousand men, Trypho was afraid to use force against him, and decided to try stratagem. He therefore persuaded Jonathan that he came only with peaceful intentions, and he advised him to dismiss his army and come with him to the neighboring city of Ptolemais. Jonathan, suspecting nothing, sent his army home, keeping only one thousand men as a guard around him, and rode with Trypho into Ptolemais. But no sooner had he reached it than Trypho closed the gates, slew the men that were with Jonathan, and cast Jonathan himself into prison. Then Trypho went to Antioch, and had the young king put to death, and caused himself to be made king in his place.

When the Jews learned what had happened to Jonathan they were in great distress. They came to Simon, his brother, asking him to become their leader, and he agreed to do so. Simon rebuilt the walls of Jerusalem and fortified them with very high and strong towers, and made everything ready for an attack.

Trypho, learning of all these things, came into Judea with a great army, and brought Jonathan along with him. He sent word to Simon that he would yield up his prisoner for one hundred talents of silver, provided two of Jonathan's children were also sent him as hostages for their father's good conduct. Simon was afraid to trust the wily Trypho, but, fearing that if he refused his offers the people might accuse him of wishing to keep his brother in bondage so that he might himself enjoy the power, he finally sent the money and the two children. Trypho acted as Simon had feared he would. He kept the money and the children and refused to give up Jonathan. The two armies watched each other for a long time. Trypho had intended to march against Jerusalem in order to assist the wicked Jews that were in the citadel, but he finally abandoned the enterprise, and, having killed the brave Jonathan, returned to his own country.

Simon sent some men to get the body of Jonathan, and he buried it with great honor. He also raised a beautiful monument to his father and his brethren, built of white and polished stone, and of so great a height that it could be seen a long way off.

When Trypho had departed, Simon renewed the siege of the citadel with fresh vigor, and soon captured it, and put to death the Jews who had defended it. In order that it might no longer serve as a place of refuge for the enemies of Judea, he pulled down the citadel, and set all the people to work to level the mountain on which it was built. After this had been done, the temple stood on the highest spot in the city.

CHAPTER CIX.

DEATH OF SIMON MACCABEUS.

KING DEMETRIUS had been made a prisoner by a nation named the Parthians, soon after Trypho drove him from his kingdom.   He still dwelt as a captive among them, and Trypho, therefore, had nothing to fear from him.   But a brother of Demetrius, named Antiochus, raised an army and made war against the usurper.   Now, Trypho had been behaving very cruelly to his subjects, and they were glad to have a pretext for rising against him.   Many of them, therefore, went over to Antiochus.   A great battle ensued, and Trypho was beaten.   He fled to a town called Dora.   Antiochus followed him thither and besieged the town.   Through the assistance of Simon, the high-priest of Judea, who sent him money and supplies, Antiochus was enabled to take Dora. Trypho fled to another town, but he was finally captured and put to death.

Antiochus made himself king of Syria, and he soon forgot the assistance Simon had afforded him in his necessity.   He put one of his generals, named Cendebeus, at the head of an army, and told him to go and ravage Judea and seize Simon. Simon was provoked at this unjust treatment, and, though he was now very old, he went like a young man to act as general of his army.   And he was successful in all his engagements with the enemy, and soon drove Cendebeus out of the country.

But after he had ruled over Judea for eight years, he was siain at a banquet by the treachery of one of his own sons-in-law, named Ptolemy.   This man also captured Simon's wife and two of his sons and threw them into prison, and he sent some men to kill the third son, who was named John Hyrcanus. In this way Ptolemy hoped to make himself master of Judea. But John Hyrcanus escaped from his intended murderers, and made haste to Jerusalem, and informed the people of what had happened. So, when a little later Ptolemy appeared at one of the gates of the city, he was driven away and forced to take refuge in a fortress called Dagon, just above Jericho.

CHAPTER CX.

JOHN HYRCANUS.

John Hyrcanus was proclaimed high-priest and ruler of Judea in the place of his father. His first act was to march against the murderer Ptolemy. He besieged the fortress of Dagon, and would soon have taken it had not Ptolemy set the mother and brethren of Hyrcanus upon the wall and beaten them with rods, threatening to kill them unless Hyrcanus would raise the siege. The brave mother, however, cried out to her son not to be moved by the injuries she suffered, since she would rather die than that Ptolemy should go unpunished. Hyrcanus was sorely tried, and knew not what to do. For his mother's courage and her entreaties to him made him set about the attack, but when he saw her body torn with stripes, his love and pity for her made him desist. In this way the siege was delayed until the year of rest, for the Jews rested every seventh year as they did upon every seventh day. Ptolemy, being thus freed, slew John's mother and brethren and fled to a foreign country.

Meanwhile, Antiochus had gathered up an army and

marched into Judea. For he had been very angry at the defeat of his general, Cendebeus, by Simon, and had determined to avenge it at the first opportunity. He laid waste the country of the Jews, and came to Jerusalem and besieged it. Hyrcanus and his followers suffered so greatly from famine that they were forced to the sad necessity of sending out of the city all who were either too old or too young to assist in its defence. The besiegers refused to let them pass, and many of them perished miserably in the ditches near the walls of the city. But Antiochus proved a generous enemy. When the time for celebrating the feast of the tabernacle came round, Hyrcanus sent messengers to him asking for a week's truce, that the Jews might be able to offer up their sacrifices. Antiochus not only granted this request, but sent Hyrcanus a number of bulls with gilded horns and cups of gold and silver to be used in the sacrifices. The poor Jews who were outside of the walls received these presents from the Syrians, and were allowed to return with them into the city. Because of this generosity, Antiochus was ever after called the Pious.

At last Hyrcanus made a treaty with Antiochus. He promised to level the walls of Jerusalem, to pay a tribute every year to the king of Syria, to assist him in his wars, and to give him hostages, among others his own brother, as security for the faithful performance of these promises.

Then Antiochus raised the siege and returned to his own country.

Four years afterwards, John Hyrcanus was sent for by King Antiochus to assist him in a war against the Parthians. That nation still held his brother Demetrius a prisoner, and Antiochus wished to make them set him at liberty. Hyrcanus collected his forces and went with Antiochus, as he had agreed. The combined armies of the Jews and Syrians met the Parthians, and defeated them in a great battle. Then Hyrcanus obtained permission to return home. Antiochus continued the war alone, but was defeated and slain by the king of the Parthians. Demetrius, however, managed to escape, and, coming to Antioch, he seized upon the throne of Syria. So much quarrelling then arose in that country, for there were others who claimed the kingdom, that Hyrcanus took the opportunity to free himself from the foreign yoke, and Judea no longer paid tribute to Syria.

Hyrcanus also made war against several of the nations around him who were the enemies of the Jews, and he defeated and subdued them. The victory which endeared him most to his people was that over the Samaritans. For several centuries the Jews and the Samaritans had looked upon one another with jealous eyes, and the mutual hatred had increased when the Samaritans built their rival temple at Gerizim. Hyrcanus first took Gerizim, and destroyed the temple there. Then he marched against the city of Samaria, where he left his army, under the command of his two sons, Antigonus and Aristobulus. The siege lasted for a long time, but, though the inhabitants called in the assistance of the king of Syria, they were at last obliged to yield, their city was entirely destroyed, and they themselves were carried off as slaves.

But though Hyrcanus prospered abroad in his wars, he found it difficult to preserve peace at home in his own city of Jerusalem. Two great parties had arisen there, called the Pharisees and the Sadducees, who were continually quarrelling because they could not agree on many questions of religion. Hyrcanus sided at first with the Pharisees, who were also at first the favorites of the people, but afterwards he left them and sided with the Sadducees.

Now he did this for the following reason: He was one day at a great banquet given by the Pharisees, and while the guests were eating and drinking Hyrcanus asked them if they had any fault to find with the way he governed. Many of the Pharisees cried out that they had no fault to find with him, for Hyrcanus was a wise and prudent prince, and they were well pleased with his government. But one among them, named Eleazar, who was of a cross temper, and who delighted in contradiction, rose and said,—

"Since thou art anxious to know the truth, if thou wilt be righteous in earnest, lay down the high-priesthood and be satisfied with the civil government of the people."

Hyrcanus, surprised, asked why he ought to lay down the priesthood. And Eleazar answered,—

"We have heard from old men that thy mother was once a captive under Antiochus Epiphanes, and was forced to marry one of the Syrians. Therefore thou art not fit to be a priest, because thou art the son of one who transgressed against the law of Moses and married a foreigner."

This story was false, and Hyrcanus was very angry with Eleazar. The other Pharisees also said that he had done wrong in making this remark.

Now there was one Jonathan, a Sadducee, who was a great friend of Hyrcanus. When he heard what had happened at the banquet he made Hyrcanus believe that Eleazar had only spoken what the other Pharisees had taught him to believe.

"To prove that this is so," said Jonathan, "ask the Pharisees what punishment the man deserves for making so wicked a speech, and you will find them willing to let him off with only a light punishment."

Hyrcanus therefore asked the Pharisees this question, and they answered, "Eleazar deserves to be publicly whipped, for it does not seem right to punish mere words with death."

Now the king thought the man deserved death for his speech; so he believed what Jonathan had told him, and was angry with the Pharisees, and left their party to go over to the Sadducees. In this way he excited the enmity of the Pharisees against him; and the people, also, who preferred the Pharisees, were less friendly to him than formerly.

Still, the remainder of Hyrcanus's reign was sufficiently peaceful and happy. He died after he had been ruler of the

Jews for thirty-one years, leaving five sons behind him. He was a very fortunate man, says Josephus, for he possessed the three most desirable things in the world,—the government of his people, the high-priesthood, and the gift of prophecy; concerning which last gift, it is related that God frequently conversed with him and revealed the future, and that among other things he predicted that his two eldest sons would not long continue in the government.

CHAPTER CXI.

ARISTOBULUS.

By the will of Hyrcanus the government of Judea was left to his wife. But Aristobulus, the eldest son, who was a wicked man, would not let her possess it, but seized upon it himself. When she would have asserted her rights he threw her into prison and let her starve to death. He also imprisoned all his brothers except Antigonus, whom he loved and made commander of his armies.

Aristobulus was the first one of his family to wear a crown, for he determined to change the government into a kingdom, and made himself king as well as high-priest.

Now, though Aristobulus loved his brother Antigonus, his wife and many others hated and were jealous of him, so they told the king many wicked stories about him. At first he would not believe them, but after a while he began to grow suspicious of his brother. It happened that on the occasion of a great festival Aristobulus lay very ill in his palace; and Antigonus returned from the army and went up to the temple, splendidly adorned, and with his officers in armor around him, to offer up prayers for the recovery of his brother.

Then his enemies went to the king and told him of the great show that Antigonus had made. And they tried to make him believe that Antigonus was very ambitious, and had come to Jerusalem with his armed men in order to slay his brother and reign in his stead.

Aristobulus was troubled, and knew not what to think. He placed guards in a dark passage leading to his palace, and ordered them to kill Antigonus if he came in armor, but to let him pass if he came unarmed. He then sent word to his brother to attend him unarmed. But the queen persuaded the messengers to tell Antigonus to come in his finest armor, for that the king had heard a great deal about its beauty, and wished to see it. Antigonus, suspecting nothing, put on the armor, and when he came to the dark passage he was slain by the guards.

Aristobulus repented of the great crime he had committed, and, brooding over his wicked deeds, he became very ill indeed. One day he vomited a quantity of blood. The servant who carried out the blood slipped and fell upon the very spot where Antigonus had been slain, and spilled the blood over the very blood-stains of the murdered brother. Then a great cry arose among the spectators. The king heard it, and asked his attendants what had happened. At first they would not tell him, but he forced them to speak. When he heard the story he burst into tears, and groaned, and said, "So I perceive I cannot escape the all-seeing eye of God, who wishes to punish me for the crimes I have committed. O thou most impudent body, how long wilt thou retain a soul that is stained with the blood of a mother and a brother? How long shall I myself spend my blood drop by drop? Let them take it all at once, and let their ghosts be no longer disappointed by a few drops offered to them." Thus speaking, the wretched king expired, having reigned barely a year.

CHAPTER CXII.

ALEXANDER JANNEUS.

THE queen now released the dead king's brethren from prison, and Alexander Janneus, the eldest, mounted the throne, having killed a younger brother who attempted to usurp it. Alexander was soon engaged in a war with Ptolemy Lathyrus, king of Cyprus, the son and deadly enemy of Cleopatra, governess of Egypt. A battle took place, in which Ptolemy was victorious. Cleopatra now came into Syria with an army to help Alexander, but Ptolemy marched into Egypt. Alexander then besieged and took Gadaia and Amathus, which contained many treasures of Theodorus, prince of Philadelphia, who immediately marched against Alexander, and totally defeated him. Alexander, however, soon recovered from this blow, and took Raphia and Gaza and Anthedon.

Many of the Jews, however, hated Alexander, and when he had returned home rose in rebellion against him, and would have overcome him but that Alexander had under him many foreign mercenaries. With the help of these he crushed the rebellion and slew six thousand Jews. He then again invaded the country east of the Jordan, forced it to pay tribute, and retook Amathus. But in a battle with Obodus, king of the Arabians, Alexander lost his entire army. He escaped to Jerusalem, where soon the Jews rose in another rebellion against him. After six years of fighting Alexander tried to bring the rebels to terms, by asking them what he might do to appease them. They cried out, by killing himself. The civil war continued, and Alexander was generally successful;

the insurgents, hard pressed, called to their aid Demetrius Euchærus, one of the kings of Syria. Alexander was routed with great loss, and fled to the mountains, where he was joined by six thousand of the rebellious Jews, who now pitied his condition. Demetrius, alarmed at this desertion from his ranks, retreated. Alexander, now master of the whole coun- try, besieged his enemies in Bethome, took it, and marched in triumph to Jerusalem. There at a banquet he cruelly cru- cified eight hundred of his enemies, and killed their wives and children before them. This horrible deed so frightened those who had opposed him that eight thousand fled from the city that very night.

Alexander again became engaged in foreign wars, and took Pella and Gerasa, and demolished Goland and Seleucia, and the fortress of Gamala. Returning to Jerusalem, he was kindly received there on account of his success. At rest from war, he was attacked by a malady which he thought he could only cure by active exercise in the field; but by overexerting himself he increased his illness, and died after having reigned for twenty-seven years.

CHAPTER CXIII.

ALEXANDER AND THE PHARISEES.

ALEXANDER left the kingdom to Alexandra, his wife, who was much beloved by the people on account of her piety, and because she had opposed the cruel measures of her husband. She had two sons by Alexander, Hyrcanus, the elder, whom she made high-priest, and Aristobulus, whom she retained near her person.

Alexandra joined herself to the Pharisees, a sect among the

Jews most strict in the observance of the laws, and who had been opposed to her husband. These Pharisees so won the queen's favor that they became the real rulers of the nation, which, as Alexandra managed affairs with great sagacity, had become very great and powerful.

The Pharisees were desirous of revenging themselves for what they had suffered at the hands of the late king and his party. So they put to death Diogenes, a friend of Alexander's, because they charged him with having advised the king to crucify the eight hundred men. And they demanded that Alexandra should put to death all who had aided the execution. Many were slain, but many who were in danger fled to Aristobulus, the younger son, and sought his intercession. He persuaded his mother to spare them, but they were obliged to leave Jerusalem and disperse themselves about the country.

Alexandra sent an army to Damascus, and under pretence that Ptolemy was always oppressing the city she captured it. Soon after this she fell ill. The young and ambitious Aristobulus seized this opportunity to gain the throne. He fled from Jerusalem, got possession of the fortresses, hired a number of troops, and made himself king. Alexandra in the mean while died, after a prosperous reign of nine years, leaving the kingdom to Hyrcanus, the rightful heir.

Aristobulus advanced upon his brother, who met him with an army near Jericho. But before a battle was fought the greater part of Hyrcanus's army deserted to Aristobulus. The rest fled, Hyrcanus with them, to a place called the Citadel, where the party of Hyrcanus had shut up the wife and children of Aristobulus as hostages. It was finally agreed between the two brothers that Aristobulus should ascend the throne, and that Hyrcanus should possess such dignities as became the brother of the king.

This state of affairs did not, however, last long. Antipater, an Idumean by birth, and a very wily man, who possessed much influence over the weak Hyrcanus, persuaded him to fly to Aretas, the king of Arabia. Aretas, having been well disposed to help the cause of Hyrcanus by the presents and eloquence of Antipater, marched an army of fifty thousand horse and foot against Aristobulus, who was deserted at the first onset by many of his army, and driven to Jerusalem, where he soon would have been captured but for timely assistance.

Scaurus, a lieutenant of Pompey the Great, had seized Damascus. Both brothers sought his aid. Aristobulus, however, sent a present of three hundred talents, which won Scaurus to his side, and Aretas was threatened with the vengeance of Rome unless he raised the siege. So the Arabian was frightened, and withdrew his forces, followed by Aristobulus, who fell upon the retreating army from the rear and completely routed it.

Hyrcanus and Antipater, being thus deprived of their hopes from the Arabians, now looked for aid to Pompey, who had come himself to Damascus, and besought him to bestow the throne of Judea upon the rightful heir. Aristobulus also sought Pompey's assistance, relying upon the presents he had formerly given to Scaurus. But Aristobulus behaved in so haughty a manner that he displeased Pompey, so he gathered together his forces and besieged Aristobulus in the strong fortress of Alexandrium. Aristobulus, frightened by Pompey's large army, tried to make peace, and came down from his fortress to parley with Pompey. Pompey forced him to sign orders for the surrender of all his fortresses. This was too much for the high spirit of Aristobulus. He fled to Jerusalem and prepared to resist the Roman general.

Pompey immediately advanced upon Jerusalem. Aristobulus, who found the city divided within itself, became alarmed, and, coming out to Pompey, promised to surrender himself and the city, and to pay a large sum of money. But when Pompey sent Gabinius to collect the money, the soldiers of Aristobulus would not allow him to enter the gates.

CHAPTER CXIV.

POMPEY was so indignant at this treatment that he imme·
diately advanced upon Jerusalem. Within the city the party
of Hyrcanus wished to admit the Roman soldiers, but the
soldiers of Aristobulus wished to fight and set their king at
liberty. The party of Hyrcanus, however, prevailed, and
threw open the gates to the invader. Aristobulus's party retired into the temple, cut off all communication between the
temple and the city by breaking down the bridge that joined
them, and prepared for an obstinate resistance.

The temple, which was built upon a very steep hill, could
not be attacked except on the north side. Pompey, therefore,
stormed it from this side. But in spite of all the efforts of his
great army, assisted by immense engines brought from Tyre,
the temple resisted for three whole months. And it might
never have been taken had not Pompey observed that on the
Sabbath-day the Jews religiously abstained from all work,
and would not fight except in self-defence. He therefore ordered his soldiers to make no attacks on those days, but employed them in filling up the valley and drawing the engines
nearer to the walls.

At last one of the largest towers was battered down; an
assault was made, and after an obstinate resistance the temple
was taken. A terrible scene of carnage followed, and a great
many of the brave defenders threw themselves headlong down
the precipices. Among all their misfortunes, nothing affected
the Jews so much as that a stranger should enter their holy

place. For Pompey entered their inmost sanctuary, called the Holy of Holies, where none were allowed except the high-priest. He took none of the great treasures which he saw there, however, but commanded the ministers about the temple to purify it and perform their accustomed sacrifices. And he appointed Hyrcanus high-priest. He then took away from the nation all the cities they had formerly conquered. He reduced Judea within its proper bounds, and laid a tribute upon it. He restored many cities within the country to their own citizens, and put them under the province of Syria. That province, together with Judea and the countries as far as Egypt and Euphrates, he gave to Scaurus to govern. Pompey then set out for Rome, taking with him Aristobulus and his two sons and two daughters as captives. Alexander, the elder son, made his escape upon the journey, but the younger, Antigonus, with his father and sisters, was carried to the city of the Cæsars.

This Alexander gathered a considerable force and overran Judea, and would soon have overthrown Hyrcanus in Jerusalem had not the Romans under Gabinius, the successor of Scaurus, hastily come to his assistance. Alexander was defeated, and fled with the remainder of his forces to Alexandrium. Here he was again attacked by Gabinius, who slew a number of Alexander's army and shut up the rest in the citadel. Gabinius left part of his army to carry on the siege, and, taking the remainder with him, rebuilt many of the neighboring cities, after which he returned to Alexandrium. In the mean while, Alexander's mother, who had come to Gabinius out of concern for her relatives in Rome, brought about a treaty, by which Alexander was pardoned on condition of surrendering his fortresses. Gabinius destroyed the fortresses, and, going to Jerusalem, committed the care of the temple to Hyrcanus, but deprived him of the title of king, and changed the political government of Judea into an aristocracy. He divided it into five independent states, each governed by a senate, whose places of sitting were Jerusalem, Gadara, Amathus, Jericho, and Sepphoris.

And now Aristobulus himself, with his younger son, Antigonus, escaped from Rome and raised the standard of revolt. Aristobulus took Alexandrium and began to rebuild its walls, but retired to Macherus before an army sent against him by Gabinius. A battle was fought, and the Jews were severely worsted. Aristobulus and a thousand of his soldiers escaped, and attempted to fortify Macherus, but the Romans fell upon them again, and though for two days the king resisted bravely, he was finally taken prisoner and sent back to Rome with his son Antigonus, who, however, was allowed to return to Judea at the request of his mother. Gabinius set out to war with the Parthians, but being hindered by Ptolemy, king of Egypt, he determined upon the conquest of that country. Alexander seized the opportunity, gathered together an army, and set about killing all the Romans that there were in the country. On the return of Gabinius, Alexander met him with a large army, but was badly defeated and forced to fly.

Crassus succeeded Gabinius in Syria. He robbed the temple of its treasures in order to carry on the war against the Parthians, but, as if in punishment for his wickedness, he and his whole army were destroyed by the nation he had expected to conquer.

CHAPTER CXV.

ANTIPATER AND HIS SONS.

JULIUS CÆSAR was now master of Rome, and Pompey was an exile. Cæsar released Aristobulus from prison. He gave him two legions and sent him to Syria, that he might conquer that country and the sections adjoining Judea. But the partisans of Pompey poisoned the king, and his gallant son, Alexander, was beheaded by Scipio at Antioch at the command of Pompey.

After Pompey's death, Antipater, who was ever on the alert to turn circumstances to his own advantage, cultivated the friendship of Cæsar, as he had done that of Pompey. He aided Mithridates, king of Pergamus, in his march towards Egypt to help Cæsar in that war which he waged in favor of Cleopatra. Mithridates was refused a passage through Pelusium, but, with the aid of Antipater and his army, he took Pelusium, and marched on until he was stopped again by those Egyptian Jews who lived in that part called the country of Onias. But Antipater persuaded them not only to let the army pass, but also to give him aid and provisions; on which account the people about Memphis would not fight against Mithridates, but joined him of their own accord. A great battle was fought against the remainder of the Egyptians at a place called the Jews' Camp. Mithridates would have been beaten had it not been for the bravery of Antipater, who led the left wing of the army. After defeating those that opposed him, he returned, and, falling upon the rest of the Egyptian forces, who had routed Mithridates, put them to flight.

Cæsar encouraged Antipater to undertake other dangerous enterprises for him; and, when he had settled the affairs of Egypt, he rewarded Antipater by giving him the right of Roman citizenship, freedom from taxes, and by making Hyrcanus high-priest.

Antigonus, the son of Aristobulus, came at this time to Cæsar and accused Antipater and Hyrcanus of injustice and extravagance, and said that such assistance as Antipater had given Cæsar was not on account of good will, but to gain pardon for formerly aiding Pompey. Upon this Antipater threw away his garments and declared that the wounds upon his body showed his good will to Cæsar, and that Antigonus only wished to obtain the government that he might stir up sedition against the Romans, as his father did before him. When Cæsar heard this he declared Hyrcanus to be most worthy of the high-priesthood. And he made Antipater procurator of all Judea, granting him leave to rebuild such walls in his country as had been overthrown. Antipater returned to Judea, rebuilt the walls of Jerusalem, and went over the country persuading the Jews to submit to the new government. But, as he found Hyrcanus to be weak and inactive, he managed the affairs of the kingdom himself, and appointed his elder son, Phasael, to the government of Jerusalem, and his younger son, Herod, to that of Galilee.

This Herod was a very active young man, and immediately won renown by capturing and killing a band of robbers that had been the terror of the country. Phasael also distinguished himself by his management of affairs in Jerusalem, so that Judea rang with the praises of these young men, and great honors were paid to Antipater.

Some of the Jews, jealous of Antipater and his sons, represented to Hyrcanus that these men were the real lords of Judea, and that they had robbed him of his authority. They persuaded the weak king that Herod had broken the law by executing the robbers without trial. Hyrcanus therefore summoned Herod to Jerusalem for trial. But Sextus Cæsar, a kinsman of the great Julius, and president of Syria, who loved Herod, sent word to Hyrcanus that Herod should be acquitted, and so he was set free. Herod went to join Sextus Cæsar in Damascus, and was made by him general of Celesyria and Samaria. Herod was very angry because he had been summoned to Jerusalem, so he got together an army and set out to overthrow Hyrcanus, but he was persuaded by Antipater and Phasael to give up his design.

CHAPTER CXVI.

HEROD KILLS MALICHUS.

A MIGHTY war now raged among the Romans just after the sudden murder of Julius Cæsar by Cassius and Brutus. The leading men joined whatever party they thought would advance their own interests best. Cassius came into Syria in order to take charge of the forces there, and laid a tax of seven hundred talents upon the Jews. Antipater divided the work of raising this sum among his sons and acquaintances, among the latter of whom was a powerful Jew called Malichus, who hated Antipater.

Herod won the favor of Cassius by bringing in his share first of all. The Roman became so angry because some of the others delayed to pay the tribute that he sold the inhabitants of several cities as slaves, and would have killed Malichus for being tardy had not Antipater prevented his ruin by bringing in a hundred talents immediately. But when Cassius had gone, Malichus forgot the kindness of Antipater and plotted against him. For Malichus wished to get the kingdom into his own hands. And although Antipater again saved his life by dissuading Marcus, the governor of Syria, from killing him on account of his plots, still Malichus finally killed Antipater by bribing a cup-bearer to give him poison at a feast.

Malichus, afraid of the vengeance of the people, made them believe that he was innocent of this crime, and proceeded to raise a troop of soldiers to protect himself from Herod, who came with an army to avenge the death of his

father. But at the advice of his brother not to punish Malichus in an open manner, lest the people should fall into a
sedition, Herod pretended for the time being to believe Malichus innocent, and, after burying his father, betook himself
to Samaria.

Herod wrote to Cassius, and received from him permission
to avenge the death of his father. He returned with his army
to Jerusalem, and upon a day of celebration invited both
Hyrcanus and Malichus to supper. They came, and Malichus was slain by some of Herod's soldiers. Hyrcanus
swooned away; but when he was told that the deed was
done at the command of Cassius, he appeared to be much
pleased, and said that Cassius had saved both himself and
his country by cutting off one that was laying plots against
them both.

CHAPTER CXVII.

HEROD AND PHASAEL ARE MADE TETRARCHS.

WHEN Cassius left Syria a new sedition arose in Jerusalem.
Cassius had protected Herod; but no sooner was he gone
than the adverse faction, assisted by Felix, the Roman general, attacked Phasael, that the death of Malichus might be
avenged. Herod was at Damascus, and too ill to come to
the assistance of his brother. But Phasael himself overcame
his enemies.

Antigonus, assisted by Ptolemy, king of Chalcis, now came
with an army to claim the throne, and advanced into Galilee.
But he was repulsed by Herod. Herod then went to Jerusalem, and was received with much enthusiasm, and there espoused himself to Mariamne, the daughter of Alexander, the
son of Aristobulus, and grand-daughter of Hyrcanus on her

mother's side. So Herod was received into general favor on account of his connection with the family of the king.

In the mean time the great battle of Philippi was fought, and Cassius was slain by Octavius Cæsar and Mark Antony. When the latter had come into Asia, the enemies of Herod sent ambassadors to him to accuse Herod and Phasael of keeping the government by force and depriving Hyrcanus of his kingly power. But the wily Herod gave such large sums of money to Antony that he would not listen to the accusations. After that a hundred more ambassadors came to Antony, who, when he had heard both sides, asked Hyrcanus which party was the fittest to rule. Hyrcanus replied, "Herod and his party." Antony then made Phasael and Herod tetrarchs of Judea. The ambassadors becoming indignant at this, Antony put fifteen of them into prison and drove the rest away. When this news reached Jerusalem the people were very angry, and a thousand more ambassadors were sent to Antony, but he became enraged at their clamors, and sent an armed force against them, who killed and wounded a great many. And as those who escaped would not keep quiet, Antony in anger slew the fifteen that he had in prison.

Two years afterwards the Parthians, led by Barzapharnes, a governor among them, and Pacorus, the king's son, possessed themselves of Syria. Lysanius, who had succeeded to the kingdom of Chalcis by the death of his father, Ptolemy, persuaded Pacorus, by promising him a thousand talents and five hundred slaves, to undertake to turn Hyrcanus out of Judea and place Antigonus upon the throne.

A great many Jews flocked to the banner of Antigonus, and he marched to Jerusalem, followed by a cup-bearer of the royal family of the Parthians, who was sent with a troop to assist Antigonus. Antigonus entered the city, and a battle was fought in the market-place, in which Herod's party beat the enemy and shut them up in the temple. Continual fights occurred; and when the multitudes came up to the Feast of

Pentecost, they embraced different sides, and daily contests took place. Antigonus at length proposed to admit Pacorus into Jerusalem to act as umpire between the two parties. Phasael consented, and Pacorus, being admitted, laid a plot, and prevailed on Phasael to go with Hyrcanus to Barzapharnes, and lay the case before him. Herod, who suspected Pacorus, besought his brother not to go. But Phasael set out, accompanied by Pacorus, who thought that by this means he would allay Herod's suspicions. Phasael and Hyrcanus were seized by the Parthians, and afterwards delivered in chains to Antigonus.

Pacorus was sent back to Jerusalem in order to entice Herod from the city and seize him. But Herod had heard of his brother's fate. And so he took with him his family and fled to Massada, a strong fortress, pursued by the Parthians, whom he several times beat back. On his way to Massada, Herod was joined by his brother Joseph. Arriving there, he left eight hundred of his men as a guard for the women of his family, and himself made haste to Arabia.

As for the Parthians in Jerusalem, they committed all sorts of cruelties and stole everything they could find. They put Antigonus upon the throne, and brought Hyrcanus and Phasael to him bound in chains. Antigonus himself bit off the ears of Hyrcanus, so that whatever might happen he could never be high-priest again. For the Jewish law required the high-priests to be without a blemish. To prevent Antigonus from torturing him Phasael dashed his own brains out against a stone. The Parthians leaving Antigonus to govern Jerusalem, took away Hyrcanus to Parthia. In the mean time, Herod, in the hope of rescuing his brother, sought the aid of Malichus, king of Arabia. But he, forgetting what he owed to Antipater, not only refused to help Herod, but ordered him from the country. Herod then set out for Rome by way of Egypt. When he arrived in Alexandria, Cleopatra, the beautiful queen of Egypt, wished to make him commander of her armies, but Herod refused this honor and hastened on to Rome. Antony was moved with compassion at the change which had taken place in Herod's fortunes. And when he remembered how hospitably he had been treated by Antipater, and Herod's own bravery, and also that he was fighting against Antigonus, who by calling the Parthians to his aid had declared himself an enemy of Rome, Antony determined to make Herod the king of Judea. Cæsar was also anxious to aid Herod against an ally of Parthia. So the senate was called together and the matter discussed, and as a result of their counsels it was agreed that Herod should be proclaimed king of Judea.

CHAPTER CXVIII.

HEROD OVERCOMES ANTIGONUS AND TAKES JERUSALEM.

HEROD hastily left Rome in order to go to the relief of Massada, which was besieged by Antigonus. Ventidius, the Roman general who had been sent out to restrain the incursions of the Parthians, came into Judea under pretence of assisting Herod's brother, Joseph, but really that he might frighten Antigonus into giving him bribes. This Antigonus did, and Ventidius went out of the country with the greater part of his army. He left his lieutenant, Silo, with a small force, that it might not be too evident that he had taken bribes. Silo also received bribes from Antigonus, and hovered between the two parties that he might enrich himself.

Herod, having come to Ptolemais, immediately raised an army and marched towards Massada, that he might relieve his bride and relatives who were shut up there. Joppa stood in his way, so he, with the assistance of Silo, who had joined him, took the city, and, marching onwards, easily relieved Massada,

and sat down before Jerusalem, where he besieged Antigonus
And now Silo showed his perfidy, for in order that Jerusalem
might not be taken he commanded his own soldiers to mutiny
against him, and to demand that they should be led into winter
quarters on account of the scarcity of provisions about Jerusalem. Herod, however, defeated Silo's plans by supplying
him with plenty of provisions. And in order that there might
be abundance for the future, he ordered the people of Samaria to bring supplies and store them in Jericho. Antigonus,
hearing of this, sent out a body of men to fight the collectors
of provisions. Herod then took with him five Jewish and five
Roman cohorts and marched to Jericho, which he found deserted. The city was plundered by the Romans under him.
This, for the time being, broke up the siege of Jerusalem.
The Roman army retired into winter quarters, and Herod
marched into Galilee, which he overran. Here he expelled
the garrisons stationed in different parts by Antigonus, and
then employed himself in delivering the country of daring
bands of robbers who infested the mountainous districts of
Upper Galilee. A great number of them he drove beyond
the river Jordan, the rest he surprised in their dens, and killed
them all by letting down armed men in chests from the precipices above. These men slew the robbers and their families,
and burnt up a great many of them in their caves. Herod
then returned to Samaria, leaving a part of his army in Galilee.
But when he had gone, a sedition arose, and a number fell
upon the general Herod had left, and slew him and laid waste
the country. Herod hastily returned, suppressed the sedition, and exacted a tribute from his enemies.

By this time the Parthians had been driven from Syria, so
Ventidius, by Antony's command, sent a thousand horsemen
and two legions, under the command of Macheras, to aid
Herod against Antigonus. The latter wrote to Macheras
promising him money for his assistance. Macheras, in order
that he might act as a spy upon Antigonus, pretended friend-

ship to him and marched to Jerusalem. But Antigonus, who suspected his designs, repulsed him from the city. At which the Roman was so enraged that he slew every Jew he met with, not sparing friends of Herod.

Herod was of course amazed at this, and set out for Samosata, which city Antony was besieging, to lay his complaint before him. Macheras, however, overtook Herod and pacified him. Still Herod marched on to Samosata, and helped Antony to take the city, who accordingly heaped more honors upon him, and commanded Sosius, the governor of Syria, to march into Judea with a large army, that he might aid Herod in taking his kingdom.

When Herod left for Samosata he put his brother Joseph in command in Judea, but charged him not to risk a battle with Antigonus during his absence. Joseph did not follow this advice. When he knew that Herod was a great distance off, he marched with five cohorts upon Jericho. Joseph was attacked upon the way by the soldiers of Antigonus, and he and all his soldiers were slain. Antigonus cut off Joseph's head from his dead body. By this victory affairs in Galilee were thrown into the greatest disorder. The men of Antigonus's party drowned a number of the principal followers of Herod in the lake. Herod heard of these calamities as he was returning from Samosata, and burned to revenge the death of his brother. He collected eight hundred men, and, with two Roman legions which Sosius had sent on in advance, he hurried into Galilee and drove his enemies from the country. Antigonus sent a large army under Pappus, one of his generals, into Samaria. Herod made an incursion into the enemy's country and destroyed five cities, and then made his headquarters at a village called Cana. Here a great multitude of Jews flocked to his standard. Pappus and his army marched upon Herod, and a great battle was fought, in which Herod was completely victorious. Herod caused Pappus's head to be cut off, and sent it to Pappus's brother,

Phernas, who was the man that had slain Joseph. Herod would have marched immediately to Jerusalem, but winter detained him. As soon as it grew warm enough he marched to Jerusalem, and pitched his camp before the temple. He gave orders for the carrying on of the siege, and then went to Samaria, in order to espouse Mariamne, who had been betrothed to him for some time. On his return he was joined by Sosius with a large army, and together they vig- orously carried on the siege. But although famine raged in Jerusalem, and the people were very hard pressed, the city held out for five months. At length a band of Herod's chosen men clambered over the walls into the city, quickly followed by Sosius's centurions. Soon the whole outside army poured into the city, and a terrible scene of carnage took place. Women, children, and feeble old men were ruthlessly put to the sword. Antigonus, frightened at the awful scene, came in great terror to Sosius and fell at his feet. But the stern Romans laughed at him, calling him by the feminine name Antigone, as if he were a girl, and put him in bonds. Having conquered his enemies, Herod now wished to restrain his foreign allies from profaning the holy places of the temple, and from entirely despoiling and depopulating the city. He complained to Sosius that the Romans, by thus emptying the city of both money and men, would leave him king of a desert, and said that he thought the dominion of the whole world too small a reward for the slaughter of so many citizens. Sosius replied that it was but just to allow the soldiers this plunder as a reward for what they had suffered during the siege. Herod made answer that he would give every one of the soldiers a reward out of his own money. He accordingly made handsome presents to all the soldiers, and gave a royal bounty to Sosius, who then went away, taking Antigonus with him to Rome, where the unfortunate captive was beheaded.

CHAPTER CXIX.

HEROD DEFEATS THE ARABIANS. HE GAINS THE FRIENDSHIP OF OCTAVIUS.

As soon as Herod was established upon the throne he conferred many honors upon those Jews in Jerusalem who had espoused his cause. But he put to death those who had aided Antigonus. He turned his ornaments into money, and sent large sums to Antony, that he might be secure of his friendship.

Antony was now in Egypt, and had become so much in love with the beautiful Queen Cleopatra that she persuaded him to do almost anything she pleased. She had all her relatives put to death, and persuaded Antony to kill the principal men in Syria, that she might be mistress of their possessions. She then longed to be queen of Judea and Arabia, and wished Antony to kill both Herod and Malichus, the king of Arabia. Antony would not consent to do this, but gave portions of both countries to Cleopatra, taking from Judea a plantation of palm-trees at Jericho, and also several cities. When afterwards Cleopatra came into Judea, Herod gave her handsome presents, and got back the places that had been torn from his kingdom by paying a yearly rent of two hundred talents.

When Antony was fighting against Octavius Cæsar for the empire of the world, Herod made ready to go to his assistance. But Cleopatra persuaded Antony to send Herod against Malichus, in order to enforce the queen of Egypt's right of tribute over the king of the Arabians; so that if

Herod won she would become queen of Arabia, or, if he were worsted, of Judea.

This scheme, however, worked to the advantage of Herod. He defeated the Arabians at Diospolis. The worsted army then retired to Kanatha, a city of Celesyria, and was joined by great multitudes. Herod gave orders to his army not to attack the Arabians, but they disobeyed, and, falling upon the enemy, at first routed them. But Athenio, one of Cleopatra's generals, treacherously sent out a force from Kanatha to the rescue of the Arabians. Encouraged by this, the Arabians turned back and completely routed Herod's army. The Jewish king hastened to bring succor, but arrived too late. He, however, revenged himself by overrunning the enemy's country. And now a great calamity fell upon the Jews. For an earthquake shook their country and destroyed an enormous quantity of cattle and thirty thousand lives; but the army escaped unharmed, because they were out in the open air, away from falling buildings.

The Arabians, believing from the reports they heard that almost all the Jews had been killed, thought they could easily capture a land almost destitute of inhabitants. So, after putting to death ambassadors who had come to them from the Jews, they marched upon Judea. The people of Judea were affrighted at this invasion, and dispirited by the calamities that had overtaken them. Herod, however, encouraged them by word and example, and led out his army to fight against the invaders. The Arabians were defeated with a loss of five thousand men, and were besieged in their camp, in which they suffered so for want of water that in five days' time four thousand of them came out and voluntarily surrendered themselves to the Jews. On the sixth day the remaining part of the army, despairing of being able to save themselves, came out to fight, and seven thousand of them were slain. Herod thus so completely crushed the power and spirit of Arabia that he was chosen by that nation to be its ruler.

In the mean time the battle of Actium had been fought, and Octavius Cæsar had defeated Antony. Herod, alarmed on account of his friendship with Antony, set out to meet the young conqueror at Rhodes. He appeared before Octavius without his diadem and in the dress of a private person, but behaved with the dignity of a king. He addressed Cæsar in a speech in which he manfully avowed the love and gratitude he bore Antony, who had made him king of the Jews, and said that he would have fought with Antony against Octavius had not the Arabian war prevented him ; and that he did not desert Antony after the battle of Actium, but advised him to kill Cleopatra and resume the war, promising him money and assistance ; that he acknowledged Octavius as his conqueror, and came to throw himself upon his mercy ; but that he wished Octavius to consider how faithful a friend, and not whose friend, he had been.

Octavius, struck by Herod's manner and address, declared he wished him for his friend, and placed the royal diadem upon his head. Herod gave Cæsar presents and returned to Judea. Afterwards, when Cæsar was going through Syria to Egypt, Herod entertained him in such a royal and generous manner that, after the conquest of Egypt, Cæsar restored to Herod the territory which Antony had given Cleopatra besides a number of cities. Nor did Cæsar's kindness cease, for he subsequently made other additions to Herod's kingdom, and appointed him procurator of all Syria.

CHAPTER CXX.

JEALOUSY LEADS HEROD TO COMMIT TERRIBLE CRIMES. HIS
UNHAPPY DOMESTIC LIFE.

In the sixteenth year of his reign Herod rebuilt the temple, which had been almost entirely destroyed during the siege. He also spent vast sums of money in improving his kingdom, by building cities and walls and temples and palaces. But although Herod was great and powerful, still, on account of his crimes, his family life was very unhappy. He loved his beautiful wife Mariamne very much indeed, and made two sons he had by her heirs to the throne. But he had committed too many wrongs against Mariamne's family to completely gain her affection in return. When the aged and unfortunate Hyrcanus, Mariamne's grandfather, returned to Jerusalem after a long captivity, Herod had him put to death because he feared the Jews might wish to make him king. He also slew Mariamne's young and beautiful brother, Aristobulus, whom he had made high-priest, but whom he feared when he saw how much the people loved him. Mariamne reproached Herod, and his mother and sister, for these crimes. The women resented this bitterly, and so, to revenge themselves, began to whisper wicked stories about Mariamne to Herod. Herod was a very jealous man, and his jealousy at times got the better of his love and made him like a demon. He began to believe the stories his mother and sister told him, and at last in a fit of jealousy he commanded his beautiful wife to be put to death. But when his passion was over he bitterly repented of what he had done, and such a fit of remorse came upon him that for a long while he acted like one gone mad. He wandered about the palace calling for his wife, and would order the servants to bring her to him. He fell very ill, and though at length he slowly recovered, the memory of his crime threw a dark shadow on his after-life. He became sullen and cruel and suspicious, while his entire life was made bitter by the quarrels which arose among his family.

The two sons of Mariamne could not but feel some bitterness towards their father, Herod, for having put their mother to death. When they grew up, Alexander, the elder, married Glaphyra, the daughter of Archelaus, king of Cappadocia; Aristobulus, the younger son, espoused Mariamne, his cousin, the daughter of Salome, Herod's sister. The sons could not at times keep from speaking out their thoughts about the cruelty of Herod in killing their mother. Salome, who had been concerned in this death, and who distrusted and disliked her nephews, began to spread evil reports, with others of her party, about the young heirs, saying that they intended to avenge the death of their mother, and that they were plotting against Herod.

The king began to suspect his sons, and in order to put a check upon them he sent for his eldest son, Antipater, begotten from his first wife, called Doris, whom he had divorced when he married Mariamne. This Antipater was a very cunning and wicked young man. He entered into plots with Salome and her brother, Pheroras. He induced Herod to receive back his mother, Doris. He so won Herod's favor that the king made him his heir; and then he set himself to work to get rid of Alexander and Aristobulus, and told so many lies and calumnies about them, and about plots he alleged they laid against Herod, that the king thought of putting them to death. So he took them before the Emperor Augustus to be judged. Alexander, however, answered the charges brought against him so well that Augustus ordered father and sons to be reconciled to each other. Herod then returned with his sons to Jerusalem, and, calling the people together, declared that Antipater should be his heir, but that the sons of Mariamne or their children should be next in succession to the throne. The anger and distrust among the brethren, however, did not diminish. Aristobulus and Alexander were grieved that the privilege of the first-born had been conferred on Antipater; while Antipater did not like the idea of having the brothers succeed him. So that before long dissensions broke out among the family with greater violence than ever. Herod was kept in a continual fever of excitement by Antipater, who continued to plot the ruin of Alexander and Aristobulus. He hired the servants, and even the friends, of the brethren to prefer all sorts of charges against them, so that the whole court soon became a scene of gloom, suspicion, and distrust. The blood of suspected persons flowed freely. Spies were everywhere. Men accused their enemies of plots so that the king would kill them; and scenes of horror were enacted every day. At length Antipater so far succeeded in his designs as to make the king believe that Alexander meant to kill him, which threw Herod into such a fright that he ordered the unhappy youth to be bound and put in prison.

Alexander occupied his time in prison in a very strange way. He wrote four long letters to his father, in which he confessed that he had been in a plot, but declared that Salome, Pheroras, and the majority of the courtiers were all concerned in it. Alexander's father-in-law, Archelaus, king of Cappadocia, becoming alarmed for the safety of his son-in-law and daughter, came hastily to Jerusalem. He won Herod's confidence by first pretending to believe all the charges trumped up against Alexander, and by feigning great indignation against his son-in-law. But by degrees he showed Herod how improbable the charges were, and succeeded in fixing the blame upon the persons mentioned in Alexander's letters, especially upon Pheroras, who had been suspected before of plotting against the king. Archelaus reconciled Herod and Alexander, and he also obtained the pardon of Pheroras, who humbly confessed his guilt. Having thus happily settled this affair, Archelaus went back to his own kingdom.

A little while afterwards there came to Jerusalem an adventurer from Sparta called Eurycles. He brought splendid gifts to Herod, and by his cunning and flattery completely won the favor of the king. As soon as he discovered the dissensions that existed in the royal family he began to turn them to his own advantage. He wormed himself into Alexander's confidence by pretending to be a friend of King Archelaus, and also took care to ingratiate himself with Aristobulus. He then hired himself to Antipater as a spy upon the brothers, and would tell him everything that they said and did, besides telling many things about them that were not true. At length Antipater hired Eurycles to charge his brethren with treason before Herod. So Eurycles went to the king and said that out of gratitude to him he would save his life, and then he pretended that he had discovered a plot. And he told Herod that Alexander had made up his mind to kill him, and then to fly with his brother Aristobulus, either to Archelaus or to Cæsar, and denounce the wickedness of Herod's reign so as to justify the murder. Herod was greatly angered at this news, and the more so when Antipater sent others to accuse the unfortunate sons of Mariamne. The king ordered the young men to be bound, and though no good proofs were brought against them, he had them put in prison. Afterwards Herod, enraged by further accusations, wrote to Cæsar, informing him of the dreadful charges against the sons of Mariamne. Cæsar wrote back and gave Herod full power over his sons, but said that he would do well to examine the matter in a public court, and take for his assessors his own kindred and the governors of his province. And he ordered the trial to take place at Berytus. Herod did not allow his sons to appear at the trial, which he conducted himself, acting as his own advocate, and seemed so eager for the death of the young princes that they were condemned by a majority of the court, although no serious charges were proved against them.

Herod hesitated about carrying out this barbarous sentence, and the whole people, and particularly the army, by whom the young men were greatly beloved, awaited in anxious suspense to see what would be done. At length a gallant old soldier by the name of Tero, whose son was an intimate friend of Alexander's, and who had himself a great affection for the princes, gave voice to the general feeling of indignation before the king. Herod caused Tero and his son to be immediately arrested, which was no sooner done than a barber in Herod's houschold rushed about in a mad sort of a way and declared that Tero had tried to bribe him to cut the king's throat, promising that Alexander would pay him handsomely for so doing. Tero and his son were immediately put upon the rack. They both denied the accusation, but when Herod gave orders that Tero should be racked more severely, the son cried out that he would confess all, if only his father should be spared from further torments. The king agreed to this, and the son confessed that his father, at the persuasion of Alexander, had determined to kill Herod. It is believed that this confession was a false one, and only made because the son could not bear to behold his father's torments. Tero and the barber and several captains were accused before the people and put to death, and the unfortunate sons of Mariamne were sent to Sebaste, and then strangled by order of their father.

CHAPTER CXXI.

DEATH OF HEROD.

ANTIPATER, having at last got rid of his brethren, went to reside in Rome, where he lived in great splendor. But although he had managed to commit many crimes without being found out, he had not been in Rome very long before one of his plots came to light in a very sudden and terrible manner. Pheroras, his uncle, who had assisted him in plotting against the young princes, fell ill, and was kindly nursed by Herod until he died. After the death of Pheroras some of his freedmen waited upon Herod, and told him that Pheroras had been poisoned by his wife. The king ordered inquiries to be made, and it came to light and was clearly proved that the wicked Antipater had sent poison to Pheroras that with it he might kill the king. The wife of Pheroras confessed the whole plot, and said that the kindness of Herod towards Pheroras while he was lying ill had melted the heart of the brother, so that he ordered the poison sent by Antipater to be thrown into the fire. But the wife only destroyed part of it, and part of it she kept. A wife of Herod's bearing the same name as the one he had killed, Marianne, daughter of Simon the high-priest, was also found to have been concerned in this plot. And so the king blotted out of his will the name of her son, Herod, whom he had appointed successor to Antipater.

Antipater, at Rome, heard of the death of Pheroras, but did not know of the discovery of the plot, for Herod had taken care that he should not be informed of it. He was

greatly grieved over the death of his uncle, or rather disappointed at the failure of his designs upon the life of Herod.
Antipater made up his mind to return to Judea, and wrote
to his father to that effect. Anxious to get the conspirator
in his hands, Herod wrote an affectionate letter to his son,
urging him to return without delay. Antipater landed at
Cæsarea, and from thence proceeded to Jerusalem. Everywhere he was met by averted looks, and sometimes open ex-
pressions of hatred. All seemed to know some secret of
which he alone was ignorant. However, it was now too late
to fly, and as Antipater had heard nothing, he was in hopes
that nothing had been discovered. Or even if anything had
been brought to light, he flattered himself that his artifice
and cunning would save him, as upon many former occasions.

Cheered with these hopes, he entered the palace at Jerusalem. But he was repulsed by Herod when he attempted to
embrace him, and charged with being a parricide. Herod
gave him one day in which to prepare his defence, and then
called him before a court over which he presided, together
with Varrus, the Roman governor of Syria. Antipater made
an artful defence, couched in such touching language that he
moved the compassion of Varrus and all those present except
Herod. Nicolaus, of Damascus, at the king's command, then
spoke against Antipater, and completely refuted everything
he had said. Such strong proofs were brought before the
court as left no doubt of the culprit's guilt. The poison
which had been kept by the wife of Pheroras was given to a
criminal under sentence of death, who expired immediately
after drinking it. Antipater was condemned, and messengers
were sent to Cæsar that he might confirm the sentence.

Herod now commenced to decline rapidly. Age and grief
increased his ailments, for he was now almost seventy years
old. As he lay upon his bed, suffering the greatest agonies
of mind and body, he was further distressed by an insurrection against him. Two of the Jews, named Judas and Mat-

thias, very learned in the laws and honored by the nation, incited a band of young men to tear down a large golden eagle which Herod had caused to be placed over the great gate of the temple in defiance of the law, which forbade the image of any living thing to be introduced into the temple. The young men were arrested in the act and brought before Herod, who ordered the ringleaders to be burnt alive and the remainder of the band to be executed.

After this Herod grew rapidly worse and suffered the most horrible torments. His sufferings seemed to make him all the more cruel. He assembled the men of distinction throughout Judea, and ordered them to be shut up in the Hippodrome, and enjoined his sister Salome that as soon as he died all these men should be killed, in order that there might be wide-spread grief throughout the country.

Scarcely had he given these orders when letters arrived from Rome giving Cæsar's assent to Antipater's execution. Herod was now suffering such terrible agony that he attempted to stab himself, but was prevented by his cousin. Instantly the palace was filled with lamentations; and Antipater, hearing them, thought the king was dead, and besought his guards to free him from his bonds, promising them large rewards. The keeper of the prison immediately went to the king and told him of Antipater's designs. Herod ordered his spearsmen to go and despatch Antipater at once, which being done, he gave orders that the body should be buried at Hyrcanium. He then again amended his will, appointing Archelaus, his eldest son, to succeed him, and Antipas, the younger brother, tetrarch of Galilee, and Philip tetrarch of Trachonitis and the neighboring territories.

Herod survived the execution of his son five days. He had reigned thirty-four years since the execution of Antigonus, when he really became master of the state; but thirty-seven years from the date of his having been declared king by the Romans.

Upon his death his sister Salome liberated the chief men
of the Jews whom Herod had shut up in the Hippodrome.
The will of Herod was then read to the people, and Archelaus was received with acclamations. Great preparations were
then made for the funeral of Herod. Archelaus spared no
expense. The bier was of solid gold, studded with precious
stones, and the bed of variegated purple. On this lay the
body, covered also with purple. On Herod's head a diadem
was placed, and over him a crown of gold. At his right hand
was a sceptre. Around the bier were Herod's sons and his
numerous relatives. Next in order were the royal guards
and hired soldiers, while in front marched the army, preceded
by the generals and officers. These were followed by five
hundred servants and freedmen, bearing aromatic spices. The
procession marched in great pomp to Herodium, which was
about twenty-five miles from Jerusalem, where the body of
the king was buried.

Archelaus mourned for his father for seven days, and
feasted the people at a funeral feast, according to the custom
of the Jews. He then prepared to set out for Rome, in order
that he might gain Cæsar's consent that he should be king of
the Jews. He called the people together, and addressed them
from a throne made of gold. He thanked the people for the
submission they had made to him, but said he would not take
upon himself the authority of king until Cæsar should ratify
Herod's will, and that he would make ample returns for the
good will the people had shown him, and that he would try
to be a better king than was his father.

The people were pleased by Archelaus's speech, and immediately put his good intentions to test by asking him to
grant them many favors. Some wished the taxes to be reduced, while others begged him to release the prisoners.
Archelaus promised to attend to these requests, in order that
he might gain the good will of the people.

In the evening great crowds of people, who had been dissatisfied under Herod's reign, collected together, and began loudly to mourn for those men whom Herod had put to death because they had attempted to cut down the golden eagle over the gate of the temple. They cried out that Herod's advisers should be put to death, and that the man whom he had made high-priest should be deprived of his office.

Archelaus was provoked by these clamors, but tried to quiet them in a peaceful manner. He sent his general among the authors of these complaints, and by him exhorted them to be quiet. But the mob threw stones at the general, and would not let him speak. In like manner they treated others whom Archelaus sent in order to quietly quell the tumult.

It was now the feast of unleavened bread, called by the Jews the Passover.

Multitudes came to Jerusalem from the country, among whom the rioters began to spread their seditious doctrines. Archelaus now saw that he must take strong measures in order to nip in the bud a terrible rebellion. He therefore sent an officer with a cohort to seize the leaders of the insurrection. But the multitude in anger stoned the soldiers and killed many of them; the officer himself escaped with difficulty. Archelaus then sent his whole army against the rioters. Falling upon them suddenly while at sacrifice, the soldiers dispersed and slew about three thousand of the rioters, and drove the rest to the mountains. The heralds of Archelaus then commanded all the strangers to return to their several homes, and so all withdrew without finishing the festival.

Archelaus, accompanied by Nicolaus, set out for Rome together with many of the royal family, who went apparently to aid Archelaus in securing the throne, but in reality to accuse him of misdemeanors against the temple, and thus in reality to assist the younger brother, Antipas, who had gone to Rome to claim the crown upon the grounds of a former will, made, as his party asserted, when Herod was in a saner state of mind, and in which Antipas was made heir.

On his way to Rome Archelaus met Sabinus, the procurator of Syria, at Cæsarea, who was marching to Judea in order to make himself master of Herod's treasures. But, at the request of Varrus, the governor of Syria, Sabinus agreed to remain at Cæsarea and leave Archelaus in possession of the treasures and fortresses of Judea until a decision had been made at Rome. But no sooner had Varrus gone away to Antioch, and Archelaus set sail for Rome, than Sabinus hurried to Jerusalem, seized the palace, and commanded the keepers of the treasures to render up their accounts, and tried to obtain possession of the fortresses. All, however, remained faithful to their charge, and refused to obey any orders until some came from Rome.

In the mean while the two brothers disputed before Cæsar their rights to the crown of Judea. Before he came to a decision in the matter news came that Judea was in a state of insurrection. The greed of Sabinus incited the people to rebellion. The feast of the Pentecost came on again, and the Jews gathered from all quarters to wreak their vengeance upon Sabinus. Dividing themselves into three sections, they encamped on the north, south, and west of the temple, and proceeded to besiege the Romans. Sabinus sent to Varrus for aid, and, greatly frightened, crawled up to the top of a high tower, and from thence ordered his troops to attack the Jews. The people mounted on the roofs of the porticoes which surrounded the outer court of the temple, and from there hurled missiles upon their enemies. The Romans set fire to the porticoes, and thus the unhappy Jews were either burned alive, or slaughtered by the enemy when they attempted to jump to the ground. The Romans then broke into the temple and plundered the sacred treasures. Maddened by this outrage, vast numbers of Jews collected together from all parts of the country, and besieged Sabinus and his forces in the royal palace

A number of the king's troops, who were aiding Sabinus,

deserted and joined the besiegers, who vigorously pressed the siege, but sent word to Sabinus to depart from the city with his soldiers and leave them to recover their national independence. Sabinus would gladly have retired, but he was afraid the Jews wished to ensnare him, and so in hope of aid from Varrus he maintained the defence.

The whole country, being without any government, became a scene of carnage and bloodshed. Two thousand of Herod's army who had been dismissed overran Judea, and drove a cousin of Archelaus's with some royal troops into the mountains. A robber chief plundered at will the country of Galilee. All over the rural districts adventurers arose, who collected together armed bodies of men and spread ruin and desolation all over the country.

Varrus, fearful for the safety of the Roman legion besieged in Jerusalem, hastened to the relief of Sabinus as soon as he received his despatches. He gathered together his forces, and assisted by an army under Aretas, king of Arabia, he hastened towards Jerusalem. Many cities were burned and sacked upon the way by the cruel Arabians. When Varrus approached Jerusalem, the forces of the Jews who were besieging Sabinus hurriedly fled to the country and dispersed. The inhabitants of the city then opened the gates to the invading army, and declared that they were not in revolt, but laid the whole blame upon the multitudes of strangers who had come into the city to attend the Pentecost. Sabinus, ashamed to look Varrus in the face after his dastardly conduct, slunk away to the sea-coast and set sail for Rome.

Varrus sent his troops all over the country in order to capture those who had been involved in the sedition. A great number were arrested, and those that appeared to be ringleaders were crucified, to the number of about two thousand; the rest were pardoned. About ten thousand of the insurgents collected together in Idumea. Varrus sent the Arabians home because he could not restrain their excesses, and with his own soldiers marched against the rebels, who immediately surrendered to him. He pardoned the common soldiers, but sent the officers to Rome for trial. Having thus settled matters, the Roman general left a garrison in Jerusalem and went back into Syria.

CHAPTER CXXI.

THE FALSE ALEXANDER.

WHILE the decision in regard to the dominions of Herod still remained in suspense, a body of fifty Jews arrived in Rome to petition for independence from all kingly rule. They were supported by eight thousand of their countrymen then residing in Rome. Cæsar called together a council in order that the cause might be heard. On one side stood the ambassadors and the Roman Jews, on the other Archelaus and his friends.

The ambassadors spoke first, and charged their former king, Herod, with the greatest extortions and cruelties. They said that the Jews were more unhappy under him than during their captivity in Babylon, and that Archelaus had shown himself to be like his father, by slaughtering three thousand Jews at the feast of the Pentecost. They therefore prayed Cæsar to allow no more kings to reign in Judea, but to annex the country to Syria and to let it be ruled by Roman governors, and said that they would show that they knew how to obey authority mildly exercised. The eloquent Nicolaus spoke for Archelaus, and refuted the charges against the royal personages; he declared the Jews to be a rebellious set, and by nature disobedient to their sovereigns. Cæsar, having listened attentively to both sides, dismissed the council, and, after having thought over the matter for a few days, he decided for the

most part to confirm the will of Herod. He therefore bestowed upon Archelaus the government of Judea, Idumea,
and Samaria, under the title of ethnarch, promising to make
him king should he prove deserving. Antipas received
Galilee and Peræa; Philip, another son of Herod, got for his
portion Batanæa, Trachonitis, Auranitis, and Paneas. Salome,
Herod's sister, obtained the government and revenues of several cities. Other members of Herod's family received such
bequests as he had left them in his will. Cæsar divided a
thousand talents which Herod had left him between two unmarried daughters of Herod, and gave them in marriage to
two sons of Pheroras, keeping for himself only a few articles
of plate in honor of his dead friend.

At this juncture another trouble arose. There suddenly
appeared in Rome a young Jew, who pretended that he was
the prince Alexander whom Herod had ordered to be killed.
He looked very much like the dead Alexander, and had been
trained to act his part by a Jew who had been much at the
court of Herod. And so well did he do it that he completely
deceived the Jews in Crete and Melos, who furnished him with
money to go to Rome and claim the Jewish throne as his
inheritance. He explained his escape from the death that
Herod had ordered by saying that the executioners had taken
compassion on both himself and his brother Aristobulus and
allowed them to escape, placing in their stead dead bodies
resembling theirs. As soon as this impostor arrived in Rome
he was received by the Jews with loud acclamations as the
true Alexander, and provided with royal attendance at their
own expense.

Cæsar, suspecting a cheat, sent one of his freedmen, called
Celadus, who had intimately known the sons of Mariamne,
to conduct the youth to his presence. When Celadus saw
the pretender, he at once knew that this was not the real
Alexander. Calling the young man aside, he told him that
he knew he was a cheat, but promised that Cæsar would

spare his life if he would point out the man who had taught
him to act the part of an impostor. The false Alexander,
finding himself detected, went with Celadus to Cæsar, and
pointed out to them his instructor. Cæsar was much amused
by this affair, and, seeing that the pretender was a stout young
man, he made him a rower in one of his galleys. But he
ordered the wicked Jew who had taught the young man to
play a false part to be put to death.

Archelaus assumed the dominion which had been granted
him, but ruled with such cruelty that he was accused before
Cæsar by both the Jews and the Samaritans. So that in the
ninth year of his rule he was banished by Augustus to Vienne,
a small town in Gaul, and his property confiscated. Judea
was made a Roman province, and was thereafter governed by
a procurator sent from Rome.

A certain Judas, a Galilean, led a revolt against the first
procurator, a man of noble family, called Coponius, but the
rebellion was soon crushed, Judas was killed, and his followers dispersed. This Judas taught his followers that the Jews
should not allow the Romans or any one else to rule them,
because they had formerly had God as a ruler, and to Him
alone should they give their allegiance.

Philip and Herod Antipas were allowed to retain the government of their tetrarchies. When Augustus died he was
succeeded by Tiberius as emperor of Rome, who confirmed
them as tetrarchs, and sent the celebrated Pontius Pilate as
procurator into Judea.

Pilate, under cover of night, secretly brought Roman standards into Jerusalem, upon which were images of Cæsar.
The Jews were greatly shocked when they saw these in the
morning, for their laws forbade the placing of any images
within the city. They hastened in crowds to Pilate, and besought him to remove the standards. Pilate rejected their
suit, and, tiring of their petitions, ordered his soldiers to surround the people, and said that he would have them all killed

if they did not withdraw their complaint. To the surprise of
the procurator, the Jews all fell prostrate, and cried out that
they would rather die than transgress their law. Pilate was
so struck by their devotion that he ordered the immediate
removal of the standards. A little while afterwards Pilate
occasioned another tumult by spending the revenue of the
temple upon the building of an aqueduct. The populace in-
terfered and stopped the workmen. Pilate dressed his soldiers
in plain clothes, and dispersed them among the multitudes of
indignant Jews, ordering them not to use swords, but to beat
the rioters with staves. He then gave a signal, upon which
the soldiers fell upon the Jews and beat them in so violent a
manner that many were killed, and the rest had all thoughts
of rebellion completely knocked out of them.

CHAPTER CXXIII.

CAIUS (CALIGULA) BECOMES EMPEROR OF ROME.

At the court of Tiberius in Rome there was a young son
of Aristobulus, the prince who had been murdered by the first
Herod, called Agrippa. This Agrippa was a very dear friend
to the young Caius, grand-nephew of Tiberius. On one occasion, while he was riding with Caius, he expressed to him a
hope that ere long he should see him master of the empire
when Tiberius should be no more. This speech was overheard by a servant, and repeated to Tiberius, who became so
angry that he threw Agrippa into prison, where he remained
for six months. At the end of this time Tiberius died, and
was succeeded by Caius, who immediately released his friend,
and made him king of the tetrarchy left vacant by the death of
Philip. Herod Antipas became very jealous because Agrippa

had been made a king, while he himself was only a tetrarch. So he set sail for Rome, in order that he might persuade Cæsar to make him also a king. But when Herod arrived in Rome, Caius, on account of some charges made against him by Agrippa, banished him to Spain, and, taking away his territory, bestowed it upon Agrippa.

Caius, who was also called Caligula, now began to grow very conceited indeed, so that he imagined himself a god, and wished to be worshipped everywhere as such. He accordingly sent Petronius with a large army to Jerusalem to place his statues in the temple, and gave him orders that should the Jews refuse to admit them, he should put all that opposed him to the sword, and enslave the rest of the nation. When Petronius had come with his army to Ptolemais, a maritime town on the confines of Galilee, the Jews assembled in crowds in a plain near by, and, coming to Petronius, they besought him to respect the laws of their country. Petronius parleyed with the Jews, and, leaving his army and the images of the emperor at Ptolemais, he went farther on into Galilee, and called together an assemblage of the Jews at Tiberias. He tried to persuade them that their request was unreasonable, for all the other subject nations had yielded to the commands of Cæsar and placed his images among their gods, so that their opposing this was little less than a rebellion. Besides, he insisted that he must fulfil the commands of his master. The Jews, on the other hand, replied that their law forbade them to allow an image of God, much less of men, not only in their temple, but even in any place throughout their country; and they declared that they were prepared to suffer and die rather than their law should be infringed.

Petronius shrank from carrying out the awful commands of the emperor. And he was indeed so struck by the fidelity of the Jews to their religion, that after trying in vain to persuade them to accede to Cæsar's commands, he resolved to risk the anger of the emperor rather than to deluge the country with blood. This noble man therefore called the Jews together, and said to them that he would try and dissuade Cæsar from carrying out his plan, or, if he failed, he would sacrifice his own life rather than destroy the lives of so many people. He then dismissed the multitude, who invoked many blessings on him, and withdrew to Antioch. From thence he wrote to Cæsar, acquainting him with the facts of his expedition into Judea, and said that unless the emperor was prepared to destroy both the country and its inhabitants, it behooved him to forego his orders and allow them to observe their law. To this letter Caius returned an angry answer, threatening Petronius with death for being so tardy in executing his commands. It so happened, however, that the messengers carrying these despatches were detained by stormy weather, while others announcing the death of Cæsar had a favorable voyage. So the good Petronius was not put to death, and did not get the letter of Caius until nearly a month after he had been informed of that wicked emperor's death.

CHAPTER CXXIV.

DEATH OF AGRIPPA.   JUDEA IS AGAIN MADE A ROMAN PROVINCE.

CAIUS was assassinated in the fourth year of his reign, and his uncle, Claudius, was declared emperor by the army. The senate, however, were bitterly opposed to the succession of Claudius, and it looked very much as if a civil war would ensue. Agrippa, who happened to arrive in Rome at this juncture, was by mutual consent made a mediator between the soldiers and the senate. Agrippa attached himself to the cause of Claudius, and succeeded in persuading the senate to withdraw their opposition to his succession. When the senate went out to present themselves to Claudius, they were met by armed bodies of soldiers with drawn swords. And there would undoubtedly have been much bloodshed had not Agrippa hastened to Claudius and persuaded him to restrain the violence of his soldiers.

For these services Agrippa received all the dominions which belonged to the great Herod, with the addition of another principality, styled the kingdom of Lysanias. Upon Agrippa's brother, Herod, the emperor bestowed the kingdom of Chalcis.

From such vast territories Agrippa began to amass great wealth, a great portion of which he spent in surrounding Jerusalem with an immense wall. But before the work was completed Agrippa died, three years after his accession to the throne of Palestine. He left three daughters, Berenice, Mariamne, and Drusilla, and one son, Agrippa. This son being under age, Claudius again reduced the kingdom to a province, and sent Cuspius Fadus as procurator, and after him Tiberius Alexander. Under these two men the country remained in a peaceful condition. Herod, king of Chalcis, died a little while after his brother, and left three sons, Bernicianus, Hyrcanus, and Aristobulus. These were all grand-children of Aristobulus, the son of Herod. The posterity of Alexander reigned in Armenia Major.

When Herod, king of Chalcis, died, Claudius raised to his uncle's throne Agrippa, son of Agrippa. Cumanus succeeded Alexander as procurator of Judea. Under him fresh disturbances arose, and a great many disasters befell the Jews. Now commenced a series of revolts against tyrannies practised by Roman governors of Judea, which finally ended in open war. A Roman soldier insulted the Jews at a festival; enraged, they not only vented their rage upon the offender, but attacked with stones the soldiers of Cumanus. The governor ordered his army to attack the Jews, who hurriedly dispersed, and in the tumult which followed ten thousand of them were crushed to death; so that the rejoicings of the festival were turned into wails and lamentations. On another occasion a Roman soldier destroyed a copy of the Law of Moses. The Jews, highly enraged, rushed in a body before Cumanus, and were only pacified by his consent that the soldier should be put to death.

Other troubles arose in this distracted country. The road by which the Jews of Galilee went to the temple led through Samaria. As a number were on their way to the festival, one of the Galileans was assassinated by a Samaritan. Cumanus was bribed by the Samaritans, and would take no notice of the crime, so a body of Jews took matters in their own hands, and, going into Samaria, slaughtered many of the people and burnt some of their towns. Cumanus marched against the invading Jews, and defeated and killed a great many of them. The survivors were persuaded by the magistrates of Jerusalem, who came out to meet them clad in sackcloth and ashes, to lay aside their arms, lest they should bring down the vengeance of Rome upon the nation.

The Samaritan chiefs waited on Numidius Quadratus, prefect of Syria, and demanded the punishment of those Jews who had laid waste their country. The Jews, on the other hand, accused the Samaritans of creating the disturbance by committing the murder, alleging also that Cumanus was responsible for all. Quadratus condemned the Samaritans, but nevertheless put to death all the Jews taken prisoners by Cumanus as rebels. He sent to Rome some of the chief men of both the Samaritans and the Jews, that they might plead the case before Cæsar, and also Cumanus and Celer, his tribune. Cæsar also condemned the Samaritans. He banished Cumanus, and sent Celer in chains to Jerusalem, with orders that he should there be beheaded.

Cæsar appointed Felix, brother of Pallas, who was afterwards the freed slave and favorite of the emperor Nero, procurator of Judea, and promoted Agrippa, king of Chalcis, to rule the more extensive dominions over which Philip was formerly tetrarch, adding to the new kingdom part of Galilee and Peræa.

Claudius died in the fourteenth year of his reign, and was succeeded by the wicked Nero.

CHAPTER CXXV.

THE REVOLT OF THE JEWS AGAINST FLORUS.

NERO confirmed Felix as procurator, and added some cities to the dominions of Agrippa. The province of Judea was much troubled at this time by robbers and assassins, who dealt death and destruction all over the country. Felix did his best to wipe out these evils, but was not completely successful.

In Cæsarea a great disturbance took place, which finally led to open rupture with Rome. This city was inhabited by two races, the Syrian Greeks, who were pagans, and the Jews. These two peoples hated each other, and each wished to rule the city. The Jews claimed the city because it was founded by Herod the Great. But the Greeks declared that Herod intended it to be a Grecian city, because he erected in it pagan statues and temples, which he would not have done had he intended the city to be possessed by Jews. Ere long the two races attempted to settle the dispute by an appeal to the sword. Every day parties of Jews and Syrians would meet and fight, although the older and more prudent men on both sides, as well as the magistrates of the city, used all their endeavors to preserve peace.

Felix himself came into the city, to preserve order; and

one day, when a party of Jews had beaten a party of Syrians, he ordered the Jews to disperse. They would not obey the order, so Felix ordered his troops to attack them, and many Jews were killed and their houses plundered in the scrimmage which followed. But as the two parties still continued to quarrel, Felix selected prominent men from each party, and sent them to Rome to argue their respective rights before the emperor.

Festus succeeded Felix as procurator, and directed his efforts to getting rid of the band of brigands that infested the country. He was not long in office before Albinus took his place, a most cruel and wicked man, who was himself a greater thief than any that infested the country. But Albinus was a saint compared to Gessius Florus, his successor. This man committed every species of rapine and injustice. He despoiled whole cities, and ruined populous communities. Entire districts were reduced by him to desolation, and many of the Jews fled to foreign countries in order to get away from his rule.

Cestius Gallus was at this time governor in Syria, but as long as he remained in his country the Jews, through fear of Florus, were prevented from sending a deputation to him with complaints against their procurator. But when Cestius visited Jerusalem to attend the Passover, the people crowded around him and besought his interference. Florus stood beside Cestius, and turned the complaints of the people into ridicule. When the governor left, Florus accompanied him as far as Cæsarea, filling his ear with calumnies about the Jews, and laying plans all the while to drive them into open revolt. For he was afraid that if peace continued, the Jews would accuse him of his evil deeds before Cæsar, but if he drove them into open war they could not do this, and he would thus conceal all his atrocities. When Florus returned to Jerusalem, therefore, he acted with greater cruelty than ever, so as to fan the flame of war.

The flame finally broke out in Cæsarea. Nero, bribed by the Greeks, had given them the government of the city. It happened that the Jews had a synagogue, the ground about which was owned by a Greek, to whom the Jews had often offered a much higher price for his lot than it was worth. He refused to sell it, and in order to insult them built some mean little workshops on the ground, and left the Jews only a very narrow approach to their place of worship. Some hot-blooded youths interrupted the builders. But, as Florus would not allow violence, some of the Jews collected eight talents and gave it to Florus as a bribe to interfere and stop the builders. Florus promised to do so, but as soon as he had got the money in his hands he set out for Sebaste, leaving the riot to take care of itself, doubtless hoping that it might bring on a war.

On the following Sabbath, when the Jews were in their synagogue, a Greek, in order to insult them, sacrificed some birds upon an earthen pot at the entrance of the temple. The more violent of the Jews, furious at this outrage, attacked the Greeks, who were already in arms and expecting an affray. Jucundus, master of horse under Florus, attempted in vain to quell the tumult. The Jews were worsted, and retired to Narbata, about seven miles distant. From thence they sent a deputation to Florus in Sebaste, imploring his assistance, and reminding him of the eight talents they had given him. But Florus threw the deputation into prison.

The news of this outrage reached Jerusalem, and although the people were very indignant, still they restrained their feelings. But Florus, determined to drive them to revolt, seized this critical time to rob the sacred treasury of the temple of seventeen talents, pretending that Cæsar needed the money. The outraged Jews flocked about the temple with loud outcries, and openly expressed their hatred and contempt of the procurator. Some passed about a basket begging in ridicule a trifle for the poor beggar Florus.

Hearing of this, Florus immediately marched upon Jerusalem, though he should have gone to Cæsarea, in order to quell the tumult there. But the Roman thought this a good chance to pillage the rich capital. The inhabitants of Jerusalem, in order to shame him from his purpose, came out to meet his army with acclamations. Florus sent forward a centurion with a body of horse, to order the people to return, and not to mock with pretended courtesy one whose name they had reviled, and to say that if they were brave men they would reproach him to his face, and prove their love of liberty by taking up arms against him. The multitude, frightened at the message, returned to their homes, and spent the night in alarm and dejection, fearing the vengeance of their ruler.

Florus fixed his quarters in the palace, and in the morning summoned the high-priests and chief men before him. He commanded them to deliver up those who had insulted him, declaring that they themselves should feel his vengeance if they did not produce the guilty ones. In reply, they represented the peaceable disposition of the people, and entreated his pardon for those who had insulted him; throwing the blame upon a few indiscreet youths, whom it was impossible to detect, as all had repented, and from fear of the consequences would not confess their guilt. It behooved him, however, they argued, to preserve the city and the peace of the nation, by forgiving the few who had offended, rather than revenge himself upon a multitude of innocent men.

Florus became all the more incensed at their words, and loudly ordered his soldiers to plunder the upper market, and to kill all they met with. The ready soldiers not only sacked the market, but broke into the houses and massacred the inmates. The city ran with blood. Neither age nor sex was spared, and men, women, and children to the number of nearly four thousand were cruelly slaughtered upon that awful day.

King Agrippa was absent in Egypt, but Berenice, his sister,

was in Jerusalem fulfilling a religious vow. Horrified at the awful sights she saw around her, she many times sent messengers to Florus, and at last herself besought him to stay the fury of the soldiers. But Florus was deaf to her prayers, and the queen was obliged to retreat quickly into the palace, in order to save her own life.

The following day the multitude gathered around the upper market-place and with loud cries lamented their dead, and gave way to fierce invectives against Florus. Alarmed at this, the chief priests and leaders went among them and implored them to keep quiet, and not again, after all they had suffered, to provoke the vengeance of Florus. Out of respect for those that exhorted them, the people complied and dispersed.

Florus was disappointed at the cessation of the disturbance. He wanted another excuse to murder and rob the people. He sent for the chief priests and leaders, and told them that as a proof of the submission of the people he desired them to go out and welcome two cohorts of troops who were advancing from Cæsarea. While the priests and leaders were exhorting the people to obey this command, Florus sent word to the advancing soldiers not to return the salute of the Jews, and if they should break out in murmurs to attack them.

The priests and leaders found it very difficult to make the outraged people obey this command. But they told them that, unless they obeyed, their country would be laid waste and their temple profaned and pillaged. At last the multitude consented, and were led out in peaceable array to meet the troops, whom they welcomed with apparent gladness. As no response was made by the cohorts, some of the Jews broke out in open murmurs against Florus. Upon this the soldiers surrounded the Jews and beat them with their clubs, while the cavalry pursued and trampled down those that fled. Many fell under the blows of the Romans, but a great many more were crushed to death by their own party. At the gates

the crush was terrible, as all strove to get into the city. Many
fell and had the life trampled out of them. The soldiers
rushed in with the people, striving to get ahead of them and
obtain possession of the temple and the fortress called Antonia. Anxious to get possession of the temple, Florus
with his soldiers sallied from the palace and tried to reach
the fortress, but was foiled by the people in the attempt.
For some so blocked up the narrow streets that he could not
cut his way through, while others assailed the soldiers from
the roofs. Florus retreated to his quarters, and the people,
fearing lest he might return and push forward through the
Antonia, and so gain possession of the temple, cut off the
porticoes and galleries which connected the two buildings.
This made Florus despair of obtaining his main object, the
plunder of the temple's treasures. He therefore gave up the
attack, and, sending for the chief priests and leaders, proposed
to go away from the city, but said he would leave a sufficient
force to guard the place. On their promising that they would
do their best to preserve the peace, he left one cohort behind
him and retired with the rest of his soldiers to Cæsarea.

CHAPTER CXXVI.

AGRIPPA VAINLY ATTEMPTS TO AVERT THE WAR.

FLORUS, in order to furnish matter for fresh hostilities, sent
a letter to his superior officer, Cestius Gallus, in which he
falsely accused the Jews of revolt, pretending that they had
raised the disturbance, and charging them with the very excesses from which they themselves had suffered. The Jews
also, on their part, through their rulers and Queen Berenice,
sent accounts of the horrible outrages committed by Florus.

They were of the opinion that Cestius should advance with his army either to chastise the malcontents among them, should a rebellion arise, or to confirm the Jews in their allegiance, should they have maintained it.

Cestius sent forward one of his tribunes, called Neopolitanus, to examine into affairs, and to report to him the sentiments of the Jews. While Neopolitanus was on his way he met King Agrippa at Jamnia, who was returning from Egypt. He informed him of the purpose of his journey, and by whom he had been sent. Before they left Jamnia a deputation of priests and leaders of the people arrived to congratulate King Agrippa upon his return. After paying their respects to the king, they deplored their calamities and bewailed the cruelty of Florus. Agrippa, though he heartily sympathized with them, artfully concealed his compassion, and even affected to reprove them, in order that he might divert them from all thoughts of revenge. For he knew that such a course would only end in their own ruin.

When Agrippa and Neopolitanus neared Jerusalem, the people poured out to meet them in a most mournful procession. The widows of those that had been slain preceded the people, and amid loud wailing and lamentations the entire populace besought Agrippa to succor them. They enumerated to Neopolitanus the many miseries they had endured under Florus; and on entering the city, they showed the market-place desolated and the houses in ruins. Neopolitanus passed through the whole city, and, finding it very peaceable, he went up to the temple, and, calling the people together, commended their fidelity to the Romans and exhorted them to maintain peace. After this he took part in the temple-worship as far as was permitted to strangers, and returned to Cestius.

The people wished to send ambassadors to accuse Florus before Nero. Agrippa, on his part, declined to encourage this embassy. And as he wished to dissuade the people from all thoughts of war, he assembled them before the Xystus. Placing his sister Berenice in view of all, he made them a long and eloquent speech. He held before them the hope of a milder government than that which had recently afflicted them, when the true state of the province should reach the ears of the emperor. He told them that their hopes of gaining independence were vain. If they could not resist part of the Roman forces under Pompey, how could they expect to make a successful struggle now when the Romans ruled the world? All other nations, he said, were held in subjection by a few Roman troops. When so many great nations had been conquered, how could the Jews hope to be victorious? Finally, he dwelt upon the horrors of war, and the destruction that would surely fall upon their city and holy temple. When the king had finished he burst into tears, and his sister wept aloud. The people were moved by his eloquence and touched by the tears of the royal pair. They cried out that they had not taken up arms against the Romans, but only to avenge their sufferings upon Florus. Agrippa replied, " But your actions are those of men already at war with the Romans. For you have not given the tribute to Cæsar, and you have destroyed the galleries which united the Antonia with the temple. You will, however, free yourselves from the blame of the insurrection if you repair the buildings and pay the tribute. For the fortress now no longer belongs to Florus, nor to Florus will you give the money."

The people obeyed. With the king and Berenice they immediately proceeded to the temple and commenced rebuilding the galleries. The magistrates and members of council were sent out through the villages to collect the arrears in taxes, and in a short time forty talents were obtained. The danger of war seemed over. Unluckily, Agrippa tried to persuade the multitude to obey Florus until Cæsar should send some one to take his place. The people, incensed at this, reproached the king, and banished him from the city.

Some of the rioters went so far as to throw stones at him. Indignant at this treatment, Agrippa sent some magistrates to Florus, who was at Cæsarea, that he might appoint some of them to collect the tribute, and withdrew to his own dominions.

And now a party of the most rebellious spirits assembled and attacked a fortress called Massada, occupied by Roman troops. They took the fortress, massacred the soldiers, and replaced them by a garrison of their own. In the temple a decisive measure was taken by Eleazar, son of Ananias the high-priest. He persuaded those priests who conducted the public worship to receive neither gift nor sacrifice from any foreigner. This was the same as directly renouncing all allegiance to Rome, for it was the custom of the Cæsars to send offerings to the temple, which were sacrificed in behalf of the Roman people.

The chief priests and influential men attempted to dissuade the people from adopting so ruinous a course. They represented that it had always been a custom to receive the offerings of strangers; that it was impious to preclude strangers from offering victims and kneeling in worship before God; such a decree would be an act of inhumanity against a single individual,—how much greater, then, must it be against the emperor and the whole Roman people! There was reason to fear also, they said, lest by rejecting the sacrifices of the Romans they themselves should be kept from sacrificing, and their city be put under the ban of the empire, unless they without delay should restore the sacrifices to their former footing, and repair the injury ere the rumor reached the injured.

They then brought forward the priests who knew the most about the customs of their worship. These all stated that the Jews had always received the sacrifices of foreigners. But the disaffected ones among the people would listen to nothing, nor would those priests whom Eleazar had persuaded perform the foreign sacrifices.

The leading men, when they saw that they could not check
the rebellion, and as they knew that they would be the first
to feel the resentment of the Romans, sent a deputation to
Florus and another to Agrippa, in order to free themselves
from blame, requesting them both to bring an army to
the city and crush the rebellion.   Florus was rejoiced at the
tidings, and, that he might further incense the Jews, he dismissed the embassy without a reply.   Agrippa, anxious to
save the city and the temple, immediately sent three thousand
horse to the aid of those opposed to the rebellion.

Encouraged by these succors, the leading men, with the
chief priests and as many of the populace as were friendly to
peace and to the Roman rule, seized on the upper town.   For
the lower town and the temple were in the possession of the
insurgents.   For seven days the two parties fought with each
other without either gaining any decided advantage.   The
following day was the festival of wood-carrying, on which it
was customary for every one to bring wood, that there might
be a constant supply of fuel for the altar, for the sacred fire was
never allowed to go out.   The insurgents refused to allow
their opponents to take part in this festival, but admitted into
the temple a large band of brigands who were eager to aid
the rebels.   A fierce attack was made upon the royal troops,
who were overpowered and obliged to retreat from the upper
city.   The victorious insurgents then set fire to the residence
of the high-priest, the royal palace, and to the public archives
in which the bonds of the debtors were registered.   They then
again rushed on to the attack.   Some of the chief priests and
leading men now hid themselves in sewers, while others fled
with the royal troops to the upper palace and shut the gates.

On the next day the insurgents attacked the Antonia.   In
two days they carried it, put the garrison to the sword, and
set fire to the fortress.   They then attacked the upper palace.
The royal troops hurled missiles upon the heads of the attacking party and killed a great many of them.   Night and

day the terrible fight went on,—the insurgents hoping that the assailed would be reduced by famine, the royal troops that their assailants would grow weary of the attack.

Meanwhile, one Manahem, son of that Judas who had revolted against Coponius, and who had upbraided the Jews for obeying the Romans after having had God for their master, accompanied by a band of followers, repaired to Massada, where he plundered the armory of Herod. Arming his own men and a number of brigands, he returned in great pomp to Jerusalem, where he became leader of the sedition, and conducted the siege. So hotly was the palace attacked that the garrison soon sued for terms. The insurgents granted safe passage to the royal troops, who accordingly withdrew, leaving their few Roman allies to face the enemy alone. The Romans retreated to three strong towers which had been built by King Herod. Manahem and his party instantly rushed into the palace, slew the few who had not yet retreated, plundered the baggage, and set fire to the encampment.

The day following, Ananias the high-priest and his brother Hezekiah were discovered hiding in a sewer of the palace, and were put to death. Manahem, inflated by his success, and believing that no one would oppose him, took upon himself the supreme authority, and began to act the part of a cruel and bloodthirsty tyrant. Eleazar, the son of the murdered Ananias, and his party would not brook this. It was unbecoming, they said, after having revolted from the Romans through love of liberty, to bow down to a master lower born than themselves. Accordingly, they attacked Manahem in the temple, where he had gone to worship, dressed in the royal robes. They were assisted by the populace, who thought that by killing Manahem they would end the sedition ; and they soon dispersed his party. All that were caught were put to death ; among them Manahem, who was dragged from a hiding-place and publicly executed with every variety of torture.

The people hoped that the death of Manahem would end the sedition; but such was not the intention of Eleazar and his party. They so vigorously pressed the siege that Metellius, who was in command of the Romans, soon sued for terms, offering to surrender arms and property if only the lives of himself and his soldiers would be spared. This was agreed to, and Metellius and his detachment came down from the towers; but just as soon as they had laid down their arms, the followers of Eleazar basely fell upon them, and butchered them to a man. Metellius alone escaped by promising that if spared he would profess the Jewish faith.

This horrible deed cut off from all the last hope of obtaining pardon from Rome. The more moderate foresaw that they would have to suffer for the misconduct of the insurgents. Jerusalem was filled with sorrow and lamentations. The crime for which all felt they would have to suffer seemed all the more horrible and atrocious because it had been committed on the Sabbath, the holy day of peace and rest.

CHAPTER CXXVII.

THE DEFEAT OF CESTIUS.

On the same day and hour, as if ordered to do so by an avenging Providence, the Cæsareans slaughtered the Jews who resided among them. In one hour over twenty thousand were massacred, and Cæsarea was emptied of Jews. The whole Jewish nation rose to avenge this outrage. Separating into bands, they laid waste the neighboring towns and villages of the Syrians, and slaughtered a great number of the inhabitants. The Syrians, on their part, slew all the Jewish inhabitants of their towns that they could capture. He who could display the largest amount of Jewish spoil was the hero of the day. The cities were filled with dead bodies; the whole province was one scene of awful calamities.

So far the Jews had been fighting against aliens, but on making an inroad into Scythopolis they found their brethren who dwelt there in arms against them, ready to assist the Scythopolitans in defence of their city. But the Scythopolitans mistrusted their Jewish allies, and, dreading that they might desert to the enemy in the midst of the attack, they requested the Jews to retire with their families into a grove near by. The Scythopolitans then, watching a good chance, attacked their allies when they were off their guard, and butchered every one of them.

The rest of the Grecian cities followed the example of Scythopolis. In all of them the Jewish inhabitants were either put to the sword or thrown into prison. In Syria, the cities of Antioch, Sidon, and Apamea alone forbade the slaughter or imprisonment of their Jewish inhabitants, while the citizens of Gerusa not only did not harm the Jews among them, but escorted into the frontiers any desirous of withdrawing.

Disturbances arose also in the dominions of Agrippa. The king, having gone to Cestius Gallus, then at Antioch, left a friend of his, called Noarus, in charge of his kingdom. This Noarus was a relation of Sohemus, tetrarch of the district about Lebanon. In the mean time a deputation of seventy leading men arrived from Batanea, requesting a military force, so that in case of any movement they might be able to repress the insurgents. Noarus cruelly put to death the entire embassy, and began to act with such tyranny over the nation that Agrippa soon relieved him of his office.

The insurgents took a fortress, called Cypros, near Jericho, massacred the garrison, and levelled the defences with the ground. At the same time another band of Jews compelled a Roman garrison at Machærus to surrender, and took possession of the place.

Cestius, thinking it high time to interfere, led out a large army from Antioch, in order to completely crush the insurrection. Agrippa accompanied Cestius, as also did Sohemus, each having supplied him with a number of troops. Cestius first attacked Zabulon, a stronghold in Galilee, which divided the territory of Ptolemais from the Jewish province of Upper Galilee. The inhabitants fled to the mountains, so Cestius sacked and burned the town, and retired to Ptolemais. Some of his Syrian allies, lingering behind to plunder, were attacked by the Jews and routed.

Cestius then advanced on Cæsarea. He sent part of his army to attack Joppa. They took it, and slaughtered the inhabitants, also laying waste the surrounding district. Another detachment he sent to Galilee to subjugate that province. The cities there threw open their gates and received the Romans. The insurgents fled to the mountains, where, favored by the ground, they made a gallant resistance, but were finally dispersed. The Roman detachment then returned to Cæsarea.

Cestius then, gathering together his forces, proceeded towards Jerusalem, and destroyed the town of Antipatris on his way, and also a fort called Aphek. When the invading army approached Jerusalem, the Jews, who were celebrating the feast of the tabernacle, broke up the festival. Although it was the Sabbath, they rushed upon the enemy with such fury that they at first carried everything before them. And had not the cavalry and a battalion of infantry come quickly to the support of part of the line which still maintained its ground, Cestius and his whole army would have been destroyed. The Jews retreated into their city, but one of their officers, called Simon, attacked the Romans from the rear, as they ascended towards Bethhoron. He killed a good many of the enemy, and captured a number of baggage-mules and led them into the town. Cestius remained quiet for three days, while the Jews kept watch from the hills, awaiting an attack.

At this juncture, Agrippa made a final effort to avert the war. He sent a deputation, offering in the name of Cestius an amnesty for all past offences if the Jews would now lay down their arms. The leading insurgents, fearing lest the whole multitude should accept the proposal, attacked the deputation, and killing one of them, drove the rest away. Such of the people as were indignant at these outrages they assailed with stones and bludgeons and drove into the town.

Cestius, taking advantage of this dissension among the Jews, attacked and routed them, pursuing them to the gates of Jerusalem. For three days he suspended operations, hoping to receive an offer of surrender. On the fourth he led his soldiers against the city. The insurgents, struck with terror, abandoned the outer walls and retired into the inner city and the temple. Cestius took possession of the upper town, and encamped opposite the palace. Had he at that moment forced his way within the ramparts, the city would have fallen and the war ended. But the camp prefect, Tyrannius Priscus, and a party of officers, bribed by Florus to prolong the war, diverted him from the attempt. A number of the leading citizens now invited Cestius to continue the attack, promising to open the gates. But Cestius, partly on account of anger, and partly on account of mistrust, delayed accepting these overtures, until the insurgents, discovering the treason, chased the party of leading men from the ramparts, and stoned them into their houses.

For five days the Romans pressed the assault without success; on the sixth Cestius, at the head of a large body of picked men, made a vigorous attack upon the north side of the temple. The Romans were at first repulsed by the Jews. But they returned, and those in the front rank fixed their shields firmly against the wall; the second rank joined theirs to these; and the succeeding ranks in like manner joined theirs to the rank preceding; forming what they called a shell. From this the darts as they fell glanced off without effect;

and the soldiers, uninjured, undermined the wall, and prepared to set fire to the gate of the temple.

A terrible panic now seized the insurgents; and many ran
from the town like rats who desert a sinking ship. Encouraged by their flight, the peaceful party began to muster in
considerable force in order to admit Cestius as a deliverer.
And had he for a short time continued the siege he would
undoubtedly have carried the town. But Cestius for some
unknown reason suddenly withdrew his troops, and retired
from the city. The insurgents at once grew bold again, and,
sallying out, cut off a number of stragglers, both horse and
foot. On the following day Cestius continued to retreat, and
invited still further the attacks of his opponents. They harassed his rear, and, advancing on either side of his route,
hurled their javelins upon his flanks. The Romans did
not dare to turn and fight, for they thought that countless
multitudes were pursuing them. Nor, being heavily armed,
did they attempt to beat off those who attacked their flanks,
for they were afraid of breaking their lines. The Jews, being
lightly armed, dashed in here and there and slaughtered the
enemy by hundreds. With difficulty and with much loss the
Romans reached their former encampment. Here Cestius
halted for two days, perplexed as to what course he should
pursue. But on the third day, seeing the numbers of the
enemy had greatly increased, he decided to retreat. To
quicken his flight he commanded the soldiers to throw away
everything that might impede their march, and to kill all the
beasts of burden, except those that carried the missiles and
military engines. The Romans then entered the pass down
to Bethhoron. As soon as they were involved in the descent
of the defiles, the Jews attacked them from all sides. One
party blocked their egress, another drove the rearmost down
into the ravine, while the main body poured down showers
of missiles from above. The infantry stood wavering, uncer-
tain how to act, while the cavalry were in a still more per-

ilous condition. They could not charge the enemy up the steep mountain-sides; while on either hand were precipices and ravines, which cut off all hope of flight. The hill echoed with the lamentations of the unhappy army and with the war-cries of the Jews. The entire Roman army would have perished had not night come on. Then the Romans took refuge in Bethhoron, while the Jews crowned every hill and guarded every pass.

Cestius now determined to save himself by flight. He selected four hundred of his bravest soldiers and stationed them upon the ramparts, with orders to raise the beacons of the camp-sentinels, so that the Jews might think the entire army on the spot. He then, with the rest of his army, silently retreated about four miles. In the morning the Jews perceived the ruse, rushed upon the four hundred who had deceived them, put them to the sword, and went immediately in pursuit of Cestius.

The Romans pushed forward so rapidly that the Jews were unable to overtake them; but in their flight they abandoned all their military engines, which fell into the hands of the enemy. The Jews continued the pursuit as far as Antipatris, and then, giving up hope of overtaking the fugitives, they secured the military engines, and whatever booty had been left behind, and with songs of triumph returned to their capital. They had hardly suffered any loss, while they slew over five thousand of the Romans and their allies.

CHAPTER CXXVIII.

JOHN OF GISCHALA.

AFTER the defeat of Cestius many distinguished Jews abandoned the city, fearing the vengeance of Rome; among them Costobarus and Saul, two brothers related to the Herodian family, who with a party took refuge with Cestius. At their request Cestius sent them to Nero, who was in Achaia, and requested them to throw the blame of the war upon Florus. For he hoped by blaming Florus to escape the anger of the emperor.

In the mean time, the insurgents called a general assembly in the temple, and appointed generals for the war. Joseph, the son of Gorion, and Ananus were given the supreme authority in the city. Eleazar, the son of Simon, was passed over, because he was suspected of aiming at kingly power. But in a short time, as he held control of much of the public treasure and the spoils taken from the Romans, the real authority fell into his hands. They sent out generals to command in the different districts; among them Josephus, the historian, was sent to command in Galilee. He ruled his district very wisely, and made it his object to promote union among the inhabitants, and to organize the whole country on one regular system. He fortified all the defensible places, and raised an army of one hundred thousand men, among whom he introduced the Roman discipline.

And now a certain native of Gischala, called John, who was very desirous of getting all the power in his own hands and of supplanting Josephus in the command of Galilee,

began to create a great deal of disturbance. He collected together a band of four hundred lawless men, and with them
he ravaged Galilee. Josephus was at first much taken with
the man's dash and energy, and at his own request allowed
him to repair the fortifications of his native city,—an under-
taking in which he enriched himself at the expense of the
opulent. After this, John received Josephus's permission to
furnish oil to the Jews living in Syria; for they would not use
the oil made by the heathens. As the crafty John bought
the oil cheap and sold it to the foreign Jews for a very high
price, he soon made a very handsome fortune. Provided
with ample wealth, he now attempted to overthrow Josephus
in order that he might be made general in his stead. He
circulated reports that Josephus was about to betray the state
to the Romans, and tried in every way to ruin the governor.

It happened that some youths took it into their heads to
lie in wait for the steward of King Agrippa as he passed
through Galilee. They caught him in an ambush and plundered him of all his baggage, which contained some valuable
treasures he was bringing to the king. Unable to dispose secretly of the booty, the robbers brought the whole to Josephus, who was then at Tarichea. Josephus reproved them
for the robbery, and put the plunder in charge of one of the
magistrates of Tarichea, to be restored to Agrippa as soon as
possible. The robbers became very angry at this, and went
about accusing the governor of being in league with Agrippa,
and stirring up an insurrection against him.

A great multitude, secretly put up to it by the crafty John,
and aided by the governor of Tiberias, assembled in the Hippodrome at Tarichea and denounced Josephus,—some crying
out to stone, others to burn the traitor. With this intent they
surrounded the governor's house, and attempted to set fire
to it. The friends and guards of Josephus, frightened at the
tumult, all ran away except four. Josephus started up from
his sleep, and was exhorted by the four to make good his

escape; but he rent his robes, and, with dust upon his head, went out to face the tumult. Some of the crowd were moved to compassion upon seeing him in such a penitent garb others called loudly to him to produce the public money and confess his traitorous compact. For they concluded from his piteous mien that he had come to sue for pardon. But this appearance of humility was only put on in order to effect a stratagem. With the design of sowing dissension among the multitude, made up not only of citizens of Taricheæ, but of men from Tiberias and surrounding towns, Josephus promised to make a full confession, and spoke as follows: " It was my intention neither to return this money to Agrippa nor to keep it for my own use. But observing your city, men of Tari-cheæ, to be destitute of defence, and in want of funds for the building of walls, and fearing the city of Tiberias, and the other cities who were lying in wait for the spoil, I determined to keep quiet possession of the money, in order to surround you with a rampart. If this displease you, however, I shall produce what you brought to me, and permit you to plunder it; but if I consulted well for you, then punish your bene-factor."

This address drew the Taricheæns all upon his side, while the Tiberians and people from the other towns murmured at and threatened him. The two parties now began to quarrel among themselves, until at last the greater number of strangers with-drew. But about two thousand remained, and these, highly incensed, rushed upon Josephus. He retreated to his house, and being beset, had recourse to another artifice. He mounted the roof, and, making a sign to his besiegers that he wished to address them, he said that it was impossible for him to hear their demands as long as they kept up such a clamor. What-ever they would order he would do, if they would send in some of their number to confer quietly with him. On hear-ing this, some of the leading rioters entered the house. Jose-phus ordered them to be dragged to the most retired part of

the dwelling, and had them scourged until their flesh was
bloody and raw. Then suddenly opening the doors, he dismissed the men covered with blood. This sight so alarmed
the rioters that they threw away their arms and took to their
heels.

John was very much disappointed because Josephus had
not been killed, and immediately formed another plot against
him. Feigning illness, he requested permission to use the
hot baths of Tiberias in order to cure himself of his complaint. Josephus did not know that John had been plotting
against him, so cunningly had he managed it, and so gave
him permission. John therefore took up his quarters at
Tiberias, and partly by bribes, partly by persuasion, he induced the inhabitants to renounce their allegiance to the governor. Silas, who commanded the city under Josephus, wrote
immediately to let him know of the conspiracy. The governor at once set out, and early in the morning arrived at
Tiberias. John, pretending illness, secured himself from paying his respects. When Josephus was addressing the people
upon the subject of the conspiracy, John privately sent a party
of men with orders to kill him. The people, seeing them
draw their swords, gave the alarm. Josephus rushed down
to the beach, and, leaping into a boat, escaped to the middle
of the lake. His soldiers, in the mean time, attacked the
band sent by John; but Josephus, fearful lest a civil war
should arise, sent orders to his men to provide only for their
own safety, and to abstain from bloodshed. John fled to Gischala, his native town. Numbers of Jews from the different
towns of Galilee flocked to Josephus, and wished him to lead
them against John, and to burn the town of Gischala. But
Josephus, being more moderately inclined, contented himself
by threatening to seize the effects of all John's adherents,
and to burn their houses and families, unless they would
withdraw within five days from his cause. Accordingly,
three thousand of John's party came over to Josephus. John

lay quiet within the walls of his native town, but all the while was hatching a plot. He sent messengers privately to Jerusalem to accuse Josephus of having too much power, and to state that he would become the tyrant of his country unless he received a timely check.

Some of the leading men and magistrates in Jerusalem, be cause they were envious of Josephus, secretly supplied John with money that he might worry Josephus. They also passed a decree among themselves for his recall, and sent an army under four leaders into Galilee, with orders that should Josephus surrender himself, they should allow him to try and justify his conduct; but if he did not, they should treat him as a foe. When the army arrived in Galilee, the four cities of Sepphoris, Gamala, Gischala, and Tiberias espoused their cause. But Josephus regained the cities without recourse to arms; and having got into his power by stratagem the four leaders and their ablest soldiers, he sent them back to Jerusalem. The people of that city, when they found out what measures had been taken against Josephus, were very indignant, and would have killed the four leaders, and also those who had commissioned them, had they not saved themselves by flight.

A little while afterwards the people of Tiberias again revolted, and invited King Agrippa to come and take possession of the town. Although the king did not come at the time appointed, a few Roman horsemen made their appearance and forbade Josephus the city by proclamation. Tidings of this defection were immediately brought to Tarichæa. Josephus when he heard the news was in a very bad fix; for he had sent his entire army away upon a foraging excursion. But he feared delaying action against Tiberias lest in the mean while the troops of Agrippa should occupy the town. He had recourse, therefore, to an artifice. He collected all the vessels upon the Lake of Galilee, to the number of two hundred and thirty, and, though there were not more than four sailors in each, made sail with all speed for Tiberias. Shortening sail

at such a distance from the town as to prevent any close in-
spection, he ordered the almost empty vessels to move to and
fro, whilst he himself, attended by seven of his guards, drew
near the shore, so that he could easily be distinguished. The
citizens, thinking the fleet full of soldiers, with imploring signs
besought him to spare the city.

Josephus, coming closer to the shore, upbraided them, but
declared he would pardon any who would come to him and
assist him in taking the town. Ten of the leading citizens
accordingly came down to him, and he put them on one of
his vessels. He sent for others of the citizens, and put them
upon the different vessels. He thus drew from the city
under different pretexts the entire council of six hundred
chief men, besides two thousand of the people. He then
gave orders to the captains of the ships to sail to Tarichæa,
and there to imprison their passengers. The remaining citizens of Tiberias loudly inveighed against a certain Clitus as
chief mover of the revolt. Josephus ordered one of his guards
to go ashore and cut off the hands of Clitus, but the guard
was afraid. Clitus, seeing Josephus on his vessel venting his
indignation and coming towards the shore, besought him to
spare one of his hands. Josephus consented on condition that
he would himself cut off one of his own hands. Clitus drew
his sword with his right hand and severed the left from his
body,—with such dread had Josephus inspired him. A few
days afterwards Josephus took Gischala, which had revolted
with Sepphoris, and gave it up to pillage. Afterwards he
collected the spoil and restored it to the citizens, acting in a
similar manner also towards those of Sepphoris and Tiberias.
For he wished first to show the citizens his power, and then to
gain their affections.

Galilee now became quiet, and the people directed their
attention to preparations against the Romans. In Jerusalem
active measures were taken for the war, although the people
were rather despondent and had little hope of being victors

In the Acrabatene territory, Simon, son of Guigas, who had been sent there as general, so robbed and oppressed the people that an army was sent against him from Jerusalem. Simon fled with his band to Massada, and began a series of robberies in Idumæa, so that the people in that country had to raise an army to protect themselves from him, and garrisoned their villages.

Such was the state of affairs throughout Judea at the beginning of their war against the power of Rome.

CHAPTER CXXIX.

VESPASIAN IS SENT AGAINST THE JEWS.

WHEN Nero, the Roman emperor, was told of the disasters that had befallen Cestius Gallus and of the open revolt of the Jews, he pretended to make light of the whole affair, but was really very much disturbed.

Accordingly, he sent Vespasian, the greatest of his generals, to assume command of the armies in Syria, and to subdue the rebellious Jews. As soon as he received his appointment, Vespasian despatched his son Titus to Alexandria to bring up two legions of Roman soldiers stationed there, while he himself proceeded to Syria. There he collected the Roman forces and a large body of allies from the neighboring princes.

While these preparations were going on, the Jews, elated by their conquest over Cestius, determined to capture Ascalon, a city rather weakly garrisoned by some Roman troops, and situated about sixty-five miles from Jerusalem.

The Jews marched out in great numbers under their commanders, called Niger, Silas, and John the Essene, and made great haste to attack the city. But Antonius, the Roman commander of the city, had heard of their approach, and was prepared to meet them.

He attacked the Jews with a squadron of cavalry and threw them into complete disorder. The Jewish forces, composed entirely of foot-soldiers, were undisciplined, and could not cope with their skilled adversaries, who rode all around them and easily slaughtered them. The vast multitude could not fight with any success, and were ashamed to fly, and so were killed by the well-trained Romans like so many sheep. Night at length put a stop to the awful carnage, but not before ten thousand Jews lay dead upon the plain; among them two of their generals, Judas and Silas. Niger escaped with the remainder, the most of whom were wounded, to a little town in Idumæa called Sallis.

In spite of this terrible defeat, the Jews, even before their wounds had time to heal, collected their forces and made another assault upon Ascalon, but were again overthrown.

Antonius placed ambushes in the passes, and suddenly surrounding the Jews with his cavalry before they had time to form for battle, he slew eight thousand of them. The Jews made scarcely any resistance. Niger retreated, and, being closely pressed, took possession of a strong tower in a village called Bezedel.

Antonius, not having time to besiege the place, set fire to tne fortress and retired, exulting in the thought that he had burned Niger up. But Niger leaped down from the burning fortress, and crept into a deep cavern under the tower. Here he was found three days afterwards by a party of his friends, who were searching for his dead body that they might bury it. The Jews were filled with joy upon seeing their leader, believing him to have been preserved by God in order to lead them to future battles.

Meanwhile, Vespasian led his army out of Antioch, where he had found King Agrippa with his whole force waiting to join him, and made a rapid march to Ptolemais.

Here he was met by a number of the citizens of Sepphoris in Galilee, who, seeking their own safety, came to assure him of their fidelity to Rome. Vespasian gave them a guard to attend them back to their native city, and to defend it from the Jews. For as Sepphoris was the largest city in Galilee, Vespasian was very glad to get it into his power so easily. It was strongly fortified, and might have been made by the Jews a bulwark to the entire province.

Vespasian accordingly sent a strong force to Sepphoris, consisting of a thousand horse and six thousand foot, which he put under command of Placidus the tribune. When the troops arrived at the plain before the city they divided; the infantry quartered in the town, but the cavalry remained outside in their intrenchments, so that they could scour the surrounding country and annoy the army of Josephus.

Josephus made a great effort to recapture Sepphoris, but the place was too strong for him, and he was repulsed. This action provoked more active hostilities against the country on the part of the Romans, who spread fire and sword over the whole region. They killed all the Jews they could find who were capable of bearing arms, and enslaved the feeble ones, so that the only places of security were the cities that had been fortified by Josephus.

CHAPTER CXXX.

SIEGE OF JOTAPATA.

Titus quickly arrived from Alexandria, bringing the Roman legions that had been stationed there with him. He joined his father in Ptolemais, where Vespasian remained for a while to get his army in order.

Vespasian was also joined by large bodies of auxiliaries

furnished by the Kings Antiochus, Agrippa, and Sohemus, and the Arabian monarch, Malchus. So that his army amounted to very nearly sixty thousand men, not counting the servants and camp-followers, who were trained to fight also when occasion demanded.

While Vespasian remained in Ptolemais, Placidus continued to overrun Galilee, and to put its inhabitants to the sword. But observing that the fighting men always fled to the fortified cities, he advanced against the strongest of them, Jotapata; for he thought that by a sudden assault he could carry it without difficulty, and that, this done, the weaker towns would immediately surrender through fear. But in this he was much deceived. For the people of Jotapata, aware of his approach, lay in wait for him in front of the town; and, eager to fight for their city and their wives and children, they fell upon the Romans with great fury and quickly routed them, without, however, killing many. Placidus, finding that he was too weak to capture the town, gave up the attempt and retreated.

When Vespasian had organized his forces he marched from Ptolemais to the frontiers of Galilee, where he encamped. He halted awhile, that he might, by displaying the greatness of his forces, strike terror into the hearts of the enemy, and, ere the sword was drawn, give them time for repentance and submission. Nor was the measure without effect; for a number of Josephus's army, who were encamped at a town called Garis, hearing of the host of Romans who were coming to attack them, became so frightened that they dispersed and fled, not only before a blow was struck, but even before they had seen their foes.

Josephus was left alone with a mere handful of men, and, perceiving that his forces were not sufficient to cope with the enemy, and that they were much dispirited, he deemed it prudent to remove as far as possible from danger, and so fled with his soldiers to Tiberias.

Vespasian advanced upon the city of Gadara, and carried it at the first assault. On entering the town he put to death all except the children. The city and all the villages and hamlets around it were burned to the ground. Thus was a terrible example made, and the defeat of Cestius avenged.

The retreat of Josephus to Tiberias filled its inhabitants with alarm, for they rightly judged that had he not despaired of the contest he would not have fled. Nor did they mistake his views, for the manner in which the war was conducted made him think resistance hopeless.

However, like a gallant commander, he determined not to give up the cause. So he despatched messengers to Jerusalem, with letters to the party in power, in which he informed them of the exact state of affairs, and advised them either to surrender at once or to send him an army which would be able to cope with the Romans.

When Vespasian heard that a large body of the enemy had fled to Jotapata, and also that it was their strongest place of refuge, he determined to capture it. And so he sent a force to level the road leading to it, which was rocky and mountainous, and very difficult to travel upon, even for infantry, and was entirely too steep for cavalry.

In four days the work was completed, and a spacious highway opened for the troops. Josephus now went from Tiberias to Jotapata, in order to revive the drooping spirits of the Jews in that stronghold.

This news was brought to Vespasian, who became all the more eager to capture the place when he heard that the general-in-chief was within the walls. He therefore despatched Placidus and Ebutius, a distinguished officer, with a thousand horse, to surround the town and cut off all means of escape. The next day Vespasian followed with his whole force, and in the evening encamped on a high hill about a mile from the town, in order that the defenders might see his entire army, and be struck with terror at its magnitude.

The Romans, wearied with their long march, did not make an immediate attack, but they entirely surrounded the city, and so cut off every hope of escape. This, however, infused into the Jews the valor of despair. For, as they were unable to flee, they had no course left but to fight to the very last.

The next day the attack began. The Jews sallied boldly forth to meet the enemy, and at first gallantly faced the Romans. Vespasian ordered the archers and slingers to charge, and he himself led the infantry up an acclivity which led to the least defensible part of the wall. Josephus, alarmed for the town, dashed forward with the entire garrison, and drove the Romans from the ramparts. Great feats of valor were performed by both sides until night parted the combatants.

The following morning and for five days the Romans continued to make their assaults, while the Jews sallied bravely forth, or fought from the ramparts with equal courage.

Jotapata stood on top of a lofty hill, on three sides surrounded by impassable ravines. On the north side only could it be approached, where the end of the ridge sloped more gradually down. On this declivity was the city built; and this part Josephus had encompassed with a wall, to prevent an enemy from occupying the summit above it.

Vespasian called a council of war, and it was decided to raise an embankment against the part of the wall that was easiest of access. The whole army was sent out to procure materials, and they stripped the surrounding mountains of timber and stone, and proceeded to build the embankment. In order to protect themselves from the missiles hurled at them by the garrison, the Romans built a kind of wicker-work roof, under the protection of which they worked with safety.

Vespasian brought out his military engines, of which he had one hundred and sixty, and brought them to bear upon the men stationed upon the ramparts. The catapults vomited forth whizzing storms of lances, and the stone-projectors hurled great rocks of enormous weight, while the archers and slingers threw their weapons, so that they soon cleared the ramparts of the enemy.

But the Jews now sallied out from below in parties. And every now and then they suddenly attacked the workmen, and pulled down the breastworks. And when they could beat back the workmen, they threw down the mound and set fire to the palisades and hurdles. Vespasian perceived that the spaces between the works afforded openings for attacks, so he united all the working-parties, and thus closing his lines, prevented these destructive sallies.

The embankment was now finished, and was almost on a level with the battlements. Josephus, in order to offset this, commanded workmen to raise the height of the wall. The workmen said that it would be impossible to build whilst they were assailed with such showers of missiles. Josephus then ordered tall stakes to be driven on top of the wall, and on them stretched fresh raw hides of oxen. From this yielding curtain the stones fell back harmless, whilst the other missiles glanced off, and even the fire-darts were quenched by the moisture of the hides. The builders, thus screened, raised the wall thirty-five feet higher. They then erected a number of towers, and defended the whole by a strong breastwork.

The Romans, who already fancied themselves masters of the town, were struck with dismay at the ingenuity of Josephus and the bravery of the besieged.

Vespasian was very much put out by this cunning stratagem, as well as by the gallantry of the people of Jotapata. For, inspired with fresh confidence by their bulwark, they sallied out in small bands and continually harassed the Romans, pillaging everything that came in their way and burning the enemy's works.

At length Vespasian determined to turn the siege into a blockade, and to starve the city into a surrender. For the

garrison, he reasoned, would either soon have to capitulate
or perish with hunger. Or if later he should wish to continue
the attack, he could more easily conquer the Jews when
wasted by hunger. So he kept his troops in their quarters,
and blockaded every avenue to the city.

The besieged were well supplied with corn and other provisions, except salt, and also suffered from a scarcity of water.
There was no spring within the city, so the inhabitants were
obliged to be content with rain-water. But in that country
it rarely rains in summer-time, and as it was now that season,
the inhabitants became very much dispirited, and looked
forward with great anxiety to the time when their supply
would fail.

As Josephus wished to protract the siege as long as possible, he measured out the water in small quantities to the
people. When the Romans saw the besieged all flocking to
one spot, and there receiving water by measure, they directed
their missiles against that place, and slew a great many.

Vespasian now thought that the garrison would soon have
to surrender, and so continued the blockade. Josephus, in
order to crush this hope, ordered a number of people to steep
their garments and hang them round the battlements, so
that the whole wall suddenly streamed with moisture. The
Roman general was dismayed when he saw so much water
wasted. For he concluded that the Jews must have an
abundant supply that they used it so freely. And so, despairing of reducing the city by want, he again ordered an
attack. This was what the Jews desired; for they preferred
to perish by the sword rather than by thirst and famine.

Josephus discovered a secret means for obtaining supplies.
By the bed of a mountain-torrent which wound along the
western side of the ravine, and which the Romans neglected
to guard, he sent letters to the Jews outside, and received in
return abundance of everything that was needed in the city.
The messengers crept on all fours, covered with the skins of

beasts, that they might look like dogs; but the guards at length detected the artifice, and secured the outlet.

Josephus now began to think of his own safety, and so resolved to fly with the leading men. But the people, hearing of his intention, surrounded him and begged him to remain, saying,—

"While you remain with us, Josephus, there is still some hope for the town, and we will fight under you bravely; but if you go away no one will dare to oppose the enemy, and the city will immediately fall."

"I cannot," said Josephus, "see what good I can do by remaining; whereas, if I escape, I can assemble the Galileans and draw the Romans from your walls. Indeed, my remaining will only stimulate the Romans to press the siege, for their chief object is to capture me; whereas, if they know that I have fled, they will naturally relax their efforts to take the town."

But the people, unmoved by these arguments, only clung to him the closer. Old men and women and children fell down in tears before him, and besought him not to leave them.

Moved with compassion at their distress, Josephus made up his mind to remain; and thinking this a good time to make an attack, he called the garrison around him, and said,—

"Now is the time to rush to an attack, when there is no hope of safety. It is honorable to exchange life for glory in doing some great deed, which will be handed down to the memory of posterity."

He then sallied out with the bravest of his troops, beat back the sentries, and, forcing his way to the Roman camp, tore away the skins which sheltered the men on the embankments and set the works on fire. For many days and nights he led these furious attacks, and kept the Romans in a constant state of alarm.

Vespasian directed his men to avoid these attacks, and not to engage with men bent on death.

" For nothing," he said, " imparts greater energy than despair, and their furious valor will die out if deprived of its
proper object, as fire without fuel. It becomes even the Romans to conquer with safety, since they war not from necessity, but to extend their dominions."

He ordered the auxiliaries alone to repel these attacks, and
finding himself, as it were, besieged in his turn, and as the
embankment had now reached close to the wall, he ordered
the battering-ram to be advanced.

The ram was a machine used by the ancients for battering
down walls. It was composed of a large beam resembling
the mast of a ship, on one end of which was forged a dense
mass of iron in the shape of a ram's head, whence it derived
its name. It was suspended by ropes tied around the middle,
so that it hung balanced from a beam above, which was supported by two strong upright posts. It was drawn back by a
great number of men, and then driven forward with such tremendous force that no wall could long withstand its blows.

The Romans now swept the battlements with a continual
discharge from their engines, as well as from their archers
and slingers, so that the Jews could not get upon the wall
and obstruct the putting up of the ram. At the first stroke
of this terrible instrument the wall was shaken, and the besieged sent up a fearful shriek, as if the city were already
taken.

Josephus, seeing the Romans constantly battering upon the
same spot, and that the wall was all but a ruin, ordered
sacks filled with chaff to be let down over the place where
the ram battered, so that they caused the head to swerve,
and weakened the blow. But the Romans then used long
poles with edged hooks at the ends, with which they cut
down the sacks, so that the ram continued its destructive
work, and soon the wall began to give way.

The Jews now hastened to defend themselves with fire as a
last resource ; and, snatching up whatever combustible matter

was at hand, they sallied out from three different points, and set fire to the machines, hurdles, and mounds of the besiegers. The Romans, confounded by this act of daring, made scarcely any defence ; and, as the timbers of the embankment were all dry, the fire spread rapidly, and consumed in one hour the labor of many days.

At this time a Jew called Eleazar performed a feat of valor which is worthy of record. Lifting up an enormous stone, he threw it with such force at the ram that he broke off the head of the machine. He then leaped down from the wall, secured his prize, and was bearing it back to the city, when he was transfixed with fire-darts. Nothing daunted, however, he climbed the battlements, displayed his trophy to all, then, writhing under his wounds, fell headlong with the ram. Two brothers, named Netiras and Philip, also distinguished themselves. Dashing out, they broke through a legion of Romans, and drove back all who opposed them. Josephus and the rest followed this heroic example, and, snatching up combustible matter, they set fire to the machines of the enemy and consumed a number of their works.

But the Romans again set up the ram, and went on battering the wall at the same place. While Vespasian was directing the assault he was slightly wounded by a javelin near the sole of his foot. This caused the greatest confusion among the Romans. Many gave up the attack and crowded around their general ; foremost of all was Titus, who was greatly alarmed for his father. But Vespasian speedily relieved their fears, and showing himself to all, roused them to greater exertions against the Jews. With loud shouts the whole army rushed to the walls, and all night the awful conflict lasted. But though the Jews fell in numbers, and though the missiles poured around them like hail, they would not abandon the walls, but continued to heave down stones and fiery combustibles upon the besiegers. Towards morning the wall, assailed without intermission, fell before the ram. The defenders, however, threw up defences opposite the breach before the Romans could apply their scaling-planks. At daybreak Vespasian allowed his troops a short repose, and then assembled them for the assault. To repel the besieged from the breach he ordered the bravest of the cavalry to dismount, and stationed them by the breach, in order that they might mount it the moment the planks were laid. In the rear of these he marshalled the flower of his infantry. The rest of the cavalry he dispersed all over the mountains which encircled the town, that they might cut off all escape; behind them he stationed an encircling line of archers, and others he directed to apply scaling-ladders to the uninjured parts of the wall in order to call off the attention of the defenders from the breach.

Josephus, seeing his design, placed the old and infirm to guard these parts of the wall, but stationed his bravest to defend the breach, while he himself took his position at their head. He commanded his men to stop their ears at the shouts of the Roman legions that they might not be terrified, and to receive the showers of missiles on bended knee under cover of their shields, and then retreat a little until the archers had emptied their quivers, but when the Romans should fix their scaling-planks they should leap upon them and fight to revenge their city. "Place before your eyes," said he, "your fathers and children and wives about to be butchered, and, anticipating the rage you will feel at these coming calamities, let it loose on those who are to inflict them."

When the helpless women and children within the town saw the awful preparations for the final conflict, and the enemy sword in hand at the breach, and the mountains above them glittering with armed men, they raised a great shriek as if the enemy were already within the town. Josephus shut the women up in their houses lest they should dispirit the men, and with threats commanded them to be silent. He then took his post at the breach and awaited the attack.

At once the trumpets of the invading army sounded, and the Romans, with a terrific war-cry, rushed to the attack. The Jews closed their ears to the noise, and guarded themselves against the flying arrows, which fell upon them in a perfect storm.

The moment the scaling-planks were laid the Jews rushed along them before the Romans could cross, and fell upon their enemies with the greatest fury; but at length the Romans, who, on account of their numbers, were able to continually pour fresh troops upon the Jews, drove them back, and began to mount the ramparts.

Still, Josephus had a last expedient. He had prepared a vast quantity of boiling oil, and at a signal this was poured upon the enemy, and the vessels, glowing with heat, were hurled at them. The ranks were broken, and the men rolled down in the greatest agony, for the burning oil trickled through their armor, and penetrated to the skin. Writhing with anguish, they tumbled from the scaling-planks, and fell upon those of their own party who were pressing forward.

But the Romans, nothing daunted by sight of the tortures which befell their companions in front of them, continued to advance upon the battlements. The Jews, however, by another stratagem checked their ascent. They poured boiled fenugreek, a slippery concoction, upon the planks, so that those retreating as well as those advancing were unable to stand up. Some were thrown upon their backs upon the scaling-planks, and were trodden to death; while many fell down upon the embankment and were despatched by the Jews.

In the evening Vespasian drew off his troops, who had suffered severely in the assault, and determined to proceed in a more slow and cautious manner. He accordingly set his men to work at raising the embankment. When this was done, he built upon it three towers, fifty feet high, and covered on all sides with plates of iron, so that they might be firm and at the same time fire-proof. In these he placed his slingers and archers and the lighter engines for hurling missiles.

From these towers a constant shower of missiles was poured upon the Jews, who were unable to harm their assailants, because the towers were too high. So they were obliged to abandon the wall. But still they sallied out in parties upon the troops who assaulted the breach, and constantly repelled them from the wall. Thus was the combat carried on by the besieged, many falling from day to day, unable to retaliate upon their foes, whose approach they could only check at the risk of their lives.

At this period Vespasian despatched Trajan, the commander of one of his legions, with a thousand horse and two thousand foot, against a town in the vicinity of Jotapata, called Japha, which was in revolt.

When Trajan drew near Japha the inhabitants advanced against him, but he soon put them to flight and chased them to the walls. The pursuers and pursued entered pell-mell within the outer gates, but when they reached the inner wall those who guarded it closed the gates, and thus shut out both their friends and enemies.

Shut up between the two walls, the miserable fugitives were slaughtered within sight of their friends, calling loudly all the while upon them to open the gates. But the people inside were afraid of letting in the enemy should they open the gates to their friends, who, discouraged by such cruelty, made no effort at resistance, and were all killed, to the number of twelve thousand.

Trajan sent a message to Vespasian requesting that his son Titus might be despatched to complete the victory. Accordingly, Titus advanced upon the city with an additional force, and, joining forces with Trajan, led the assault.

The Jews almost immediately abandoned the walls, and Titus and his soldiers leaped into the city. Then a fierce struggle took place, in which even the women joined, and hurled from the windows whatever missile came to hand. At length the fighting-men among the defenders were all killed; the rest were massacred, and none except the infants and the women were spared. They were carried off into slavery.

Misfortunes also befell the Samaritans. These people had not openly joined in the revolt, but still, made no wiser by the misfortunes of their neighbors, they looked forward for an occasion to rebel, and had collected in great force in the sacred mountain of Gerizzim. For most of their cities were garrisoned by the Romans.

Vespasian, in order to nip the insurrection in the bud, sent Cerealis, one of his prefects, with an armed force against the Samaritans. Cerealis surrounded the base of the mountain, and kept watch during the whole day. It was midsummer, and the Samaritans, who had laid in no provisions, suffered terribly for want of water, so that some died of thirst, and others deserted to the Romans.

Cerealis, learning from the deserters that the Samaritans were greatly enfeebled by their sufferings, ascended the mountain, and completely encircling the enemy, offered them pardon should they surrender. Unable to prevail with them, however, he attacked and massacred them to a man, to the number of eleven thousand six hundred.

And now the fall of Jotapata drew near. For forty-seven days the brave garrison had held out and resisted the attacks of the powerful Roman army. They were worn out with fatigue and wounds, when one of their number deserted to Vespasian and informed him that those left in the town were so few and enfeebled that they could not now repel a vigorous assault. In the early morning, he said, the sentinels were apt from sheer exhaustion to fall asleep at their posts, and at that hour the town should be attacked.

Vespasian hardly believed the man, so faithful had all the other Jews been to their cause; but still what he said appeared to be probable, and at all events no harm could come from making the attack. So the general marshalled his army for the assault, and at the hour named the Romans approached the ramparts in silence, under cover of a dense fog.

Titus was the first to mount them, followed by a tribune and a few soldiers. They killed the sentries and stole quietly into the city, followed by Placidus and Cerealis with the troops under their orders. The citadel was surprised and taken. Though the day had begun, the inhabitants were still unconscious of the capture, for the greater number of them were asleep, and those who were awake saw nothing through the heavy mist. By this time the whole army was within the gates, and the Jews were aroused only to receive in death the first evidence of their capture.

The Romans, remembering what they had suffered during the siege, showed no mercy to the unhappy defenders. Pressed together in the streets, they were ruthlessly slaughtered, a great many falling by their own hands. All who showed themselves were slain, and during the ensuing days the Romans searched the hiding-places, slaughtering all the men, and sparing none but the women and children. Of these twelve hundred prisoners were taken. During the capture and siege forty thousand men perished. Vespasian ordered the town to be razed, and reduced all its forts to ashes. Thus fell Jotapata.

CHAPTER CXXXI.

THE CAPTURE OF JOSEPHUS.

THE Romans sought in vain among the dead for the body of Josephus, and then looked among the secret recesses of the city, but without success, until they began to fear that the wily general had escaped them. During the massacre Josephus had leaped down in a deep pit, in the side of which was a large cavern invisible to those above. Here he found forty persons of distinction concealed, provided with necessaries sufficient to support them for a considerable time. He lay hidden during the day, and at night attempted to escape from the city, but, as every avenue was closely guarded, he was obliged to return to the cavern. For two days he escaped detection, but on the third a woman who had been with the party in the cave was captured, and betrayed the secret.

Vespasian at once despatched two tribunes with orders to offer Josephus protection and to induce him to leave his retreat. Repairing to the mouth of the cavern, they called to him to come out, and pledged themselves for his safety. But Josephus, being suspicious, would not leave his retreat until Vespasian sent another tribune, called Nicanor, known to Josephus, and formerly an associate of his.

Nicanor discoursed upon the generosity of the Romans to an enemy once subdued, and assured Josephus that on account of his valor he was rather an object of admiration than of hatred to the Roman officers. He said that Vespasian wished to save a man who had showed such courage, for did he wish to kill him he had it now in his power to do so; moreover, he would not have sent a friend to him for the purpose of deceiving him.

While Josephus was hesitating, the Roman soldiery in their rage rushed forward to throw fire into the cavern, but Nicanor, anxious to take the Jewish leader alive, restrained them. Josephus, hearing the tumult, and knowing that if he remained he would be killed anyway, consented to Nicanor's terms, and was about to leave the cave.

But here an unexpected difficulty arose. The Jews who were with Josephus, drawing their swords, declared that he must not surrender himself; that such a course would be cowardly and against the Jewish laws, and rather than see him fall into the hands of the Romans, they would slay him themselves.

Josephus, between his enemies outside the cavern and his friends within, found himself in a very tight fix indeed. He, however, attempted to persuade the Jews that it was right to save one's own life when it could be done without dishonor; indeed, that it was a great sin to throw away life unless in open warfare against an enemy. But the Jews would not listen to arguments. Upbraiding him with cowardice, they ran at him from all sides and tried to kill him. The general thrust aside their strokes as best he could, and by persuasion and command induced them to put up their swords, and then with his usual sagacity saved himself by a stratagem, speaking thus to his assailants :

"If we must die, let us not die by our own, but by each other's hands. Let us cast lots, and thus fall one after another; for if the rest perish it would not be just for any one of us to survive."

To a proposal apparently so fair they readily assented, and Josephus himself cast the lot. Each one in turn bared his throat to the next, until Josephus and one other alone remained. Josephus persuaded this man to surrender along with himself to Nicanor. The Jewish chieftain was immediately brought to Vespasian, while the Romans crowded from all quarters to obtain sight of him. Those who were at a distance from him cried out that he should be killed; but those near him thought of his exploits, and were struck with pity at his reverses. All the Roman officers, even those who had been most furious against him, were touched by the fortitude with which he bore his misfortunes, and relented towards him. Titus in particular was struck by his noble mien, and interceded for him with Vespasian, who ordered the general to be closely guarded, that he might be sent to Nero at Rome.

Josephus demanded a private interview with Vespasian,

which was granted, and all retired except Titus and two of his friends. The Jewish chieftain then addressed Vespasian thus :

"You think, Vespasian, that you have possessed yourself merely of a captive in Josephus; but I come to you as a messenger of greater things. Why do you send me to Nero? For who will succeed Nero but yourself? You, Vespasian, are Cæsar and emperor,—you, and this your son. For you, Cæsar, are master not only of me, but of sea and land, and of the whole human race."

Vespasian at first mistrusted this declaration of Josephus, thinking it flattery, but gradually was led to believe it. One of the friends of Titus who was present expressed his surprise that Josephus should have been unable to predict either the fall of Jotapata or his own captivity. Josephus replied that he had predicted both these things.

Vespasian, having privately questioned the prisoners respecting these statements, and finding them true, began to believe that Josephus was really a prophet. He, however, still kept him in chains, though he presented him with raiment and other articles, and treated him with much kindness and attention.

CHAPTER CXXXII.

THE DESTRUCTION OF JOPPA.

VESPASIAN returned to Ptolemais, whence he marched to Cæsarea. Here the army and its commander were received with great acclamations, both on account of the friendship of the inhabitants to the Romans and their hatred towards the Jews. Accordingly, they loudly demanded the punishment of Josephus; but Vespasian refused this request. He remained with two of his legions in Cæsarea for the winter, and ordered the rest of his army to quarter in Scythopolis.

Meanwhile, a large body of insurgents had gathered together from different parts, and as a rallying-point rebuilt Joppa, which had been destroyed by Cestius Gallus. As the Romans occupied the country, they had recourse to the sea. They built a number of piratical vessels, and plundered all the merchant-vessels trading between Syria, Phœnicia, and Egypt.

Vespasian sent a considerable force against Joppa. The Romans, finding the city unguarded, entered it by night. The inhabitants fled in terror to their ships, where they passed the night out of reach of the enemy's missiles. Joppa had no safe harbor. Its shore was rugged and lined with rocks, which extended into the sea. When the north wind blew, it beat full in upon the coast and dashed the waves against the rocks, making the port more dangerous than the open sea.

The next morning a terrific wind, called by the sailors "the black norther," dashed the ships of the unfortunate insurgents against one another and against the fatal rocks. The poor Jews could neither sail away nor remain where they were with safety; for on account of the wind, which blew directly shoreward, the ships could not escape to the open sea, nor could the navigators land, on account of the Romans, who occupied the coast.

A number of the ships foundered in the rough waters, whilst a greater number were dashed against the rocks. If any on board were cast on shore, they were immediately massacred by the Romans. Over four thousand of the people perished. Joppa itself was razed to the ground, but the citadel was garrisoned by the Romans, lest it should again become a nest of pirates.

At first vague rumors of the fall of Jotapata reached Jerusalem. These were generally disbelieved, for not an eye-witness to the fact had escaped to tell the tale. But, as bad news travels fast, these rumors were ere long confirmed, and, moreover, it was stated that Josephus had been slain. Jerusalem was filled with the deepest sorrow. Every house bewailed some private affliction in the loss of a friend or a relative, but the whole city mourned for the general.

By degrees, however, the whole truth became known, and the wailing for Josephus gave way to the fiercest indignation when it became known that he was alive and had surrendered to the Romans. He was called a coward and a traitor; and, stirred by their indignation, the people began to prepare all the more eagerly for a fierce resistance to the Romans, in order to avenge themselves upon Josephus.

But Vespasian did not advance at once upon the rebellious capital. He accepted an invitation from Agrippa to come into his dominions, for the king wished to allay by the terror of the Roman arms the disorders in his own kingdom.

Vespasian advanced to Cæsarea Philippi, where the army reposed for twenty days. Being informed that disaffection was showing itself in Tiberias, and that Taricheæ had already revolted, and as both towns were in Agrippa's kingdom, he resolved to subdue them.

Advancing with three legions, he encamped near Tiberias, and sent forward Valerian, an officer, at the head of fifty horse, to propose peaceful measures to the citizens. For he had heard that the people were desirous of peace, but had been compelled to revolt by a small turbulent party. When Valerian came near the city he and his troops dismounted, that they might not appear like a body of skirmishers. But, before he could utter a word, a party of insurgents, led by a brigand chief called Joshua, charged him with great fury.

Not wishing to fight without orders from his general, Valerian fled on foot, and five others in like manner abandoned their horses. Joshua seized the steeds and led them back to the town in triumph.

Dreading the consequences of this affair, a number of the

leading men repaired in haste to the Roman camp, and besought Vespasian not to punish the entire city for the crime of a few. For the majority of the people, they said, were friendly to the Romans, and his vengeance should fall on the authors of the revolt, by whom the people had been kept under guard, anxious as they were for his protection. Vespasian, principally because he did not wish to despoil one of Agrippa's fairest cities, yielded to these entreaties, and gave the deputation a pledge of protection for the people. Joshua and his party, thinking it unsafe longer to remain at Tiberias, made off to Taricheæ.

The next day Vespasian led his army into the city, and was received with acclamations. In compliment to Agrippa, he did not allow his soldiers to plunder the city. And as that king pledged himself for the future fidelity of the inhabitants, the fortifications were not destroyed.

CHAPTER CXXXIII.

THE FATE OF THE PEOPLE OF TARICHEÆ.

VESPASIAN then advanced upon Taricheæ, where not only the insurgents who had escaped from Tiberias had fled, but multitudes of the disaffected from all quarters, for they confided in its strength. It had been fortified by Josephus, and was situated on the lake called Gennesareth, upon which they could take refuge by means of their ships, should they be defeated on shore.

While the Romans were throwing up their intrenchments in the neighborhood of the town, Joshua and his band boldly sallied from the walls, and, dispersing the workmen, levelled the intrenchments and fell back before they had suffered any loss. The Romans pursued and drove the Jews to their ships, in which they sailed out a little way, and, casting anchor, hurled their missiles at their enemies from the water.

News was brought to Vespasian that a great number of Galileans had assembled on the plain before the town, so he sent his son Titus with six hundred picked cavalry to disperse them. Titus found the Jews in such large numbers that he sent back for reinforcements. But, remarking that many of his men were anxious to charge before any succor arrived, he exhorted them all not to be dismayed by numbers, but to secure the victory before their fellow-soldiers should come up to share their glory.

He inspired his men with such ardor that they were not pleased when Trajan, at the head of four hundred horse, made his appearance to assist them. Vespasian likewise despatched two thousand archers to occupy the side of a hill opposite the city, in order to keep the enemy on the ramparts in check and prevent them from giving any assistance.

Titus now led the charge against the enemy, who withstood for a short time the attack, but were soon dispersed and fled towards the city. The Romans pursued and killed a great number of them; the rest escaped into the town.

But here a fierce contention awaited them. For the citizens, anxious on account of their property, were inclined to peace, and wished to surrender, but this the insurgents, who were all strangers, violently opposed. The two parties were on the point of appealing to arms, when Titus, who heard the noise of dissension outside the walls, cried out,—

"Now is the time for an attack, while they are distracted by civil discord."

He leaped upon his horse, dashed into the lake, and, followed by his men, entered the city. Terror-struck at his daring, those on the ramparts abandoned them without waiting to fight. A number rushed towards the lake and were killed by the advancing Romans. Great was the slaughter in the city. The strangers who resisted, and many of the peaceful citizens, fell beneath the sword. At length, Titus, having punished the guilty, was touched with compassion for the inhabitants, and put an end to the slaughter. Those who had taken refuge on the lake, when they saw the city taken, withdrew as far as possible from danger.

Titus sent word of this signal victory to his father, who was exceedingly gratified at the intelligence. Repairing immediately to the city, he placed guards over it, that none might escape. Going down to the lake, he gave orders that rafts should be fitted out against the fugitives. And, as wood was plentiful, these were soon built.

Vespasian then embarked some of his troops, and ordered them to attack the fugitives. The poor Galileans in their light boats could not cope with the well-armed Romans on their heavy rafts. They sailed around them and flung stones at them from a distance, but without doing any damage. For if they came near enough to attack them, the Romans were so much better armed that they easily gained the advantage.

All the shores were lined with armed men, so that the fugitives had no means of escape, and they were pursued into every inlet and creek. The Romans boarded their vessels, or slew them from the rafts by means of their long lances; the boats of others were crushed or swamped, and the people drowned. If they attempted to swim, their heads were hit by an arrow or by the prow of a raft; if they clung to the side of a raft, their hands or their heads were hewn off. The few survivors were driven to the shore, where they met with no mercy. They were slain by the Romans, who lined the shores, so that not a man escaped.

The beautiful waters of the lake were tinged with blood; the shores were lined with the wrecks of boats and the carcasses of men. Such was the issue of this naval battle. The killed, including the number who had fallen in the city, amounted to over six thousand.

After the battle, Vespasian took his seat on a tribunal in Taricheæ, and sat in judgment over the strangers, whom he had separated from the inhabitants, consulting with his generals whether their lives also should be spared. The officers, however, were in favor of putting them all to death. For they said that the strangers were desperate men, who, if let loose, would stir up insurrection wherever they went. Vespasian then deliberated concerning the manner in which he should put them to death. Should he order the massacre to be performed in the streets of Taricheæ, he feared lest such a sight would incite the inhabitants to insurrection, especially as he had pledged protection to the city. But the officers urged that every act was lawful against the Jews, and that right must give way to expediency.

Vespasian, in order therefore to get the insurgents out of the city, granted them an amnesty, but ordered them to leave the city by the road which led to Tiberias. Trusting to his word, the strangers fearlessly pursued their journey along the permitted route, while the Romans lined the road to the very gates of the city, in order to cut off all escape, and shut them up in the town.

Vespasian entered Tiberias soon afterwards, and, driving the insurgents in a body into the circus, ordered the old and feeble, to the number of twelve hundred, to be put to death. From the youth he selected six thousand of the most robust and sent them to Nero, to be employed as workmen. The rest, amounting to thirty thousand four hundred, he sold as slaves, with the exception of some who were subjects of Agrippa, and whom he allowed that king to sell. Thus was a terrible example given to the whole of Galilee.

CHAPTER CXXXIV.

TAKING OF ITYBARIUM AND GAMALA.

AFTER the fall of Taricheæ, nearly all the garrisons and towns of Galilee returned to their allegiance to the Romans. Three cities alone still defied the conqueror, Gamala, Gischala, and Itybarium, the place which Josephus had fortified on Mount Tabor.

Gamala belonged to the kingdom of Agrippa. It was built upon a long and rugged ledge of mountains, which sloped downward at each end and rose in the middle into a sudden ridge like the hump of a camel. It could only be approached from behind, where it joined the mountain-ridge. On this side a deep trench had been dug, and rendered the approach more difficult. The houses were built one above the other on the steep hill, and the whole city seemed as if hanging on a sharp precipice.

Josephus, when fortifying the town, had rendered it still more impregnable by digging mines and trenches. So that though the garrison was not so numerous as that which had defended Jotapata, the people felt so secure on account of their position that they would not admit any more outsiders within their walls to help them. This city had already held out for seven months against the troops of Agrippa, and was filled with fugitives.

Vespasian, breaking up his camp, advanced upon Gamala. Its situation not permitting him to surround it with a line of troops, he stationed sentries in those places that were accessible, and occupied the mountain that overhung it. When the legions had fortified a camp upon this mountain, Vespasian commenced operations by throwing up mounds in the rear of the town, and on the east, where there was a lofty tower. One legion was employed against the centre of the town, and another in filling up the trenches and ravines.

King Agrippa approached the ramparts and attempted to persuade the people to surrender, but he was struck with a stone upon the right elbow by a slinger, and was immediately carried off by his followers. The Romans were greatly enraged at this insult to their ally, and pressed the siege with renewed vigor.

The mounds were quickly completed, and the engines were brought up. Chares and Joseph, the commanders in the city, drew out their forces, though the men were somewhat dispirited on account of a want of water and other necessaries in the city. Still, they bravely manned the walls, and for a short time kept at bay the men who were fixing the machines. But at length they were beaten off by the catapults and stone-projectors, and fell back into the town.

The Romans now advanced the rams from three different quarters, and beat down the wall. Rushing in the breach, the soldiers with loud shouts fell upon the defenders. These, however, for a time gallantly repulsed the Romans, until, overpowered by force of numbers, they were obliged to retreat to the higher parts of the town. Here, turning upon their assailants, they charged with great fury, drove them down the declivities, and made great havoc among them, embarrassed as they were by the narrowness and steepness of the streets.

As the Romans could not repel the enemies who rushed upon them from above, nor yet make their way through the throngs of their own party who forced them on from beneath, they took refuge on the roofs of the houses, which rose one above the other on the hill.

The houses, which were lightly built, could not bear the weight of so many heavy armed soldiers, and gave way. As the houses were built one above another, they knocked each other down like nine-pins, each one falling upon the one beneath it.

Many of the Romans were buried in the ruins, while multitudes died of suffocation from the dust. The people of Gamala took advantage of this confusion to fall upon their besiegers. The ruins afforded them stones, and they caught up the weapons of the dead. Terrible was the havoc they made among the Romans as they fell amid the ruins of the houses or slipped about the steep and narrow streets. So dense were the clouds of dust and so great the confusion that many of the besiegers slew their own comrades and fell around each other in heaps.

Those who through the blinding dust could find the road retreated from the city. Vespasian himself, who had entered with his soldiers, hardly knowing where he was going, fought his way to the highest quarter of the city. Here he found himself in the thick of the danger, with but a few followers around him. However, disdaining to fly, he formed a compact body around him, and ordered the soldiers to lock their shields over their heads, so as to protect himself and them from the falling ruins and darts. In this manner he retreated step by step, with his face to the foe, until he was outside the ramparts. The loss of the Romans in this affray was very great. Among the slain was Ebutius, one of their bravest officers. Another officer, named Gallus, with ten soldiers, crept into a private house and concealed himself there. At night he killed all the inmates, and with his comrades escaped to the camp.

The Romans were greatly depressed by the disasters that had befallen them, and were particularly ashamed that they had allowed their general to be exposed to great danger. But Vespasian encouraged them by word, saying that their repulse was due to accident and to their own too impetuous ardor, which had led them to fight with the frantic fury of the Jews rather than with the steady discipline of Roman troops. In this way he revived their drooping spirits.

The people of Gamala, meanwhile, were for the moment greatly elated by their signal success. But when they considered that they were now cut off from all hopes of pardon and that their supplies were giving out, they became very dejected; yet they did not entirely lose their courage and activity. The bravest guarded the breaches, and the rest defended what still remained of the wall.

Still, while the Romans were completing their works and preparing for a second assault, multitudes escaped from the city down pathless ravines, where no watch was kept, and through underground passages. As many, however, as remained in the town through fear of capture slowly perished from want, for the scanty provisions that were left were reserved for the use of the garrison.

At this time Vespasian sent Placidus with six hundred horse to attack Itybarium upon Mount Tabor, where a vast multitude had congregated. Thinking it unwise to attempt to ascend the heights, Placidus invited the assemblage to terms, holding out the hope of his protection and influence with Vespasian. He did this as a ruse to get them down into the plain, where he could capture them.

The Jews pretended to agree to these terms, and came down with a design of falling upon the Romans when off their guard. The craft of Placidus, however, succeeded, for when the Jews commenced the action he pretended to fly. When he had drawn his enemies far down into the plain, he ordered his cavalry to wheel round, and, falling upon his pursuers, routed them with dreadful slaughter and cut off their retreat to the mountain. Those who escaped fled to Jerusalem. The inhabitants of Itybarium, under promise of protection and because they were distressed for want of water, surrendered to Placidus.

In the mean time the garrison of Gamala still made a vigorous resistance, while the people pined away with hunger. At length three Roman soldiers stole up early in the morning and undermined a lofty tower, without being perceived by the sentries. The soldiers, without noise, rolled away five of the supporting stones and sprang away. The tower fell with a tremendous crash, carrying the guards with it headlong. The rest of the sentinels fled on all sides. Many were slain by the Romans, among them Joseph, who was killed while trying to escape through the breach. The whole city was in an uproar, and the people ran about in the greatest fright.

Charres, the other commander, was lying sick in his bed and was so disturbed by the noise that he died. The Romans, warned by their former disaster, did not make an attack at once, but waited for some days.

Titus, who had been away on an expedition, now returned. He was very angry when he heard of the loss which the Romans had sustained during his absence, and immediately entered the city with two hundred horse and a body of infantry. The people flew quickly to arms. Some, catching up their children and dragging their wives along, fled to the citadel with loud lamentations; others, who encountered the enemy, were slain without mercy. Terrible was the slaughter, and blood flowed down the steep streets like a waterfall.

Vespasian entered the city with his entire force to aid his son, and led his men against the citadel. The rock upon which it stood was rugged and jagged and surrounded on all sides by precipices. The Jews crowded upon this crag, the top of which the Roman darts could not reach, and hurled stones and missiles upon their assailants.

But to seal their destruction a tremendous storm arose, and blew full in the faces of the unfortunate Jews, which, while it carried against them the Roman darts, turned their own aside and rendered them harmless. Nor could they stand on the edges of the rock, having no secure footing, nor yet see the enemy as they scaled the crag. Thus they were surrounded and slaughtered.

The Romans, savage on account of their former defeat, spared no one, not even the women and children. Multitudes threw themselves headlong down the precipices. Their despair was even more fatal than the weapons of their enemies. For four thousand fell by the sword, while five thousand hurled themselves down from the heights.

Two women who had hidden themselves alone survived the general carnage. Thus fell Gamala, upon the 23d of September, in the year A.D. 67.

CHAPTER CXXXV.

THE SURRENDER OF GISCHALA.

GISCHALA, a small town in Galilee, now alone remained in arms against the Romans. The inhabitants, indeed, were an agricultural people, and little inclined to war; but the crafty John, son of Levi, the old rival of Josephus, commanded a strong faction in the city, headed by his own band of robbers, who compelled the people to assume an attitude of defiance.

Vespasian sent his son Titus with one thousand horsemen against the town, and directed the tenth legion to proceed to Scythopolis, while he himself, with the other two legions, went into winter quarters at Cæsarea, in order to recruit his men before attacking Jerusalem.

Titus, on riding up to Gischala, ascertained that it might easily be carried by assault. But, as he desired to shed as little blood as possible, and knowing that many of the people wished to submit, he offered the inhabitants terms, promising them pardon and protection should they surrender.

Not only were none of the citizens allowed to reply to these terms, but they were not even allowed to ascend the wall while they were offered, for the brigands had completely taken possession of it. John replied that he was satisfied with these conditions and would surrender the town, but, as the day was the Sabbath, when it was not lawful for the Jews either to fight or to treat of peace, he would wish Titus to wait until the day following, when the terms could be concluded.

Titus was not only prevailed upon to grant this delay, but was induced to withdraw his troops to the neighboring town of Cydessa.

At nightfall John, seeing no Roman guard about the town, escaped with his band towards Jerusalem, followed by many others with their families, who had determined to seek refuge in the capital. The women and children marched on steadily for about two or three miles, but then their strength began to fail them. Finding that they would impede his flight, John abandoned them, and urged his followers to save themselves.

The poor women and children were in a dreadful state of fright, and started at the sound of one another's footsteps as if the Romans were upon them. Many strayed into pathless wastes, while many fell from fatigue and were trampled to death. Those who marched the fastest called upon their friends and relations to turn back and help them, but in vain. For John called out to the men,—

"Save yourselves, and flee to some place of security, where we may avenge ourselves upon the Romans, if they plunder those we leave behind."

So the men hurried forward, and the women and children were left in the darkness all alone.

When day broke, Titus appeared before the wall of Gischala to propose terms. The people threw open their gates and hailed him as a liberator; they informed him of John's flight, and entreated him to spare them, but to punish whatever insurgents yet remained. Titus immediately despatched a troop of horse to overtake John; but the chase proved fruitless, and he escaped in safety to Jerusalem. Of those who accompanied him, however, the horsemen slew six thousand, and brought back three thousand women and children into the city.

Titus, although he was greatly disappointed because he did not capture John, still behaved with great lenity to the remaining inhabitants of the city. He put none to death, but merely threatened any disaffected ones with future punishment should they attempt to disturb the peace. He then ordered, according to the law of capture, a small part of the wall to be thrown down, and left a garrison to preserve the peace. Thus, after giving the Romans an immense amount of trouble, was the whole of Galilee subdued.

CHAPTER CXXXVI.

THE ZEALOTS.

No sooner had John set foot in Jerusalem than the whole population poured forth in crowds and surrounded the several fugitives, eagerly inquiring what calamities had happened without. The heat and broken breathing of John's party showed that they had come at a very quick pace. But still they put on a blustering air, and said they had not fled from the Romans, but had come to defend the capital, not thinking it worth while to risk their valuable lives in defence of a little place like Gischala.

When, however, they related the fall of Gischala, it became evident to many that their retreat was no better than a flight;

and when they heard the awful details of massacre and captivity, they foreboded the fate that would overtake themselves.

John, however, put on a bold air, and went about inciting the multitude to warlike measures, setting forth in false colors the weakness of the Romans, and saying that even had the Romans wings like birds, they could never surmount the ramparts of the capital; that they already had had trouble enough in subduing the villages of Galilee, and could never take so strong a city as Jerusalem.

The young men eagerly believed him, and were easily incited to take up arms; but the old and prudent men mourned over the prospect of the future. The metropolis now began to be divided into two hostile factions,—one desirous of peace and submission to the Romans, the other desirous of war.

The whole province, indeed, was torn by civil dissension, and everywhere, in every city, the peace party and the war party fought for the supremacy. Whenever the people had time to breathe from the assaults of the Romans, they turned their swords upon each other. Every family was divided against itself.

In the country, bands of brigands collected, and robbed and ravaged the district. The Roman garrisons in the different towns looked on in indifference, and let the people fight it out among themselves, affording no relief to the distressed and those who desired peace.

At last the brigands, satiated with pillage, collected together in one band, and crept into Jerusalem; for this city, according to ancient custom, received all people of Jewish blood. These robbers were a useless burden to Jerusalem, for they consumed those supplies which might have long supported the garrison, and brought upon the people the miseries of sedition and famine.

The different bands of robbers joined together formed a powerful faction, and soon began to exercise their old calling. They grew so bold that they committed robberies and murders in the open daylight; and, wishing to become masters of the city, they slew some of the most distinguished citizens.

Their first victim was Antipas, a man of royal birth, and the treasurer of the city. They seized him and detained him in custody, and then in like manner arrested a number of leading men. The people looked on in dismay, but refrained from interference, each one fearing for his own personal safety.

As the brigands feared that an attempt might be made to rescue the prisoners, they decreed that they should be put to death, and sent one of their number, called John, a desperate villain, with ten men into the prison to execute their orders. John and his band accordingly despatched those in custody. As an excuse for this atrocious act they pretended that the prisoners had held conferences with the Romans to treat about a surrender of Jerusalem; and they gave out that they had slain the betrayers of their liberty. In fact, they gloried in their wicked deeds, as if they had been the benefactors and preservers of the city.

Finding that the people were thoroughly cowed beneath their sway, these robbers took a step even more daring. They assumed authority to appoint to the high-priesthood. Accordingly, they annulled the right of those families from which by succession the high-priests had been elected, and ordained to the office the ignoble and low-born, that they might make them accomplices in their impious proceedings. Moreover, by artifices and slanderous stories they set at odds persons formerly in authority, and so, by creating divisions, increased their own power, united as they were for evil.

The multitude at last, instigated by Ananus, the oldest of the chief priests, were goaded to resistance. The robbers took refuge in the temple of God, and sacrilegiously turned it into a fortress to protect them against the outburst of popular violence, making the holy place their asylum. To these bitter evils they added mockery, which the people felt more deeply than even their violent acts. They pretended that, according to ancient law, the high-priest should be chosen by lot, although the succession was really hereditary.

And so they cast a lot, and the office fell upon a coarse clown called Phannias, who scarcely knew what the high-priesthood meant. Yet they dressed him in the priestly robes, and taught him how to act when offering sacrifice. This shocking impiety, which to them was a subject of merriment, drew tears from the other priests, who beheld from a distance their law turned into ridicule, and wept over the profanation of the holy office.

This insult aroused the people. Some of the chief men went among them and urged them to punish these destroyers of liberty, and to purge the sanctuary of its polluters. An assembly of the people was convened, and Ananus addressed them, his eyes filling with tears every time he looked towards the temple. He reproached the multitude with their tame endurance of a tyranny more cruel than that of the Romans. Would they, who would not submit to the masters of the world, bear the tyranny of their own countrymen? It was a cause for bitter tears to see the offerings of the heathen in the Holy Place; how much worse to see the arms of murderers who had slain their own people, those even whom the Romans would have spared! The Romans had always remained reverently without in the court of the Gentiles; those who were bound to observe the law, who called themselves Jews, trod with polluted feet the very Holy of Holies, their hands reeking with the blood of their brethren.

Stirred by the eloquent harangue, the people demanded to be immediately led against the Zealots, for so the robbers styled themselves,—as if they were zealous in the cause of virtue, while indeed they were noted for their pursuit of vice. The Zealots had sent spies to the assembly, and from them received news of what was going on.

While Ananus was mustering his forces they rushed from

the temple, and spared none that came in their way. Ananus
hastily collected the populace, who, though superior in numbers, were inferior in discipline to the robbers. The two parties fought with the greatest fury, and the slaughter on both
sides was enormous.

At first the better discipline of the Zealots gave them the
advantage, but before long they were obliged to retire before
the superior numbers of their opponents, and they retreated
into the temple, Ananus and his party breaking in with them.
The Zealots fled into the inner court and closed the gates.
Ananus was prevented from improving his advantage, because
he deemed it wrong to assail the sacred gates, or to introduce
the multitude unpurified into the inner temple. He therefore
contented himself with stationing six thousand men as sentinels about the cloisters and gates of the inner court, that
they might keep guard over the party within, and he made
arrangements that this guard should be regularly relieved.

The ruin of Ananus and his entire party was caused by
John of Gischala, whose flight from his native town has been
related. This crafty man, always plotting to get power for
himself, pretended that he sided with the populace, and daily
attended the councils of Ananus and the leaders of his party.
But at night when he visited the watch he would betray his
secrets to the Zealots. To conceal his treachery, he pretended
the greatest anxiety for the success of the people. But he
rather overacted his part, and as the people found out that
their movements were disclosed to the Zealots, John fell under
suspicion. Yet it was no easy matter to punish him, because
he was too sly to be detected, and he had a large band of
followers.

It was deemed advisable, therefore, to bind him by oath to
keep good faith with the people. Without any hesitation
John swore that he would be true to the people, and that he
would not betray either counsel or act to their enemies, but
would assist both by his personal exertions and advice in con-

quering their assailants. Relying on his oath, Ananus and
his party now admitted him without suspicion to their de-
liberations, and even sent him to treat with the Zealots.

John, however, as if he had sworn fealty to the Zealots, instead of against them, entered the temple and spoke to them
like a sworn friend. He represented the dangers he had
incurred in rendering them secret service, and informed them
that negotiations were going on for the surrender of the city to
the Romans; also that Ananus had appointed a purification
service on the following day in order that his followers might
enter the temple and attack the Zealots. Nor, said he, did
he see how they could hold out for any length of time against
so many opponents. They must either, therefore, sue for pardon or obtain some external aid. And he warned them
against the danger of trusting to the mercy of the people,
who had not forgotten their daring deeds. He hinted, therefore, at obtaining succor from the Idumeans; and in order to
make the leaders of the Zealots angry, he stated that Ananus
made them the special objects of his threats. The leaders
were Eleazar, son of Simon, and Zacharias, son of Phalek.
These men, on hearing the threats directed against themselves,
and, moreover, that Ananus had invited the Romans to aid him,
for so John had falsely stated, were deeply perplexed as to
what course of action they should take.

It was finally resolved that they should call the Idumeans
to their aid, and so they despatched some swift messengers
with letters, saying that Ananus was about to betray the
city to the Romans, and that they had revolted in the cause
of freedom, but were now shut up in the temple, and that un
less they received immediate aid they would be soon overcome and the city be surrendered to the Romans.

The Idumeans were a warlike people, and as soon as they
knew the contents of the letters they flew to arms, and marched
towards Jerusalem with an army of twenty thousand men. Ananus heard of their coming, and closed the gates. He was op-

posed, however, to warlike measures, and so determined to try persuasion before recourse was had to arms. Accordingly, Joshua, the chief priest next in age to Ananus, addressed the Idumeans from a high tower. He endeavored to persuade them to do one of three things,—either to unite with them in the chastisement of the robbers, to enter the city unarmed and act as judges between the two parties, or to depart and leave the city to settle its own affairs.

But the Idumeans would not listen to the proposals of Joshua, and were greatly irritated because they were not allowed to enter the city at once. Simon, one of their leaders, sternly answered Joshua that they had come as true patriots and defenders of their country against men who were in a conspiracy to sell the liberties of the land to the Romans. " Here before these walls," he said, " we will remain in arms until the Romans grow weary of listening to your proposals, or a change of sentiment leads you to espouse the cause of freedom."

The Idumeans loudly applauded these words, and Joshua withdrew in dejection, finding them opposed to all moderate measures, and anxious on account of the city, now threatened with war from two quarters. The Idumeans on their part began to grow uneasy; they were greatly irritated at being shut out of the city. But when they perceived no aid at hand from the Zealot party, whom they supposed to be in considerable strength, they became perplexed, and many repented that they had come. Still they were ashamed to return without having accomplished their purpose, so they encamped before the walls. With night came on a terrific storm of wind and rain, lightning and terrible thunder. The Idumeans huddled up together in order to keep each other warm, and locked their shields over their heads to keep off the rain. The Zealots became greatly concerned about their allies exposed to this terrible storm, and held a consultation to devise means for their relief. The most impetuous wished to force the sentries, sword in hand, and boldly rush forth and open the gates to the Idumeans. But the more prudent restrained them from making this attempt, because the sentries had been doubled, and they expected Ananus would be going the rounds at all hours. This had been his practice every night, but this night alone, trusting probably to the strength of his doubled sentries, Ananus neglected all precaution. As the night advanced, a great many of the sentries in the cloisters about the inner court fell asleep. The watchful Zealots perceived this, and, taking a lot of saws belonging to the temple, they severed the bars of the gates, the noise of the tempest aiding their purpose by preventing them from being heard.

A few of them stole out secretly from the temple, and when they reached the wall, they sawed open the gate nearest to the Idumeans. They, supposing themselves attacked by Ananus and his party, were at first seized with alarm, and every man drew his sword for defence, but quickly recognizing their visitors, they entered the city with them. Had they turned immediately upon the city, so ungovernable was their rage that nothing could have prevented the entire destruction of the people; but they hastened first to liberate all the Zealots from custody, at the request of those who had let them into the city. These men besought them not to neglect those for whose sake they had come, surrounded as they were with difficulties, nor yet to put them in still more serious danger. Were the guards mastered, they said, it would be easy to conquer the city; but if they first attacked the people, the citizens would rally around the guards, and would form an irresistible force to keep the invaders from the temple, wherein the Zealots were shut up.

In obedience to these requests, the Idumeans marched to the temple. As they were entering, the Zealots inside took courage and attacked the sentries from the rear. Some of them who lay in front they killed in their sleep, till the entire force, roused by the cries of those who were awake, snatched up their arms and hastened to the defence. So long as they supposed themselves assailed only by the Zealots, the guards fought with spirit, hoping to overcome them by numbers, but when they discovered that the Idumeans were in the city, most of them threw down their arms and gave way to lamentations. A few of the younger ones, however, fencing themselves in, gallantly fought the Idumeans, and for a time protected the feebler crowd, who by their cries informed the people in the city of the calamities that had befallen them. But the people were too frightened to venture to their assistance. All the houses resounded with lamentations and the piercing shrieks of women. The Zealots joined in the battle-cry of the Idumeans, and the shouting on all sides was rendered still more fearful by the howling of the storm.

The Idumeans gave no quarter. They slaughtered all the guards, and when day dawned the sun shone on over eight thousand corpses. Then the invaders rushed upon the city, pillaging all the houses and killing all who came in their way. The high-priests, Ananus and Joshua, were killed, and their bodies denied the rite of burial, although the Jews were so attentive to the rites of sepulture that even malefactors who had been crucified were interred before sunset.

The bloody work went on for days. The Zealots and their cruel allies butchered the people as if they were a herd of beasts. A great many youths of noble birth they threw into prison, hoping to induce them to join their party. Not one, however, listened to their proposals, all preferring to die rather than array themselves with the wicked against their country. Twelve thousand young men were thus doomed to destruction.

At length, weary of slaughter, the Zealots began to affect the forms of law, and set up mock tribunals and courts of justice. There was a certain distinguished man, called Zacharias, whom they wished to get rid of, because they dreaded his influence with the people and wished to possess themselves of his wealth.

They therefore formed a court composed of seventy of the leading men in the character of judges, but really without authority, and before them charged Zacharias with treasonable correspondence with Vespasian in order to betray the state to the Romans. They brought forth neither proof nor witnesses, but insisted that he should be convicted upon their charges alone.

Zacharias boldly ridiculed their accusations, and in a few words refuted the charges brought against him, and then rebuked the wickedness of his accusers. Stung by his taunts, the Zealots with difficulty restrained themselves from killing him then and there. But they were anxious to see if the judges would obey their will. The seventy, however, preferred to die with the accused rather than be guilty of condemning an innocent man, and so brought in a verdict of acquittal.

The Zealots raised a cry of indignation, and two of the most daring rushed upon Zacharias and slew him in the midst of the temple, crying out in derision as he fell, "You have now our verdict, and a more effective acquittal." They then threw him headlong from the temple into the ravine below. The judges they beat with the flat blades of their swords, and drove them in disgrace back to the city.

The Idumeans, dissatisfied with these proceedings, now began to regret that they had given aid to such a band of murderers as the Zealots. A man attached to the Zealot party called them together privately and pointed out to them the lawless acts of those who had invited them, and set forth in detail the injuries they had inflicted upon the city. He urged them to return home and no longer give countenance by their presence to the murders and atrocities of the Zealots, who had deceived them into becoming their accomplices by representing Ananus and his party as guilty of treason,—a groundless charge, since no treason was feared, and the Roman army had not appeared before the city.

Induced by these arguments, the Idumeans returned home from Jerusalem; but first they liberated about two thousand prisoners, who fled from the city to Simon, the son of Gioras, of whom we shall hear more presently.

The people, ignorant of the repentance of the Idumeans, supposed themselves relieved from enemies, and began to feel more easy. The Zealots, on the other hand, as if released from control rather than deprived of assistance, became all the more audacious, and continued in their wicked courses. They put to death all the brave and noble men, the leaders of the people. For they thought that their own safety depended on leaving none of those in authority alive. No one escaped death but those whose safety lay in the utter meanness of their birth or fortune.

Hearing of the dissensions in Jerusalem, many of the Roman officers urged Vespasian to march immediately upon the city, thinking it a good time for an attack. But the politic general replied that an attack from the Romans would instantly extinguish these internal dissensions and unite the Jews against the common enemy; while if they were let alone, they would go on destroying each other and give the Romans later an easy victory.

Every day people fled from the tyranny of the Zealots in Jerusalem, although flight was difficult, because all the outlets were guarded, and every one caught in them was instantly put to death unless he could pay a certain sum for his freedom, in which case he was allowed to go. Hence it followed that, as the rich purchased escape, the poor alone were slaughtered. In the city and in the roads they lay dead in heaps. For to such an excess of cruelty and impiety did the Zealots proceed that they forbade the rites of burial. He who interred a relative was put to death. But the living under so awful a rule deemed themselves less blessed than the unburied dead.

The Zealots laughed at every human law, and scoffed at the oracles of the prophets as the fables of mountebanks. Yet did these very men bring down upon their country the fulfilment of an ancient prophecy, which declared that when civil war should break out in the city and native hands defile God's hallowed temple the city would be taken and the sanctuary burned to the ground.

CHAPTER CXXXVII.

THE ZEALOTS WRANGLE AMONG THEMSELVES.   VESPASIAN TAKES
GADARA.   PLACIDUS GAINS A VICTORY.

AND now the Zealot party itself split into two factions. For John of Gischala, whose aim all along had been to gain the supreme power, withdrew from them with a band of the most desperate men whom he had attached to his person, and over whom he ruled as a king. Those who were too proud to submit to his authority, and who dreaded lest John should be made king, formed an opposite party.

The two parties watched each other closely, but rarely, if ever, appealed to the sword. They both, however, assailed the populace, and vied with each other in the quantity of plunder they could extort.

The capital was thus afflicted with the three greatest of evils,—war, tyranny, and sedition,—while a fourth evil was soon added to complete the nation's ruin. Not far from Jerusalem was a fortress of very great strength, called Massada, erected by the ancient kings as a treasury for their wealth and a place of safety during war. Of this the Sikars, or Assassins, had taken possession some time before. They had hitherto confined themselves to marauding expeditions through the surrounding districts. But when they heard that the Roman army was lying inactive, and that in Jerusalem the people were distracted by sedition and tyranny, they attempted more daring enterprises. And so at the feast of the Passover they surprised by night a small town called Engaddi, drove the men from the town before they could seize their arms, and put the women and children to the sword. They then rifled the houses, seized great quantities of corn, and, when they had laid waste the whole region, carried back their booty to Massada. These bold robbers were daily strengthened by multitudes of wicked men who flocked to them from every quarter. Other bands of robbers collected in other parts, until the whole province became a scene of plunder and confusion.

The Jewish refugees who had fled from the capital to the camp of Vespasian besought him to march upon the city and succor its inhabitants, who, they said, were in great peril because of their friendliness to the Romans. Vespasian thought it best to first reduce the rest of the country, and so broke up his camp and marched upon Gadara, the capital of Peræa. The leading men, who wished to save their property, sent a deputation to treat of surrender. The insurgents, despairing of being able to defend the city, put to death one of the leading men who was to have advised that the deputation be sent, and fled from the city.

The Gadarenes then threw open their gates to Vespasian, and welcomed him with every demonstration of joy. The general left them a garrison for protection; for they had demolished their own walls, in order that their want of power to make war might be a sign that they would remain peaceful for the future.

Vespasian sent a force of cavalry and foot under Placidus against those who had fled from Gadara. He himself returned with the remainder of the army to Cæsarea.

The fugitives took possession of a village called Bethenna-

bris, and, being joined by a number of the young men, they
rushed at random upon the troops of Placidus.

Placidus feigned a retreat, in order to lure them a distance
from their walls, then faced round and killed a great number
of them. The remainder fled back to the village, so closely
pursued by the Romans that they almost entered the town
with them. The assault was immediately made, and by evening the ramparts were scaled, the inhabitants slaughtered, and
the village reduced to ashes.

Some fugitives, however, escaped, and created great excitement throughout the country by stating that the Roman
army was advancing in full force. Accordingly, the whole
population fled towards Jericho, where, from the strength of
its defences and from its numerous inhabitants, they hoped
for safety. Placidus pursued them to the Jordan, putting all
he overtook to the sword. The river was swollen and impassable, so the Jews were compelled to turn and fight. Placidus charged them with his cavalry, cut them down by thousands, and drove multitudes into the river, where they were
drowned. Fifteen thousand perished, while over two thousand were captured, together with an immense booty of asses
and sheep, camels and oxen.

Placidus, following up his good fortune, rapidly took town
after town, and soon reduced the whole of Peræa and the
coast of the Dead Sea as far as Machærus.

Meanwhile, Vespasian received tidings that disturbances
had broken out in Gaul and that a chief called Vindex, with
many others, had revolted from Nero. He foresaw the civil
dissensions which threatened the empire, and was persuaded
that he had better put an end to the war in Palestine at once,
that his army might be at liberty for any further service.

He therefore employed himself during the winter in garri-
soning the villages and smaller towns that he had reduced;
and as soon as spring broke he marched to Antipatris.
Spending two days in reducing this town to order, he ad-

vanced upon Jericho, wasting all the places around with fire and sword. He captured a number of cities and towns, fortifying some and destroying others, and at length encamped before Jericho, where he was joined by the troops who had reduced Peræa.

Before the Romans arrived, the inhabitants escaped to a mountainous range which lies over against Jerusalem, so that the city was deserted. Vespasian placed a garrison here, and another in Adida, in order to invest Jerusalem on all sides. And he also despatched Lucius Annus, one of his officers, with a large force, against the city of Gerasa.

Annus carried the city at the first assault, burnt it to the ground, and advanced against the villages in the neighborhood. All who could fly from these towns did so; the feeble people perished. The whole country was overrun, and all egress from Jerusalem was prevented. For those who wished to desert were closely watched by the Zealots, while those who did not yet favor the Romans were kept in check by the army, which hemmed in the city on all sides.

While Vespasian was preparing to march upon Jerusalem in full force, tidings reached him of the violent death of Nero, the emperor of Rome. This news deferred his expedition, and he waited anxiously to learn who would be the new emperor. When he learned that Galba had been called to the throne, he despatched his son Titus to receive his commands in regard to the Jews. While Titus was on his way, Galba met a violent death, and Otho succeeded to the throne. Titus returned to his father at Cæsarea without going to Rome. Being thus in suspense while the empire was in such a state of change, they refrained from carrying on the war. For they thought it unwise to attack a foreign country while filled with apprehension for their own.

But Jerusalem during the interval did not remain at rest. Another war broke out, which was caused by Simon, son of Gioras, a Gerasan by birth. He was not as artful as John, who was now master of the city, but was his superior in bodily strength and daring, qualities which had led Ananus the high-priest to drive him from the territory of Acrabattene, which he once held. Thus expelled, he betook himself to the brigands, who had seized on Massada.

At first he was regarded by them with suspicion, but gradually he gained their confidence and joined them in laying waste the country about Massada. He could not, however, induce them to attempt larger conquests, so he withdrew to the mountainous districts, and there gathered robbers from all quarters around him in such numbers that he was emboldened to descend to the lowlands. Becoming at length very formidable, he was joined by many men of rank, and overran the Acrabattene territory as far as Idumea. He fortified a village called Nain, and deposited much booty and provisions in caves near by, and made it evident that he soon intended to attack Jerusalem.

The Zealots, alarmed at his designs, marched out in considerable force against Simon, but were routed and chased into the city. He did not, however, attempt to take the city, but at the head of twenty thousand men marched towards Idumea, in order first to subdue that province.

The Idumeans assembled twenty-five thousand men and met Simon at the frontier, where for a whole day a battle was fought, but neither party gained the victory. The next day Simon returned to Nain, and the Idumeans disbanded to their homes.

Not long after, however, Simon returned with a larger force, and, encamping at a village called Thecoe, he sent one of his followers, named Eleazar, to persuade the garrison of Herodium, which was near by, to surrender. Eleazar was admitted by the garrison, but when he spoke of surrender, the soldiers indignantly rushed upon him with drawn swords; upon which he threw himself from the ramparts into the ravine below and was killed.

The Idumeans, now much alarmed at Simon's strength, thought it well to find out how strong his forces were before they gave him battle. For this purpose James, one of their generals, offered his services. But in his heart he meditated treachery. He went to Simon and promised to betray the Idumeans on condition of receiving a post of honor under him. Simon consented, and loaded James with presents, who returned to his own people and frightened them by telling them stories about the great numbers of the enemy, and said it was better to surrender without a struggle. He then sent a message to Simon, inviting him to advance. Upon the approach of his army, James sprang upon his horse and took to flight, followed by a number of his dupes. Seeing this, the whole multitude was seized with a panic, and before a blow was struck they hastily dispersed to their homes.

Simon made himself master of the city of Hebron, where he obtained immense booty, and from this point advanced through Idumea, laying waste the entire country. Besides his regular forces, he had forty thousand followers, so that his supplies were not sufficient for such a multitude. They therefore stole all they could find, and passed over the whole district like a swarm of locusts, leaving no sign of life or vegetation behind them.

The Zealots, afraid to meet Simon again in open warfare, placed ambushes in the passes, and captured Simon's wife with a numerous band of attendants. With these they returned to the city, thinking that Simon would lay down his arms and beg them to give him back his wife. Her seizure, however, only roused Simon's ire. He advanced to the walls of Jerusalem, and vented his rage upon every one he could capture without the city. Old and unarmed men who ventured outside to gather herbs or wood were seized, tortured, and put to death. Many of them Simon sent back into the city with their hands cut off, telling them to say that Simon had sworn an oath that unless the people restored his wife to him without delay he would break down the wall and inflict a like punishment on every one within it. These threats so terrified not only the people, but also the Zealots, that they sent his wife back to him. Simon was then somewhat soothed, and paused in his career of slaughter.

It was now the spring of the year 69, and Vespasian broke up from winter quarters in Cæsarea and advanced upon those places in Judea which had not yet submitted to his arms. He subdued two provinces called Gophnitis and Acrabattene, and advanced with his cavalry as far as the walls of Jerusalem. Cerealis, one of his generals, meanwhile entered Idumea, and took Caphetra, Capharabim, and Hebron. There remained nothing now to conquer except Herodium, Massada, and Macherus, which were held by the brigands, and Jerusalem itself. But not yet did Vespasian think it wise to attack the capital. He laid waste the country about it, and returned to Cæsarea.

Simon had remained in Massada while Cerealis laid waste Idumea. He then marched forth again, entered Idumea, and drove a number of the unhappy people to Jerusalem, pursuing them to the city. He again encamped without the walls, and put to death all who came in his way. Thus, to the people was Simon without more formidable than the Romans, and the Zealots within more oppressive than either. The unfortunate city was in the most dreadful condition. The Galileans, who belonged to John's party and who had raised him to power, were allowed by him to commit every excess. They robbed, murdered, and committed every crime. Thus was the city besieged within and without. Those who stayed were tyrannized over by John and his party; those who fled were massacred by Simon.

At length John's party divided. The Idumean portion of it detached themselves and made an attack upon the tyrant, as well from envy of his power as from hatred of his cruelty. An engagement took place, in which many Zealots fell, and the rest were finally driven into the temple. There they assembled in great numbers, and John prepared to lead them against the people and the Idumeans. The latter did not so much dread the attack, but feared lest the Zealots should steal from the temple by night and set fire to the city. A council was therefore held with the chief priests, and it was resolved that they should call in Simon to their aid,—a measure which only added to the miseries of the city by admitting a second tyrant.

Simon was admitted, and was received with acclamations by the people as their savior and guardian. His first care was to collect a lot of plunder left in the city by John, and then he attacked the temple. The Zealots posted themselves on the colonnades and battlements, and from the advantage of their higher position ably defended themselves against their assailants, and created great slaughter in the ranks of Simon. To increase their advantage they reared four large towers, that they might hurl their missiles from a still greater height. Upon these they put their engines of war and their archers and slingers. These made great havoc among Simon's troops, so that he, although he still held his ground, in some measure relaxed his assaults.

In the mean while, the great empire of Rome itself was torn by civil dissensions. The emperor Galba was murdered, and Otho ascended the throne. But this honor was disputed by Vitellius, who was chosen emperor by the legions of Germany. Otho was conquered by the troops of Vitellius, and committed suicide. Vitellius then marched in triumph to Rome. But the army under Vespasian declared that he should be emperor. Mucianus, the president of Syria, also declared for Vespasian, as did the legion of the East and of the central provinces. Vespasian took possession of Egypt, and sent one of his generals, Antonius Primus, and Mucianus, into Italy. They overcame the army of Vitellius, took possession of Rome, and put the emperor to death.

Vespasian thus became emperor of Rome, and, delighted that the prophecies of Josephus had come true, he loaded him with honors and delivered him from his bonds. When he felt secure of his throne he again turned his attention to the rebellious capital of Judæa, and sent his son Titus to complete the subjugation of Palestine by the conquest of Jerusalem.

CHAPTER CXXXVIII.

TITUS SURROUNDS JERUSALEM.

Titus passed through Egypt and Syria, and at length arrived at Cæsarea, where he determined to organize his forces before he commenced the campaign. While he was still on his way, the unhappy city of Jerusalem, daily weakened by civil dissensions, was torn by still another faction. It was a sedition within a sedition, which, like a ravenous wild beast, preyed upon its own flesh.

That Eleazar who was mentioned some time ago as being the first cause of the Jewish revolt, because he had persuaded the people to reject the offerings of the Roman emperors, became very jealous of John. And because he could not brook submission to a tyrant of lower birth than himself, he seceded with a considerable body of the Zealots, and seized upon the inner court of the temple.

They were well supplied with provisions, but, because their numbers were fewer than John's, they confined themselves to their retreat, from whence, on account of the height of their position, they could easily repel his attacks. John, in his rage, although he lost heavily, made continual assaults upon them; so that clouds of missiles flew about the temple, and the sacred pavement was strewn with dead.

Simon, who was now master of the upper and a great part of the lower city, carried on his attacks upon John with greater vigor, because he knew his party to be divided, and that he was threatened by Eleazar from above. But John had the same advantage over Simon which Eleazar had over John. From the superior height of his position he easily repelled all attacks from below by hand-weapons, while with his machines he hurled missiles against the party above him.

The missiles hurled by these machines flew all over the temple, and slew priests and worshippers at the very altar itself. For, notwithstanding all the horrors of war, the sacrifices went on, and pious Jews from all quarters still came to make offerings, and to worship at the altar of their God, around which many of them fell, and sprinkled it with their blood.

At times, when the party above through fatigue refrained from hurling down their missiles, John would sally out against Simon and his adherents. And as far as he was able to drive them before him he would set fire to the storehouses filled with corn and provisions over that extent. Simon in his turn would drive him back with fire and sword, so that the space around the temple became a mass of ruins, and a great quantity of corn, which might have sufficed the besieged for many years, was burnt up. So that the city was finally reduced by famine, which could hardly have been possible had not the Jews brought it upon themselves.

The people, harassed by the bloody contentions of the three factions, groaned in secret, and many prayed that the Romans might come and deliver them from these internal dissensions. For them there was no other hope of escape, for the three parties, disagreeing in everything else, united in putting to death all who showed any desire of peace with the Romans, or whom they suspected of intentions to desert the city.

Day after day the fearful strifes went on, each party devising new means for mutual destruction. John seized upon some sacred timbers, which Agrippa had brought from Mount Lebanon some time before the war, in order to raise the sanctuary, and converted them into towers, that he might fight on even terms with the faction of Eleazar. But before he could bring his impiously-constructed towers into play the Romans appeared before the walls of Jerusalem.

Titus had drawn together part of his troops and marched from Cæsarea, ordering the others to meet him at Jerusalem. He had under him the three legions which his father had commanded, and also the twelfth legion, which had formerly been defeated under Cestius, and which now burned for revenge. And besides these he had a number of hired soldiers from Syria and from Egypt. Tiberius Alexander, a former governor of Egypt, distinguished for his wisdom and integrity, accompanied Titus, and on account of his age and experience acted as his adviser during the war.

Titus encamped with his army about four miles from Jerusalem, in a valley called the valley of Thorus. Taking a body of six hundred horsemen with him, he rode forward to reconnoitre the strength of the city, and to ascertain the disposition of the Jews. For he was persuaded, as indeed was the fact, that the body of the people were desirous of peace with the Romans, and were only kept from making overtures through fear of the brigands.

While he continued to ride along the direct route which led to the wall, not a soul appeared before the gates. But on his filing off from the road to the right towards a tower called Psephinus, the Jews suddenly rushed out in great numbers, and broke through his ranks. They then placed themselves in front of the troops who were still advancing along the road, and prevented them from joining their comrades who had filed off, thus intercepting Titus with only a handful of men.

Titus could not advance, because the ground was covered with orchards and gardens, divided by stone walls, and intersected by deep ditches, which reached to the city walls. To retreat was almost as difficult, because the enemy lay in great numbers across his road. Still, he saw that his only course was to cut his way through to his own party, who were retreating, not knowing their prince's danger, but thinking that he had turned back with them. Titus wheeled his horse round, called to his handful of warriors to follow him, and charged fiercely through. Darts and arrows fell in showers around him, but, although he had on neither helmet nor breast-plate, he escaped uninjured. The Jews shouted at his bravery, and cheered one another on against him, anxious to secure such a prize. But wherever Titus directed his course they shrank back through fear, and made way for him. His followers formed around him as well as they could, and at length they cut their way through, and reached the camp in safety. Two of their number, however, were killed by the enemy. The Jews were greatly elated by the success of this attempt, and it inspired them with much confidence for the future.

Titus was joined during the night by the legion from Ammaus, and advanced the next day to a flat called Scopus (the Prospect), about a mile from the northern quarter of the town. Here he formed a camp for two legions, and stationed the fifth legion a little way in the rear. While the troops were engaged in building intrenchments the tenth legion arrived, and took up its station at the Mount of Olives, which rises to the east of the city, and is separated from it by a deep intervening ravine.

The three factions within the city beheld with dismay the three fortifications which were going up without the walls, while no attempt was made to check them. They began to feel the necessity of becoming united against the common foe.

"We are courageous, then," they exclaimed, "only against ourselves, while the Romans, through our dissension, will make a bloodless conquest of the city."

Assembling together, and encouraging one another with language such as this, they seized their arms, and sallying forth, made a sudden attack upon the tenth legion. Bursting through the ravine with a terrific shout, they fell upon the Romans while at work upon their intrenchments.

The legion was divided into two parties for the purpose of carrying on the work, and the men had for the most part laid aside their arms. Indeed, they had no idea that the Jews would make an attack. They were in consequence taken by surprise, and thrown into disorder. Abandoning their works, some instantly retreated, while many, who ran to arms, were slaughtered before they could turn on their assailants.

Encouraged by the success of the first assault, great numbers of Jews flocked out to aid their brethren. Accustomed to fight only in array, the Roman soldiers were thrown into confusion by this wild mode of warfare. Taken unawares, they gave way before the attack, and were driven from the camp. The entire legion would have been defeated had not Titus, hearing what had happened, instantly hastened to its succor.

Bitterly upbraiding their cowardice, Titus rallied the fugitives, and falling on the flank of the Jews with his picked men, he drove them headlong down the ravine. Still, rallying upon the other side, the Jews renewed the combat, and thus the battle raged until about noon. Then Titus planted the troops who came with him in front, across the valley, to repel any further sallies, and despatched the rest to proceed with their intrenchments upon the upper part of the mount.

The Jews mistook this movement for flight, a watchman upon the battlements gave a signal, and a fresh crowd of Jews rushed from the city with the fury of wild beasts. The Romans could not sustain their onset; but, as if struck from an engine, they broke up their ranks and fled to the mount. Titus was left with a few followers about half-way up the steep hill. These besought him to retreat, and not to risk his valuable life against the mad courage of the Jews.

But the brave Titus disdained to fly; he fell upon the thickest of the mass as they advanced, and drove them back down the declivity. But still the Jews rushed up the hill on both sides of him, and pursued those who were fleeing up the hill. Meanwhile, the soldiers who had resumed work on the intrenchments upon the upper part of the mount became alarmed as they saw their comrades below in flight, and fled upon all sides.

They fancied that the charge of the Jews was irresistible, and that Titus himself was among the fugitives; for the rest, they thought, would never have fled while he maintained his ground. But a few, perceiving the general in the thickest of the fight, and greatly alarmed upon his account, with loud shouts intimated his danger to the whole legion. Shame rallied them, and, reproaching one another for their base desertion of their general, they fell in full force upon the Jews, and drove them down the hill into the valley. The Jews contested the ground as they retreated; but the Romans, having the advantage of a higher position, drove them in a body down into the ravine.

Titus, pressing still upon those who opposed him, ordered the legion back to complete their fortifications, while he maintained his ground and kept the enemy in check. Thus did this brave general save the legion from defeat, and give them an opportunity of fortifying their camp without being troubled by the enemy.

CHAPTER CXXXIX.

A SUCCESSFUL STRATAGEM.

WHILE the Romans were at work upon their fortifications they did not make any attacks; and, left at rest, civil dissension soon broke out again among the Jews. It was now the feast of the Passover, and Eleazar and his party opened the gates of the inner temple, that any who wished might worship.

John made the festival a cloak for his wicked designs. He armed with concealed weapons a number of his followers, and introduced them by stealth into the inner temple, with a view of seizing upon it. Scarcely had they entered, when, throwing aside their garments, they suddenly appeared in full armor. The worshippers feared a general massacre. Eleazar's party, knowing the attack was made upon them, scattered and took refuge in the vaults of the temple. The multitude cowered round the altar; some were slain out of mere wantonness or from private hate, while a great many were trampled to death in the confusion.

Having glutted their vengeance upon those with whom they had no feud, the partisans of John came to terms with their real enemies. Possessed of the inner temple and all its stores, they could now bid defiance to Simon. Two factions thus were united; and now but two parties, instead of three, divided the city.

Meanwhile, Titus cautiously advanced his approaches, and levelled the ground from Scopus to the walls. Outside the walls were blooming gardens and orchards, which had for-

merly delighted the Jews, but which were now swept away
by the Roman soldiery, together with fences and hedges,
until the whole space was reduced to a level.

While this work was going on, the Jews concerted the following stratagem. A body of insurgents issued out of one
of the gates, as if they had been expelled from the city by
the advocates of peace, and stood cowering alongside of one
another close to the wall, as if in fear of an attack from the
Romans. A number of others stationed themselves upon the
wall and cried aloud for peace, calling upon the Romans for
protection, and promising to open their gates. Moreover,
they assailed the portion of their own party outside with
stones, as if to drive them from the gate. The latter made
feints of attempting to force the entrance, and of petition-
ing those within, every now and then rushing towards the
Romans, and again retreating, as if in extreme agitation.

The Roman soldiers were taken in by this ruse, and, thinking that they had one party in their power, and that the other
would open the gates to them, they were about to charge in
a body, but were restrained by the wary Titus. For he had
the day before, through Josephus, invited the Jews to terms,
but had found their demands exceeding all reason. He therefore ordered the soldiers to remain in their position.

Some of them, however, who were stationed in front, had
already snatched up their arms, and run forward towards the
gate. The Jews at first retired before them; but when the
soldiers were between the towers of the gate they turned
upon them. Then others sallied from the city and surrounded
them, while those upon the wall hurled down stones and missiles on their heads. After suffering great loss in killed and
wounded, the Romans at length retreated, and were pursued
for quite a distance by the Jews, who, when they did pause,
stood and laughed at the Romans, heaping ridicule upon
them for having so easily become dupes, and, brandishing
their shields, danced and shouted for joy. The soldiers who

had escaped were received with a reprimand from their officers, and with indignation on the part of Titus, who addressed them sternly thus:

"The Jews, who have no leader but despair, do everything with the utmost coolness and precaution, lay ambushes, and plot stratagems; while the Romans, to whom fortune has always been a servant on account of their steady discipline, are become so rash and disorderly as to venture into battle without command."

He then threatened to put into execution the military law which punished such a breach of order with death. But the other troops came round him and petitioned him for their fellow-soldiers, imploring him to pardon, in consideration of the obedience of the many, the rashness of a few, and promising to redeem the disaster by future regularity and discipline.

Moved by these entreaties, Titus pardoned the offenders, but commanded them to act with more prudence for the future. He then began to think how he could best avenge himself for this artifice of the Jews. The approach to the city was now complete, and Titus ranged the flower of his troops opposite the northern and the western wall, drawing them up, the infantry in front, the cavalry in the rear, and the archers in the middle.

The sallies of the Jews were thus checked, and the beasts of burden with the camp-followers came up to the camp in security. Titus himself encamped about a quarter of a mile from the ramparts, near the tower called Psephinus. Another division of the army was intrenched at about the same distance opposite the tower called Hippicus, while the tenth legion still continued to occupy its position on the Mount of Olives.

CHAPTER CXL.

THE JEWISH FACTIONS UNITE.

THE whole number of fighting-men and insurgents in the city of Jerusalem was as follows: Simon had under him ten thousand men, not counting his allies, the Idumeans, who numbered five thousand. John, now that he was joined by Eleazar and his party, was in command of a force of eight thousand two hundred men-at-arms. Had these forces been united from the start, and had they, instead of turning their attention to mutual slaughter, turned it to preparing the city for defence, they might long have kept the Romans at bay.

It was not long before they relapsed into their former quarrels, and continued in the work of destroying one another, much to the satisfaction of the besiegers. While affairs within the city were in this condition, Titus, with a detachment of horse, rode round the wall, to see where he could best make his attack. He determined to assault the town at a point opposite a monument erected to the memory of John, a former high-priest. For here the outer wall was lower, and there was easy access to the two inner walls, for they were not as well fortified as at other portions of the town. While Titus was riding around, one of his friends, called Nicanor, who had approached near to the walls with Josephus, was wounded by an arrow as he was addressing some of the Jews upon the ramparts upon the subject of peace.

Titus was very angry at this, and commenced at once to prosecute the siege with vigor. He gave the legions permission to lay waste the suburbs, and ordered them to collect the timber together for the building of mounds. Dividing his army into three divisions for the works, he put the javelin-men and archers between the mounds. In front of these he placed the military engines, so as to check with them the sallies of the enemy and all attempts to impede the building of the mounds from the ramparts.

Though his partisans were burning with impatience to be led against the enemy outside the walls, John, through fear of Simon, remained quietly in the temple. Simon, however, as he lay nearer the scene of attack, was not inactive. He placed those engines upon the ramparts which had formerly been taken from Cestius, and those also which had been captured from the garrison of the Antonia. These, however, did but little damage, for the Jews did not know well how to work them. However, his men assailed from the wall, with stones and arrows, the soldiers employed in raising the mounds, and, rushing out in parties, engaged them in hand-to-hand combat. The workmen were protected from the arrows of the Jews by wicker-work hurdles, while the military engines defended them against the sallies of the besieged.

All the engines constructed by the Romans were possessed of great force, but those belonging to the tenth legion were the most powerful. From their position upon the Mount of Olives, at a distance of about a quarter of a mile, they hurled missiles and tremendous stones with terrific force over the ramparts. The Jews set men to watch the huge rocks which came thundering down upon their heads, for they could be seen coming by their shining whiteness. These watchmen, when they saw the stone discharged, would call out, "The bolt is coming;" on which they all bowed their heads and the stone fell harmless. It then occurred to the Romans to blacken it, by which means, as it could no longer be easily seen, they swept down many at a single discharge.

When the mounds were completed, the battering-rams were brought up, and the engines were moved closer to the walls, so as to protect those working the rams. Suddenly, at three different quarters, they began their thundering work, and a tremendous noise echoed round the city. A cry was raised by those within, and the factions themselves were seized with alarm. Seeing that they were exposed to a common danger, both now turned their thoughts to a common defence. The two parties cried aloud to each other that they must for the present at least stop fighting with each other, and unite in arms against the Romans.

Simon proclaimed an amnesty to all John's followers who wished to come out from the temple and man the wall. John, though still suspicious, did not oppose their going, and the two parties, burying their private differences, fought side by side. They threw showers of torches against the machines and assailed the men who worked upon the rams. The more courageous dashed out in bands, tore the hurdles from the engines, and fell upon those who fired them off.

Titus always came up in person to succor those who were hard pressed. He placed the horsemen and archers on either side of the engines, and repelled the Jews as they attempted to set them on fire. He drove back others who sallied from the towers, and so made the storming-engines effective. The wall, however, did not yield to the strokes, save that one battering-ram knocked down the corner of a tower.

The Jews paused for a while in their sallies, but watched their opportunity; and when the Romans, who thought the Jews had paused through fear and fatigue, were dispersed about the works and off guard, they suddenly poured forth with their whole force. They carried fire to burn the works, and were bent on advancing to the very intrenchments of the Romans. The besiegers gathered hastily, but the daring valor of the Jews at first prevailed over the discipline of their enemies. The Romans, however, quickly rallied, and a terrible conflict ensued around the engines, one party striving to set them on fire, the other to prevent them.

The Jews fought with such desperate valor that they were gaining the victory, and would soon have succeeded in burning the works and engines had not a body of picked troops from Alexandria made a determined stand and bravely held their ground. This gave Titus, at the head of his cavalry, time to rush to their assistance. Titus with his own hand slew twelve of the foremost Jews; the remainder gave way in alarm, and were driven into the city.

One of the Jews was taken prisoner in this engagement, and Titus had him crucified before the wall, hoping that the rest would be so terrified by the spectacle that they would be led to surrender. After the retreat, John, the general of the Idumeans, while talking with a soldier in front of the ramparts, was shot in the breast by an arrow, and instantly expired. His death was greatly mourned by the Jews, for he was a man of great bravery and distinguished for ability and resolution.

That night, when the tired Roman soldiers had gone to rest, they were suddenly wakened up by a crash. Titus had ordered three towers to be built upon the several mounds, in order that from them they might fight the Jews upon the ramparts. One of these fell of its own accord in the middle of the night. It made a tremendous noise, and threw the soldiers for a time into a panic. But Titus, having learned what had happened, gave orders that the news should be generally spread, and thus allayed the alarm.

The archers and slingers that were placed in the towers did great damage to the Jews, while they themselves, on account of the height of the towers, were perfectly safe. Nor could the Jews overthrow these towers, on account of their weight, or set fire to them, because they were plated with iron. If they withdrew beyond the range of the missiles, they could not impede the strokes of the battering-rams, which, by their continual strokes, were gradually taking effect. At length the wall began to totter before the strokes of a tremendous ram, which the Jews themselves named the Conqueror. Worn out with fatigue and grown somewhat careless, the Jews abandoned their posts and retreated to the second wall, —for Jerusalem was surrounded by three walls,—and there took up their positions.

The Romans laid a great part of the outer wall in ruins, and took up a position before the second wall just out of range of the missiles, and from there carried on their attacks. The Jews, dividing their forces, made a vigorous defence from the wall; John and his party defending the Antonia and the northern cloister of the temple, while Simon guarded the rest of the wall, as far as a gate through which an aqueduct passed to a tower called Hippicus.

The Jews made continual sallies, and though beaten in these, and driven back by the superior discipline of the Romans, still, in their contests from the walls, they gained a decided advantage. Both parties passed the night in arms, the Jews because they feared to leave the wall defenceless, the Romans because they dreaded a sudden attack. Thus both parties were ready for battle at the break of day.

The defenders fought with the greatest bravery, and rivalled each other in daring deeds. Simon inspired his men with such awe and reverence that they were ready to die by their own hands at his command. The Romans, on the other hand, were incited to valor by the remembrance of all their former victories, by pride in the vastness of their empire, and, above all, by Titus, who was everywhere present, and always ready to reward a display of valor.

Upon one occasion while the Jews were forming for a sally, Longinus, a Roman cavalry soldier, rushed single-handed against them and dashed into their midst. The Jewish ranks were broken by his charge, and two of their bravest fell beneath his arm. He then retreated in triumph to his own party, out of the midst of his foes. So much praise did he gain for his valor that many were led to emulate his example.

The Jews were entirely reckless of life if they could only involve an enemy in their fall. Before long the Romans began to thunder with their great ram against the central tower of the second wall. The defenders all fled, except a crafty Jew by the name of Castor, with ten others. For some time these men remained quiet, crouched beneath the breast-works; but when the tower began to totter they rose up, and Castor stretched his hands out to Titus and implored his mercy in a piteous voice. Titus, hoping that the Jews were beginning to repent, stopped the playing of the ram, forbade the archers to shoot at the suppliants, and bade Castor speak and acquaint him with his wishes. The Jew replied that he wished to come down under promise of protection. Titus answered that he was ready to give protection to the whole city if it would surrender. Five of the ten Jews joined in the pretended supplication; the others cried out that they would never be vassals of the Romans as long as they could die free. A fierce dispute seemed to arise, during which the assault was suspended.

Meanwhile, Castor sent word to Simon to arrange his plans for defence, as he would keep the Roman general at play for some time longer. All the time he seemed to be urging the unwilling five to accept the offered pledge. They, as if moved with indignation, brandished their swords above the battle-ments, and, striking their breastplates, fell down as if slain. The Romans, who could not see very clearly from below, were amazed at the courage of the men, and even pitied their fate.

During the parley Castor was wounded on the nose by an arrow, which he drew out and showed to Titus, complaining of unjust treatment. The general sternly rebuked the archer, and directed Josephus, who was standing beside him, to go forward and offer Castor protection. But Josephus wisely declined to go. Æneas, a deserter, however, said that he would go. Castor called to him to come near and catch some money which he wished to throw down. Æneas opened the folds of his robe to receive it, and eagerly ran forward; but Castor threw a big stone at him, which Æneas dodged, and it wounded a soldier near by.

Titus, seeing through the trick, made up his mind to show no more mercy to the Jews, and, angry at being duped, ordered the engines to be worked more vigorously than ever. The tower giving way, Castor and his companions set fire to it, and plunged through the flames into a vault beneath, inspiring the Romans, who thought they had jumped into the fire, with a high idea of their courage.

CHAPTER CXLI.

THE ROMANS SUFFER A REPULSE.

On the fifth day after the taking of the first wall the Jews retreated from the second. Titus then entered that part of the lower city which was within it with his body-guard and a thousand men. Instead of throwing down the wall and laying waste as he advanced, Titus gave orders that none who fell into their hands should be put to death, nor any of the houses burned. At the same time, he promised to restore their property to the people, for he wished to gain them over to him.

The people indeed had long been ready to listen to overtures of peace, but to the insurgents the humanity of Titus seemed weakness, and they looked upon his overtures as proofs of his inability to take the remainder of the town. They threatened death to any of the people who should breathe a word about surrender, and killed all who made any mention of their desire for peace

They then attacked the Romans who had entered. Some confronted them in the streets; some attacked them from the houses; others, sallying from the upper gates, so frightened the Roman guards at the ramparts that they jumped down from the towers and retreated to their camp. All was confusion. The Jews constantly increasing in numbers, and possessing a decided advantage because they knew every lane and alley of the city, appeared on every side, and drove the Romans before them by repeated charges. But the Romans, owing to the narrowness of the breach, could only retire very slowly. And had not Titus brought in fresh succors, all who had entered would probably have been cut down. Titus stationed his archers at the ends of the streets, and, taking his post where the enemy were in greatest force, he kept them at bay until his soldiers had retired.

Thus were the Romans, after gaining possession of the second wall, driven out. The spirits of the war-party in the city were greatly elated by this success, for they thought they could drive out the enemy every time they attempted to enter the town. But they did not know that an immense force of the Romans had not been engaged in this assault, nor yet that famine was slowly but surely creeping in upon the city.

Many were already sinking on account of the scarcity of provisions; but the insurgents only rejoiced to see the people die, deeming it a good riddance to themselves. For they desired that those alone should be preserved who were adverse to peace, and who wished for life only to employ it against the Romans. As for the breach, they manned it boldly, and walled it up with their own bodies. For three days they kept the enemy at bay, but on the fourth they were obliged to give way before the intrepid assaults of Titus, who, entering a second time, threw down the whole northern portion of the wall, and placed garrisons in the towers of the southern portion.

Before attacking the third wall, Titus suspended the siege for a few days, in the hope that terror of his conquests, and of famine, might induce the insurgents to surrender. He employed the time in making a magnificent review of his troops and paying them their salaries. The space in front of the city gleamed far and wide with the shining arms of the Romans, presenting a terrible spectacle to their enemies, who eagerly watched from the house-tops the numberless hosts of the besiegers.

When they beheld the entire force thus assembled in one place, and the beauty of their arms, and the admirable order of the men, even the most daring were struck with fearful dismay. Still the insurgents, thinking over their evil deeds, felt that for them there was no hope of pardon, and as they knew they would have to die anyway, they preferred to die in battle.

In four days the several legions of the Romans had all been paid off in order. On the fifth, as the Jews had not sued for peace, Titus formed the legions into two divisions, and commenced raising embankments, both at the Antonia and at John's monument. At the latter point he designed to carry the upper town, and the temple through the former; for unless the temple was secured the city could not be retained without danger. Simon and his troops impeded by continual sallies those at work beside the monument, while John and his party obstructed those before the Antonia.

The Jews, by long practice, had now become skilled in the use of their military engines, and directed them with terrible effect against the besiegers. Titus, anxious to preserve the city from destruction, continually during the siege used every means to induce the Jews to surrender, and sent Josephus to address them in their native tongue. Josephus with difficulty found a spot from whence he might be heard and at the same time be out of reach of the missiles. From thence he harangued his countrymen at great length, using every argument

in his power to induce them to surrender; but all in vain.
The war-party remained obdurate; but the people, however,
made up their minds to desert. All that could elude the
vigilance of the insurgents escaped to the Romans. Most
of them were granted a free passage by Titus, which further
encouraged the people to desertion, as thus they would be
freed from the tyrants within the city, and yet not be enslaved
by the Romans. The insurgents, however, began to guard
the outlets from the city with still stricter vigilance, and put
to death all whom they even suspected of a desire to escape.

Famine now began to rage in the city in a terrible manner.
The insurgents took for themselves all the food they could
lay hands upon, and the poor people starved to death in thousands. Rich people gave all their wealth for a little measure
of wheat, and were obliged to eat it hastily and in secret lest
it should be snatched from them. Numbers of the rich were
put to death by Simon and John; while the poor died by
hundreds every day from want and starvation. Indeed, the
sufferings of the people were so fearful that they cannot be
told.

CHAPTER CXLII.

THE JEWS DESTROY THE ROMAN WORKS.

IN the mean while, the Roman soldiers went on steadily
building the mounds, although they were greatly bothered by
the insurgents upon the ramparts. Titus, in order to frighten
the Jews into surrender, laid parties of his men in ambush.
These soldiers captured all the poor stragglers, who, because
they were very hungry, came out from the city in the evening
to look for food. These poor wretches the general crucified

before the walls, that they might be a terrible warning to the people within.

But the insurgents dragged the people and the relations of the crucified ones to the walls, and, pointing to the dead upon the crosses, said that this was the way the Romans treated those who sought their protection. This was not true, because those whom the Romans crucified had not sought their protection, but had been taken prisoners. Still, the people for some time believed the insurgents, and a great many who wished to desert remained in the city for fear of being crucified. Some, however, fled immediately, because they thought they would rather run the chance of being put to death at once than to die slowly and surely of starvation in the city.

Titus then ordered a number of those who had been taken captives to have their hands cut off, and to be sent in this state to John and Simon, to tell them that they were not deserters, but captives, and to exhort them to pause and not compel him to destroy the city, but to surrender at once, and thus save their own lives and their city and temple. At the same time he went around to each mound, urging on the workmen, to show that he would quickly follow up his threats.

But the insurgents in reply to his messages only howled at him from the ramparts, and called down curses upon himself and his father. They said that they preferred death to slavery, and that as long as they breathed they would continue to fight against the Romans.

At this time the son of the king of Commagena, a young prince, called Antiochus Epiphanes, arrived at the Roman camp. He came to help the Romans, and brought with him a number of heavy-armed men, and a band of chosen youths, dressed and armed in the Macedonian fashion.

Antiochus, who was very brave and strong, expressed his surprise that the Romans should delay attacking the ramparts. Titus hearing him, said, with a smile, " There is a fair field for

everybody." Upon this Antiochus with his band immediately
rushed to the wall. As he was very skilful and strong, he
managed to ward off all the missiles that the Jews hurled
at him, but all his comrades were either killed or wounded,
so he was very soon compelled to return to the camp, without
having accomplished his object of taking the wall.

After seventeen days of hard toil, the Romans at length
finished the mounds, four in number, and the engines were
brought up. But John had secretly undermined the mounds
opposite to him, and had put upright beams in the excavations
that he had made, so that they would support the mounds
until the Romans should place their military engines upon
them. And so, when they brought up the engines, John set
fire to the beams below the mounds, and they soon fell in
with a tremendous crash, and the engines and embankments
were either buried or burnt up. The Romans were greatly
discouraged at seeing the results of so many days' labor so
quickly destroyed.

Two days after, Simon and his party made an effort to destroy the mounds near to him, for the Romans had brought up
their engines in that quarter also, and were already shaking
the wall. Three of his band rushed out with torches in their
hands and set fire to the military engines, though the Roman
guards did their best to prevent them. The flames spread,
and the Romans rushed from their camp to the rescue, while
the Jews ran out to meet them, and attacked them with great
fury.

The Romans tried to drag their rams away from the fire ;
but the Jews, heedless of the flames, caught hold of them,
and would not let go, although the iron upon the rams was
red-hot. From the engines the fire burned onwards to the
mounds, and began to destroy the works.

The Romans, surrounded on all sides by the flames, gave
up all hopes of saving their works, and retreated to their
camp. The Jews, flushed with success, dashed forward, and.

advancing to the very intrenchments, engaged in a hand-to-hand conflict with the sentries. These men resisted bravely and held their ground, because Roman sentries were punished with death if they quitted their posts. A good many of the Romans who were running away returned to the battle when they saw their comrades standing firm. But so fierce was the attack of the Jews that before long the Roman forces began to waver.

At this moment Titus, who had been searching for a site upon which to build new mounds by the Antonia, arrived upon the spot, and, with a picked band of men, charged the enemy in the flank. The Jews, though attacked in front as well, turned and bravely faced him. The hostile forces became mixed up, and such a dust and noise arose that neither side could any longer tell friend from foe. At length the Jews retreated into the city, but not before the mounds had been completely destroyed.

The Romans were greatly cast down, because in one short hour they lost the fruits of all their labors by the destruction of the mounds, and many were led to despair of ever taking the city by the ordinary means.

CHAPTER CXLIII.

TITUS BUILDS A WALL AROUND JERUSALEM.

Titus held a council of war, in order to fix upon some plan of action. Some of his officers wished him to lead his whole army to the wall and endeavor to take the ramparts by storm. Others wished to rebuild the mounds; while others, more cautious still, wished the passes to be guarded and the city reduced by famine.

Titus, because he thought it would be useless to fight against desperate men who would soon destroy each other or be destroyed by famine, made up his mind to blockade the city, and to cut off all hopes of relief by surrounding the city with a wall. For he thought that if he contented himself with guarding the passes the Jews would find out hidden paths, by which they would get provisions into the city and thus prolong the siege. But if the city were surrounded by a wall every path would be thus blocked up, and the Jews would soon have to succumb to famine.

Accordingly, he set his soldiers to work; and so quickly did they labor and with such ready good will that the whole work was finished in three days,—an almost incredibly short time, when it is considered that the wall was very nearly five miles long. Around the wall, at certain distances from each other, thirteen forts were built. In these Titus placed garrisons, and during the night sentries paced up and down between the forts until daylight.

Thus all hope of escape and all means of getting food into the city were cut off from the Jews. Famine raged among them with terrible violence, and thousands upon thousands died. The houses were full of dying women and children, and the streets were choked with the bodies of the dead. The insurgents, suffering now themselves from the pangs of hunger, plundered the dead and became more cruel than ever to the living. Not a sound of mourning was heard throughout Jerusalem, for the people were too weak from hunger even to wail aloud, and an awful silence brooded over the city. Silently the people died by thousands, and their bodies, too numerous to bury, were hurled from the walls into the ravines below.

When Titus, as he went his rounds, beheld these multitudes of dead bodies, he groaned aloud, and, lifting up his hands, called God to witness that this was not his doing. His army, meanwhile, were in the highest spirits, because the insurgents

were now too weak to attack them, and they themselves had
plenty of food. Sometimes they would approach the ramparts and make their enemies feel their hunger all the more
by showing them quantities of tempting viands.

Titus, touched with the suffering of the people, and anxious
to save those who still survived, ordered some new mounds
to be raised, although materials for them could only be procured with great difficulty. For all the trees for over ten
miles around had been cut down in order to raise the first
mounds. The new mounds were raised at four points opposite the Antonia.

The Roman general went the rounds of his legions and
urged on the works, in order to show the insurgents that
they were in his power. But nothing could subdue these
men. Even their own sufferings did not soften their hearts,
but, like dogs, they worried the people even after death, and
crowded the prisons with the feeble.

The cruel Simon even tortured and put to death the feeble
old Matthias, the chief priest, who had persuaded the people
to let him into the city that he might aid them to conquer
John. This good old man was accused of being a partisan
of the Romans, and, without allowing him to utter a word in
his defence, Simon condemned him to death, with three of
his sons.

Matthias begged that he might be put to death before his
sons, but the cruel Simon refused him even this, and ordered
him to be slain last. And so the sons were butchered first,
before the eyes of the father, in full view of the Romans; and
then the aged priest was killed. After these, a priest named
Ananias, and Aristeus, the secretary of the council, with fif
teen eminent men, were executed. The aged father of Josephus was thrown into prison; and an order was sent throughout the city that none should converse together, or gather in
small parties, for fear of treason. All who lamented together
in parties were immediately put to death.

On seeing these cruelties, Judas, one of Simon's officers, who had custody of a tower, called ten of those under him together and said to them,—

"How long shall we tolerate these evils? Or what prospect of saving ourselves is there as long as we obey this wicked man? Is not famine already upon us? The Romans are all but in the town, and Simon is unfaithful even to his friends. Have we not now reason to fear him, while the Romans will surely give us protection? Come, then, let us surrender the ramparts, and save ourselves and the city."

The ten agreed with Judas in these views, and early in the morning they called to the Romans from the tower, and offered to surrender it. But the Romans, because they had been so often fooled before, were suspicious, and hesitated about coming at once. While Titus was slowly advancing to the wall with some troops, Simon, who had heard what was going on, came up to the tower, and seizing the ten men and Judas, he killed them in sight of the Romans, and threw their bodies over the ramparts.

It happened that as Josephus was going round the wall, trying to persuade the insurgents to surrender, he was struck on the head by a stone, and instantly dropped down senseless. On his fall the Jews sallied out, and he would have been dragged into the city had not Titus sent a body of soldiers to protect him. During the conflict that followed, Josephus was removed, not knowing what had happened.

The insurgents thought they had killed Josephus, and shouted aloud in their joy. And so news of his death was spread through the city, and was carried to the mother of Josephus, who was in prison, and she was very much cast down by the news. But she was not long distressed by these bad tidings, for Josephus quickly recovered from the stroke; and he again came before the wall and cried aloud,—

"I will have my revenge upon you before long for this wound."

And he again exhorted the people to accept the protection of the Romans; so that some leaped down at once from the ramparts, while others went out of the gates, carrying stones, as if they meant to hurl them at the enemy, and then quickly fled to them. When they came to the Roman camp they were swollen with hunger, and a good many of them ate so much that they died; but some knew that they must eat moderately at first, for their stomachs were tender, because they had had no food for days, so they ate but a little at a time, and in this way gradually became well and strong again.

But even these were doomed to death. For the Arabians and Syrians, who were with the Romans, found out that the deserters had gold hidden about their persons, and so began to kill and rob them in order to get their treasures. In one night two thousand were slain.

Titus was very angry on hearing of this outrage, and was on the point of putting his allies to death, but was kept from doing so because their numbers were far greater than the number of Jews slain. He, however, threatened with instant death any one caught thereafter in the act of killing a Jew. Still, the love of gold was stronger with many of the barbarians than the fear of punishment, so that what before they did openly they now did in secret. They went forward to meet deserters, and killed them in out-of-the-way places, where they could not be seen by the Romans. Fear of being thus slaughtered caused numbers of deserters to return to the city.

When the people of Jerusalem had been plundered of all they possessed, John began to strip the temple itself of its golden vessels and dishes and tables. He seized the rich offerings which in times past the Roman emperors had made, and even stole the sacred wine and oil and gave them to his followers to drink. The people looked upon this sacrilege with the greatest horror, and felt it even more than the sufferings the wicked John had brought upon them.

Most awful were the sufferings now within the city. It became like one vast sepulchre, and its dead far outnumbered its living. Over six hundred thousand bodies had been thrown over the ramparts. But still the insurgents, as if drunk with crime, tramped over the dead bodies, and manned the walls with wild despair, though everywhere death stared them in the face.

CHAPTER CXLIV.

THE ROMANS MAKE AN ASSAULT UPON THE ANTONIA.

THE Romans went steadily on building the mounds, and finished them in twenty-one days. They stripped the whole district for nearly eleven miles around of its trees, so that the formerly beautiful suburbs of the city looked like a wilderness. Where before there had been parks of trees and beautiful pleasure-grounds, now all was desolate and waste; nor would a stranger, who had known the place in all its former beauty, now have ever recognized it.

The new mounds caused anxiety to both the Romans and the Jews. For the Jews were afraid that they would not be able to destroy them, and so that the city would surely be taken; while the Romans feared that should these mounds also be destroyed, they would have to give up all hopes of ever taking Jerusalem. They were also depressed because the Jews had not already sunk beneath the weight of the awful calamities that had overtaken them.

Before the rams were brought up, John and his party made a descent from the Antonia and tried to destroy the Roman works. But the attempt was not successful, and the Jews were driven back before they had reached the mounds. For they rushed out in small parties in a helter-skelter sort of manner, without united design, and so were easily repulsed by the well-trained Roman guards. These stood firmly by their posts, knowing that all their hopes would be cut off should the works be burned; besides, they felt ashamed that Jewish artifice should prove superior to their valor, and Jewish desperation to Roman skill and arms.

The Roman engines at the same time greatly aided the soldiers, for their missiles killed numbers of the sallying parties. Each Jew as he fell blocked up the way for the man in the rear, so that the danger of advancing chilled the ardor of the Jews. Many who ran up within range of the missiles became frightened when they beheld the perfect order and firm array of the Romans, and turned round and fled before they came to close quarters. Others rushed on, but were repulsed by the guards, so that before long the Jews retreated to the Antonia, and gave up the attack.

Upon the retreat of the Jews the Romans brought up the storming-towers, though they were assailed from the Antonia with stones, fire, iron, and every kind of missile which the Jews could pick up and hurl at the besiegers. Soon the engines began to thunder against the Antonia; but, though the Romans worked their largest ram, the wall seemed to resist firmly every shock.

The Romans locked their shields over their heads, and set to work with hands and crow-bars to undermine the foundations, and at length succeeded in getting out four large stones. Night put an end to the conflict. But while the soldiers were at rest the wall suddenly fell in with a terrific crash, for it had been shaken by the rams in that part which John had undermined when he had destroyed the former mounds. The ground above the mine, beneath which John had dug, suddenly caved in, and so the wall gave way.

But in the morning, when the Romans rushed to the breach, their ardor and joy were damped by seeing still another wall, which John had built inside. However, this wall appeared much weaker than that of the Antonia, and the Romans thought that it could easily be destroyed. Still, none ventured to mount it, for death surely awaited those who should first make the attempt.

Titus drew the bravest of his troops around him and exhorted them to make the attack, promising large rewards to the man who should lead the assault. Still the soldiers hesitated, knowing only too well the danger of the attempt. At length a soldier named Sabinus, a Syrian by birth, offered to scale the wall. Sabinus was distinguished for his bravery and strength, although he was withered and very thin. Any one looking at him would have thought him unfit to be a soldier, but in his small body there dwelt an heroic soul. He arose and said to Titus,—

" I cheerfully devote myself to you, Cæsar. I will be the first to scale the wall, and if I die in the attempt, know that for your sake I willingly give up my life."

Having thus spoken, he lifted high his shield, drew his sword, and advanced towards the wall. Only eleven men had the courage to follow him. The Jews hurled their darts at them from the ramparts, pouring at the same time showers of missiles from all quarters, and rolling down vast stones, which overthrew some of the eleven. But Sabinus still marched boldly on, far in advance of his comrades, and paused not in his onset until he had gained the summit of the wall and routed the enemy ; for the Jews, panic-stricken at his boldness, and thinking that more had followed him, took to flight.

But in the very moment of his triumph Sabinus slipped upon a stone, and fell headlong over it with a loud crash. The Jews turned, and, seeing Sabinus alone and prostrate, assailed him on all sides. Rising upon his knee, he made a gallant defence and wounded many of the enemy, but at length, overpowered by numbers, he fell, pierced by a thousand wounds. Three of his comrades were crushed by the stones and slain. The rest were carried back, wounded, to the camp.

Two days after, twenty of the guards stationed upon one of the mounds, together with a standard-bearer, a trumpeter, and two horsemen, crept silently through the breach during the dead of the night. They scaled the wall, slew the sentinels as they slept, and then ordered the trumpeter to sound his horn. On this the other guards started up from their sleep, and fled before any one had taken note of the numbers of the enemy. For the panic, and the peal of the trumpet, led them to suppose that the Romans had mounted in great force. When Titus heard the trumpet he immediately ordered the troops to arms, and, with his body of picked men, was the first to mount the ramparts. The Jews fled in dismay to the temple.

John and Simon united their forces, and made a desperate defence at the entrance to the temple. For they thought all would be lost should the Romans enter the holy place. A fierce battle took place; the Romans pressing in to get possession of the temple, the Jews thrusting them back to the Antonia. Missiles and spears were alike useless to both parties. Drawing their swords, they engaged in a hand-to-hand combat, and so closely and fiercely did they fight that the troops of both parties got mixed up with each other, so that it was hard to tell on which side they were fighting.

At length, after fighting for ten hours, the Jews, who fought with the greatest fury and desperation, succeeded in driving back the Romans. They had the advantage in numbers, besides; for as yet only a portion of the Roman army had come up to the attack. And so for the present the Romans were satisfied with the possession of the Antonia.

But while the Romans were slowly retreating into the Antonia, a Bithynian centurion, called Julian, a man distinguished for his strength and valor, sprang forward, and singly drove back the Jews to the corner of the inner temple. The mul-

titude fled in crowds before him, thinking his strength and
courage something more than human. Julian dashed through
the scattered ranks, and slew all who came in his way. But,
unfortunately for him, his shoes were thickly studded with
pointed nails; he slipped upon the pavement as he was rushing along, and fell upon his back with a loud noise. The
clanging of his armor upon the pavement caused the Jews to
look back, and seeing his plight, they rushed upon him. The
Romans upon the Antonia raised a loud shout as they saw
the valiant Julian surrounded by his enemies, but none of
them ventured to his assistance.

The Jews attacked him with swords and spears, and thrust
him back when he attempted to rise. Yet even upon his
back the brave man defended himself gallantly, and wounded
many of his enemies with his sword. At length, however, he
was hacked to pieces, and the Jews dragged the body into the
temple, and again repulsing the Romans, they shut them up
in the Antonia.

CHAPTER CXLV.

THE ANTONIA IS DESTROYED.

In order to prepare an easy ascent for his whole force,
Titus ordered that the fortress of the Antonia should be razed
to the ground. He had heard that the daily sacrifice had
ceased to be offered in the temple for want of men to make
the offerings, and that the people were very sad on this account.
And so he sent Josephus forward to say to John that Titus
would willingly allow him to come out of the temple and
fight somewhere outside, so as no longer to pollute the holy
place; and that also he gave him permission to perform the
daily sacrifices, with the aid of such Jews as he should select.

Josephus therefore came forward, and, standing where he might be heard not only by John, but by the multitude as well, delivered Cæsar's message. He also besought them to spare their country and to save their temple. But John, in reply, bitterly reviled Josephus, and said that he did not fear capture, because Jerusalem was the city of God.

Josephus then upbraided John, and declared that because of the wickedness of the insurgents God was giving over the city to capture and destruction. Very angry at this, John and his party rushed out and tried to seize Josephus. Many of the higher class among the people, however, were greatly moved by his words, and a party of chief priests and nobles deserted to the Romans.

Titus received the fugitives with great kindness, and sent them to the city of Gophna, with directions to remain there for the present, promising that as soon as the war was over he would restore to them their possessions. When they had gone to Gophna, the insurgents spread a report that they all had been slaughtered by the Romans. The people for a time believed this, because they noticed that the deserters were no longer to be seen at the Roman camp, and this kept the people from going over to the besiegers.

But Titus, in order to give the lie to this rumor, recalled the men from Gophna, and ordered them to march around the wall with Josephus, in order that they might be seen by the people. Upon this, a great number fled to the Romans. The deserters then all grouped together, and, standing in front of the Roman line, they besought the insurgents with tears in their eyes to surrender, or at least, if they would not surrender, to retire from the temple and save it from ruin, for that the Romans would not set fire to the holy places unless the insurgents compelled them to do so.

But these entreaties were in vain. The insurgents only shouted curses upon the deserters, and ranged their military engines over the sacred gates, so that the temple looked like a warlike citadel. They rushed in arms about the holy places, and even shocked the Roman soldiers by the impiety of their conduct. Titus again upbraided John and his followers, saying to them,—

" Was it not you who put up a barrier to prevent strangers from polluting your temple ? And this barrier the Romans have always respected, and allowed you to put to death any who attempted to pass it. Why, then, O guilty ones, do you trample even dead bodies under foot within it ? Why do you defile your holy place with the blood of strangers and of your own countrymen ? I call on the gods of my fathers, I call on the God who once watched over your temple,—for now, I think, it is guarded by none,—I call on my army, I call on the Jews who are with me, I call on yourselves, to witness that I do not force you to commit these crimes. Come forth and fight in any other place, and no Roman shall profane the holy places. Nay, I will save the sanctuary for you, even against your will."

Josephus translated for the Jews this address of Titus, but the insurgents, thinking that Titus only wished them to leave the temple that he might enter it without danger, treated his offers with scorn.

The Roman general, finding all his efforts of mercy in vain, began at once to prepare for an attack. He could not make the assault with his whole army, because the approaches to the temple were too narrow; and so he selected the thirty best men out of each century, and appointed a tribune to take command of every thousand. He placed Cerealius in command of the whole, and gave orders that the attack should be made after midnight. He would himself have led the attack had not his officers persuaded him not to run such a risk, and that it would be wiser for him to take his station on the Antonia, and from there guide and watch his troops, for that all would conduct themselves as brave soldiers under the eye of Cæsar.

And so when the night was about three-quarters over Titus sent the troops to the attack, and mounted a watch-tower of the Antonia, telling the soldiers that he would watch them in the fight, so that he could reward the brave and punish the cowards among them.

The Romans did not find the guards asleep as they expected. The Jews sprang to arms with loud cries, and a fierce battle immediately began. The Romans at first had the advantage in the fight, because they kept together in a compact body, while the Jews attacked in small parties, and often in the confusion and darkness they fell upon each other by mistake. But when morning broke, and they could see clearly, they drew together, and fought in good order.

For eight hours the battle raged, but neither party were able to beat the other. At length, tired out, they stopped fighting, and the Romans for the time being gave up the attack.

The rest of the army, meanwhile, overturned the foundations of the Antonia, and within a week prepared a wide ascent as far as the temple. They then erected mounds against four places of the outer court. These they built with great difficulty, because they had to bring the timber from a distance of over twelve miles.

During the building of these works the troops suffered greatly from the constant attacks of the Jews, who, because they had no hope of safety, had become all the more daring. Some of the Roman cavalry, when they went out to collect wood or fodder, took the bridles off their horses and turned them loose to graze while they were foraging. The Jews often sallied out in bands and stole the horses.

As the cavalry in this way lost a number of horses, Titus determined to make them more careful of their steeds by making a severe example. And so he put to death the next man that lost his horse. After this the men no longer allowed their horses to graze at random, but kept close by them, and so prevented the Jews from carrying them off.

The Jews thought their one hope of safety was to break down in some place that wall which the Romans had built around the city. And so they made a sudden attack upon the Roman posts at the Mount of Olives. They rushed out at meal-time, thinking to find their enemies off their guard. But the Romans saw them coming, and hurried to the spot from the adjacent forts, and checked their attempts to scale the wall or throw it down.

A fierce contest took place, and many gallant deeds were done on both sides. But the Jews were at length repulsed and driven down the ravine. While they were retreating, a Roman horseman, called Pedanius, dashed into their midst, and, stooping from his horse, seized by the ankle a young Jew of robust frame. He carried the Jew off by main strength and threw him at the feet of Titus, who greatly admired this wonderful feat of strength.

Beaten back, and having suffered much in their contests, the Jews now set fire to the portico which led from the Antonia to the temple, and made a breach of from twenty to thirty feet. Ten days afterwards the Romans set fire to the adjoining colonnade, and burned about twenty feet more. The Jews then cut away the roof and destroyed all connection between themselves and the Antonia. Still the conflicts between the Romans and Jews went on about the temple, and every day a contest took place.

One day, during a lull in the battle, a Jew by the name of Jonathan advanced to the monument of the high-priest John, and challenged any one of the Romans to single combat. Jonathan was a mean-looking little Jew, and the Romans allowed him for some time to yell out his jibes and insults without taking any notice of him.

But at length one of the troopers, disgusted at the impudence of Jonathan, and thinking he could easily whip so small a fellow, came forward and attacked him. The trooper was getting the best of the fight, but all of a sudden he slipped and fell down.   Jonathan immediately ran him through with his sword, and then he danced about in high glee, yelling and jibing at the Romans who were looking on.   Then a centurion took aim and shot the little Jew with an arrow as he was insanely dancing up and down.   Jonathan, writhing with pain, fell upon the body of his fallen foe, and thus the Jew and the Roman lay together in that sleep that knows no waking.

CHAPTER CXLVI.

THE DESTRUCTION OF THE TEMPLE.

IN order to destroy as many of their enemies as possible, the Jews made use of a stratagem.   Along the western cloisters they filled the space between the rafters and the ceiling with dry wood, bitumen, and pitch, and then, as if worn out, they retreated from the cloisters.   On this a number of Romans put up their scaling-ladders and mounted to the roof, without waiting for orders.   But the more prudent suspected that a trap had been laid for them, and did not follow their comrades.

When the roof was filled with those who had clambered up, the Jews set fire to the whole range of cloisters from below.   The flames rushed roaring upwards among the besiegers.   They were thrown into a terrible fright.   Some of them jumped down into the city, others into the very midst of the enemy.   There they lay bruised to death or with broken limbs.   Most of them, in trying to escape, perished in the flames, while many fell upon their own swords when they saw they could not save themselves.

Titus, though very angry at all who had mounted the roof without waiting for orders, still was touched with pity when he beheld them burning up and dying before his eyes. He sprang forward and exhorted those around him to make every effort for their rescue. But nothing could be done to save them. A few of those who had mounted retired to a broader part of the roof, out of reach of the flames; but they were surrounded by the Jews and killed to a man, after having made a valiant resistance.

Towards the close of the struggle one of them, called Longus, was called upon by the Jews below, who said they would spare his life if he would come down and surrender. But his brother from among the Romans called out to him not to tarnish the honor of the family or that of the Roman arms by surrendering to the Jews. Longus then raised his sword in view of both armies and stabbed himself to the heart.

Among those who were entangled among the flames, one Artorius saved himself by his cunning. He called aloud to one of his fellow-soldiers below,—

"I say, Lucius! I will leave you heir to my property if you will come near and catch me."

Lucius ran up, and Artorius threw himself upon him, and was saved. But poor Lucius was dashed by the weight of his friend upon the pavement, and killed upon the spot.

The Roman soldiers were much cast down in spirits by the death of so many of their comrades, but still it made them all the more cautious and wary against the wily stratagems of the Jews. As the western gallery or cloister had been destroyed, they themselves set fire to the northern one, and laid it in ashes as far as the northeast corner, which was built over the ravine called Cedron.

In the mean time the famine raged with such fierceness that countless thousands died of hunger. In every house where there was the least morsel of food the inmates fought over it like dogs. The dearest friends fought for the most miserable little scraps. Gaping with hunger, the insurgents prowled about, and gnawed at anything that might seem like food. They chewed their belts and shoes, and tore off the leather from their shields. They ate up wisps of hay, and all sorts of nasty things,—in fact, anything that might help to sustain life.

When some of the mounds were finished, Titus ordered the battering-rams to be brought up at the western wing of the inner temple. For six days before, the largest of the rams had battered against the wall without effect. A part of the army tried to undermine the foundations of the northern gate. After a great deal of labor, they at last rolled out the front stones, but the gate itself, supported by the inner stones, still remained firm, so that the Romans gave up trying to force an entrance to the temple in this manner, and instead fixed their scaling-ladders to the galleries.

The Jews allowed the Romans to mount, but as soon as they reached the top, they hurled them down headlong, or slew them before they could cover themselves with their shields. Several ladders filled with armed men coming up to the attack they pushed aside from above, and thus hurled all the soldiers to the ground. All who had mounted fell by the swords of the Jews, and some of the Roman ensigns were captured. As Titus saw he could not force an entrance in this way, he ordered the gates to be set on fire.

At this time two of the insurgents belonging to Simon s body-guard deserted to Titus. They hoped for pardon because they surrendered in a moment of success. Titus had a great mind to put them both to death, because he thought that they had only surrendered through necessity, to save themselves from that ruin which they had helped to bring upon their native city. However, as he had promised protection to all who came to him, he kept his word, and allowed the deserters to depart without punishment.

The soldiers had already set the gates on fire, and the flames spread quickly to the galleries. When the Jews saw the circle of fire hem them in on every side, they lost courage, and stood gaping at the flames, without trying to put them out. Through the whole day and the following night the fire continued to burn the range of cloisters.

The next morning Titus gave orders that the fire should be put out and the gates thrown down, so as to admit the troops. He then called his generals together and held a council of war. Some of them wished to destroy the temple at once, because they said as long as the Jews had the temple to take refuge in they would continue to be rebellious. Others advised that if the Jews would leave the temple at once it should be spared, but if they would continue to fight from it as if it were a fortress, it should be burned to the ground.

But Titus declared that, whatever happened, so magnificent a work as the temple ought to be spared, because it would always be an ornament to the Roman empire. Three of his principal generals agreed with him in this view, and the council was dissolved. Some of the cohorts were immediately ordered to open a way through the ruins and put out the flames, while the rest of the army were allowed to repose, that they might be the more vigorous for action.

Upon the next day the Jews made a furious sally upon the guards who were posted in the outer court. The Romans closed up their ranks, locked their shields together in front like a wall, and bravely withstood the attack. But the Jews came pouring forth in such tremendous numbers that Titus was afraid the guards would be defeated, and hurried with his picked body of cavalry to assist them. The Jews could not withstand his charge, and retreated. But when he turned to go, they rallied and rushed again to the attack. The cavalry then charged, and the Jews were driven back, and shut up in the inner court of the temple.

Titus then withdrew into the Antonia, intending the next morning to make an attack with his entire force upon the temple. But the beautiful edifice was upon that day doomed to destruction.   The fated day had come, the tenth of August, the very day on which the former temple had been destroyed by the king of Babylon.

When Titus retired, the insurgents again charged the Romans.   A conflict took place between the Jewish guards of the sanctuary and the Roman troops who were trying to put out the flames in the inner court.   The Jews were routed, and pursued even to the sanctuary.

At this moment a soldier, neither waiting for orders nor awed by so dread a deed, snatched up a burning brand, and, lifted by one of his comrades, he threw the brand through a small golden door on the north side which opened on the apartments around the sanctuary.   As the flames caught, a fearful cry was raised by the Jews.   They rushed to the rescue, caring nothing for their lives, now that their temple was burning.

Titus was lying down in his tent, when some one rushed in and told him that the temple was in flames.   Starting up as he was, he at once ran to the spot in order to stop the flames. But there was such a noise and confusion that the soldiers either could not or would not hear the commands of their general, or heed the waving of his hand.   Nothing could check the headlong fury of the soldiers.   Many were trampled down by their own comrades about the entrances, and falling among the burning ruins of the outside galleries, they shared the fate of their enemies.

Mad with rage, and pretending not to hear the orders of their general, the soldiers rushed on, and hurled their torches into the sanctuary.   The insurgents now were helpless, and made no attempt at defence.   On every side was slaughter and flight.   Numbers of feeble and unarmed citizens were butchered.   Around the altar were heaps of slain ; down its steps flowed a stream of blood which washed down the bodies that lay about.

As Titus could not restrain the fury of his soldiers, he

entered with some of his generals into the holy place of the sanctuary, and looked upon all the splendors that it contained. As the flames had not yet reached the interior, but were still feeding upon the apartments around the temple, Titus made one last effort to save the beautiful structure.

He hurried out, and again exhorted the soldiers to put out the flames. At the same time he ordered one of his centurions to beat with his staff those who would not obey him. But neither respect for their general nor fear of punishment could check the soldiers. The din of battle, their rage, and hatred of the Jews, and hope of rich plunder, all combined to make the Romans ungovernable. For they saw that all about the temple was made of gold, and they believed that within it they would find immense treasures.

Though Titus rushed out to restrain the soldiers, one even of those who had entered with him thrust fire amid the darkness between the hinges of the gate that opened into the inner temple. The whole building was in flames in an instant. Titus and his generals withdrew, and the beautiful building was left to its fate.

CHAPTER CXLVII.

THE WARNINGS GIVEN TO THE JEWS BEFORE THE DESTRUCTION OF THE TEMPLE.

WHILE the temple was in flames, the Roman soldiers stole everything they could lay their hands upon, and killed every Jew that came in their way. No pity was shown to any one; old men and children, women and priests, all fell beneath the sword. The flames roared upward from the temple, and as it stood high upon a hill, and burned with tremendous fury, it seemed from a distance as if the whole city were in a blaze.

The din about the temple was something fearful. There arose the war-cry of the Romans, the shrieks of the insurgents, surrounded as they were by fire and sword, and the wailing of the people over their misfortunes. The mountains about the city echoed the cries and swelled the uproar. It seemed as if the hill on which the temple stood was one blaze of fire. All over the ground was covered by bodies of the slain, over heaps of which the soldiers jumped in pursuit of the Jews who were still alive. A band of the insurgents forced their way through the Romans into the outer court of the temple, and from thence into the town.

Some of the priests at first tore up spikes from the sanctuary and hurled them at the Romans, but afterwards, retreating before the flames, they took refuge on a part of the wall. Two of the priests plunged into the fire and perished in the flames of the temple.

The Romans now set fire to all the buildings around, to the remains of the cloisters or colonnades, to the gates, and to the treasure-chambers, where immense wealth had been collected. Upon a small part of the cloister of the outer court a crowd of defenceless people had taken refuge, to the number of about six thousand. These had been induced to gather there by a false prophet, who told them that God had commanded all the Jews to the temple, where He would display His power to save His people.

Before Cæsar had made up his mind what to do with these people or had given any orders, the soldiers set fire to the colonnade, and the whole multitude perished in the flames.

There were at this time a number of false prophets, who were hired by the insurgents to deceive the people by bidding them wait for help from God, and so keep them from deserting; though, indeed, before the siege there had appeared signs and wonders enough that foretold the awful fate that hung over Jerusalem. And yet they had not regarded the warnings of God.

A star in the shape of a fiery sword had stood over the city
for a year. And just before the revolt, when the people were
coming together for the feast of the Passover, a bright light
shone around the altar during the night and made the temple
as light as day. The people thought this a good omen, but
the sacred scribes told them that it boded no good.

Moreover, the eastern gate of the inner court, which was
fastened with iron bars, and was so heavy that it took all the
strength of twenty men to move it, suddenly flew open of its
own accord during the night.

Not many days after the festival there appeared in the skies,
just before sunset, a number of chariots poised in the air, and
armies of soldiers speeding through the clouds. And at the
feast of Pentecost, when the priests entered the inner court
of the temple, they heard a great noise, and after this a loud
voice as of a multitude, saying, "We are departing hence."

But the most wonderful story remains to be told. About
four years before the war, while the city was enjoying all the
blessings of peace, there came up to a festival a rusti who
stood up in the temple and called aloud,—

"A voice from the east, a voice from the west, a voice from
the four winds, a voice against Jerusalem and the sanctuary,
a voice against bridegrooms and brides, a voice against all
the people."

Day and night he walked up and down the streets with
this cry. Some of the people, bothered by his noise, caught
hold of him and beat him, but he only kept on crying out
as before. At length the rulers brought him before the
Roman procurator, who caused him to be scourged until his
flesh was bare to the bone. He neither sued for mercy
nor shed a tear, but cried aloud at every stroke, "Woe, woe
to Jerusalem!"

When the procurator asked him who he was and whence
he came and why he uttered these words, he made no reply,
but only repeated over and over again, "Woe, woe to Jerusa-

lem!" Until the breaking out of the war he continued this cry, and spoke to none of the citizens, neither thanking those who gave him food nor cursing those that beat him. For seven years and five months he continued his wail, nor did his voice become feeble, nor did he grow weary. At length, as he was going round upon the wall during the siege, crying with his piercing voice, "Woe, woe once more to the city, to the people, and to the temple!" he suddenly added, "Woe, woe also to myself!" and was immediately struck dead by a stone.

CHAPTER CXLVIII.

TITUS TAKES THE UPPER CITY.

THE insurgents fled into the city from the burning temple, and the Romans pitched their standards among the smoking ruins. They offered sacrifice for their victory, and with joyful shouts hailed Titus as emperor.

The priests who had escaped were still perched upon the walls of the sanctuary. A boy who was with them called out to the Roman guards that he was suffering from thirst, and asked their protection while he came down and got a drink of water. The soldiers took pity on his youth and granted his request. And so the boy came down among them; but when he had quenched his thirst, he suddenly filled a vessel with water and hurried back to the priests with such speed that the guards could not catch him.

The guards thought that when he asked protection the boy meant that he would surrender himself, and they charged him with breaking his word. But he answered from the wall that he had only asked for protection while he got some water, and that he did not say that he would stay with them. The soldiers were rather crestfallen at having been outwitted by so young a boy.

Five days afterwards the priests became so hungry that they came down and surrendered themselves to Titus, praying him to spare their lives. But Titus said that for them the hour of mercy had passed; their temple was destroyed for the sake of which alone he would have saved them; now it was but fitting that they should perish with the temple. And so he ordered them all to be killed.

And now the insurgents, seeing that there was no hope of escape and nothing left to fight for, sent word to Titus that they would like to confer with him. As Titus wished to save what remained of the city from destruction, he granted their request, and invited the insurgents to appear before him. When they came he spoke to them through an interpreter. He reproved them for having been so long so stubborn and cruel, but offered to spare their lives on condition of instant surrender.

To this they replied that they would never surrender, because they had sworn not to do so; but they begged Titus to let them pass through his lines, with their wives and children, and promised that they would depart into the wilderness, and leave the city to him. But Titus was very angry because they would not accept his terms, but instead offered terms of their own, and said to them,—

" Do not hope for protection from me, for I will spare none of you; but fight and save yourselves if you can, for now I shall be governed only by the laws of war."

He then ordered the troops to plunder and burn the city. Then fire blazed all over the lower part of Jerusalem, and many beautiful buildings and houses perished in the flames.

The insurgents now rushed to the palace, where, because it was very strong, a large amount of treasure had been stored up. They drove back the Romans who surrounded it, and when they had entered they slew a number of people who had taken refuge there, and plundered all the treasures.

They captured two Roman soldiers, one a trooper, the other a foot-soldier. The latter they slaughtered on the spot, and dragged his body about the city in their rage. The trooper pretended to have something important to say to Simon, so he was brought before him ; but having really nothing to say, he was delivered to one of the officers to be executed. The officer bound the prisoner's hands behind his back, put a bandage over his eyes, and led him forth so as to behead him in view of the Romans.

But while the Jew was drawing his sword, the trooper managed to escape to the Romans. Titus ordered his arms to be taken from him, and dismissed him from his legion in disgrace, because he thought him unworthy to be a Roman soldier who could allow himself to be taken alive.

The next day the Romans drove the Jews from the lower city, and set the whole of it on fire. The insurgents were cooped up in the upper city. There they dispersed themselves about and lay in ambush amid the ruins, putting to death all who attempted to desert.

As a last hope, the insurgents thought to find a safe refuge in the underground passages beneath the city. They thought that when the Romans should force an entrance into the upper city they could escape to these caverns, and there lie hidden until the city was entirely destroyed and the Romans had departed. And so, in order to aid their plan, they set fire to the city, and so helped their enemies in the work of destruction.

Because the ascent to the upper city was very steep, Titus thought it well to build some mounds. And so he set his soldiers to build some, although it was a very difficult task, because the country for over twelve miles around had been stripped of timber. But at length two mounds were built, the one opposite the palace, the other near the Xystus.

And now the Idumean chieftains, who had all along fought with Simon, met secretly together to consult about surrendering themselves to the Romans. They sent five of their number to Titus to ask his protection. Titus, because he thought if the Idumeans deserted the tyrants also would surrender, sent the men back with a promise that he would protect all who would come to him.

But while the Idumeans were making ready to escape Simon found out their intentions, and immediately put to death the five who had gone to Titus, and he threw all the chieftains into prison. The Idumean soldiers, being thus deprived of their leaders, did not know exactly what to do. They were narrowly watched by Simon, who put more trusty soldiers to defend the walls.

Still these guards could not prevent desertion. For although a good many were killed while trying to escape, still a great number fled to the Romans. The citizens of the city who came to him were allowed their freedom by Titus, but all the rest were sold as slaves. About forty thousand of the citizens were thus spared, but the numbers of people sold into slavery could not be counted.

About this time one of the priests received a promise of protection on condition of giving up certain treasures of the temple which he had secured. And so he handed from the wall two candlesticks, and tables and cups, all of solid gold, and also gave up the veils, and other vestments of the high-priests, with the precious stones and many other articles used by them.

Another priest, who had been the keeper of the temple treasury, pointed out the place where the tunics and girdles worn by the priests were hidden, together with a lot of precious spices used in offering incense. This priest had been taken prisoner, but because he pointed out these treasures his life was spared, as if he had been a deserter.

The mounds were finished in eighteen days, and then the

military engines were brought up to batter down the last bulwark of the besieged. A number of the insurgents now gave up all hope and retired from the ramparts; others crept down into the caverns; while some endeavored to repel the Romans who were bringing up the military engines. But these the Romans easily drove back.

A part of the wall and some of the towers were soon battered down by the rams. The defenders then took to flight, and the tyrants themselves were seized with a panic. Before the Romans had mounted the breach the insurgents had given up all hope. Rumors flew about that the Romans had knocked down the whole of the western wall, and that they were already in the town. The fierce leaders who had before led their men to commit all sorts of daring and desperate deeds now stood trembling and afraid. Many fell upon their faces, bewailing their fate, and were so weak from fear that they were unable to fly.

Even Simon and John became panic-stricken, and came down with their followers from three strong towers and fled into the valley of Siloam. These three towers had been built by King Herod the Great, and were so strong that the Romans never could have battered them down, so that John and Simon could have held out until they were reduced by famine. But so great was their fright that they did not even wait for an attack. So that when the Romans came into the town they were surprised as well as delighted to find the towers empty. For against these their machines would have been useless.

Afterwards, when Simon and his followers had recovered a little from their panic, they tried to break down the wall which the Romans had built round the city and escape. But the Roman guards beat them back and dispersed them, and they then crept down into caves.

The Romans entered the upper city with great rejoicing over so easy a victory. They spread through the streets and killed all who fell in their way, burning the houses, with all who had taken shelter in them. So great was the slaughter that in many places the flames were put out by streams of blood. Towards evening the soldiers, tired of killing, sheathed their swords. But all night the fire burnt fiercely, and when morning broke it beheld the whole of Jerusalem in flames.

CHAPTER CXLIX.

JERUSALEM IS DESTROYED.

WHEN Titus entered the city he was struck with wonder at its strength, and especially at the towers which the tyrants had abandoned. Indeed, when he saw how high and solid they were, and of what huge stones they were built, he said, "Surely we fought with God upon our side, and God it was who brought the Jews down from these bulwarks; for what could human hands or engines avail against these towers?"

Titus freed all those whom he found in the prisons, where they had been thrown by the tyrants. And when he afterwards destroyed what was left of the city and razed the walls, he left the towers standing as monuments of his victory.

The soldiers at length became weary of killing people, and Titus ordered them for the future to kill only those whom they found in arms, or who made a show of resistance, and to make prisoners of the rest. Still the troops killed the old and feeble, because they could not be sold as slaves. Those who were young and fit for service they drove into a space of the temple called the Court of the Women.

Titus placed a guard over them, and ordered a friend of his, called Fronto, to decide what should be done with them. While Fronto was making up his mind, eleven thousand of the unfortunate prisoners perished from hunger,—part of them because the guards, through hatred, would not give them food, and part because they would not take the food when it was offered to them. Moreover, there was not a sufficient supply of food for so vast a multitude.

Finally all those known to be insurgents were put to death, except the tallest and most handsome of the youth, who were reserved to grace the triumph of Titus, which took place when he returned to Rome. Of the remainder, those above the age of seventeen were sent to Egypt to work in the mines, or sent through the provinces to appear in gladiatorial shows.

The number of prisoners taken during the war was ninety-seven thousand, while during the siege there perished one million one hundred thousand people. The greater part of these were of Jewish blood, but they were not all natives of the city. For just before the siege people had flocked into Jerusalem from all parts of Judea, to take part in the feast of the Passover, and many had come to it as a place of refuge.

Therefore there was in the city during the siege a vast number of people who were not natives of the place. These were shut up as in a prison from which they could not get away, and were obliged to suffer all the horrors of famine and of the siege.

The Romans now went down into the caverns and killed all they lighted upon in these retreats. In them they came across numbers of the dead bodies of people who had either fallen by their own hands or had died of hunger.

At length John and his followers, worn out with hunger, came out from one of the caverns and implored the Romans for that protection which he had so often rejected with scorn. He was condemned to pass the rest of his days in prison. The Romans set fire to the extreme quarters of the city, threw down the walls, and levelled them with the ground.

Thus was Jerusalem taken in the second year of Vespasian's reign, on the second of September, seventy years after Christ.

It had been captured five times before, and was now for the second time laid in ruins. Shishak, king of Egypt, and then Antiochus, then Pompey, and then Sosius and Herod, had taken the city, but preserved it. Before their times it had been laid waste by the king of Babylon, fourteen hundred and sixty-eight years and six months from the date of its foundation.

It was first built by a prince of Canaan, called Melchisedek, or "the Righteous King," for such, indeed, he was. He was the first priest of God, and he first built the temple, and then called the city Jerusalem. For before he built the temple the city was called Salem.

The Canaanites were driven from Jerusalem by King David, the king of the Jews, who then lived in it with his own people. Four hundred and seventy-seven years and six months after David's time the city was destroyed by the Babylonians. Titus destroyed the city one thousand one hundred and seventy-nine years after the time of David and two thousand one hundred and seventy-seven years since its first foundation. Neither its age, nor its vast wealth, nor the number of its people, nor the glory of its religious service could save it from ruin. And so ended the siege of Jerusalem.

CHAPTER CL.

TITUS REWARDS AND DISMISSES HIS ARMY.

WHEN the beautiful city of Jerusalem had been destroyed, there were left standing only the three high towers as monuments of the Roman victory, and a part of the western wall, which was left as a defence for the Roman camp. For Titus left the tenth legion, with some cavalry and infantry, to keep

guard over the ruins of the city. But before he went he called
his army together, that he might praise them for their bravery
and confer rewards upon those who had particularly distinguished themselves. And so a high tribunal was erected in
the middle of the former encampment, and upon this Titus
took his stand with his principal officers. He thanked the
army for the good will they had shown to him, and praised
them for their prompt obedience and courage. He then
caused a list to be read of those who had performed any
splendid feat during the war. Calling them by name, he applauded them as they came forward, placed crowns of gold
upon their heads, and presented them with golden neck-
chains, long golden lances, and silver ensigns. He also gave
them shares out of the spoils which had been taken,—silver
and gold, and vestments, and other booty.

When each had been rewarded according to his deserts, he
wished every happiness to his army in general, and stepped
down, amid loud applause, from the tribunal. He then sacrificed a great number of oxen in thanksgiving for his success,
and gave the carcasses to the troops for a banquet.

For three days Titus joined in festivities with his officers,
and then dismissed his army. The tenth legion, however, he
left to guard Jerusalem, and because the twelfth legion had
formerly been defeated under Cestius, he banished it from
Syria altogether, and sent it to a country called Meletene.
Two legions he thought proper to keep with him until his
arrival in Egypt. With them he first went to Cæsarea upon
the sea-coast, and here he directed his prisoners to be kept in
custody, for, the winter having set in, he was prevented from
sailing immediately for Italy.

Titus proceeded from Cæsarea upon the coast to Cæsarea
Philippi, as it was called, and here he remained for some time.
Many of the prisoners were killed, during his stay, in gladiatorial shows. Some were thrown to wild beasts, while others
were compelled to fight with one another in combats. It was

here that Titus heard of the capture of Simon, the son of Gioras, which was effected in the following manner:

While the Romans were laying waste the upper city, Simon, with a body of his most faithful followers, and a party of miners, had leaped down in a cave, taking with him enough provisions to last for several days. The party advanced until they had reached the end of the cave, and then they attempted to dig their way out beyond the walls and escape. But the work went on very slowly, and the provisions gave out.

Simon then gave up all hope of making his escape in this manner. He dressed himself in white robes, threw a cloak of purple over his shoulders, and, walking to the mouth of the cave, suddenly appeared amid the ruins of the temple. Some soldiers who were lounging about were at first very much frightened at seeing him, and stood and gazed at him in awe. At length they came nearer to him, and, forming a circle about him, they asked him who he was. This Simon refused to tell them, but bade them to go and call their general.

Upon this the soldiers ran quickly to Terentius Rufus, who had been left in command, and to him Simon told his story and surrendered himself. Rufus put him in chains, and wrote to Titus to inform him of Simon's capture. On the return of Titus to Cæsarea upon the coast, Simon was sent to him in chains, and was kept to appear in the triumph which Titus was preparing to celebrate in Rome.

CHAPTER CLI.

VESPASIAN AND HIS SONS CELEBRATE A TRIUMPH.

WHILE Titus remained at Cæsarea he celebrated his brother's birthday with great splendor, and put to death a great number of the prisoners. After this he removed to Berytus, a Roman colony in Phœnicia. Here he made quite a long stay, and celebrated his father's birthday by killing many more of his Jewish captives.

While Titus was besieging Jerusalem, his father, Vespasian, had set out from Alexandria to Rome, and Titus now obtained news of the splendid manner in which he had been received by all the Italian cities. When he drew near Rome, the people poured out in crowds to meet him, and joyfully hailed him as their emperor. The city was hung with garlands, and for days the multitudes feasted, and offered sacrifices to their gods that the empire of Vespasian might long be preserved.

After hearing this good news, Titus left Berytus and marched towards Antioch, passing through many cities of Syria, in which he put to death many more of his prisoners by making them fight one another as gladiators.

When Titus drew near Antioch, the people hastened forth to meet him, and received him with loud acclamations; and at the same time they besought him to drive all the Jewish inhabitants out of the town.

Now, there were a great many Jews in Antioch, and they were much attached to the city, because they had always enjoyed equal rights with the native Syrians. And they had built there a very large and magnificent temple.

But at the time when the war had first broken out, and Vespasian had just landed in Syria, and when hatred of the Jews was everywhere at its height, a man of their own race, called Antiochus, the son of the chief magistrate of the Jews in Antioch, excited much hatred against his brethren in Antioch by bearing false witness against them. For he charged the Jews, and among them his own father, with having formed a design to burn the whole of the city during a certain night, and he delivered up some foreign Jews as accomplices in the plot.

The native inhabitants of course became very much incensed, and they immediately put to death those Jews that had been delivered up to them. The people then rushed against the other Jews, thinking that by putting them all to death they would save their city from being burned down. A number of them were massacred, and those that escaped this fate were cruelly persecuted. Antiochus, aided by a body of Roman troops sent by the governor of Syria, lorded it over the Jews, and would not even allow them to rest upon the Sabbath.

In a little while it happened that a fire broke out in the market-place, which burned down a number of the public buildings, and was with difficulty kept from spreading over the whole town. Antiochus charged the Jews with this deed. Upon this the Syrian inhabitants attacked the poor Jews with the greatest rage. Cneus Collegas, the commander of the Roman troop, interposed and saved the Jews from a general massacre, and allayed the fury of the inhabitants, promising to lay the matter before Cæsar.

Collegas began to investigate the affair, and found out that the Jews were not to blame, but that the market-place had been set on fire by some wicked men who owed large sums of money, and who thought if they could destroy the public buildings in which the records of their debts were kept they would escape from having to pay them.

Still the inhabitants hated the Jews; so when Titus came they begged him to drive them from the city. Titus, however, did not give any answer, but went immediately on to Zeugma, a town upon the Euphrates.

But he very soon returned to Antioch, and visited the theatre, where all the people had assembled to receive him. There they again besought him to expel the Jews from the city. But Titus answered,—

"The country of the Jews is destroyed; thither they cannot return. It would be hard to allow them no home to which they can retreat. Leave them in peace."

Failing in this request, the people then asked that the rights of the Jews should be taken away from them. But this Titus also refused, and, leaving the Jews every right that they had formerly enjoyed in Antioch, he set out for Egypt.

On his way thither Titus passed by Jerusalem, and, as he surveyed the ruins, he could not help thinking of the beautiful city that had formerly stood there. And he felt very sorry that he had been compelled by the insurgents to destroy so great and splendid a city.

Titus now made haste towards Egypt, and, crossing the desert with great speed, he soon reached Alexandria. Here he dismissed his two legions, and set sail for Italy. The two leaders, Simon and John, with seven hundred Jewish captives, whom he had selected on account of their beauty and height, he ordered to be sent after him, that they might grace his triumph in Rome.

Titus enjoyed a safe and speedy voyage, and received a warm welcome in Rome. His father and his younger brother, Domitian, who had lately returned to Rome after quelling a revolt among the Germans, came out to meet him. The people were overjoyed to see the father and his sons united, and great rejoicings took place.

Vespasian and his sons agreed that they should celebrate their successes in war upon the same day by one common triumph, although the senate had decreed a separate day for each. When the day arrived, the whole multitude poured out to view the pageant.

Before sunrise all the military forces marched out in companies and divisions under their officers, and drew up around the gates, near the temple of Isis, where the imperial family had reposed for the night.

When morning broke, Vespasian and Titus came forth, crowned with laurel and clothed in purple garments, and ascended a high tribunal which had been erected for them. Instantly a joyous shout burst from the troops, and Vespasian bowed his head to his soldiers, and then made them a signal to be silent. The emperor then rose, and, covering his head with his cloak, he, together with Titus, offered up prayers to the Roman gods. This done, Vespasian made a short speech to the soldiers, and then dismissed them to a repast he had provided.

After the repast the pageant entered the city, passing through the theatres, that the assembled crowds might have a better view. Words could not describe the beauty and magnificence of the procession which took place, and the splendor of the articles which were displayed to view,—gold and silver and ivory, wrought in various forms, beautiful tapestries, worked in Babylon, jewels and crowns of gold, and images of gods made of costly materials.

Different kinds of wild animals were led along by men clad in splendid garments, and numbers of captives dressed in the costumes of their nation. But nothing in the pageant excited so much wonder and admiration as some huge structures rising to the height of three or four stories. These were divided into platforms rising one above the other, and on each was represented some feature of the war.

Here was to be seen a happy country laid waste, and there

an army slain and routed; some again in flight, others being led into captivity; high walls laid in ruins by engines; strong fortresses battered down; populous cities overrun by armies; houses thrown down, and their owners buried in the ruins; rivers running through lands laid waste and wrapped in flames on every side.

On each of these platforms was placed the governor of one of the captured cities. A number of ships also followed. Then the spoils of the war were displayed in confused heaps, and among them, and placed where all could see, were the sacred treasures taken from the temple of Jerusalem. Last of all was borne the Jewish Book of the Law. Next came a body of men carrying images of Victory made of gold and ivory; and next Vespasian was driven along in a chariot, followed by Titus, while Domitian rode beside him upon a beautiful horse.

The procession stopped before the temple of Jupiter Capitolinus, and waited until the Jewish general Simon had been put to death. For he had been led along by a halter, and was now dragged to a place overlooking the Forum, and there was executed. When the tidings spread that Simon was no more, the people gave a shout of joy, and, after offering up sacrifices, they dispersed.

Some were entertained at a banquet by the emperor and princes themselves, while all had feasts prepared at home, for all the Romans kept festival that day in celebration of the victories gained by the imperial family.

When the triumphs were over, Vespasian commenced to build a beautiful temple, which he dedicated to Peace. When it was finished, he stored in it beautiful statues and paintings, taken from different countries, and for a sight of which men had before wandered over the whole world. Here he placed also the golden vessels taken from the temple of Jerusalem. But the purple veils of the sanctuary and the Book of the Law he kept in his own palace.

CHAPTER CLII.

THE CONQUESTS OF BASSUS.

LUCILIUS BASSUS was sent to Judea as legate, and theie took command of the Roman army. Although Jerusalem was in ruins, yet three strong fortresses, garrisoned by Jews, still remained in arms against the Roman Empire. These were Herodium, Massada, and Machærus.

Bassus soon gained over the fortress of Herodium, and then drew around him the Roman forces scattered throughout Judea, and, together with the tenth legion, marched against Machærus.

Because Machærus was a very strong fortress, and well fortified by nature, Bassus thought that it ought to be destroyed, lest its very strength should induce many of the Jews to revolt. For so long as it stood they would feel that they had a place of safety to which they might retire.

It was built upon a high and rocky hill, which was surrounded on all sides by deep ravines, which could not be easily crossed, and which it was nearly impossible to mound up. Remarking the natural advantages of the spot, Alexander, king of the Jews, first erected a fortress there. But this was destroyed by Gabinus in his war with Aristobulus.

Afterwards, when Herod was king, he surrounded a space of ground upon the hill with ramparts and towers, and built there a city, with an ascent leading upwards to the summit of the hill. On the very brow of the hill he raised a wall, and at the angles built high towers. In the centre of the enclosure he built a beautiful palace, and around it he placed a number of cisterns in order to receive the rain and thus keep the city supplied with water in case of a siege; and also he stocked the place with missiles and engines, so that a gallant defence could be made.

After Bassus had examined the place from every point, he determined to fill up the ravine upon the east, and from thence make an attack upon the town. The Jewish natives of the town separated themselves from the strangers who had taken refuge within the walls, and shut themselves up in the citadel. But they compelled the strangers to defend the lower town.

Many fierce conflicts took place about the walls, for the Jews every now and then would sally out upon the Romans while they were employed upon their works. The garrison sometimes caught the Romans off their guard, but at other times they were repulsed with great loss. These combats, however, did not decide the fate of the town, but it was suddenly decided by a remarkable chance.

Among the garrison there was a young man called Eleazar, who was very brave and bold. He had greatly distinguished himself in the sallies that the Jews had made, and had killed a great many of the enemy. Always the last to retreat, he had often checked by himself the onset of the Romans. One day it happened that just after a fight, and when both parties had retired, Eleazar remained alone outside the walls of the town, chatting with some friends upon the ramparts, and giving his attention entirely to them.

Suddenly an Egyptian called Rufus, who was serving in the Roman army, and was renowned for his strength, rushed swiftly up to Eleazar while off his guard, and, picking him up armed as he was, he succeeded in bearing him off to the Roman camp. For the Jews upon the ramparts were too much taken by surprise to attempt his rescue.

The Roman general ordered Eleazar to be stripped and taken to a spot where he could be seen by all his friends in the city, to be there scourged in sight of all. When the Jews saw this sight they began to weep and groan, for Eleazar was very dear to them. When Bassus saw how much they were affected by this, he thought he might force the town to surrender by a stratagem. Nor was he disappointed.

He ordered a cross to be put up, as if he were about to crucify Eleazar. Then the friends and relatives of the youth set up loud wails and gave themselves up to the most violent ' grief. And rather than see him perish thus before their eyes they sent messengers to the Romans, saying that they would surrender the fortress if only they might be allowed to depart in safety and take with them Eleazar.

Bassus agreed to these conditions. When the multitude of strangers in the lower town heard of the agreement which the citizens had made, they determined to steal away quietly during the night. But as soon as the gates were thrown open, those who had come to terms with Bassus told him of the design the strangers had in view. Bassus then fell upon them and slaughtered the greater part of the men, and enslaved the women and children. A few of the bravest men managed to cut their way through the Roman forces and escape. All the natives were spared, according to the agreement, and allowed to depart with their beloved Eleazar.

Bassus then marched to a forest, called the forest of Jarden, and proceeded to surround it. For here a number of those Jews had collected who had escaped from Jerusalem and Machærus while they were being besieged. Bassus posted his cavalry all around the forest, and then set the infantry to chopping down the trees, among which the fugitives had taken refuge.

The Jews were thus compelled to fight, for their only chance of escape was to cut their way through the enemy. And so they collected together, and rushed upon the troops that hemmed them in. But the Romans were well armed and prepared for the attack. Upon their side only a few fell, while the Jews were slaughtered to a man; and at the end of the fight three thousand lay dead among the woods of Jarden.

At this time Cæsar wrote to Bassus, and to Liberius Maximus, the procurator, directing them to sell the whole of the Jewish territory. For he kept it all as his own private property, without sharing the conquered land with his army. To eight hundred veterans, however, he gave as a dwelling-place a town called Emmaus, about seven or eight miles from Jerusalem. At the same time he ordered that every Jewish man would have to pay an annual tax of two drachms for the support of the Capitol; this being the amount that each Jew had formerly paid for the support of the temple.

CHAPTER CLIII.

THE FORTRESS OF MASSADA.

BASSUS died in Judea, and was succeeded in his government by Flavius Silva. When Silva arrived in Judea the whole country was subdued except one fortress,—that of Massada.

Massada was held by a band of Sikars or Assassins, and their commander was Eleazar, a descendant of Judas the Galilean, who held that as the Jews bowed to God as their master, they should not submit to the rule of any man. Eleazar and his followers believed in this doctrine, and so would not submit to Cæsar. Silva gathered together all the Roman forces, and immediately marched against Massada. That none of the besieged might escape, he built a wall around the fortress and guarded it with sentinels.

Massada stood upon a high rock, which was surrounded by deep ravines. It could be reached only by two narrow and difficult paths from the east and from the west. On the east the path led up from the shore of the Dead Sea, and, winding upwards by the verge of frightful precipices, finally opened upon a plain at the summit, upon which Massada stood.

The fortress was first built by the high-priest Jonathan, but it was afterwards made stronger and added to by King Herod. Herod surrounded the summit with a high wall, which he fortified with thirty-seven strong towers. Herod also built a beautiful palace upon the western ascent. He cut in the rock a number of cisterns, so that the place should never want for water. The fortress was thus very strong, and well fortified both by nature and art. For the path on the east was so steep and narrow that it could not be used by an attacking party, while that on the west was barred by a huge tower built at the narrowest part. It was not possible to pass this tower, nor was it easy to reduce it.

The fortress was well stocked with provisions (enough to last for years), and there was also a vast quantity of arms (enough for ten thousand men), with great stores of unwrought iron, brass, and lead. For King Herod had provided this fortress as a refuge for himself in case of a revolt among his subjects, and also because he feared Cleopatra, the queen of Egypt, who had always desired his throne. Because of this twofold danger Herod had fortified Massada, little thinking that one day it would be the last refuge of the Jews in a war against Rome.

CHAPTER CLIV.

THE FALL OF MASSADA.

WHEN Silva had blockaded the town so that none could escape, he commenced to build a mound upon a rock called the White Cliff. This rock jutted out to the westward, below the tower that barred the western passage to Massada. First a high mound was built of earth, and upon this a second bank, made of enormous stones, built in the shape of a platform. Then upon this a high tower was raised, completely cased with iron. From this tower the Romans hurled missiles and darts by means of their military engines, and cleared the ramparts of their defenders.

Silva brought up a battering-ram and commenced to batter against the wall, and at length battered down a portion of it. But in the mean while the Sikars had thrown up another wall inside. This they built of wood and earth, which, being soft, did not give way before the blows of the ram, but only became all the firmer from the blows.

When Silva saw that the ram was useless against this wall, he ordered his soldiers to throw lighted torches upon it. The wood-work soon caught on fire, and before long the whole wall was one vast sheet of flame. At the beginning the north wind blew the flames in the faces of the Romans, and they were much alarmed on account of their military engines, which seemed likely to be burned up.

But on a sudden the wind shifted and blew fiercely from the south, driving the flames inward, and soon the wall fell down, after the woodwork was all destroyed. The Romans then returned rejoicing to their camp, intending to attack the enemy on the following day. During the night they kept vigilant watch lest any of the besieged should escape.

Eleazar, however, did not intend to fly, nor would he allow any of his followers to do so. When he saw the wall in ruins and no hope of safety left them, he thought it would be nobler for all to die by their own hands than to be cut down by the swords of the enemy.

And so he called his followers together in the palace, and urged them to set the city on fire and perish with it, rather than to wait for death at the hands of the Romans, who would carry off their wives and children into slavery.

Some of his followers were eager to obey Eleazar at once, but others could not bear the thought of putting their wives and children to death, and tears stole down their cheeks.

Seeing them wavering, Eleazar addressed them again. He spoke of the endless life of the soul and its freedom after death, and of the horrors of slavery which their wives and children would have to endure if they did not destroy them with their own hands. "Let us," he said, "depart from life in freedom with our wives and children, and thus we will disappoint the Romans of their victory. Let us deny them the joy and triumph of seeing us conquered, and rather strike them with awe at our death and with admiration of our valor."

While Eleazar was still speaking, he was cut short by his hearers, who became filled with ardor and with haste to commit the deed. They rushed away like men possessed, and began the bloody work. While they embraced their wives and stooped to kiss their children they stabbed them to the heart.

When they had put them all to death, they gathered together their effects and set fire to them. Then they chose by lot ten of their number to slay the rest. They lay down beside their dead wives and children and were slaughtered by the ten. The ten then cast lots, and nine of them fell by one another's hands. Then he who was left single and alone looked about to see that all were dead, set fire to the palace, and with his own hand drove his sword into his heart, and fell dead beside his family.

Two women, however, and five children escaped by hiding themselves in an underground cavern. But all the rest perished, to the number of nearly a thousand.

Early the next morning the Romans formed in close array and advanced to the wall with great caution, for they expected to meet with a fierce resistance. They formed bridges of planks from the mound to the fortress, and rushed to the assault. But no enemy appeared, and an awful silence hung over the city. When the Romans saw fire burning the palace they did not know what to think. At length they shouted aloud, in order to call out some of the enemy.

Hearing the noise, the two women who had saved themselves came out of their retreat and informed the Romans of what had taken place. At first they would not believe the story, until, putting out the flames, they made their way into the palace and there beheld the heap of slain.

The Romans did not rejoice over this victory, since their own arms did not win it. But they could not help admiring the contempt of death which their enemies had shown. With the fall of Massada the war in Judea was completely ended, and not an enemy remained to dispute the power of Rome.

CHAPTER CLV.

THE TEMPLE IN EGYPT IS CLOSED.

A LITTLE while after the conquest of Judea it happened that a number of Sikars who had escaped from that country tried to incite a revolt among the Jews in Alexandria in Egypt. They went around among the Jews in that city, and said to them, "You should assert your freedom, and not be ruled by the Romans, for they are no better than you, and you should regard God alone as your master."

Some of the leading men among the Jews in Alexandria opposed the Sikars, whereupon they were murdered by the Assassins, who then tried to persuade the rest of the Jews to revolt.

Then a number of the council of elders among the Jews called together all their people, and exposed to them the madness of the Sikars. "These men," they said, "because they know that they will be put to death by the Romans whenever they are recognized as Sikars, wish to make us all sharers in their danger, who have not been sharers in their crimes." And they exhorted the people to give up these Sikars to the Romans, and thus save themselves from punishment.

The people agreed to this, and, rushing upon the Sikars, they captured six hundred of them. All the rest who escaped from the city were pursued and brought back. They were given up to the Roman governor, Lupus, in Alexandria, and astonished every one by their firmness and strength of purpose. For they were put under every kind of torture to try and force them to acknowledge Cæsar as their lord and master. But, in spite of all the torments they were forced to suffer, no one of them would do so. And so they all perished upon the rack or were burned to death. Even the little children among them preferred to die rather than to say that Cæsar was their lord.

Lupus sent word to Vespasian about this commotion. The emperor then ordered Lupus to destroy the temple of Onias, in order that the Jews might not collect there and raise another revolt.

This temple stood in Heliopolis, a city of Egypt, and had been built in former times by Onias, one of the chief priests of the temple at Jerusalem. This Onias had fled to Alexandria at the time that Antiochus, king of Syria, was at war with the Jews. Onias was well received by Ptolemy, the king of Egypt, who hated Antiochus.

One day Onias said to Ptolemy,—

"If you will grant me one favor I will make the Jews your allies."

"I will do all in my power to grant the favor," said the king.

"Then," said Onias, " give me permission to build a temple in some part of Egypt, and to worship God according to the ways of my country, for Antiochus has laid waste the temple of Jerusalem. The Jews will then love you, and many will gather around your standard, if you allow them to worship as they please."

Ptolemy then gave Onias a tract of country called the prefecture of Heliopolis. And here Onias built a temple. The king also gave him a large tract of land, that the priests might have plenty of necessaries for the service of God.

When Lupus received Cæsar's order he went to this temple, and, taking away some of the offerings, he shut up the building. Lupus soon afterwards died, and was succeeded as governor by Paulinus.

Paulinus took away all the offerings from the temple, forbade any one from worshipping in it, and blocked up the entrance. The temple had been open for three hundred and
forty-three years.

CHAPTER CLVI.

THE SEDITION IN CYRENE.

THE last attempt at revolt took place in the city of Cyrene.
Here an abandoned Jew, by the name of Jonathan, who had
found a refuge in that city, persuaded a multitude of the
meaner classes of Jews to follow him out of the city into a
desert. He pretended that he would show them great signs
and wonders. But the men of rank among the Jews of Cyrene
sent word to Catullus, the governor of the Libyan Penta-
polis, about Jonathan's march into the wilderness.

Catullus despatched a body of horse and foot, who obtained
an easy victory over Jonathan and his followers. A great
many of the latter perished in the fight, and the rest were
brought back to Cyrene. Jonathan for a while managed to
escape capture, but at length he was taken prisoner. When
he was brought before Catullus, he said that a number of the
wealthiest among the Jews were accomplices in his plot.

Catullus listened eagerly to his charges, and pretended to
believe them all, because he hated the Jews. Moreover, he
wished to make the affair appear as big and dangerous as
possible, that he too might seem to have ended a Jewish war.
And he even named some of the Jews whom he was anxious to kill, and made Jonathan and some of his followers
swear that they were in the plot. In this way he put to death
a Jew, named Alexander, with whom he had quarrelled, and
also his wife. After this he slew all the wealthiest Jews, to

the number of three thousand, and added their property to the revenues of the emperor.

Lest any of the Jews elsewhere should expose his crimes, Catullus got Jonathan and his associates to charge the leading Jews in Alexandria and Rome with being aiders in the sedition. Among those charged with sedition in Rome was Josephus, the historian.

Catullus went to Rome with his witnesses. But Vespasian made strict inquiry, and found out that all the charges were false. He acquitted the accused Jews, and condemned Jonathan to be burnt alive. Catullus was allowed to live, but was soon after seized with a terrible disease, and died in great agony. For God punished him for his wicked deeds.

The feeble sedition led by Jonathan was the last attempt made by the Jews to revolt from the power of Rome, and with it ends the history of the Jewish war.

THE END.

www.ingramcontent.com/pod-product-compliance
Lightning Source LLC
Chambersburg PA
CBHW052333110726
47901CB00005B/1228